STUDIES IN EAST ASIAN BUDDHISM 25

Patrons and Patriarchs

REGIONAL RULERS AND CHAN MONKS DURING THE FIVE DYNASTIES AND TEN KINGDOMS

Benjamin Brose

A KURODA INSTITUTE BOOK

University of Hawai'i Press
Honolulu

First printing, 2015

Library of Congress Cataloging-in-Publication Data
Brose, Benjamin, author.
Patrons and patriarchs : regional rulers and Chan monks during
the Five Dynasties and Ten Kingdoms / Benjamin Brose.
pages cm — (Studies in East Asian Buddhism ; 25)
"A Kuroda Institute book."
Includes bibliographical references and index.
ISBN 978-0-8248-5381-5 (cloth : alk. paper)
1. Zen Buddhism—China, Southeast—History—To 1500.   2. Buddhism and
state—China, Southeast—History—To 1500.   3. Buddhist monks—China,
Southeast—History—To 1500.   4. China—History—Five dynasties and the
Ten kingdoms, 907–979.   5. China—Politics and government—907–979.
I. Title.   II. Series: Studies in East Asian Buddhism ; no. 25.
BQ9262.9.C52B76 2015
294.3'927095109021—dc23
2015003419

ISBN 978-0-8248-9784-0 (paperback)

The Kuroda Institute for the Study of Buddhism and Human Values
is a nonprofit, educational corporation founded in 1976. One of its primary
objectives is to promote scholarship on the historical, philosophical,
and cultural ramifications of Buddhism. In association with the University
of Hawai'i Press, the Institute also publishes Classics in East Asian
Buddhism, a series devoted to the translation of significant texts in the
East Asian Buddhist tradition.

For Jennifer, Walker, and Kalina

The Min Commander [Wang Shenzhi] sent [Xuefeng Yicun] a folding silver chair. A monk asked, "The master accepts this sort of offering from the great king. How do you intend to repay him?"

The master placed his hands on the ground and said, "Hit me a few times."

Jingde-Era Record of the Transmission of the Flame

We must give back more than we have received.

Marcel Mauss, *The Gift*

Contents

Figures, Maps, and Tables

FIGURES

MAPS

TABLES

Acknowledgments

HAVING BEEN PREOCCUPIED for some time with the workings of patronage, I am acutely aware of the debts owed my own benefactors. This book began as a Ph.D. dissertation at Stanford University, where I benefited from the erudition and kindness of my advisors, Carl Bielefeldt and Bernard Faure. Fabrizio Pregadio also guided me along the way, and I remain grateful for his generosity as a scholar and a friend. Thanks are also due to Paul Harrison and John McRae, who sat on my committee, and to my wonderful cohort—Megan Bryson, George Klonos, Kenneth Koo, Dominic Steavu-Balint, and Zhaohua Yang. James Robson and Wendi Adamek, senior members of the Stanford lineage, were also unstinting with their time and counsel. John Kieschnick was kind enough to share his translation of the *Song Biographies of Eminent Monks* with a graduate student he had never met.

The first phase of research for this project was carried out in Kyoto, under the guidance of Tonami Mamoru at Otani University and Funayama Tōru at Kyoto University. Their selfless hospitality and impeccable scholarship set a standard I still aspire to. My time in Kyoto was also greatly enriched by Thomas Yūhō Kirchner, who opened many doors—including his own—for me; Robert Rhodes, who helped to arrange my visit; Ken Rodgers and the *Kyoto Journal* community; and the late Monica Esposito, whose infectious love of life and scholarship will not soon be forgotten. I also incurred a deep karmic debt from the kindness showed to me by Kobori Taigen Roshi, Shū-san, and the monks of the Kennin-ji sōdō, and Shōdō Harada Roshi, Chi-san, and the monks and nuns of the Sōgen-ji sōdō.

The first drafts of these chapters were written at Shōbō-an, in the foothills of the Sierra Nevada mountains. Gary Snyder's generosity, great wit, and delicious cooking made our time there especially enjoyable. Nelson Foster, likewise, was an exemplary host (and a hawk-eyed editor), keeping me alert with plenty of tea, chocolate, and other food for thought. The greater Ring of Bone community sustained me with their encouragement, their good sense, and their critical feedback on different aspects of this project.

A host of other scholars and friends have read through drafts of this work at various stages, made excellent suggestions, or pointed me in the proper direction. I am much obliged to James Benn, Raoul Birnbaum, Jinhua Chen, Paul Copp, Daniel Getz, Eric Greene, Paul Groner, Mark Halperin, George Keyworth, Miriam Levering, Jason Protass, Robert Sharf, Nicolas Tackett, and Albert Welter. Special thanks go to Peter Gregory and T. Griffith Foulk, who have offered encouragement and sage advice throughout the writing and publication process. My colleagues in the Department of Asian Languages and Cultures at the University of Michigan have, both through casual conversations and focused comments, also done a great deal to help me to refine my writing and broaden my thinking. I am particularly grateful to Donald Lopez, Micah Auerback, Juhn Ahn, William Baxter, Varuni Bhatia, Deirdre de la Cruz, Miranda Brown, Maki Fukuoka, David Rolston, Christian de Pee, and Xiaobing Tang for their assistance. While errors in fact and interpretation undoubtedly remain, this book has been much improved through the work and insight of all these scholars.

Like the monks who populate these pages, I have survived for many years off the alms of various public and private institutions. This work would not have been possible without the generous support of Stanford University, the Ho Center for Buddhist Studies, the Andrew W. Mellon Foundation, the American Council of Learned Societies, the Freeman Spogli Institute for International Studies, the Japanese Ministry of Culture, and the Lieberthal-Rogel Center for Chinese Studies at the University of Michigan. At the University of Hawai'i Press, I have been kept on track by Stephanie Chun and my writing has been (mostly) tamed by Molly Balikov. Michael Brackney gets all the credit for the index.

My parents, Barry and Wendy, and the greater Brose clan have been unflaggingly supportive, often, no doubt, against their own better judgment. Dorothy Muñoz was a constant source of encouragement and inspiration. She will be greatly missed. Finally, I am deeply grateful to Jennifer, Walker, and Kalina, who have kept me sane while cheerfully enduring all manner of deprivation so that I might indulge this peculiar interest in a handful of monks and monarchs who lived more than a thousand years ago on the other side of the world. Though I don't expect they'll make it much past this page, this book is dedicated to them.

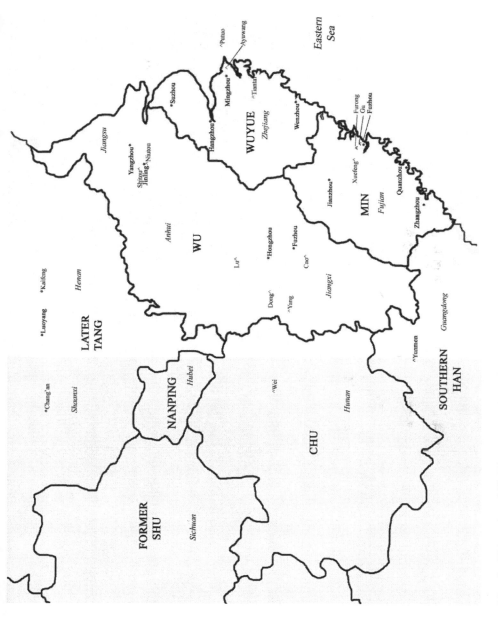

Map 1. China circa 930. The names of modern provinces are provided in italics; approximate locations of mountains are indicated by carets; cities are marked with asterisks.

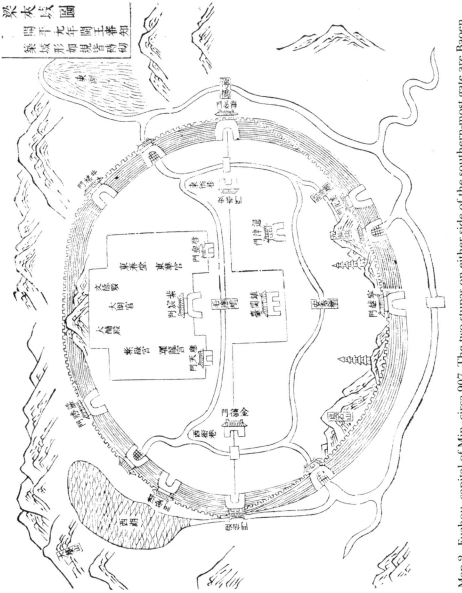

Map 2. Fuzhou, capital of Min, circa 907. The two stupas on either side of the southern-most gate are Baoen (right) and Chongmiao (left). *Min du ji*, n.p.

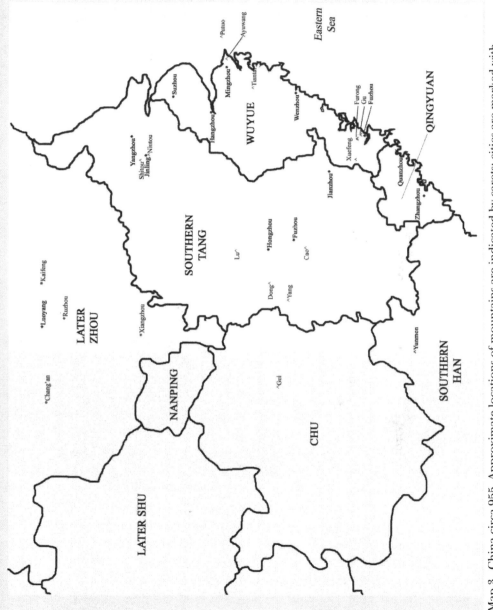

Map 3. China circa 955. Approximate locations of mountains are indicated by carets; cities are marked with asterisks.

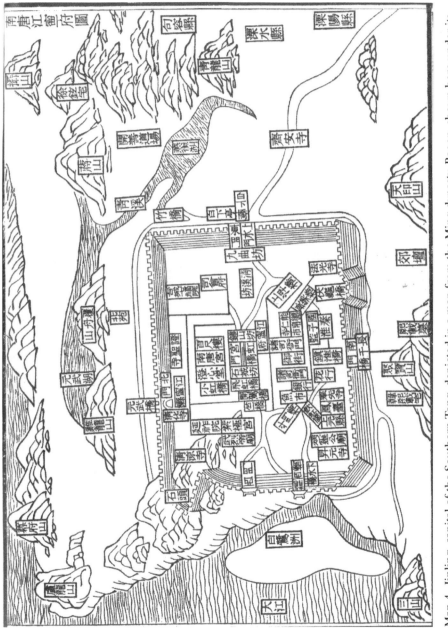

Map 4. Jinling, capital of the Southern Tang, depicted in a map from the Ming dynasty. Baoen, shown here under its later name of Nengren, is located in the bottom right quadrant of the city. Qingliang si is shown in the northwestern corner. Fengxian si is shown to the left of the southern gate, within the city wall. Shengyuan si is in the bottom left corner of the city. *Jinling gujin tukao*, 1:19.

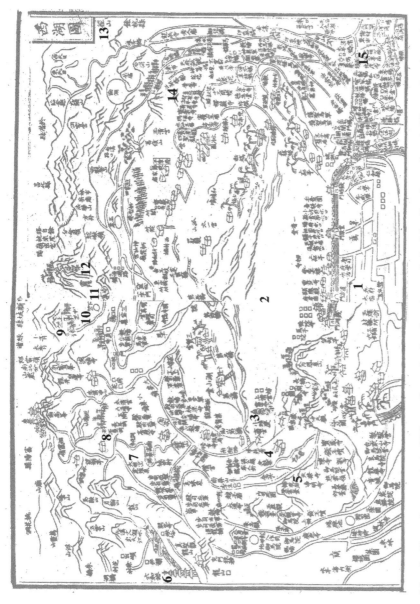

Map 5. Hangzhou, capital of Wuyue (here depicted as the capital of the Southern Song). Illustration from the *Xianchun Lin'an zhi*. Clockwise from bottom center: 1. Imperial compound; 2. West Lake; 3. Leifeng stupa; 4. Yongming si; 5. Longhua si; 6. Liuhe stupa; 7. Mt. Daci; 8. Shiwu cave; 9. Upper Tianzhu si; 10. Middle Tianzhu si; 11. Lower Tianzhu si; 12. Lingyin si; 13. Mt. Jing; 14. Baochu stupa; 15. Huadu si.

Introduction

THIS BOOK IS A STUDY of elite Chan monks and their patrons in southeastern China during the Five Dynasties and Ten Kingdoms (907–960). It seeks to address two closely related issues in the history of Chan Buddhism. The first is how Chan clerics, who represented a relatively minor undercurrent in mainstream Buddhism during the Tang dynasty (618–907), rose to become some of the most culturally and politically significant clerics of the Northern Song dynasty (960–1127). The second is the extent to which the Chan institutions and traditions of the early Northern Song derived from developments in southeastern China during the Five Dynasties and Ten Kingdoms.

I should be clear up front about what this book does not attempt to do. First, it is not a comprehensive history of Chan Buddhism—let alone Buddhism writ large—during the Five Dynasties and Ten Kingdoms. While I do discuss some aspects of clergy-court relations in other regions, this book focuses primarily on *saṃgha*-state relations in three kingdoms located in southeastern China: Min 閩 (corresponding roughly to present-day Fujian province); the Southern Tang 南唐 (Jiangsu, Anhui, and Jiangxi provinces); and Wuyue 吳越 (Zhejiang province). My decision to concentrate on these regions stems from several factors: the royal families of these kingdoms supported large numbers of Chan monks, many of whom belonged to the same lineage family; the cultural traditions of these three states played a formative role in the creation of Northern Song imperial culture; and the source material for monks living in these kingdoms is relatively abundant. Other regions—particularly Hunan, Hubei, Guangdong, and Sichuan— also hosted large populations of Chan monks during this period and deserve to be studied in detail, but they are touched on only briefly here. Moreover, among the tens of thousands of monks living in southeastern China, I have limited my discussions to those known to have received some form of material or symbolic support—temple appointments, administrative positions, titles, purple robes, and resources like land, silk, cash, and food—from regional rulers. This book does not, therefore, directly examine the lives of ordinary monks or nuns, or aspects of regional religious cultures such as Daoist traditions, deity cults, or lay societies. While these

1

individuals and institutions were all integral to the religious life of local communities, they are not as well documented in existing sources and are mentioned only in passing in this study. Finally, this book is not intended as an intellectual history of Chan during this period.[1] Prominent Buddhist texts, doctrines, and practices will be discussed in some detail, but my primary goal is to assess the effects of political, social, and economic forces on the development and distribution of Chan lineage networks and their traditions.

The monks at the center of this study were dharma-descendants of Xuefeng Yicun 雪峰義存 (822–908) and Xuansha Shibei 玄沙師備 (835–908), two Chan masters active in northern Fujian at the turn of the tenth century. With the backing of a host of regional rulers, the disciples and granddisciples of these two monks first spread to all of Min's major cities and then came to prominence in the neighboring kingdoms of the Southern Han, Southern Tang, and Wuyue. All told, more than eighty members of this lineage received some form of support from three generations of kings in four different kingdoms over the course of roughly one hundred years. These clerics dominated the abbacies of major, state-sanctioned monasteries, served as national teachers and royal preceptors, and trained thousands of young monks. Together with their patrons, they transformed a small, localized monastic movement into a transregional religious phenomenon. The history of this network of monks and monarchs—the history this book attempts to survey—serves as a case study in the movement of Chan monks from the peripheries of Chinese society to its center.

What does it mean to study the historical development of Chan? "Chan" is a notoriously slippery word that has meant different things to different people in different times and places. For the purposes of this study, I have adopted T. Griffith Foulk's definition of the Chan school as a "group of people—monks, nuns, and lay followers—who were united by a shared belief in a multi-branched Chan lineage, conceived as an extended spiritual clan that was founded in India by the Buddha Śākyamuni and transmitted to China by a first ancestor named Bodhidharma."[2] This school or movement consisted of men and women connected only informally through their devotion to texts documenting the history of an exclusive spiritual genealogy and their dedication to monks who were heir to that lineage. Chan lineages can be more narrowly defined as genealogies of mythical and historical ancestors that were promoted and perpetuated by a small number of living "patriarchs" who had been adopted into the lineage by senior members and who would, in most cases, go on to produce heirs of their own.[3] This definition of Chan hinges on the notion of lineage (zong 宗)—whether one accepted its existence and basic premises; whether one aspired to or attained membership—rather than distinctive soteriological systems. As such, it is a particularly apt characterization of the clerics that came to dominate the Buddhist landscapes of southeastern China during the tenth century. Although these men all claimed the same spiritual ancestors, they championed a wide range of doctrines and disciplines. Their ideological affinities coalesced most consistently and most distinctively around the concepts of lineage, transmission, and inheritance.

Perspectives on the Five Dynasties and Ten Kingdoms

Most of the people discussed in this book lived during the period of political division that spanned the dissolution of the Tang dynasty and the consolidation of the Song, an era known as the Five Dynasties and Ten Kingdoms (see table 1). The conventional dates for this period are somewhat misleading. Officially, 907 marks the year that the Tang dynasty ended while 960 is the date the Song dynasty was first established; however, the Tang lost *de facto* control of their empire decades earlier, in 881, and the Song did not complete the process of unification until 979. In addition to issues of chronology, assessments of this period's character and significance also span a wide range. The Song scholars who wrote the first comprehensive histories of the Five Dynasties and Ten Kingdoms portrayed it as a brief and unfortunate interruption in an otherwise continuous succession of virtuous, unified rule.[1] The very name "Five Dynasties and Ten Kingdoms," coined retrospectively by the celebrated Song literatus Ouyang Xiu 歐陽修 (1007–1072), itself conveys certain presumptions about political continuity. "Five Dynasties" refers to the succession of regimes that controlled much

TABLE 1   Dates for the Five Dynasties and Ten Kingdoms

Tang dynasty 唐, 618–907	
Five Dynasties 五代	**Ten Kingdoms 十國**
	Wu 吳, (892) 902–937
	Wuyue 吳越, (895) 907–978
	Former Shu 前蜀, (891) 907–925
Later Liang 後梁, 907–923	Min 閩, (892) 909–946
Later Tang 後唐, 923–936	Southern Han 南漢, (905) 917–971
Later Jin 後晉, 936–946	Nanping 南平, (907) 925–963
Later Han 後漢, 946–950	Chu 楚, (896) 927–951
Later Zhou 後周, 951–960	Later Shu 後蜀, (925) 934–965
	Southern Tang 南唐, 937–975
	Northern Han 北漢, 951–979
Song dynasty 宋, 960–1279	

Sources: The dates for this period, particularly the origin dates of the southern kingdoms, are imprecise and vary from source to source depending on the criteria used. This table provides the dates listed in the *Tōhō nenpyō* and indicates the year northern courts officially recognized the rule of the southern "kings" or "emperors." Dates from Ouyang Xiu's *Xin Wudai shi* are provided parenthetically and show the date when a region came under the control of the families that ruled over southern kingdoms.

of northern China. According to the dictates of dynastic succession, these governments represented the only legitimate line of political authority after the Tang and before the Song. "Ten Kingdoms" refers to the smaller states that, with the exception of the Northern Han, concurrently occupied the south. These kingdoms were typically cast as illegitimate, rogue regimes and were of secondary interest to court historians despite the fact that they were on average more politically stable and economically prosperous than their northern counterparts.

In the first official history of this era, the [*Old*] *History of the Five Dynasties* [舊]五代史, Xue Juzheng 薛居正 (912–981) devoted only 5 of 151 fascicles to southern kingdoms. A second and more widely read account of the Five Dynasties and Ten Kingdoms was privately compiled by Ouyang Xiu a century later. In this work, the coverage of southern states was nearly doubled, but as Ouyang's preface to the section on these "hereditary houses" makes clear, the expanded coverage did not stem from some new appreciation of the political or cultural significance of southern states. Instead, it represented a new opportunity to contrast the "perpetrators of darkness" with the bright "sun and moon" of the Song dynasty. Ouyang writes:

> After the decline of Tang rule, bandits across the world with tattooed faces and shaved heads exploited conditions to assume the costumes and trappings of royals. The domains of Wu and Southern Tang usurped power through a mixture of villainy and valor. Insularity for Shu created prosperity while isolation for Southern Han caused destitution, yet the poor became entrenched while the prosperous met an early end. Uncouth were overlords of Min and exploitive were those at Jinghu, while barbarian submission motivated men of Chu. The worst in insufferable plunder occurred at Wuyue, although Lingnan peoples seemed grist for sacrifice under Liu overlords.[5]

In this way, Ouyang and other Chinese historians portrayed the Five Dynasties and Ten Kingdoms as a chaotic interlude between two great dynasties. But with the birth of modern sinology in late nineteenth-century Japan, the tenth century came to be identified as a major watershed in the historical evolution of China, a divide separating the medieval and modern eras. Naka Michiyo 那珂通世 (1851–1908), in his *General History of China* (*Shina tsūshi* 支那通史, 1888–1890), was the first to apply European periodization schemes to Chinese history to arrive at three distinct stages: an ancient period, beginning with the legendary Three Emperors and ending in the Qin dynasty (221–207 BCE); a medieval period, lasting from the Qin through the Tang dynasty; and a modern period, extending from the Song to contemporary times.[6] Naka's scheme was subsequently adopted in history textbooks in both Japan and China and was later developed by Naitō Konan 内藤湖南 (1866–1934), a leading historian of China in Japan.[7] Naitō identified specific changes in the realms of politics (the shift from aristocracy to autocracy), social structure (from aristocracy to populism), economics (from silk to coins), art (from formalism to free expression), and literature (from classical to vernacular) during the Northern Song as signaling the first stirrings of modernity.[8] This European inflected understanding of Chinese history was, not surprisingly, embraced by Western sinologists with the result that the Five Dynasties was often glossed as a period of violent contractions preceding the birth of modern China.[9]

Aspects of this teleology are evident in twentieth-century surveys of Chinese Buddhist history as well. In the 1930s, for example, Hu Shih 胡適 (1891–1962) described the shift from the medieval to the modern period as the transition from the Buddhist Age (300–1100) to the Age of the Chinese Renaissance (1000–present).[10] Just like the Enlightenment in Europe, China's evolution into a rational, humanistic society was thought to have necessarily entailed the gradual demise of religion.[11] During the Northern Song, according to Hu, secular, Neo-Confucian thought triumphed over medieval superstition. Buddhism had been a great cultural invasion from India that "dazzled, baffled, and conquered" the inherently rational Chinese mind, and its elimination was a critical step in China's modern development.[12] Paradoxically, Hu held that the demise of Buddhism had been hastened by Chan monks, who, though Buddhist, were part of a subversive movement that sought to reassert indigenous Chinese values. "The razor of Chinese Ch'an" cut off and destroyed "the medieval ghosts, the gods, the *bodhisattvas* and the Buddhas, the four stages of *dhyāna*, the four formless states of *samādhi*, the six divine powers of the attained yoga practitioner, etc."[13] By dismembering Indian Buddhism, Chan monks opened the way for Neo-Confucian scholars in the eleventh century who finally put an end to the period of Indian intellectual colonization and reclaimed China for the Chinese.[14]

Although modern Japanese scholars of Chinese Chan firmly rejected the idea that the rise of Chan was merely a transitional stage in the philosophical evolution of China, most agreed that the Song dynasty marked the onset of spiritual dissolution and creative decline. Scholars like Daisetz Teitaro (D. T.) Suzuki 大拙貞太郎鈴木 (1870–1966), Ui Hakuju 宇井伯壽 (1882–1963), Kagamishima Genryū 鏡島元隆 (1912–2001), and Yanagida Seizan 柳田聖山 (1922–2006) noted that, by the Song, Chan clerics had come to wield significant economic and political power and had established strong ties with the ruling class. As the new leaders of state-sanctioned Buddhist establishments, Chan monks appeared to have taken on the trappings of court clerics, and their once vibrant, free-spirited tradition devolved into a sclerotic institution of empty forms led by monks who could only parrot the words and deeds of past masters. Whereas Hu Shih had argued that Chan monks destroyed mainstream Buddhism, Japanese scholars contended that it was mainstream Buddhism that sapped the life out of the Chan movement.[15] Either way, post-Tang Buddhism was little more than the tarnished shell of a lost golden age.

With some significant exceptions, the narrative of post-Tang decline has been completely abandoned in contemporary scholarship.[16] The political and ideological agendas that colored Chan scholarship in the postwar period are now well known, and research conducted over the past twenty-five years has sought to reveal and revisit the blind spots of previous generations.[17] One of the most significant developments in the field of Chan studies in recent decades has been the shift in focus from the origins and development of Chan doctrines and practices during the Tang dynasty to the formulation and normalization of Chan traditions and institutions during the Song.[18] Scholars of Chinese Chan now contend that the "mature" or "classic" Chan tradition—the style of Chan that was transmitted to Japan, Korea, Vietnam, and eventually the West—flowed from the confluence of political unification, cultural consolidation, and philosophical innovation of the Northern Song. This was when some of most influential and enduring works of Chan literature—flame records (*denglu* 燈錄), discourse records (*yulu* 語錄), and *gong'an* (J. *kōan* 公案) collections—were produced.[19] These texts, we now know, were often compiled and promoted with the help of Song scholar-officials, some of whom counted themselves members of Chan lineages. The backing of these and other powerful benefactors raised the stature of Chan monks and facilitated the spread of their discourses among the lay elite.[20] It was also during the early Northern Song that the court began to designate public (as opposed to private or hereditary) monasteries. These institutions were supported and regulated by the state, and leading members of Chan lineage families received the lion's share of imperial appointments to their abbacies. Chan monks were thus accorded significant political and economic advantages by the Song government.[21] Given the influence of Song Chan literature, practices, and institutions on the construction of a distinctive Chan identity, several scholars have suggested that Chan, as a self-conscious sectarian movement, might best be understood as a product of the Song dynasty.[22]

Studies of the sociopolitical contexts of Chan's institutional success during the Northern Song have revolutionized our understanding of Chan history and thought, but they also risk reinforcing the idea that the Five Dynasties and Ten Kingdoms was merely a period of cultural stagnation or, at best, subterranean ferment. The tenth century, once dismissed as posterior to the golden age of the Tang, is now often elided as anterior to the golden age of the Song. Over the last ten years, however, new research has demonstrated that past portrayals of the Five Dynasties and Ten Kingdoms as a brief and chaotic interregnum have seriously underestimated the extent to which the developments of this period laid the foundations not only for Song unification but also for distinctive Song institutions and traditions.[23] With the destruction or obsolescence of old forms, new systems are improvised and, when successful, institutionalized—processes that are particularly apparent in the emergence and development of relatively stable states in southern China after the fall of the Tang. In contrast to their counterparts in the north, southern kings were able to build their economies through land reclamation, agricultural innovations, and regional and interstate trade. Surpluses were invested in cultural as well as military initiatives, and traditions of literature, poetry, and landscape painting flourished. Following Song unification in 979, literati, officials, and artisans from southeastern states became some of the primary architects of a new imperial culture, and it is now becoming clear that many of the economic, political, military, and cultural systems initially implemented by the Northern Song court were legacies from the Five Dynasties and Ten Kingdoms.

To what extent can the same be said of Buddhist traditions? While there is no doubt that Chan monks flourished in the political, economic, and intellectual climate of the Northern Song, this book argues that many of the literary traditions, monastic institutions, and political privileges commonly associated with Song-dynasty Chan were in fact already in place in southeastern China during the Five Dynasties and Ten Kingdoms. The history of clergy-court relations during this period is thus important not only for understanding the processes by which Chan clerics moved from the margins to the center of the Chinese Buddhist world but also for distinguishing between the inheritance, adaptation, and innovation of Chan traditions in the Northern Song.

This book, with its focus on the history of Chan from the late Tang through the early Song, covers some of the same ground as Albert Welter's pioneering *Monks, Rulers, and Literati: The Political Ascendancy of Chan Buddhism*, but the approach and perspective are somewhat different. Welter's work examines the development of Chan flame records to determine how and why they were produced, how they shaped conceptions of identity and orthodoxy, and how they influenced later interpretations of Chan history. For Welter, "Chan's rise from 'outsider' to 'insider' status" was closely associated with the compilation and imperial endorsement of these literary collections in the early Northern Song.[24] The present study looks more closely at the cultural and social milieux from which these texts and traditions initially emerged. The most important flame records of this period—the *Patriarch's Hall Collection* (*Zu tang ji* 祖堂集); the *Jingde-Era Record of the Transmission of the Flame* (*Jingde chuan deng lu* 景德傳燈錄; hereafter *Transmission of the Flame*); and the *Tiansheng-Era Extensive Flame Record* (*Tiansheng guangdeng lu* 天聖廣燈錄)—were all produced by monks and laymen who were already well established in positions of significant power. Although these collections spread Chan discourses across regional and linguistic boundaries, they were not the cause of Chan monks' success in the Five Dynasties and early Song but rather one of its effects. This book, therefore, explores the forces that first propelled Chan monks to positions of influence, focusing on the patronage practices of regional rulers and the sociopolitical functions of the clerics they served and were served by.

Despite some differences in orientation and interpretation, Welter's work on the historical development, content, and influence of flame records, together with his studies of the life and teachings of the famous tenth-century cleric Yongming Yanshou 永明延壽 (904–975), has served as an indispensable guide through this difficult and often thorny terrain. As will become clear in the chapters that follow, the same is true for Yanagida Seizan's landmark studies of Chan monks and their patrons in the kingdoms of Min

and the Southern Tang and for Suzuki Tetsuo's voluminous research on regional Chan movements during the Tang and Five Dynasties. The purpose
of the present study is neither to rehash nor reevaluate the contributions
of these or other scholars but to build on their research and insights in an
effort to offer new perspectives on a complicated but critical phase in the
historical development of Chan.

Sources

The material for this study has been pieced together from a diverse array
of sources, none of which are particularly concerned with the kinds of questions raised here. Many tenth-century sources have been lost, but several
temple and stupa inscriptions, private and official histories, and collections
of monastic biographies remain.[25] These sources, broadly speaking, fall into
two categories: those written by monks and laymen and those written by
men not affiliated with Buddhist traditions. The former, as one might expect, are highly sympathetic to the *saṃgha*, underscoring the extraordinary
discipline, supernormal powers, and social benefits of the clergy. The latter group of materials is more disparate and includes both celebrations of
virtuous clerics and acerbic accounts of immoral monks and the inept monarchs who supported them.

The most detailed accounts of clergy-court relations during the Five
Dynasties and Ten Kingdoms are contained in three collections of monastic
biographies: the *Patriarch's Hall Collection*, the *Transmission of the Flame*, and
the *Song Biographies of Eminent Monks* (*Song gaoseng zhuan* 宋高僧傳; hereafter
Song Biographies). Since our views of tenth-century Buddhism have largely
been framed by and filtered through the editorial choices and ideological
agendas of these texts' editors, it is worth briefly introducing these works
here.

Among the three extant Buddhist biographical collections from this
period, the *Patriarch's Hall Collection* is thought to be the oldest. The core of
the collection appears to have been composed at Zhaoqing si 招慶寺 in the
city of Quanzhou in 952.[26] The texts' editors—known only as Jing 靜 and
Yun 筠—and their master, Zhaoqing Wendeng 招慶文僜 (892–972), were the
dharma-descendants of Xuefeng Yicun and thus belonged to the preeminent Chan lineage of the region (see appendix 1). The work they produced
is the earliest surviving example of a multi-lineage compilation of Chan biographies and discourse records, though it belongs to a genre of Chan genealogical literature that reaches back to the early eighth century.[27] The
Patriarch's Hall Collection disappeared in China not long after it was produced
and resurfaced only in 1912, when the wooden printing blocks were discovered in the storehouse of Haein-sa 海印寺, in Korea. The received edition
consists of twenty fascicles with 256 "biographies"—some quite lengthy and
detailed, some little more than brief dialogues—for mostly Chinese but also
some Korean monks. The content and history of this collection has been

studied in detail by Yanagida Seizan, Kinugawa Kenji, Ishii Shūdo, Albert Welter, and others.[28] Although most scholars now agree that the *Patriarch's Hall Collection* was compiled in several stages, beginning in 952 and culminating in Korea sometime in the early eleventh century, it preserves a wealth of information on the history of Chan during the late Tang and early Five Dynasties. This is especially true for the Fujian region; twenty-one of Xuefeng Yicun's disciples and seven of his grand-disciples are represented in this work.

Members of Xuefeng Yicun's lineage appear to have been particularly concerned with issues of lineage and are credited with producing two other genealogical collections during this period: the now lost *Xu baolin chuan* 續寶林傳, compiled by Xuefeng Yicun's disciple Nanyue Weijing 南嶽惟勁 (n.d.) sometime during the Kaiping era (907–911), and the *Transmission of the Flame*, completed roughly a century later.[29] While the *Patriarch's Hall Collection* does not appear to have been widely read in China, the *Transmission of the Flame* became the model on which all subsequent flame records were based and established the archetypes for what would become classic Chan dialogue and behavior. Very little is known about Daoyuan 道原 (fl. 1004), the original compiler of this collection, but it is widely accepted that he was a disciple of Tiantai Deshao 天台德韶 (891–972), the national teacher of Wuyue and leading representative of Xuefeng Yicun's lineage in that kingdom.[30] Daoyuan's work, originally titled *Collection of the Shared Practice of Buddhas and Patriarchs* (*Fozu tongcan ji* 佛祖同參集), was submitted to the throne in 1004 and then edited by a group of Song scholar-officials before it was issued in 1009.[31] The final version totaled thirty fascicles and contained information on 1,760 people and 1,169 entries for individual clerics associated with the Chan tradition. Like the *Patriarch's Hall Collection*, the *Transmission of the Flame* is organized according to lineage and its entries consist largely of verbal exchanges occasionally interspersed with biographical details. Although many of the monks included in the *Transmission of the Flame* also have entries in the *Patriarch's Hall Collection*, the accounts in each collection are distinct and the latter text does not seem to have served as a source for the former. (Scholars have speculated that the editors of both texts may have structured their collections on the model of the earlier *Baolin chuan* 寶林傳 or drawn from the same inscriptions, veritable records, or discourse records circulating in manuscript form.[32])

We do not know what sources Daoyuan used for his collection or the precise nature and extent of later revisions, but in his preface to the text, Yang Yi 楊億 (974–1020), a Song scholar-official and lead editor of Daoyuan's manuscript, offers a few comments on his own editorial process: "In the case of dialogues involving officials and lay people, of those with well-known titles and names, we checked calendars for errors and consulted historical records for [other] mistakes—all such errors and mistakes were effectively eliminated in order that what it conveys be reliable."[33] Despite Yang's assurances of historical accuracy, however, the need to generate

entries for every member of an extensive lineage and the necessity of including dialogues for each subject all but required authors and editors to
incorporate or generate material that was demonstrably fictional.[34]

The *Patriarch's Hall Collection* and the *Transmission of the Flame* share many
of the same sectarian agendas and literary conventions, but they were compiled in different places under different circumstances and thus provide
slightly different perspectives on their subjects. The *Song Biographies*, in
contrast, while homologous to these two texts in many ways, adheres to a
wholly different tradition of monastic biography. This thirty-fascicle text
was compiled under imperial order by the monk Zanning 贊寧 (919–1001)
between the years 982 and 988 and contains 531 primary and 125 subsidiary
biographies of monks who lived between the Zhenguan 貞觀 era of Tang
Taizong (627–649) and the inaugural year of Song Taizong's Duangong 端
拱 era (988), a period of nearly 340 years.[35] Zanning was not affiliated with
a Chan lineage, and he organized his collection along the more conventional thematic model, with biographies grouped together on the basis of
their subjects' primary area of expertise—exegesis, translation, supernormal
powers, vinaya, self-sacrifice, recitation, fundraising, meditation, or preaching. While Zanning included many biographies of prominent Chan monks,
the *Song Biographies* is a pan-Buddhist work that strongly rejects sectarian
rhetoric and portrays all facets of the Buddhist tradition as equally valid.
Zanning's biographies of Chan clerics are thus less concerned with recording instances of awakening and transcribing dialogues between masters
and disciples than with documenting prestigious temple appointments,
relationships with prominent lay people, unusual abilities, erudition, and
discipline.

Zanning was born in Wuyue and enjoyed a long and productive career
as one of the highest-ranking clerics in that kingdom.[36] His broad learning
and literary talents earned him an appointment to the prestigious Hanlin
Academy 翰林院 during the Song dynasty, and in compiling the *Song Biographies* he, like his fellow academician Yang Yi, claimed to have employed a
rigorous historical method: "We based some of the biographies on stele inscriptions. For others we sought out written accounts and records. For some
we questioned official envoys, while for others we interviewed local elders.
We did research to match this information against treatises and scriptures,
did editing work to compare this information with historical documents,
and compiled it all into three cases in order to assist the palace. We have
narrated these wondrous accounts of the clergy that [the reader] may know
of the wealth and value of the house of Buddha."[37] As his own interjections
in the text make clear, Zanning himself served as one of the sources for
the *Song Biographies*; he had known several of his subjects personally, especially the court clerics of Wuyue, and had seen many of the images and sites
described in his work.

Accounts of tenth-century monks preserved in the *Song Biographies*, the
Transmission of the Flame, and the *Patriarch's Hall Collection*, while not homoge-

neous, share the common goal of illustrating and advertising the efficacy of the Buddhist tradition. Fortunately, these partisan accounts can often be compared with secular inscriptions, official and private histories, and local gazetteers to arrive at a more nuanced picture of *saṃgha*-state relations during the tenth century. While Buddhist canonical texts predictably praise the close ties between the clergy and the court as indicative of rulers' virtue and monks' purity and power, secular sources written during the Song dynasty often assert that southern kings' excessive support of the clergy was a symptom of incompetence and a source of political and social unrest.

Many of the authors of these accounts took a rather dim view of Buddhist monks and their lay supporters. Ouyang Xiu, the author of the most influential history of the Five Dynasties and Ten Kingdoms, famously viewed Buddhist monks as parasites who leeched the life out of the empire. Others, like Sima Guang 司馬光 (1019–1086), the preeminent historian of his generation, and Lu You 陸游 (1125–1210), a prominent Song poet and literatus, argued that Buddhism was a tradition noble in principle but often corrupt in practice. In their histories of the Five Dynasties and Ten Kingdoms, these men celebrated the virtues of Song emperors by exposing the inadequacies of their immediate predecessors, chronicling the seemingly incessant violence and betrayals at the northern courts and the administrative and military incompetence of southern regimes. Buddhist clerics appear only infrequently in these works, but when they do they are typically portrayed as unproductive, ignorant, and avaricious men who hastened the demise of kingdoms and dynasties.[38]

Evidence of the economic hardship and social disorder brought on by regional rulers' overzealous support of Buddhist monks functioned as a foil to the prosperity and moral rigor of the Song, but it also served as an object lesson for the Song administration. Almost every critique of tenth-century clerics and laypeople written by Song literati is also a lament about the excessive size, wealth, and influence the clergy attained during the Five Dynasties and Ten Kingdoms. Authors railed against the rulers who funneled cash, land, and other resources into the hundreds of temples they built and restored. They argued that the misguided piety of southeastern kings encouraged large monastic estates to monopolize arable land and hoard precious resources, creating an economic imbalance that persisted into the Song. Accounts of the impropriety of monastics and the credulity of southeastern rulers during the Five Dynasties and Ten Kingdoms can thus also be read as veiled warnings to the Song court against investing too much wealth or too much faith in Buddhist institutions.

Despite divergent interpretations of the moral character and social value of Buddhist monks and their traditions, however, secular historical accounts tend to reinforce, rather than refute, the general historical narrative found in Buddhist biographical collections. Both groups of sources demonstrate that, particularly in southeastern China, the numbers of monks and monasteries, the wealth of monastic institutions, and the political influence of elite clerics had steadily increased during the late ninth and tenth centuries. By all accounts, Buddhism was flourishing in southeastern kingdoms after the fall of the Tang.

Methods

Given the abundance of biographical material and the dearth of firsthand accounts like temple records, official documents, or personal correspondences, I have pursued a prosopographical approach, attempting to uncover the shared characteristics of elite clerics by means of a collective study of their individual biographies.[39] Prosopography, in Lawrence Stone's classic definition, seeks to "establish a universe to be studied, and then to ask a set of uniform questions about birth and death, marriage and family, social origins and inherited economic position, place of residence, education, amount and source of personal wealth, occupation, religion, experience of office, and so on. The various types of information about the individuals in the universe are then juxtaposed and combined, and are examined for significant variables. They are tested both for internal correlations and for correlations with other forms of behavior or action."[40] As a general model, this approach is well suited to the study of tenth-century Buddhism because monastic biographies contain a wealth of personal data—native places, family backgrounds, tonsure masters, places of training, primary masters, texts studied, texts lectured on, texts authored, practices engaged in, teachings, monastic appointments, lay supporters, disciples, circumstances of death, and posthumous honors. Read collectively, these biographies reveal patterns of movement, association, and engagement that are hidden at the individual level. They make it possible, for example, to identify when and where monks affiliated with Chan lineages first began to receive regular patronage from regional rulers. We are able to chart with some precision the spread of monastic networks across regions and to identify which cities, mountains, and monasteries served as centers and conduits for the generation and transmission of doctrines, practices, and material cultures. These sources also reveal trends in practice, teaching, and patronage across generations, as well as correlations between the fortunes of monastic networks and shifting political and economic conditions in specific regions.

The sample size for this study is, however, relatively limited. Nearly all monks honored with memorial inscriptions or with entries in canonical collections belonged to a very small segment of the monastic elite, but in this book I have focused on an even more select group of clerics—those known to have received some form of material or symbolic support from regional rulers. The vast majority of monks patronized by southeastern kings were linked not only by state support but also by affiliation with the same Chan lineage family, a correlation that seems to indicate a direct relationship between lineage and patronage, or between monks' professed ancestry and lay donors' perceptions of efficacy. In thinking through issues of patronage and lineage, the methods and conceptual models associated with historical social-network analysis have also offered some guidance. This relatively recent cross-fertilization of the fields of sociology and history seeks to connect the lives of individuals with larger social, demographic, and cultural processes. Its basic premises have been described by Charles Wetherell: "First, actors in all social systems are viewed as 'interdependent rather than independent'. Second, the linkages or relations among actors channel information, affection and other resources. Third, the structure of those relations or ties among actors both constrain and facilitate action. Fourth, and finally, the patterns of relations among actors define economic, political and social structure."[41]

Buddhist monks, of course, were embedded in multiple, overlapping social networks based on a range of associations—native region, biological family, monastic residence, tonsure family, lineage family, patrons, official appointments, and schools of thought, craft, and practice. Extant sources make it possible to reconstruct, albeit in a limited way, portions of these complex relational webs. Mapping these connections is particularly important for assessing the lives of Chan clerics, because the identity and authority of these men derived in large degree from both their affiliation with and promotion of exclusive lineages and their positions within elite social and institutional hierarchies. These clerics and their allies belonged to multiple communities with distinctive social structures, expectations, values, and traditions. To appreciate the careers and contributions of individual monks, it is necessary to locate them within their larger social, clerical, and intellectual networks and to chart the development of these larger collectives over time.

Admittedly, relying on hagiographical sources to chart the historical development of monastic networks poses several interpretive, methodological, and evidentiary problems. To begin with, monastic biographies contain a creative mix of fact and fiction. Buddhist biography, like all Chinese historiographical writing, is unapologetically allegorical and didactic; the past is something to be framed and interpreted as a commentary on the present and a guideline for the future.[42] These accounts are thus shaped by the moral imperatives of their compilers and constrained by the dictates of their genres. Their purpose was not to produce objective historical records but to exemplify the awakened state and exhibit the efficacy of the tradition. They are polemical works, and the individuals they portray conform to certain archetypes. The lives of saints, as Michel de Certeau noted long ago, can be read as individual manifestations of a tradition's collective ideals: "The same features and the same episodes are passed along from one proper name to another; from all these floating elements, like an array of words and jewels, the combinations make up a given figure and charge it with meaning."[43]

While certain narrative themes and personality types do recur throughout the biographies studied here, the monks represented in these texts were clearly more than just fictional constructs.[44] We are often fortunate enough to have multiple biographies for the same monk preserved in different sources, and when canonical narratives can be compared against inscriptions and secular histories, basic biographical information generally tallies across accounts, though there are certainly exceptions. This consistency may mean that different biographies were based on the same root sources or it may reflect common knowledge about the major milestones of prominent monks' lives. After all, the compilers of all three of the biographical collections used in this study lived in southeastern China and were familiar with many of their subjects or their direct disciples. Nevertheless, without letters, diaries, or original manuscripts, the best we can say is that these accounts, if not demonstrably accurate or objective portrayals of their subjects, were at the very least collectively accepted representations of them.

A second risk inherent in this approach is that extent sources, even if we grant them historical value, present an extremely limited perspective and offer only a very narrow and highly filtered view of the past. The motives of authors, whether scholar-officials or Buddhist clerics, not only shaped the way events and individuals were portrayed but also determined what was included and excluded from the historical record. The vast majority of extant Buddhist texts were produced by a small fraction of the clerical elite, working in a handful of major, state-sanctioned monasteries, often under imperial supervision. Those texts that were (by imperial order) inducted into the Buddhist canon had been self-censored by their authors as well as vetted and, in some cases, edited by secular officials.[45] References in inscriptions, letters, and private histories to other, clearly prominent clerics—monks not mentioned in canonical sources—make it clear that major figures were omitted from biographical collections, the memory and significance of their lives effectively lost to later generations.

The accounts that were collected and preserved thus tell a particular kind of story. The *Patriarch's Hall Collection* and the *Transmission of the Flame* were compiled by Chan monks associated with Xuefeng Yicun's lineage who were active in southeastern China. Both texts document the rise of Chan monks, with a particular, though not exclusive, emphasis on the descendants of Yicun. The editors of these collections had an obvious interest in promoting Chan lineages in general and embellishing the credentials of this network of clerics in particular. We might dismiss these texts as sectarian self-promotion if accounts in the *Song Biographies*, memorial inscriptions, and private histories did not also confirm (in somewhat less detail) the prominence of this same lineage of Chan monks in southeastern China. So, while there is no doubt that regional Buddhist cultures were far more complex and diverse than our sources allow, we can be reasonably confident that accounts of Chan prominence were not simply the wishful thinking or retrospective creation of Chan monks themselves.

Chapter Overview

This book is divided into six chapters, arranged roughly chronologically and regionally, beginning in the northern capitals during the late Tang dynasty, moving on to the cities and mountains of the kingdoms of Min, the Southern Tang, and Wuyue, and concluding in the capital of the Northern Song. It spans a period of nearly two hundred years, from the time of the anti-Buddhist Huichang persecutions in the mid-ninth century to the publication of the *Tiansheng-Era Extensive Flame Record* in 1036, but it focuses most intensively on the years between 881 (when Chang'an fell to Huang Chao's rebellion) and 978 (when the last of the southern kingdoms submitted to the Song).

The first two chapters address the social and political transformations of the late ninth and early tenth centuries and their effect on regional cultures. Chapter 1 offers a broad, historical overview of the rebellions leading to the collapse of the Tang dynasty and the economic and political autonomy of southern territories. While the overthrow of the Tang court and the decimation of the aristocracy are frequently equated with the onset of debilitating disorder, the loss of centralized control effectively freed southern provinces from the political restraints and economic obligations imposed by the Tang court, ushering in a period of relative peace and prosperity. This chapter focuses on the early histories of the kingdoms of Wuyue, the Southern Tang, and Min with particular attention paid to the patronage practices of the first generation of rulers. In their efforts to transition from military to civil rule, southern kings sought political legitimacy through the promotion of both regional and transregional cultural traditions—a process that reshaped Buddhist institutions in major southern cities.

Chapter 2 examines some of the ways the Tang–Five Dynasties transition impacted Buddhist monastics, their traditions, and regional religious cultures. During the late Tang, economic development, population growth, and increased political independence in southern provinces helped to swell monastic populations and initiated an upsurge in temple construction. With the onset of the Five Dynasties, just as some southern rulers recruited former Tang officials and local leaders to their administrations, they also appointed Chang'an's displaced court clerics and prominent native monks to the abbacies of major monasteries in their territories. Drawing on the biographies of monks active during this period, this chapter demonstrates that traditions of learning and practice popular in the northern capitals during the late Tang were disseminated to and reconstituted in the capitals of southern kingdoms, most notably Shu and Wuyue. The continuity of elite Tang Buddhist traditions is then contrasted with the elevation of local clerics, many of whom belonged to Chan lineages, in less developed regions like Jiangxi and Fujian. The political empowerment and economic development of southeastern regions situated resident Chan monks at the centers of newly sovereign states, and the rapid ascent of Chan clerics to positions of power and influence in these kingdoms can be understood as part of a larger process of political and geographic reorientation set in motion by the fall of the Tang and rise of regional powers.

Chapters 3 through 5 survey clergy-court relations in the three southeastern kingdoms of Min, the Southern Tang, and Wuyue, respectively, charting the relationships formed between these kingdoms' royal families and the lineage of monks descended from Xuefeng Yicun and Xuansha Shibei. Chapter 3 examines the origins of this religio-political network in Min and argues that some of the defining features of the mature Chan tradition—the compilation of flame records, monasteries whose abbacies were reserved for members of Chan lineages, sustained governmental support, and association with the imperial ancestral cult—are evident in this kingdom. The first half of this chapter introduces Yicun and Shibei—their biographies, teachings, lineage affiliations, monasteries, and their relationships with Min's rulers. The second half details the divisions that formed among these monks' disciples. For a period of roughly fifty years, as members of Min's royal Wang family occupied the throne or assumed governing posts in Min's major cities, they consistently recruited the disciples of Yicun and Shibei to major monasteries within their territories. After the death of Min's first king, however, power struggles between members of the Wang clan appear to have led to schisms among monks loyal to and dependent on different patrons.

Infighting among members of Min's royal family eventually crippled the kingdom of Min, and it was subsequently invaded and conquered by the Southern Tang and Wuyue in 946. By that time, many clerics had already left Min for the security and opportunity Min's more stable neighbors could provide. In the mid-tenth century, the Southern Tang stood as the most prosperous and powerful southern kingdom, and chapter 4 discusses how the descendants of Yicun and Shibei rose to become its preeminent clerics. This chapter begins by charting the movement of monks from the cities of Min to the capital of the Southern Tang as they received successive temple appointments from increasingly powerful patrons. The area within the Southern Tang's borders had long hosted major centers of Buddhist learning, but the influx of largely non-native Chan monks does not seem to have disrupted established traditions. As clerics from Min assumed control of well-established monastic institutions with large resident populations, rather than transform the character of the region's normative Buddhist cultures, they appear to have embraced and embodied it. The activities of these monks in the capital of the Southern Tang, particularly those gathered around the eminent cleric Fayan Wenyi, suggest that they were able to differentiate themselves from other monks by means of both their distinguished pedigree and their ecumenical approach to teaching and practice. As abbots of major monasteries and advisors to the ruler and his court, these monks promoted a range of regional Buddhist traditions while fulfilling the responsibilities of court clerics. Their teachings thus took on a catholic, literary, and conservative quality that was well suited to the urbane audiences of the capital.

When the fortunes of the Southern Tang began to decline after a failed war with the northern Zhou dynasty in 958, the center of this Chan movement shifted yet again. Several of Fayan Wenyi's leading disciples relocated to the kingdom of Wuyue, a politically stable and economically prosperous state with a reputation for generously supporting the *saṃgha*. The patronage practices of Wuyue's kings described in chapter 5 provide perhaps the clearest illustration of what might be called the Chanification of Buddhism during this period. Wuyue's first kings nurtured an eclectic array of Buddhist and Daoist monks and monasteries; it was only during the reign of the last king, Qian Chu 錢俶 (r. 948–978), that court patronage was channeled to monks affiliated with specific sub-branches of Xuansha Shibei's lineage—primarily the dharma-descendants of Fayan Wenyi. As in the Southern Tang, where many of these monks had initially trained, the teachings and practices of Chan clerics in Wuyue encompassed a spectrum of normative Buddhist traditions—from classic *zhiguan* meditation, to *Avataṃsaka* and *Lotus Sūtra* devotion, to Pure Land faith and esoteric practices. The broad interests of this closely connected network of clerics highlight the ecumenical and inclusive nature of Wuyue's Buddhist culture, but they also raise questions about the function of lineage and the nature of Chan identity—issues that are explored in detail in this chapter.

At the end of the Five Dynasties and Ten Kingdoms, the descendants of Xuefeng Yicun and Xuansha Shibei occupied the abbacies of monasteries throughout much of southeastern China. Then, just as quickly as they ascended to prominence, they seem to have disappeared. After Song reunification, the prestige of this clerical network began to be undercut by monks affiliated with other Chan lineages based in northern China. The sixth and final chapter begins with a sketch of *saṃgha*-state relations in northern China over the course of the Five Dynasties and then explores the effects of the Five Dynasties–Song transition on Chan monks in and around the Song capital at Kaifeng and in southeastern cities. As is well known, beginning in the early decades of the Song dynasty, the dharma-heirs of the renowned Tang-dynasty Chan master Linji Yixuan 臨濟義玄 (d. 866) consistently won the support of prominent Song officials. The biographies of Linji clerics and their patrons in northern cities recounted in the final section of this chapter indicate that the processes of political unification and cultural consolidation influenced a shift in imperial patronage from monks affiliated with the lineages of Yicun and Shibei to the descendants of Linji. By highlighting the shared characteristics of Chan monks and their traditions in southeastern kingdoms during the tenth century and their successors at the turn of the eleventh, I hope to show that the Chan institutions of the early the Northern Song rested on foundations laid during the Five Dynasties and Ten Kingdoms.

The eminent sinologist Jacques Gernet once observed that after the destruction of the anti-Buddhist Huichang persecutions, monastic communities regained and even increased their power in southeastern China during the Five Dynasties and into the Song. In his estimation, however, this "was a church that had outlived itself and seems to have lost its soul."[46] This book is a search for that lost soul. It is perhaps fitting, then, that it begins with a murder.

1

Disintegration

The Tang–Five Dynasties Transition

ON THE EVENING of September 13, 904, the assassin Li Yanwei 李彦威 (d. 904) led a hundred troops into the imperial precincts of Tang emperor Zhaozong 昭宗 (r. 888–904). Knocking at the palace gates, he feigned some urgent business, and when one of the emperor's wives appeared, she was killed. Li's men rushed into the inner quarters, and Emperor Zhaozong, drunk at the time, tried to flee but was slain. Hundreds of his family members were also put to death, their bodies thrown unceremoniously into a common grave.[1] This assault on the Tang imperial family was carried out on the orders of Zhu Wen 朱溫 (852–912), a former lieutenant of the rebel Huang Chao 黃巢 (d. 884) and formidable rival to the Tang house.[2] Zhu installed Zhaozong's eleven-year-old son Li Zhu 李柷 (892–908; r. 904–907) on the throne for three years before declaring himself emperor of the new Liang dynasty (907–923), drawing the final curtain on nearly three centuries of Tang rule.

At the beginning of the tenth century, no one could be certain if the Tang dynasty would be restored, if a new regime would reunify the empire, or if the continent would continue to be divided into smaller states. Most post-Tang regimes aspired to preside over an empire as extensive and prosperous as the early Tang. Each envisioned itself as the heir to the imperial legacy and attempted to replicate the Tang's accomplishments while avoiding its errors. Disunity brought difficulties, of course, but it also created opportunities. The coexistence of numerous independent kingdoms allowed for multiple sources of authority, and rival regimes competed with one another for cultural as well as military superiority, driving developments on both fronts. Rulers' efforts to recruit and retain men of talent and means opened new avenues for patronage and fostered the development of distinctive regional cultures. Later chapters will deal in detail with the effects of balkanization on Buddhist communities in southeastern China. This chapter briefly outlines some of the key events precipitating the fall of the Tang and the establishment of the Five Dynasties and Ten Kingdoms. Several excellent studies on the history of this period are now available in English; the present discussion therefore focuses on strategies of legitimization and governance employed by the founding figures of the kingdoms of Min, the Southern Tang, and Wuyue.[3] As will become clear in subsequent chapters, political and social forces influenced the development of regional monastic communities during the late ninth and early tenth centuries and helped to elevate Chan clerics to positions of unprecedented authority.

The Fall of the Tang

Zhu Wen's overthrow of the Tang dynasty was merely the *coup de grâce* for a gravely ailing empire.[4] The onset of the Tang's decline is conventionally traced to the political and economic disruptions caused by the An Lushan 安祿山 rebellion (755–763). Among the many changes the court instituted in the aftermath of An Lushan was the granting of increased authority and autonomy to regional commissioners. Men holding the titles of military commissioner (*jiedushi* 節度使) and surveillance commissioner (*guanchashi* 觀察使) were posted first in the northern provinces and later in the south. The shift in the administration of the hinterlands, designed to increase border security, had the unintended consequence of concentrating military, civil, and economic powers at a far remove from the capital in Chang'an. Although the Tang court managed to retain control of the empire (with the exception of Hebei 河北) up until the onset of Huang Chao's rebellion in the 870s, its hold on the provinces had grown tenuous.[5]

Huang Chao's rebellion was by far the most devastating insurrection of the late Tang, but it was not the first. By the early decades of the ninth century, the Tang administration was operating at a fiscal deficit and responded by increasing the taxes levied on an already overburdened peasantry.[6] Efforts to regain financial solvency led to civil unrest. Bandits took to raiding towns and villages, compounding the difficulties of the populace and depriving the government of much-needed revenue and resources. Many of the tens of thousands of men who took up arms to fight against Tang troops in the second half of the ninth century had been forced off their land through tax default or a succession of natural disasters that hammered the countryside. Government reports claimed that, in order to pay taxes, some men were selling the lumber from their homes, hiring their wives out as servants, and selling their children into slavery.[7] Banditry and smuggling offered an alternative; a thriving black market in salt operated at the expense of a government-imposed monopoly. Faced with bleak futures or famine, destitute peasants were recruited by rebel leaders. Disparate groups were eventually united and organized by warlords like Qiu Fu 裘甫 (d. 860), whose band of thirty thousand men ravaged southeastern China before he was finally killed in 860. The Tang court regained control after Qiu's uprising, but the rebellion initiated by Wang Xianzhi 王仙芝 (d. 878) in 874, and later led by Huang Chao, was not so easily overcome. After six years of warring and pillaging throughout the empire, Huang's army of six hundred thousand men marched on Chang'an in 880, forcing Emperor Xizong into exile in Sichuan early the next year. Huang's capture of Chang'an in 881 plunged the city into chaos. The capital was subsequently destroyed and the aristocracy decimated. Poets would later describe the carnage in apocalyptic terms: "In house after house blood flows like boiling fountains; / In place after place victims scream: their screams shake the earth. / Dancers and singing girls have all disappeared, / Babies and young girls are abandoned alive."[8]

The capital was recaptured in 883 and a cornered Huang Chao was killed the following year, but it was a pyrrhic victory for the Tang; the rebellion had laid bare the frailty of the regime. Henceforth, all pretense of control over the provinces was dropped, so that, for all intents and purposes, the Tang relinquished control over most of its former empire in 881. This date marks the effective end of the Tang dynasty, though it existed in name for another quarter century. After 881, military strongmen in the provinces challenged and overthrew Tang-appointed governors. By the final decades of the Tang, the positions of military and surveillance commissioners, formerly strictly mandated and controlled by the court, had in many cases become hereditary. These powerful posts passed from father to son or from mentor to protégé, making those who held them more akin to kings than commissioners—a situation that culminated with the establishment of autonomous states during the Five Dynasties and Ten Kingdoms.

The Formation of Southern Kingdoms

The demographic and economic weight of China had begun to shift south during the second half of the Tang—a process that only accelerated after Huang Chao's rebellion. Census figures for the years 742 and 1080 show a 328 percent population increase in southern China compared with just 26 percent in the north.[9] While the precise extent of north-south migration following the destruction of Chang'an and Luoyang 洛陽—the secondary or "eastern" capital—is unclear, there is little doubt that a significant portion of the northern population sought refuge in the south during the late ninth and early tenth centuries. The governors of southern territories relied on the influx of skilled labor as well as local talent to staff their nascent administrations and transform erstwhile provinces into independent states. Regional rulers' efforts to draw reputable and talented men to their courts brought symbolic as well as tangible benefits. An upright official's willingness to serve a ruler was conventionally taken as a sign of good governance. According to the famous passage from the *Analects*, "He who governs with virtue is like the North Star, residing in his place while the multitude pay tribute."[10] Men of honor were supposed to gravitate toward noble monarchs but keep their distance from unjust rulers. By receiving patrons' largesse, recipients acknowledged their authority and enhanced their credibility, and newly crowned kings in southern states were understandably eager to exploit the social and political capital men of means could convey.[11]

The founding patriarchs of the southern kingdoms were not the most natural allies of northern nobility, however. The first generation of southern rulers had risen from humble origins and secured their positions not through formal education and familial influence but through superior military strategy and strength.[12] Song literati would later scorn the patriarchs of southern kingdoms as base commoners, unworthy of the power they had seized through insurrection. Though a southerner himself, Ouyang Xiu showed no nostalgia for the period of southern independence. In his *Historical Records of the Five Dynasties,* he dismissed the rulers of southern states as "tattooed bandits and baldheaded smugglers" who had turned to insurrection and "anointed themselves through prodigies and omens" in order to delude the credulous masses into accepting their oppressive rule.[13] He characterized Wang Jian 王建 (r. 907–918), the first ruler of Shu (in modern Sichuan province—Ouyang's birthplace) as "a wastrel in youth, who made a living butchering cows, stealing donkeys, and pirating illegal salt, such that fellow villagers dubbed him 'Wang the Bastard.' "[14] Ouyang may have downplayed the accomplishments of southern rulers, but warlords like Wang Jian were clearly savvy enough to subdue competitors and lay the foundations of robust, if short-lived, states.[15]

Once established as regional rulers, many of these men went to great lengths to distance themselves from the warlord image. Instead, they cultivated the persona of a civilized sovereign, who ruled not though force or fear but by sound governance, economic development, and the promotion of high culture. To that end, Wang Jian and other regional rulers recruited former Tang courtiers to help administer their territories. Sima Guang wrote that when the kingdom of Shu was first established, "the clans of many Tang capped-and-gowned officials fled the upheavals and came to Shu. The emperor [Wang Jian] revered and employed them there, and he had them manage the affairs of his government. Thus, the civil elements [of government], such as the institutions and documents [of Shu], retained an air of the Tang."[16] This same strategy—staffing regional courts with experienced Tang bureaucrats—was pursued by the founding patriarchs of other southern kingdoms as well. It was a process that would have important implications for the development of regional monastic communities; in addition to recruiting former Tang officials, local rulers also sought out many of the Buddhist monks and Daoist adepts who had formerly served the Tang court.

Wuyue

At the same time that Wang Jian was coming to power in Shu, Qian Liu 錢鏐 (852–932), the first king of Wuyue, was consolidating his control over the Zhejiang region.[17] Ouyang Xiu characteristically claimed that Qian Liu had been a salt smuggler with a weakness for drinking and gambling. Whatever the dissipations of his youth, Qian went on to battle elements hostile to the Tang in the Zhejiang area for nearly twenty years, pacifying the region after much bloodshed and earning the gratitude of the Tang court.[18] In 895 Tang emperor Zhaozong appointed Qian military commissioner of the Zhenhai and Zhendong commanderies, awarding him an "iron pledge" that granted immunity for up to nine capital offences.[19] Such gestures were largely symbolic, intended to affirm the authority already commanded by men like Qian while maintaining the fiction that they served at the pleasure

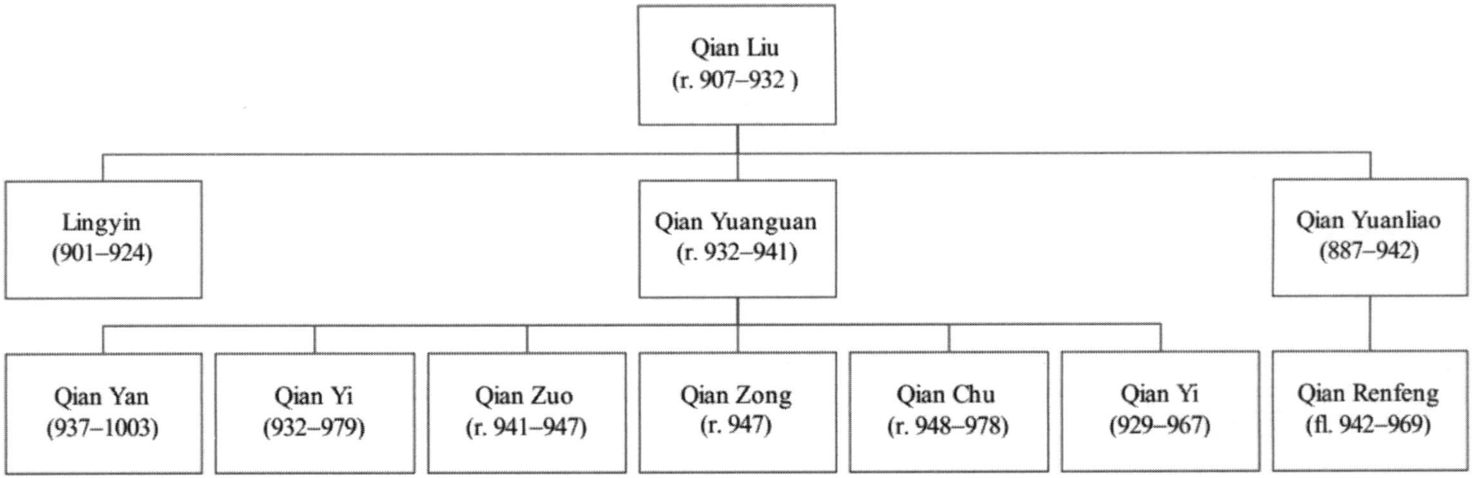

Figure 1. Prominent members of Wuyue's royal family

of the Tang emperor. When the Tang was finally overthrown in 907, Zhu Wen, now Liang emperor Taizu 太祖 (r. 907–912), invested Qian as Prince of Wuyue.[20] With the establishment of the Later Tang dynasty (923–936), Emperor Zhuangzong 莊宗 (r. 923–926) went even further, awarding Qian the jade registers and gold seal typically reserved for emperors. Qian thereafter declared himself King of Wuyue and converted his homes into palaces and his administrative offices into a court befitting his royal status.

Qian Liu, like the early rulers of Min, Chu, and Nanping, maintained a façade of loyalty to northern courts, sending tribute, obeying sumptuary and taboo restrictions, and using suitably deferential language in official communiqués. While referencing their own reign periods for domestic affairs, Qian and his heirs (fig. 1) observed the reign designations of northern courts in diplomatic correspondence, thus paying lip-service to northern control. Despite these gestures of fealty, the north had no real power to enforce its will in the south, and southern kingdoms essentially functioned as sovereign states.

At any given time, as many as seven states coexisted in the south, and interstate relations were accordingly fluid and complex (see map 1). In Wuyue, Qian Liu entered into marriage alliances with the ruling families of Min and the Southern Han to his south, but his relationship with the kingdom of Wu to his north and west was strained. Wu (and its successor, the Southern Tang) controlled overland transport routes to the northern capitals as well as access to major river passages, including the Yangzi.[21] These roads and rivers, together with the Grand Canal that linked Hangzhou Bay with Luoyang, Kaifeng, and cities further north, were the primary channels for interstate travel and trade during the tenth century, but Wuyue had no direct access to any of them.[22] Despite this disadvantage, Wuyue did control a major seaport at Mingzhou, which allowed for tributary and diplomatic missions to travel by sea to the northern capitals and beyond to the Koryŏ and Khitan empires. Ocean access also opened up opportunities for lucrative trade with Southeast Asia and Japan. The combination of trade, land reclamation and agricultural development, and local industries made Wuyue the most secure and wealthy state of the post-Tang period.[23] For over eighty years, the region enjoyed a peace and prosperity that proved elusive to other kingdoms in that volatile era. A reputation for political stability and economic affluence attracted emigrants from all over China, making Wuyue's capital at Hangzhou one of the most densely populated cities in southern China. The Qian family's generous support for monks and monasteries also established their capital as a major center of Buddhist culture.

Wu and the Southern Tang

During Qian Liu's reign, Wuyue was bordered to the north and west by the kingdom of Wu 吳 (902–937), a short-lived and volatile state, controlled by the Yang 楊 family from its capital at Yangzhou.[24] Known as Jiangdu 江都 (River Capital) during the Tang, Yangzhou was situated at the intersection of the Yangzi River and the Han Conduit of the Grand Canal, making it *the* commercial hub of the Tang empire. During the late Tang, this region had been administered by the celebrated Tang general and Buddhist layman Gao Pian 高駢 (ca. 821–887). Until his assassination in 887, Gao was one of the few Tang-appointed commissioners to maintain control of his territory both during and after Huang Chao's rebellion.[25] The murder of Gao destabilized the area, however, and the ensuing struggle for control reportedly took a grizzly toll on the populace. According to Ouyang Xiu, "Starving residents murdered each other for food—husband and wife, father and son sold one another to the butcher to be trimmed like sheep or swine."[26] By 892, Yang Xingmi 楊行密 (852–905), a former Tang military commander, had taken control of Yangzhou and much of the former Huainan circuit. Yang received the titular title of surveillance commissioner for Xuanzhou 宣州 from the Tang court in 889, and his position as regional ruler was confirmed in 902, when Tang emperor Zhaozong named him Prince of Wu.

The subsequent succession of rulers in Wu is somewhat complicated (fig. 2). After Yang Xingmi's death in 905, he was succeeded in title by his eldest son, Yang Wo 楊渥 (886–908). Control of the region, however, was assumed by Xu Wen 徐溫 (862–927), one of Yang Xingmi's senior military commanders. Xu Wen had Yang Wo assassinated after just three years on the throne and installed Yang Xingmi's second son, Yang Longyan 楊隆演 (897–920), who at the time was only eleven years old. Like his brother before him, Yang Longyan answered to Xu Wen, who arranged the prince's elevation to King of Wu in 919 and simultaneously secured his own appointment to the position of grand counselor and protector-general of armed forces for the kingdom.[27] Yang Longyan died of illness shortly thereafter, at the age of twenty-four, and was succeeded, again through Xu Wen's orchestration, by his younger brother Yang Pu 楊溥 (900–938).

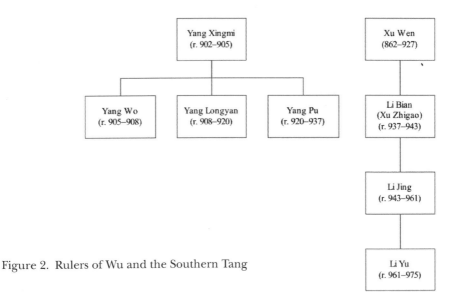

Figure 2. Rulers of Wu and the Southern Tang

With Yang Pu on the throne, Xu Wen continued to pursue his imperial ambitions. In 926 four generations of his ancestors received posthumous titles and were honored with ancestral temples in Jinling (present-day Nanjing), the kingdom's second largest city after Yangzhou.[28] After Xu Wen's death the following year, all of his sons were invested as princes. In time, his adopted son Xu Zhigao 徐知誥 (889–943) assumed Xu Wen's position as regent and effective ruler of the kingdom of Wu. Xu Zhigao seized complete control in 937, usurping Yang Pu's throne and establishing the new Kingdom of Qi 齊. Shortly after the fall of the Later Tang dynasty in the north, Xu Zhigao took the further steps of changing his kingdom's name to the Great Tang (Datang 大唐) and his own name to Li Bian 李昇, adopting the surname of the former Tang imperial clan, from which he claimed descent. (Song historians made certain to distinguish this short-lived kingdom from its illustrious predecessor, dubbing it the "Southern Tang" or the "Illegitimate Tang" 偽唐.) As Li Bian's re-designations made clear, he did not see his kingdom simply as one among many sovereign states occupying the old imperium but rather as the sole legitimate heir to the temporarily disrupted Tang dynasty. In accord with these lofty aspirations, Li Bian moved his court from Yangzhou to Jinling, a city with a long history as an imperial capital.[29] In contrast to Qian Liu in Wuyue, Li Bian abandoned any pretense of subservience to the northern courts, declaring himself emperor and laying plans for the reunification of the empire.

As part of that process, Li Bian, like other southern rulers, labored to transform his image from that of usurper to noble and righteous sovereign. According to the Song literatus Ma Ling 馬令 (fl. 1105), "When the Wu kingdom was first stabilized, local officials were all of military background and taxes were levied to aid the military. Only Xu Zhigao [Li Bian] was fond of scholarship. He welcomed those who practiced Confucian ritual and was personally able to promote frugality. His administration was humane, and [people] were attracted to it from far and near."[30] Even Ouyang Xiu, while predictably noting Li Bian's unremarkable origins, conceded that he went on to become a benevolent ruler who did not capitalize on the weakened positions of neighboring kingdoms, preferred aid to invasion, and offered economic relief to the destitute among his own subjects.

Such sentiments conform to the trope of the disadvantaged yet virtuous first ruler (the counterpoint to the indulgent and ineffective last ruler) common in official historiography, but there is no cause to doubt that the rulers of the Southern Tang promoted the principles of both wen 文 (civil) and wu 武 (martial) society. In pursuit of the former, Li Bian amassed a vast library of Tang texts as well as collections of Tang paintings, board games, and musical instruments. Some of the most celebrated poetry, literature, and painting of the tenth century was produced by men of the Southern Tang. The promotion of high culture, carried on by Li Bian's successors, was not just an expression of the family's love of literature and learning, but also an effective means of attracting scholars from other regions to their court and adding luster to their imperial credentials.[31] As part of Li Bian's

efforts to turn the Southern Tang into the civilized center of a war-torn empire, he also nurtured the growth of the region's already substantial population of Buddhist monks and Daoist adepts. Although Li Bian himself
demonstrated some fascination with Daoist traditions (some Song historians claim that he, like several Tang emperors, died after consuming al-
chemical elixirs), Buddhist monks—many of whom will be discussed in
chapter 4—were the most numerous and influential religious specialists
in the kingdom.[32]

Min

The histories and cultures of Wuyue and the Southern Tang were closely
tied to those of their mutual neighbor, the kingdom of Min (909–946),
whose capital lay at Fuzhou near the mouth of the Min River.[33] Min was
ruled by the Wang 王 family (fig. 3), which wrested its lands from the Tang
domain by force of arms. As the ninth century drew toward its close, the
Tang-appointed surveillance commissioner for Fuzhou, Chen Yan 陳巖
(d. 891), inherited the onerous task of restoring order to the area after the
devastation wrought by Huang Chao's rebellion.[34] With the authority of
the Tang court continuing to wane, his position was challenged by a band
of brothers led by Wang Chao 王潮 (846–897). In 886 the Wang brothers,
originally from Guangzhou 光州 in Henan, entered the Min region with
five thousand troops and established a military base in the strategic port
city of Quanzhou, along the southern coast. Chen Yan's death in 891 triggered a fierce struggle for control of the regional seat at Fuzhou, from which
Wang Chao and his brothers emerged victorious.

Wang Chao assumed Chen Yan's position in the capital, appointing his
brothers and other kinsmen to governing posts in the new kingdom's other
prefectures. On his death five years later, Wang Chao was succeeded as surveillance commissioner by his younger brother Wang Shenzhi 王審知 (862–
925).[35] As uncontested ruler of the region, Wang Shenzhi received a series
of titles, first from the Tang court and then from the Liang. He was officially enfeoffed as Prince of Min by Liang emperor Taizu in 909, some years
after neighboring rulers had been elevated to similar positions.

When the Wang family first entered Fujian in 886, the region was less
developed than Sichuan, Jiangsu, or Zhejiang. During the reign of Wang
Shenzhi, however, cities along the coast of Fujian grew into prosperous
cultural and economic centers. The transformation was accomplished in
large part through new agricultural techniques, exploitation of sea trade,
and skillful management of the large numbers of emigrants streaming into
southern China from the north. The population of southern Fujian, according to some estimates, increased fivefold between the eighth and the tenth
centuries.[36]

Consistent with his accounts of other southern kings, Ouyang Xiu
described Wang Shenzhi as a "brigand" who reinvented himself as a frugal
and compassionate ruler.[37] Rather than seek to expand his territory, Shenzhi sued for peace with the neighboring kingdoms of Wuyue and the

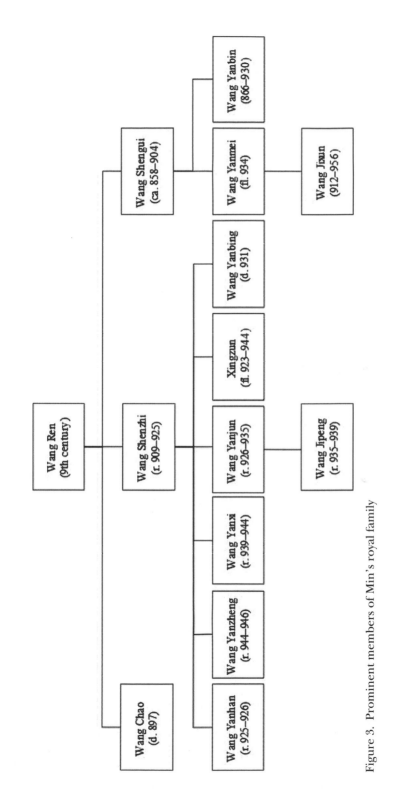

Figure 3. Prominent members of Min's royal family

Southern Han.[38] Like Qian Liu, Li Bian, and others, once his position was secured, Wang Shenzhi exchanged his battle armor for the robes of a gentleman scholar. In addition to recruiting some members of the former Tang aristocracy, Shenzhi also established schools to educate "refined men" indigenous to Min.[39] Importantly, efforts to transform local leaders into cultured officials suitable to serve in an imperial administration were paralleled by Wang Shenzhi's strategic cultivation of prominent local Buddhist clerics to serve both as counselors to his court and as abbots of major monastic estates in his capital and other major cities.

Min's first king was by all accounts a great benefactor of Buddhist monks and monasteries. Wang Shenzhi styled himself in the image of a Cakravartin (Wheel-turning) king—the secular counterpart to a buddha—and his Buddhist affinities were celebrated in steles recording his devotion to the Buddhist teachings and describing his pious acts: personally copying Buddhist texts, authorizing the construction of temples and stupas, and doling out resources to convert those near and far.[40] The inscription for Shenzhi's ancestral temple records that, as a result of his benevolent rule, "sages without outflows [i.e., free of all defilements] and monks were scattered in every direction. Having established the proper conditions, Buddhist temples filled his joyous kingdom."[41]

Shenzhi's imperial destiny, according to legend, was even foreseen by a Buddhist cleric. In a cryptic poem, the monk Suishi 碎石 (n.d.) reportedly predicted: "The cliff is high but falls before the tidal waters. / The tide recedes and an arrow and mouth come forth."[42] Interpreted—or more likely written—with the benefit of hindsight, the cliff (yan 巖) represents the deceased surveillance commissioner for Fuzhou, Chen Yan, whose regime Wang Chao swept away, in keeping with the last character of his name, meaning "tide" (chao 潮). Wang Chao was in turn succeeded by his brother Wang Shenzhi, whose name (zhi 知), unites the characters for arrow 矢 and mouth 口.[43] Prophecies of this sort were a common feature of dynastic transitions; there are similar stories of Buddhist monks foreseeing the fall of the Sui dynasty, the rise of the Tang, and the founding of other southern states during the Five Dynasties and Ten Kingdoms. As John Kieschnick has observed, "while purporting to provide a link between present and future, such stories were in fact providing a link between the present and the past."[44] In the case of Min, Suishi's augury asserts the Wangs' destiny to rule the region and implies that Buddhist monks both acknowledged their authority and served their interests. By the time prophecies of Wang Chao's preordained rule were circulating in print at the end of the tenth century, the close relationship between Min's royal family and Buddhist clerics was already the stuff of legends.

Other members of the Wang family were also stalwart benefactors of the clergy, and at least one of Wang Shenzhi's sons was later ordained as a Buddhist monk.[45] But not everyone was enthusiastic about the close ties that linked the clergy and the court in Min. Shenzhi's adopted son Yan Si 延嗣 (n.d), for example, reportedly tried to curtail his father's support of the *saṃgha*, but the king famously—some would say infamously—continued to sponsor large ordinations, to donate land to monasteries, and to underwrite the construction and expansion of temples and stupas, the casting of gold and bronze images, and the copying of Buddhist canons in precious metals.[46] Wang Shenzhi seems to have been particularly supportive of local Chan clerics. According to a biography of Xuefeng Yicun—one of Min's most influential clerics and a close confidant of the king—after Wang Shenzhi vanquished his political rivals, he "washed his weapons in the rain of the Law and paid obeisance before the forest of Chan."[47]

Wang Shenzhi's metamorphosis from fearsome warlord to pious king and his kingdom's transformation from provincial backwater to affluent and autonomous state were part of the larger social, political, and geographic reorientation of China at the turn of the tenth century. This period was undoubtedly a devastating time for the residents of Chang'an and Luoyang, but the collapse of the Tang dynasty brought increased economic prosperity, regional development, and political autonomy to the residents of many southern provinces. While the fall of the Tang is often associated with the onset of chaos, Nicolas Tackett has pointed out that "the abdication of the last Tang emperor in 907 actually marked the point at which relative stability had returned to most of the territory of the Chinese heartland. Indeed, it was only by reestablishing order that new regimes acquired the political legitimacy that would allow them to proclaim new dynasties and kingdoms."[48] After over a quarter century of upheaval and uncertainty, relatively stable regimes emerged to pacify and govern large swathes of southern China. Northern emigrants, drawn toward the promise of security and opportunity, joined with native southerners to transform former provinces into sovereign states. The political authority of regional rulers was demonstrated not through aristocratic ancestry but through the expansion of agricultural and industrial production, the formation of effective and efficient administrations, and the promotion and preservation of cultural traditions.

   With the disintegration of the old empire, moreover, there was no longer a single normalizing force—no one standard of political authority or ideological orthodoxy—and new states struck a balance between laying claim to the legacy of the Tang and asserting their own unique regional identities. The staffing of regional courts and the construction of imperial cultures also involved the recruitment of prominent clerics to the abbacies of state-sanctioned temples and the promotion of both local Buddhist traditions and those associated with the Tang court in Chang'an. The processes of state construction played out differently in different regions and, as we will see, the patronage practices of southern kings effectively determined the leadership of regional monastic communities and directly influenced the development of regional Buddhist cultures.

2

Improvisation

The Transformation of Regional Buddhist

Cultures in Southern China

THE PERSECUTION OF BUDDHISM launched by Tang emperor Wuzong 武宗 (r. 840–846) in 842 lasted nearly three years and resulted in the laicization of more than 260,000 monks and nuns, the destruction of over 4,600 monasteries and 40,000 small temples and shrines, the loss of tens of millions of acres of monastic property, and the return of some 150,000 monastic servants to the tax registers. Scholars have long assumed that Wuzong's purge (also known as the Huichang persecutions) did irreparable damage to the scholastic Buddhist traditions that prevailed in the northern capitals. Kenneth Ch'en, in his influential survey of Chinese Buddhist history, summed up the scholarly consensus of the 1960s when he wrote, "Even before [Wuzong's] persecution, Buddhism already showed signs of decay and slackening of faith and intellectual vigor in some areas, but the suppression of 845 supplied the crippling blow. That year is therefore the pivotal date, marking the end of the apogee and the beginning of the decline of the religion."[1]

Extensive research on Buddhism during the Song and later eras has subsequently upended the notion of a post-Tang decline, but the Huichang persecutions are still regularly credited with instigating a major shift in the trajectory of the tradition. The prevailing narrative of Chinese Buddhist history traces the political ascent of Chan clerics to the late Tang, when the elite Buddhist institutions in the capitals and major cities were destroyed during the purges and rebellions that precipitated the fall of the dynasty. Unlike exegetes who were dependent on textual traditions and political patronage, Chan monks were thought to have weathered the difficulties of the ninth and tenth centuries and increased their influence. By the time the empire was reunified under the Song, a new social and political climate favored the more robust, sinified form of Buddhism championed by Chan monks. Chan had emerged, almost by Darwinian default, as the dominant force in Chinese Buddhism.[2]

This chapter draws on demographic and biographical data to reassess this narrative, taking a closer look at how the Huichang persecutions and the Tang–Five Dynasties transition impacted the lives of Buddhist clerics and the broader development of regional monastic communities and cultures. I argue, in short, that the normative Buddhist traditions of the capitals did in fact continue after Wuzong's persecutions and the fall of the Tang. The rise of Chan monks, moreover, does not appear to indicate a turn away from scholastic Buddhism toward some more direct and unmediated approach to awakening. Rather, the growing support for members of Chan lineages in certain regions can be understood as a consequence of the political and economic restructuring that culminated in the formation of autonomous kingdoms, making it possible for previously marginal monastics to become the standard-bearers of new imperial cultures.

Persecutions, Rebellions, and the Destruction of the Capitals

Over the course of the Tang dynasty, the center of Chinese Buddhism began to slowly shift, along with the population, from the northern capitals to southern cities. A survey of canonical and secular sources conducted by the Chinese scholar Li Yinghui 李映辉 suggests that, while the total number of Buddhist temples in China decreased by roughly 20 percent from the first to the second half of the Tang, the number of temples in southeastern cities—the Jiangnan region—rose by nearly 25 percent (see table 2).[3] A similar trend emerges from analysis by Yan Gengwang 嚴耕望 (1916–1996)

TABLE 2   Relative temple distributions for the Tang before and after the An Lushan rebellion

Route 道	District 州		618–755	755–907
Guannei 關內	Jingzhao Prefecture 京兆府	Chang'an	124	79
		Mt. Zhongnan	21	7
		Other areas	17	9
		Total	162	95
	Total for all districts		**181**	**112**
Henan 河南	Henan Prefecture 河南府	Luoyang	29	14
		Mt. Song	6	7
		Other areas	21	7
		Total	56	28
	Total for all districts		**119**	**62**
Hedong 河東	Dai Prefecture 代州	Mt. Wutai	17	17
		Other Areas	6	2
		Total	23	19
	Taiyuan		21	16
	Total for all districts		**96**	**74**

(*continued*)

TABLE 2 *(continued)*

Route 道	District 州	618–755	755–907
Heibei 河北	Xiangzhou	16	4
	Youzhou	10	10
	Total for all districts	**57**	**41**
Longyou 隴右	Qiuci	3	6
	Total for all districts	**17**	**10**
Shannan 山南	Xiangzhou	25	3
	Jingzhou	17	13
	Total for all districts	**60**	**33**
Huainan 淮南	Yangzhou	18	20
	Total for all districts	**33**	**36**
Jiangnan 江南	Suzhou	19	31
	Hangzhou	12	20
	Runzhou	28	20
	Changzhou	8	13
	Yuezhou	23	28
	Fuzhou	4	6
	Quanzhou	5	6
	Hongzhou	2	12
	Total for all districts	**184**	**249**
Jiannan 劍南	Chengdu	30	19
	Total for all districts	**56**	**37**
Lingnan 岭南	Guangzhou	7	6
	Total for all districts	**31**	**10**
	Sum Total	**834**	**664**

Sources: These approximate data are derived from a tabulation of temple names that appear in historical sources (including the Buddhist canon, inscriptions, literature, poetry, and official histories). This table is intended to demonstrate general trends and relative quantities, not actual numbers of temples in existence, which would have been much greater. Adapted from Li Yinghui, *Tangdai Fojiao dili yanjiu*, 88–91.

of the monks' residences recorded in the *Song Biographies*. For the second half of the Tang, the number of northern monks represented in this collection decreased significantly while those based in the south increased.[4] Such statistics are far from precise, but they do seem to indicate that just as the economy and population of China began migrating south after the An Lushan rebellion, the cities and mountains of southeastern China were becoming increasingly important centers of Buddhist culture.

The Huichang persecutions were devastating for the clergy and lay devotees. But while the destruction was widespread—monks and monasteries in the south were not spared, as is sometimes assumed—recovery appears to have been swift.[5] After Emperor Wuzong's death in 846, temples were rebuilt and many monastics returned to their robes. Wuzong's nephew and successor, Emperor Xuanzong 宣宗 (r. 846–859), worked to repair the damage his uncle had done. The twelve Daoist priests who had instigated the persecution were clubbed to death, their severed heads put on public display. Decrees lifting restrictions on ordinations and granting laymen and monks the right to restore or build monasteries alarmed some officials, at least one of whom reportedly lamented that since Emperor Xuanzong ascended the throne, "the sound of axes at the construction sites of monasteries has never stopped! With respect to the ordination of the clergy, we have virtually returned to the situation that prevailed before Huichang."[6]

Biographies of court clerics included in the *Song Biographies* and other sources suggest that the Buddhist culture in the Tang capital before and after the Huichang persecutions was more or less continuous. Many of the monks who filled honorific and administrative posts in Chang'an under Emperor Xuanzong and his successors belonged to the same group of elite, scholastic Buddhists that had served under previous emperors. The career of the monk Zhixuan 知玄 (811–883) exemplifies how the Huichang persecutions disrupted but did not derail the careers of prominent court clerics.[7] Learned in both Buddhist and classical literature, Zhixuan was first called to the court of Emperor Wenzong 文宗 (r. 826–840) and, early in the Huichang era, was summoned again, this time to debate Daoists before Emperor Wuzong on the occasion of the emperor's birthday. Zhixuan's critique of both the emperor's support for Daoism and his reckless quest for immortality was doomed to fail, and the next we hear of Zhixuan, he is living in Shu as a layman. After Wuzong's death, however, Zhixuan was summoned a third time to the capital to celebrate the birthday of the new emperor, Xuanzong. The emperor demonstrated his pleasure with Zhixuan by awarding him a purple robe, the position of director of the three teachings, and a new residence within the imperial compound.[8] Xuanzong also appointed Zhixuan's disciple Sengche 僧徹 (n.d.) to the position of monastic recorder on the left, and named his grand-disciple Juehui 覺輝 (n.d.) monastic recorder on the right. Both Zhixuan and Sengche went on to author commentaries and subcommentaries on a range of sutras, a fact that, together with the catalogue of texts collected by the Japanese pilgrim Enchin 圓珍 (814–891) during this same period, testifies to the continued presence of canonical texts and the commentarial tradition in the capital and provincial centers directly after the Huichang persecutions.[9]

The careers of Zhixuan and his disciples, along with those of several other court clerics of the late Tang, demonstrate not only that Wuzong's campaigns did not eradicate the Buddhist traditions favored by Chang'an's monastic elite but also that these clerics exhibited a tenacious staying power in the face of persecutions and political instability.[10] Huang Chao's rebellion, by contrast, appears to have been much more disruptive to monastic communities, particularly those based in the northern capitals. Despite the increasing significance of the south, Chang'an and Luoyang constituted the twin centers of the Chinese Buddhist world throughout most of the Tang dynasty. For centuries, clerics from throughout China and greater East Asia traveled to these cities in search of erudite masters as well as scriptures and commentaries, miraculous images, relics, and patronage. The translations, treatises, doctrinal innovations, and rituals originating in or imported to the capitals then flowed out from those metropoles to the provinces, where a network of imperially sanctioned Buddhist monasteries extended into every prefecture and functioned as veritable organs of the state, charged with regulating the *saṃgha* and serving the needs of the emperor and his empire. While the provinces were never merely passive recipients of the capital's culture, the literature, artistic forms, and fashions of Chang'an set a standard of sophistication that people in the provinces must have aspired to emulate.

Huang Chao's capture of the capital in 881 put an end to that. The razing of Chang'an and later Luoyang all but eradicated the great aristocratic clans that had dominated governmental posts for hundreds of years and severed the administrative structures and patronage networks that had so long supported elite Buddhist institutions in the capitals. Former patrons lost their fortunes, their court positions, and sometimes their lives, and the ties of material and political support that once bound the clergy to the court were frayed and broken. The empire's most opulent and best endowed monasteries were destroyed. One observer reported that thousands of monks were systematically executed.[11] Those monks that survived or evaded the sieges and purges of the capitals were left without shelter or support.

With Chang'an in ruins, many of the capital's elite clerics took to the road in search of safe havens. Northern monks joined the lines of refugees fleeing Chang'an and other northern cities for urban centers in the south. During the second half of the Tang, the upper and lower Yangzi River regions—corresponding to modern Sichuan province in the southwest and southern Jiangsu and northern Zhejiang provinces in the southeast—were the two most densely populated regions of southern China.[12] The biographies of court clerics living in the capital at the time of Huang Chao's rebellion indicate that, like the northern refugees that fled the disorder of the Sui-Tang transition, many of these men made their way to major southern cities like Chengdu in Sichuan and Hangzhou in Zhejiang.[13] With the arrival of prominent northern clerics in these cities, the Buddhist institutions and traditions of Chang'an were transplanted to southern capitals.

The Continuity of Chang'an's Buddhist Traditions

Despite the quelling of Huang Chao's rebellion, the Tang court never regained control over the provinces, and the governors of southern cities began to transform what had been provincial centers into imperial capitals. Like Chang'an, these cities were envisioned as centers, often *the* center, of both political and spiritual authority, and Buddhist monks and other religious specialists played a small but vital role in establishing and maintaining the integrity of these new capitals. According to long-standing tradition, the inauguration of a virtuous ruler was accompanied by the appearance of auspicious omens in and around his capital, and the founding legends of the kingdoms of Shu and Wuyue predictably assert that their regimes were divinely sanctioned.

The place of prophecy in establishing the political authority of southern rulers irritated Song historians such as Ouyang Xiu, who, in the conclusion to his history of Wuyue, charged, "Since antiquity, not only have occultists been favored for the novel, but ultimately valorous men turning to insurrection have anointed themselves through prodigies and omens. Such upstarts would scarcely have succeeded in deluding the gullible masses, if not for exploiting such superstitions."[14] Ouyang laments that his contemporaries in the Song still "delight in perpetuating myths" about the rulers and prophets of southern kingdoms, but prophecies and omens were stock elements in the imperial narratives of new regimes after the fall of the Tang. In Shu's capital, Chengdu, for example, Du Guanting 杜光庭 (850–933), the preeminent court Daoist of the late Tang period, augmented the authority of Shu's first patriarch, Wang Jian, by performing prophylactic rituals, announcing sightings of immortals and unusual celestial phenomena, and declaring that regional and transregional deities both recognized and protected Wang's heavenly mandate. For his services, Du was appointed to some of the highest political and religious posts in the kingdom, including preceptor to the heir apparent and vice-president of the board of finances.[15]

At the same time that Du Guanting was testifying to Wang Jian's divine right to rule in Shu, on the other side of the empire, the new king of Wuyue and his ministers were sanctifying their realm and legitimizing their reign through the power and presence of the Buddha.[16] The spiritual centrality of Wuyue's capital, Hangzhou, was proclaimed in a number of ways with recourse to a range of religious traditions, but none more imposing than the construction of towering stupas to enshrine the relics of Śākyamuni Buddha.[17] Tang emperors had famously venerated a finger bone of the Buddha, but Wuyue initially lacked a relic of comparable power and pedigree. That changed in 916, when Wuyue's founding patriarch, Qian Liu, sent his younger brother Qian Hua 錢鏵 (d. 945) and the monk Qingwai 清外 (n.d.) to Ayuwang si 阿育王寺 (King Aśoka Temple) in Mingzhou to retrieve a small reliquary—believed to be one of eighty-four thousand crafted by the Indian king Aśoka (ca. 300–232 BCE)—that contained a piece of Śākyamuni's skull.[18] The relic was brought to Hangzhou and kept for a time at Luohan si 羅漢寺, whose abbot, Lingyin 令因 (901–924), was none other than Qian Liu's son.[19] Shortly thereafter, the relic was interred in the newly built Baota si 寶塔寺 (Precious Stupa Temple) within the palace grounds.[20] Over the course of the tenth century, Baota would develop into one of the most prominent temples in the capital, housing not only the Buddha-relic but also an ornate copy of the Buddhist canon brushed in gold and silver ink, two *dhāraṇī* pillars, and an ancestral hall enshrining statues of Wuyue's former kings. As if to underscore the association between Baota si and Famen si 法門寺—the imperial temple outside of Chang'an that housed the Buddha's finger bone—Qian Liu's son and successor, Qian Yuanguan 錢元瓘 (r. 932–941), appointed a monk from Famen to reside at Baota.[21]

Baota was also known as Southern Stupa Temple (Nanta si 南塔寺), to distinguish it from the stupa that Qian Liu later constructed in the north of his capital. The Northern Stupa Temple (Beita si 北塔寺) housed two additional Buddha relics, discovered in 929 in an ancient well that monks claimed dated back to the time of the mythic Chinese emperor Shun 舜.[22] Such discoveries belong to a phenomenon that Hubert Durt has called *archaeologia sacra*.[23] They claimed an ancient Buddhist presence in Wuyue's capital and implied that the appearance of the Buddha's relics was not a fortuitous accident (or a publicity stunt) but a sign that Śākyamuni himself sanctioned the rule of Wuyue's king. The presence of these relics in Hangzhou also associated Qian Liu with both the celebrated Indian emperor Aśoka—a monarch who, like Qian Liu, became a great benefactor of Buddhism after a violent struggle for power—and the legendary Chinese emperor Shun, who, also ostensibly like Qian Liu, rose from humble origins to assume the throne by virtue of his filial devotion and unswerving loyalty. The Buddha's relics and teachings may have originated in India, but they, like honorable officials and accomplished clerics, were attracted to benevolent rulers and thus drawn to Wuyue—even a portion of Numinous Vulture Peak had miraculously flown from Rājagṛha in India to Hangzhou.[24] Symbolically then, the congregation of relics, along with apparitions of the bodhisattva Guanyin, visions of Indian arhats, and the growing population of eminent monks, situated Hangzhou as the center of the Buddhist world.

The rulers of Wuyue may have envisioned Hangzhou as the new political and cultural capital of China, but Hangzhou was only one of many southern cities contending for that title. Biographical sources give some indication of how Buddhist monks responded to the proliferation of "imperial" capitals in southern China at the turn of the tenth century. One of the effects of decentralization seems to have been disorientation as monks tried to navigate unsettled and unpredictable political terrain. The career of the celebrated poet-monk Guanxiu 貫休 (832–912) typifies the peripatetic lives of monks searching for safe harbor and stable patronage during this chaotic period. Born in the city of Jinhua 金華 (present-day Zhejiang province), Guanxiu became a monk at the age of seven, just six years prior to the Huichang persecutions. Although his adult life unfolded amid the rebellions and political intrigue that plagued much of China during the late ninth and early tenth centuries, Guanxiu developed into a skilled poet, calligrapher, and painter (most famously of Buddhist arhats).[25] Had he been born a century earlier, he probably would have found his way to Chang'an to carry out his work under the auspices of the Tang court. Instead Guanxiu drifted from one regional capital to another in search of a benefactor. One of his poems captures the bleakness of the times:

> Battlefield bones ground into dust
> fly into soldiers' eyes.
> Yellow clouds turn suddenly black:
> Wailing ghosts of war are forming ranks.
> Evil winds howl on the great desert,
> Bugles urgent, but we dare not go out!
> Who will stand before the Son of Heaven
> And sing *this* frontier song?[26]

Guanxiu, it seems, was himself determined to sing before the Son of Heaven. He first sought but failed to secure the patronage of Qian Liu, who was at the time the most powerful warlord in Guanxiu's native region.[27] He next traveled to Jingnan 荊南 (also known as Nanping 南平 or Northern Chu 北楚, in present-day Hubei province), where the military commissioner Cheng Rui 成汭 (d. 903) "treated the monk with the utmost ceremony," and appointed him abbot of a temple within the capital. Guanxiu fell out of favor, however, and was banished. Finally, "in a deep depression," he made his way to Shu, where "Wang [Jian] was plotting to usurp the throne and attempting to gather worthy men from all directions. He was exceptionally pleased to obtain Guanxiu and treated him with great ceremony, bestowing numerous gifts and the name 'Great Master Chan Moon' [禪月]."[28] After spending years wandering from one southern capital to another, the elderly monk had finally secured the patronage necessary to carry out his work.[29]

Guanxiu, of course, was just one of many clerics set adrift during this period, and his biography illustrates both the obstacles and opportunities encountered by monks of his generation. Monastics would flee one collapsing city for another whose fortunes were on the rise, hoping to ingratiate themselves with prominent and powerful patrons. Regional rulers, for their part, were often eager to secure the symbolic and material benefits prominent clerics could convey. Like officials and administrators, monks were expected to maintain the social, political, and cosmic order, but the presence of eminent monks at regional courts was also interpreted as a testament to rulers' virtue and proof of their capacity to govern. Biographies are explicit in this regard; when the warlord Gao Jixing 高季興 (858–929) was invested as Prince of Nanping in 925, for instance, he reportedly "searched the land for men of reputation and integrity and obtained [the monks] Yifeng [義豐] from Qi [齊] and [Qi]ji [齊己] from the Nanyue [南嶽]. He considered this proof that he had started to build the golden walls [of an imperial palace]."[30] The very fact that venerable monks were willing to serve warlords like Gao Jixing implied that their authority was recognized not just by accomplished clerics but also by the entire pantheon of ancestors and deities they represented. The accumulation of this kind of cultural and spiritual capital, coupled with the real need for skilled administrators, compelled regional rulers of southern kingdoms to seek out clerics of experience and reputation to staff their major monastic institutions.

During the late Tang and the early Five Dynasties, the governors of densely populated, economically prosperous regions like Sichuan and Zhejiang were able to attract some of the same clerics who had served in the former Tang administration. Of all the cities in southern China, Chengdu had perhaps the strongest claim on the title of imperial capital. This city had served as the temporary seat of the Tang government in exile from 881 to 885, and during that period many of the Buddhist monks and Daoist masters in the service of the Tang court also relocated there. After the fall of the Tang, some of these same clerics, along with former courtiers and literati, remained in or returned to Chengdu to offer their services to the new emperor of Shu, Wang Jian. The eminent court Daoist Du Guanting is probably the best known example, but he was joined in Chengdu by several Buddhist monks who had also previously held official posts in Chang'an. These included the aforementioned Zhixuan and his grand-disciple, Guangye 光業 (n.d.), who was awarded the title of national teacher and named to the post of monastic recorder in Shu.[31] Wang Jian and his successors relied on these and other religious specialists to embellish their imperial credentials and safeguard their rule, just as these men depended on Wang Jian's patronage to ensure the survival of their traditions.[32] Along with the heavenly mandate, some of the cultural traditions and clerical networks of Chang'an were thus transferred to and reconstituted in the capital of Shu.

Chang'an's Court Clerics in Wuyue

Chengdu was not the only southern city to attract prominent members of Chang'an's displaced population. A very similar process was playing out in Hangzhou, another major population center at the other end of the old empire. Just as the rulers of Wuyue enshrined the bones of eminent monks in their new capital, they also recruited living masters to assume positions within their monastic administrations. Some of these were clerics of local renown, but a significant number had previously served the Tang court in Chang'an. The monk Xushou 虛受 (d. 925), for example, had served as the inspector of the doctrine on the left (*Zuojie jianyi* 左街鑑義) on the birthday of Tang emperor Yizong 懿宗 (r. 859–873) and was later appointed supervisor of the ordination platform, selection, and training (*Jiandan xuanlian* 監壇選練) in Wuyue by king Qian Liu. The king also petitioned the Later Tang emperor Zhuangzong to award Xushou a purple robe.[33] Another monk, Bianguang 辯光 (d. ca. 930), had been awarded a purple robe by Tang emperor Zhaozong and later traveled to Wuyue to stay as Qian Liu's guest in the imperial palace.[34]

The clerics favored by Qian Liu represented a broad spectrum of Buddhist traditions. Like the court clerics of the Tang, most specialized in distinct groups of texts and practices, but others ranged more broadly, studying the *Lotus Sūtra*, Maitreyan devotional scriptures, Yogācāra treatises, Avataṃsaka doctrine, and meditation, as well as Confucian and Daoist texts.[35] The culture of Wuyue Buddhism during this early period was multifaceted, but Nanshan Vinaya masters hailing from Chang'an occupied a particularly prominent place. As is well known, the Nanshan, or South Mountain, tradition based itself on commentaries by Daoxuan 道宣 (596–667) on the *Four-Part Vinaya* (*Sifen lü* or *Dharmaguptaka-vinaya*), which had become the standard interpretation of the Vinaya by the second half of the Tang dynasty.[36] At the onset of the Five Dynasties, several of the Nanshan Vinaya masters who had served the Tang court relocated to Wuyue, where they were appointed to posts within Qian Liu's administration. Many of these monks were the disciples and grand-disciples of the eminent Chang'an Vinaya master Xuanchang 玄暢 (797–875), who had been living in Chang'an when Emperor Wuzong first implemented his restrictions on the clergy. In a series of events that closely paralleled the trials of Zhixuan, Xuanchang was forced to return to lay life after submitting a memorial to the throne detailing the precedents for the imperial support of Buddhism. Following Wuzong's death, however, Emperor Xuanzong recalled Xuanchang to the imperial palace on the occasion of the emperor's birthday, granted him a purple robe, and appointed him to the position of preceptor both inside and outside the palace. Emperor Yizong subsequently awarded him the title "Fabao" 法寶 (Dharma Treasure).[37] Xuanchang's legacy was such that with the retrospective creation of a Nanshan Vinaya lineage he came to be honored as its sixth patriarch.

The subsequent relocation of Xuanchang's heirs from Chang'an to Wuyue can be summarized briefly, beginning with the putative seventh patriarch of the Nanshan lineage, Xuanchang's disciple Yuanbiao 元表 (n.d.). Yuanbiao fled Chang'an the same year that Huang Chao's forces entered the city. In Wuyue, he was lauded for his extensive knowledge of both Buddhist and classical literature.[38] King Qian Liu later summoned one of Yuanbiao's disciples, Jingxiao 景霄 (fl. 927), to the capital to preside over the ordination platform at Beita si, and then appointed him to Baota si— the two temples in the capital that enshrined Buddha-relics.[39]

A second branch of Xuanchang's Nanshan "lineage" also relocated to Wuyue. The monk Huize 慧則 (835–908), like Yuanbiao, had studied with Xuanchang in Chang'an, where he earned a reputation for his broad learning in the *Abhidharma-kośa* and the Confucian classics.[40] Tang emperor Xizong appointed Huize assistant administrator of the precept platform (*Lin tan zheng yuan* 臨壇正員), but after the occupation of Chang'an, Huize headed south. He stopped first in present-day Jiangsu, where he was courted by the military commissioners of the region, Gao Pian and Yang Xingmi. Huize left Jiangsu, however, to settle in Wuyue, first at Guoqing si 國清寺 at the base of the Tiantai mountains and later at nearby Ayuwang si 阿育王寺

in Mingzhou, the former home of the Baota Buddha-relic. As with other eminent Vinaya masters in Wuyue, Huize was ordered by the king to administer a precept platform, this one in Yuezhou.[41]

One last member of this group of Vinaya specialists needs to be introduced: Xijue 希覺 (864–948), Huize's most prominent disciple in Wuyue. Xijue came from a family of scholar-officials whose status had declined along with the fall of the Tang. Poverty-stricken, he first worked as an amanuensis for the Wuyue official and Daoist adept Luo Yin 羅隱 (833–910).[42] His path to political office blocked, Xijue became a monk in 888, studied with Huize on Mt. Tiantai, and later succeeded him as abbot of Ayuwang si. Like his master, Xijue was both respected and protected by Wuyue's royal family, but in addition to his close ties to the court, Xijue is important to our story because his students went on to become some of Wuyue's most influential clerics.[43] The best known was Zanning, the compiler of the *Song Biographies* and monastic controller (*sengtong* 僧統) of Wuyue, but Xijue also instructed the monk Haoduan 皓端 (890–961), a leading disciple of Xuanzhu 玄燭 (n.d.), once considered the tenth patriarch of the Tiantai school.[44] Importantly, Xijue also mentored Fayan Wenyi 法眼文益 (885–958), a Chan master whose descendants became some the most powerful Buddhist clerics in the kingdoms of the Southern Tang and Wuyue.[45] Xijue thus served as preceptor and mentor to many of the leaders of Wuyue's Chan, Tiantai, and Vinaya traditions. Although these monks specialized in different disciplines, the personal connections between them make it clear that they participated in a common Buddhist culture that took the *Vinaya* as its basis.

The presence of these Nanshan Vinaya masters in Wuyue is significant for several reasons. To begin, it demonstrates that although Nanshan Vinaya exegetical traditions were briefly disrupted during the fall of Chang'an, they were reconstituted in the southern kingdoms, most notably Wuyue. Out of a total of thirteen *Vinaya* commentaries composed during the Five Dynasties and Ten Kingdoms, eight were written by monks living in the kingdom of Wuyue, indicating that the Zhejiang region had become the new center of the Nanshan Vinaya tradition after the fall of the Tang.[46] A second, closely related point is that the relocation of Vinaya masters from Chang'an to Hangzhou during the early decades of the tenth century appears to have been part of a deliberate strategy by Qian Liu and his court to preserve and lay claim to the Buddhist culture of the former Tang capital. By the turn of the tenth century, the territory within Wuyue's borders hosted one of the largest populations of monastics in China. Some of these monks were no doubt well qualified to assume positions of leadership under Qian Liu's regime. The king, however, appears to have favored monks who had held officials posts in Chang'an. There may have been practical reasons for this, but the symbolic value—the fact that these monks had served the last Tang emperors and now served the first king of Wuyue—could not have gone unnoticed. Finally, the prominence of Vinaya specialists in Wuyue during the early decades of the tenth century is noteworthy not only because it establishes continuity with the Buddhist cultures of Chang'an but also because by the second half of the tenth century the role of Vinaya masters as arbiters of orthodoxy in Wuyue would be ceded to monks affiliated with Chan lineages—a point that will be taken up in detail in chapter 5.

Chan Monks and Regional Rulers in Southeastern China

The southern cities of Chengdu and Hangzhou attracted some of the more pedigreed refugees of Chang'an and Luoyang. In less populated and less economically developed regions like Hongzhou in Jiangxi and Fuzhou in Fujian, however, rulers of necessity relied on clerics of local renown to staff their state-sanctioned temples and to serve as personal advisors. Importantly, many of the leaders of these regions' monastic and lay Buddhist communities were associated with Chan lineages.

During the Tang, southeastern and south-central China were major centers of the Chan movement. An analysis of temple locations for Chan monks listed in Song-dynasty flame records shows that the greatest concentrations of these clerics were (in descending order) in Zhejiang, Jiangxi, Hunan, Jiangsu, Hubei, Fujian, and Anhui (table 3). With the exception of Zhejiang, which was a major population center, there appears to be an almost inverse relationship between population density and the presence of Chan monks. Areas that were relatively sparsely populated during the mid-Tang—including most of southern China with the exception of the upper and lower Yangzi regions—were home to the largest populations of Chan monks. The areas of northern China that were most densely populated during the mid-Tang, by contrast, record the smallest number of Chan clerics, at least as represented in Song flame records. These kinds of statistics convey only a very rough and relative sense of actual populations, but they indicate that throughout the Tang most Chan monks were based in the hinterlands of southeastern China, at a far remove from major urban centers in the north. The political and economic transformation of these provinces empowered local monks and elevated their traditions. Because the careers of politically connected clerics were closely bound up with those of their benefactors, however, the ever-shifting political conditions of the Tang–Five Dynasties transition frequently cut short the influence of some clerics while thrusting others into positions of significant power. The outcome of political conflicts thus had a direct and enduring impact on the development of regional Buddhist traditions.

During the Tang, some Chan monks did famously establish themselves in the northern capitals, winning the recognition of emperors and the support of the court, but the influence of Chan clerics in Chang'an and Luoyang was limited. Among the several descendants of the putative fifth Chan patriarch Hongren 弘忍 (602–675) who were active in the capitals, the most prominent were undoubtedly Shenxiu 神秀 (605?–706) and Shenhui 神會 (684–758), the leading representatives of the so-called Northern and Southern schools.[47] As John McRae has shown, the imperial attention showered on Shenxiu, Shenhui, and their disciples made minor celebrities of monks

TABLE 3   Temple locations of Chan monks listed in flame records

Province	JDCDL	TSGDL, JTPDL	JZJGXDL	Average
Zhejiang	170	349	422	314
Jiangxi	206	264	295	255
Hunan	142	210	228	193
Jiangsu	55	194	201	150
Hubei	124	161	159	160
Fujian	134	157	170	148
Anhui	44	111	150	102
Sichuan	50	132	86	89
Henan	63	73	57	64
Guangdong	62	35	28	42
Shaanxi	71	11	12	31
Guangxi	no data	48	10	29
Hebei	42	26	8	25
Shanxi	47	8	8	21
Shandong	6	8	17	10

Sources: Jingde chuandeng lu (JDCDL) data are taken from Yan Gengwang, "Tang dai pian."
Those from the Tiansheng guang deng lu (TSGDL), Jiatai pudeng lu (JTPDL), and the
Jianzhong jingguo xudeng lu (JZJGXDL) are derived from Suzuki T., "Kenchū seikoku
zokutōroku no jūchi betsu jinmei sakuin" and "Tenshō kōtōroku." The totals of Suzuki Tetsuo's
tabulation of the residences of Chan monks given in the Zu tang ji, Jingde chuan deng lu,
and Song gaoseng zhuan differ only slightly from the figures given here, with the top six
provinces being Jiangxi (238), Zhejiang (204), Hubei (192), Hunan (163), Fujian (137), and
Jiangsu (119). The raw data are can be found in Suzuki's contributions to the Aichi gakuin
daigaku bungakubu kiyō, vols. 3, 5, 8, 10, 12–14, and 16.

that traced their spiritual ancestry through Hongren, but the influence of
the Northern school peaked in the 770s and declined thereafter.[48] As for
Shenhui's disciples, apparently lacking their teacher's charismatic oratorical
skills and thus the ability to raise substantial funds for the court, they too
were unable to maintain imperial support.[49]

A number of other Chan monks, most notably the disciples of Mazu
Daoyi 馬祖道一 (709–788), were successful in developing close ties with Tang
officials and literati, but those few who were summoned to court enjoyed
only brief periods of imperial recognition, and those honors rarely extended
to their disciples.[50] This pattern of sporadic support of individual Chan
masters stands in marked contrast to the patronage networks that would
develop in southern China during the tenth century, in which a succession
of kings supported multiple generations of distinct Chan lineage families.
The next three chapters detail the careers of Chan clerics at the courts of
Min, the Southern Tang, and Wuyue. The remainder of the present chap-

ter offers a brief overview of the patronage relationships between Chan
monks and regional rulers in southeastern China during the late Tang,
both to provide necessary historical context for later developments and to
highlight the intersections between place, patronage, and the fates of regional monastic networks.

Chan Monks and their Patrons in Jiangxi

By the ninth century, the Jiangnan region had developed into a major
stronghold of the Chan movement, with several of the most prominent
Chan factions of the Tang dynasty—the Oxhead, Hongzhou, and Caodong
lineages—hailing from Jiangsu and Jiangxi.[51] Tang officials and administrators posted to cities in these regions inevitably interacted with the leaders of local monastic communities and, for reasons both personal and political, some of these men developed close ties with prominent members of
Chan lineages.

The fortunes of the monastic communities in general and Chan lineages in particular were directly tied to the favor and fate of their benefactors, a fact illustrated by the decline of Mazu Daoyi's descendants and the
ascent of the heirs of Dongshan Liangjie 洞山良价 (807–869) in Jiangxi during the latter half of the ninth century. The history and teachings of Mazu's
Hongzhou school during the Tang have been studied in detail by Mario
Poceski and Jia Jinhua and can be summarized briefly here. About a decade before the Huichang persecutions, the scholar-official and Buddhist
layman Pei Xiu 裴休 (ca. 791–864) was transferred from the Secretariat in
Chang'an to a series of posts in southern China.[52] This was a boon to local
Chan communities; Pei was a devout layman with a particular interest in
the teachings of Chan monks. In Chang'an he had studied closely with
the erudite Chan cleric Guifeng Zongmi 圭峰宗密 (780–841), a fourth-
generation descendant of Shenhui, and later composed Zongmi's stele inscription as well as the preface to his *Chan Chart* (*Zhonghua chuan xindi Chan-
men shizi chengxi tu* 中華傳心地禪門師資承襲圖).[53] Pei's assignment to Hongzhou,
however, brought him in close contact with the grand-disciples of Mazu
Daoyi. In contrast to the court clerics of Chang'an, Mazu famously eschewed
an intellectual and gradual approach to awakening in favor of a direct and
spontaneous realization of one's buddha-nature. This approach alarmed
more conservative clerics like Zongmi, who, in a text written specifically
for Pei, charged that the radical nondualism preached by Mazu and his disciples advocated "giving free reign to the mind," and thus did not properly
distinguish right from wrong.[54] Despite the unintended but potentially
corrosive ethical implications of Mazu's teachings, they appear to have struck
a chord with Pei and other members of the Tang aristocracy.

Prior to the early ninth century, Mazu's influence was confined to the
Hongzhou region (present-day Nanchang 南昌, northern Jiangxi province). Some of Mazu's disciples claimed that their isolation was a matter of
principle—fame and fortune were unwelcomed distractions from practice
and realization—but whether in violation of such lofty ideals or in service

of them, it is clear that many of Mazu's disciples did indeed actively seek to secure imperial recognition for their master and his legacy.[55] They found their primary patron in Tang emperor Xianzong 憲宗 (r. 805–820), who awarded posthumous titles to Mazu and several of his immediate heirs and invited at least three of Mazu's surviving disciples to the imperial palace.[56]

Pei Xiu arrived in Hongzhou several decades later and, disregarding his teacher Zongmi's warnings about the teachings of Mazu and his heirs, fell under the spell of Huangbo Xiyun 黄檗希運 (d. 850), one of Mazu's grand-disciples. Pei became an ardent supporter of Huangbo and his teachings. When Pei was recalled to the capital shortly after the death of Emperor Wuzong, Emperor Xuanzong bestowed additional posthumous titles on Mazu and several of his disciples.[57] These imperial honors marked the Hongzhou lineage as the most politically prominent Chan movement of the late Tang period.

Despite such success—or perhaps because of it—the descendants of Mazu Daoyi were only rarely and inconsistently patronized by regional rulers during the Five Dynasties and Ten Kingdoms. Monks associated with the Hongzhou school seem to have been relegated to the margins of state-sanctioned Buddhism for most of the tenth century, returning to the limelight only after Song reunification. In their studies of the Hongzhou school, both Poceski and Jia note that by the end of the Tang, the prominence and cohesion of Mazu's monastic network was eroded by the emergence of regional traditions.[58] Jia reads this division as a result of doctrinal differences among Mazu's heirs, which may be so, but the fall of the Tang and the demise of the Hongzhou school's chief benefactors must have also played a part in the diffusion and decline of this monastic network.

After Huang Chao's rebellion, the Hongzhou region came under the control of Zhong Chuan 鍾傳 (d. 906), a Tang-appointed surveillance commissioner for the Jiangxi circuit. Zhong was from the town of Gaoan 高安, not far from the city of Hongzhou, and from this home base he managed to carve out and maintain what was essentially an independent state that endured for more than twenty years. Like other regional rulers at that time, Zhong sought out northern refugees as well as local leaders to build his territory into a political and military stronghold.[59] Not surprisingly, these new recruits included local Chan clerics as well as military strategists and statesmen.

The *Patriarch's Hall Collection* and the *Transmission of the Flame* both list Zhong Chuan as the disciple of the clairvoyant Chan monk Shanglan Lingchao 上藍令超 (d. 890).[60] Shanglan was himself a disciple of Jiashan Shanhui 夾山善會 (805–881), but among the many other recipients of the commissioner's largesse, the disciples of Jiashan Shanhui's better-known dharma-cousin Dongshan Liangjie appear to have been particular favorites.[61] Zhong converted one of his residences into a temple for one of Dongshan Liangjie's disciples, Jiufeng Puman 九峰普滿 (d. 896), and appointed two others to the abbacy of Puli Chan Temple 普利禪院, Dongshan's monastery on Mt. Dong, located about 130 kilometers northwest of Zhong's hometown.[62] When Daoying 道膺 (d. 902), another of Dongshan's heirs, visited the commissioner at court, Zhong reportedly "cleaned the Ganzi Hall [甘子堂] out of respect for the master. He also submitted a memorial to Tang emperor Zhaozong, requesting that Daoying be granted a purple robe and a master's title."[63] Daoying received additional donations from Cheng Rui, the previously mentioned military commissioner of neighboring Nanping, and Daoying's biographers claim that he attracted more than a thousand disciples, many of whom went on to hold the abbacies of important temples throughout the greater Hongzhou region.[64]

The point to emphasize here is that the demise of Mazu Daoyi's network of disciples coincided with the loss of prominent patrons both locally and at the Tang court, while the rise of Dongshan Liangjie's descendants in Jiangxi was made possible by the support of the region's new ruler. As the political regime changed, so too did the network of monks supported by those in positions of power. Importantly, there is little indication that Mazu's and Dongshan's heirs advocated significantly different doctrines or practices; their respective fortunes appear to have been driven less by the efficacy of their teachings than by the outcomes of their political allegiances.

Zhong Chuan died in 906, just after Yang Xingmi. At that time, Xu Wen became the *de facto* ruler of the new kingdom of Wu, and his generals quickly moved to seize Zhong's former territory. Many of the officials appointed by Zhong in northern Jiangxi maintained their positions under the tenures of Wu's rulers, and it appears that the disciples and grand-disciples of Dongshan Liangjie also retained control of major monasteries in and around Hongzhou throughout this volatile period.[65] However, as will be discussed in chapter 4, with the establishment of the Southern Tang three decades later, a new regime assumed control of the region and its leaders installed yet another network of Chan clerics. At that time, the heirs of Dongshan forfeited the abbacies of their temples and made way for a new family of Chan monks spreading northwest from Fujian.

Support for Chan Monks in Fujian during the Late Tang
As the post-Tang political landscape began to settle and the positions of regional rulers grew more secure, monks allied with dominant regimes were established in positions of authority. The first enduring alliance between a royal family and a single Chan lineage—an alliance that in many respects marked the beginning of the sustained political ascent of Chan clerics— took shape in Fujian in the late the ninth century. For much of the Tang dynasty, the Fujian area was little more than a distant backwater to the political and cultural centers located well over a thousand kilometers of hard travel away to the northwest. Although there had been a long history of Buddhist activity along Fujian's coast, the province's position on the economic and cultural fringes of the empire kept it from developing into a significant Buddhist center until the late Tang period. Only after the Huichang persecutions were substantial numbers of Buddhist temples built in Fujian; in contrast to other areas of China, Fuzhou saw its number of temples actually

TABLE 4   Buddhist temples built or
restored in northern Fujian during
the ninth and tenth centuries

Year Constructed/Restored	Number
801–810	2
811–820	4
821–830	3
831–840	4
841–850	29
851–860	37
861–870	70
871–880	30
881–890	32
891–900	64
901–910	43
911–920	40
921–930	45
931–940	7
941–950	35
951–960	59
961–970	85
971–980	78

Sources: Data from *San shan zhi,* fascicles
33–38. Chart modified from Chikusa,
Chūgoku Bukkyō shakaishi kenkyū, 189.

increase dramatically in the second half of the ninth century (see table 4).[66]
In a trend that closely parallels population estimates for the same period,
the number of Buddhist temples in Fujian grew slowly over centuries, increased sharply in the second half of the ninth century, and peaked during
the latter half of the tenth century, when Song gazetteers record that well
over two hundred temples were built or restored in northern Fujian alone.

As in Jiangxi, the rulers of Fujian had little choice but to rely on local
leaders to help establish their credibility and govern their populations.
Perhaps because of the region's isolation and relative poverty, there are
no records of eminent scholar monks traveling to Fujian after the fall of
Chang'an. Instead, the Wang family that would eventually rule over the new
kingdom of Min aligned itself with leaders of local Buddhist communities,
most of whom were affiliated with Chan lineages.

During the second half of the ninth century, Mazu Daoyi's descendants
were still influential in Fujian. Before settling in Hongzhou, Mazu himself

had resided for a time in Fujian and some of his students remained in the region. Several of Mazu's disciples in the Quanzhou area were initially honored, either during their lives or posthumously, by the Wang family during the brief period that Quanzhou served as their base of operations.[67] The honors bestowed on Hongzhou monks in Quanzhou suggest that the Wang family, like the emperors of the late Tang and the early governors of both Jiangxi and Zhejiang, recognized the significance of this group of clerics and sought the legitimacy they could confer. But monks affiliated with the Hongzhou lineage were soon overshadowed by Chan monks based in northern Fujian, in closer proximity to Min's capital at Fuzhou. While many of these clerics were closely connected to both Nanshan Vinaya masters and monks of the Hongzhou school, they claimed other influences and asserted alternative lines of descent. Their story is taken up in chapter 3.

The evidence gathered here runs counter to the claim that the rise of Chan monks during the late Tang and early Five Dynasties resulted from the demise of normative, text-based traditions in the capitals. The Buddhist cultures and elite clerical networks of Chang'an were disrupted and dispersed during the political upheavals of the late Tang, but they were subsequently preserved in major southern cities, particularly Chengdu and Hangzhou. In these regional capitals, rulers reconstructed elements of the Tang court by appointing former Tang courtiers and court clerics to prominent positions within their administrations. Collectively, the patronage practices of these cities' governors reflected the general trend of court Buddhism during the thirty-five years spanning the end of the Huichang persecutions to the destruction of Chang'an, with Vinaya and exegetical traditions prevailing and Chan monks representing a relatively minor undercurrent. The increased prominence of Chan clerics at the turn of the tenth century appears to be more closely linked to the geographical restructuring and political transformation set in motion by the decline and fall of the Tang dynasty.

In contrast to the major cities of Chengdu and Hangzhou, in less populated, less affluent areas of southeastern China, regional rulers allied themselves with respected local clerics, many of whom counted themselves members of Chan lineages. These monks, who had formerly dwelled along the margins of elite, urban Buddhist cultures, now found themselves at the center of powerful new states. The growing economic and political autonomy of southeastern cities increased the prominence and prestige of resident monastic communities as regional rulers conferred material and symbolic support in return for their sanction and service. As a result of a series of political transitions, the dominant Chan movement in these regions during the late Tang, the Hongzhou school, was surpassed by other clerical networks—the Caodong lineage in Jiangxi and the heirs of Xuefeng Yicun in Fujian—each backed by different political and military factions. Like the royal families they served, these Chan monks rose quickly from humble, obscure origins to become some of the most powerful figures in the Buddhist cultures of southeastern China.

3

Founding Fathers

The Kingdom of Min

IN THE SPRING OF 945, a monk from a large monastery in the mountains of northern Fujian was brought to the capital of the kingdom of Min and installed as emperor. His name was Zhuo Yanming 卓巖明, and he was reputedly endowed with double pupils and exceptionally long arms, which some interpreted as signs of his divine origins and imperial destiny.[1] He hailed from Xuefeng si 雪峰寺, one of the kingdom's most prestigious monastic estates. For more than seventy years, monks associated with this monastery had served as the counselors and confidantes of Min's royal family and its ministers, but it was only during the brief reign of Zhuo Yanming that the overlapping spheres of Min's elite monks and monarchs became so fully fused.

Portents aside, this confluence of authority was far from auspicious. Zhuo was little more than a pawn in Min's brutal political endgame; he was assassinated after just two months on the throne, his erstwhile kingdom vanquished less than two years later. The events surrounding the life and death of Zhuo Yanming exemplify the blurred boundaries delineating the *saṃgha* and the state in the kingdom of Min. They also mark the dual foci of Min's clergy-court alliance: Xuefeng si and Min's capital at Fuzhou (see map 2). The relationships forged between these two centers established a model that would be replicated throughout southern China for the duration of the tenth century.

This chapter examines the formulation and institutionalization of what became the most powerful monastic network in southeastern China during the Five Dynasties and Ten Kingdoms. Certain aspects of this history are already fairly well known. Tokiwa Daijō and Chikusa Masaaki were among the earliest scholars to examine the social history of Buddhism in Min and to note the close relationship that existed between Min's first king, Wang Shenzhi, and local Buddhist clerics, most notably Xuefeng Yicun and his disciples.[2] It was Yanagida Seizan, however, who first recognized the significance of this kingdom for the historical development of Chan. Yanagida's point of entry into Chan studies, in the early 1950s, was the *Patriarch's Hall Collection*, a text that continued to fascinate him for the remainder of his life. The *Patriarch's Hall Collection* was initially composed in the mid-tenth century in the city Quanzhou, and Yanagida's early studies were devoted to annotating and explicating the collection's contents and uncovering the historical context in which it was produced. For Yanagida, the *Patriarch's Hall Collection* was not only an early, unedited, and previously unknown history of the Chan movement, it also represented the first truly sinitic form of Buddhism.[3] After the disruptions of the late Tang and Five Dynasties put an end to the old secular and clerical aristocracy, "tradition was upended, scriptures were superseded, temples were left, and doctrines were abandoned."[4] This reorientation, according to Yanagida, created the conditions for Chan monks to flourish. They "were always together with the common people. No, they were the common people. Their feet never left the ground. Dwelling among the vicissitudes of daily life, they shared the worries, sorrows, and afflictions of the people."[5] The era of spontaneity and authenticity reflected in the *Patriarch's Hall Collection* represented a time when "'Zen monasteries' and 'the Zen sect' did not yet exist, and there was no separation between kōan and zazen. People just cultivated the earth and ate, pursued the Way and went on pilgrimage, posed questions and got answers. Each person lived Zen his or her own way, and non-professional buddhas were hidden here and there. No need for some third person to wrap it all up, and no time to preach about its benefits. One's own inner realization, sanctioned by one's own conscience, was everything."[6] While such sentiments might strike modern readers as overly idealistic, Yanagida's efforts to elucidate what he saw as "the period of pure Zen"—the time before the movement was institutionalized and politicized in the Song—resulted in a series of pioneering studies on the monks, monasteries, and officials that were included in the *Patriarch's Hall Collection* or involved in its production.[7]

Several scholars have since followed in Yanagida's footsteps, refining and elaborating on his work. Suzuki Tetsuo, for example, has tracked the geographical distributions, lineal affiliations, temple histories, and political associations of Chan monks throughout the kingdom of Min.[8] Through careful linguistic analysis of the *Patriarch's Hall Collection*, Kinugawa Kenji has demonstrated that the text must have been compiled in stages, beginning with a core of one fascicle in 952 and expanding to its current twenty-fascicle form in Korea sometime in the early eleventh century.[9] Ishii Shūdō has drawn on information contained in later gazetteers to paint a more complete picture of the monk presumed to be the driving force behind the text's compilation—Zhaoqing Wendeng 招慶文僜 (also known as Shengdeng 省僜; 892–972)—and his place of residence, Zhaoqing Cloister 招慶院 in Quanzhou, where the *Patriarch's Hall Collection* appears to have been first compiled.[10] More recently, Albert Welter has analyzed the content of this text and provided a detailed discussion of the individuals and institutions involved in its creation.[11]

Since the historical context of the *Patriarch's Hall Collection* has been studied so thoroughly, there is no need to reexamine it here. Moreover, although the *Patriarch's Hall Collection* is invaluable for understanding the development of both Chinese linguistics and Chan literature and thought during the late Tang and early Five Dynasties, it does not appear to have been a particularly influential text during the later tenth century or thereafter. Unlike the *Transmission of the Flame*, there is no evidence that it either served as a model for subsequent texts or that it enhanced the social status of Chan clerics. With the exception of Xuefeng Yicun, the monks most often discussed in connection with the text—Zhaoqing Wendeng and his teacher Baofu Congzhan 保福從展 (d. 928)—were not the most significant figures in Min's Buddhist establishment, and neither they nor their disciples seem to have had a lasting impact on the later development of Chan in Fujian or elsewhere.

While this chapter does not examine the compilation of the *Patriarch's Hall Collection*, it does draw heavily from this text, supplementing and contextualizing its accounts with material from the *Song Biographies*, the *Transmission of the Flame*, and epigraphical sources to chart the origins and evolution of Min's most prominent Chan lineage. It begins with overviews of the biographies of Xuefeng Yicun and Xuansha Shibei, and then surveys the careers of these monks' leading disciples in Min's major cities, the alliances forged between members of this Chan lineage and segments of the Wang family, and the factions that formed among branches of the broader lineage. The history of this clerical network in Min is important not only because its descendants would later come to dominate the Buddhist cultures of neighboring kingdoms but also because many of these monks established or developed traditions that we now recognize as defining features of the later Chan movement.

Xuefeng Yicun

Xuefeng Yicun is a towering figure in the legends of Chan Buddhism, lauded for his stubborn perseverance as a young student and for his dynamic instructions as a mature master.[12] The earliest account of Yicun's life, a memorial inscription composed by the Min literatus Huang Tao 黃滔 (ca. 840–911), forms the first of several biographical strata that by the Ming dynasty had accumulated into the two-fascicle *Discourse Record of Xuefeng Yicun*.[13] There are important differences between the various versions of Yicun's life story—notably a gradual accretion of dialogues and an elision of biographical detail—but early accounts are in broad agreement regarding the basic chronology of his life.

Xuefeng Yicun was born in Quanzhou in 822 and entered the nearby Yurun Temple 玉潤寺 at the age of twelve to study with the Vinaya Master Qingxuan 慶玄 (n.d.). After taking the tonsure five years later, he went to Mt. Furong 芙蓉山 outside of Fuzhou, where he studied with Furong Lingxun 芙蓉靈訓 (n.d.), one of Mazu Daoyi's grand-disciples.[14] Yicun's time on Mt. Furong coincided with the Huichang persecutions, and his biography in the *Patriarch's Hall Collection* records that he returned to lay life during this period.[15] After the persecutions had run their course, however, Yicun returned to his robes and traveled widely throughout China, stopping for a time in Hebei to take the complete precepts at Baocha Temple 寶剎寺 in Youzhou 幽州. It was during this period of peregrination that he met

Deshan Xuanjian 德山宣鑒 (782–865) in Hunan.[16] According to his memorial inscription, on arriving at Deshan's temple, Yicun "took one look at Deshan, exchanged greetings and left. Deshan had several hundred disciples but none of them could fathom this. Deshan announced, 'I have found one who cannot be placed at any level.'"[17]

The author of Xuefeng Yicun's inscription was careful to note his Chan credentials, but he made no mention of the kind of dramatic enlightenment experiences that later became *de rigueur* in biographies of Chan masters. In Huang Tao's account, Deshan simply verifies Yicun's accomplishments and the narrative moves on to the next phase of Yicun's travels. As time passed, however, more details were added to this exchange, emphasizing Yicun's sudden transformation from a searching monk to a fully realized Chan master. In the *Patriarch's Hall Collection*, on meeting Deshan, Yicun asked, "As for the Great Matter that has been passed down [from ancestor to ancestor], do I have a share in it or not?" Deshan got up and hit Yicun, scolding, "What are you saying?" With that, Yicun is said to have immediately "obtained the essential point."[18] In this telling, Deshan's blow and abrupt words trigger Yicun's sudden awakening.

This kind of exchange—earnest student caught off guard by a fierce yet skillful and compassionate master—was already becoming something of a set piece in Chan hagiographies by the time the *Patriarch's Hall Collection* was composed, but later authors felt compelled to burnish Yicun's story even further. In the *Transmission of the Flame*, Yicun is represented as struggling for years as a young monk, visiting various teachers multiple times without resolving his sense of doubt. He was chided for his slowness and was famously referred to as a "tub of lacquer."[19] Still later flame records celebrate Yicun's dedication, noting that he suddenly became "like a dead man" after being struck by Deshan. His "great awakening" was reportedly triggered shortly thereafter while discussing his encounter with Deshan with another of Deshan's students, Yantou Quanhuo 巖頭全豁 (828–887).[20] Such stories, subsequently repeated in countless Chan commentaries and sermons, reflect the changing image of the archetypical Chan master over the course of the tenth and eleventh centuries. While every source, from Yicun's early stupa inscription to his later discourse record, represented him as the rightful heir of Bodhidharma and Huineng 慧能 (638–713), representations of Chan patriarchs had yet to be codified and continued to evolve throughout the Five Dynasties and Northern Song.

Hongzhou Connections

Xuefeng Yicun's memorial inscription passes over his tutelage under Deshan in the briefest of terms, and it is only in Yicun's *Discourse Record* that we are told he was with Deshan for four years, from 861 to 865.[21] After Deshan's death, Yicun went back to his former teacher Lingxun's community on Mt. Furong, where he remained for several more years. Yicun's return to Furong suggests that his relationship with Lingxun—and thus the Hongzhou movement—may have been more important than has been previously recognized. Albert Welter has suggested that Yicun and his disciples sought legitimation by laying claim to the legacy of Mazu Daoyi and the Hongzhou school.[22] The doctrinal similarities between the two groups may have cut across lineage boundaries, as Welter has proposed, but there were also direct and meaningful connections between Yicun and members of the Hongzhou lineage. Yicun spent two extended periods as a member of Lingxun's assembly on Mt. Furong. One of Yicun's students, Ruti 如體 (n.d.), assumed the abbacy of the monastery on Furong sometime after Lingxun's death, which, if succession followed the conventional hereditary model, implies that Yicun's disciple (and thus Yicun himself) may have belonged to the same lineage family as Lingxun—the lineage of Mazu Daoyi.[23] Moreover, two documents written by Yicun near the end of his life also highlight his connections to Lingxun. In the rules he set down for his monastic community on Mt. Xuefeng and in his last words to his disciples before his death, Yicun exhorted the monks to rely on the regulations set down by "my late master Furong" 芙蓉先師.[24] This seems to indicate that, at one point, Yicun considered himself a disciple of Lingxun and thus presumably a member of the Hongzhou movement. At the very least, it is clear that Yicun modeled his own monastery not on Deshan's temple in Hunan but on Lingxun's community at Mt. Furong.

The relationship between Xuefeng Yicun and Furong Lingxun suggests that lineage did not necessarily function as a conduit for doctrines or practices. If it had, Yicun or his disciples could have easily claimed him as a disciple of Lingxun and thus a member of Mazu Daoyi's influential network. Instead, Yicun was identified as an heir of Deshan Xuanjian, who appears only briefly in Yicun's memorial inscription but who becomes an increasingly prominent figure in later retellings of Yicun's life. Deshan was the fourth-generation heir of Qingyuan Xingsi 青原行思 (d. 741), a purported disciple of the famous sixth ancestor of the Chan lineage, Huineng. Yicun's affiliation with this lineage ran counter to the prevailing current of Chan genealogy during the ninth century as represented by the Hongzhou, Guiyang, and Linji branches of the Chan lineage, all of which claimed descent from another of Huineng's heirs, Nanyue Huairang 南嶽懷讓 (677–744). Jia Jinhua, in her work on the history and doctrine of the Hongzhou school, has noted a general movement of Chan monks away from the lineage of Nanyue Huairang and toward that of Qingyuan Xingsi during the second half of the ninth century, and it is possible that Yicun's assignment to this line was an attempt on the part of his disciples or patrons to downplay his association with Hongzhou monks and forge a new, independent identity.[25]

There is some circumstantial evidence to support such a reading. Yicun's memorial inscription records that during his second stay at Furong, another of Mazu Daoyi's disciples, a monk named Yuanji 圓寂 (n.d.), moved from Mt. Wei 潙山, an important center of the Hongzhou school in Hunan, to Mt. Yi 怡山 in northwestern Fuzhou.[26] Mt. Yi was renowned as the location where a Daoist sage known as the True Lord Wang (Wang zhen jun 王眞君) ascended to the realm of the immortals.[27] A monk named Shu

熟 (n.d.), who had also studied under Deshan Xuanjian but later became a disciple of Yuanji, repeatedly requested that Yicun also relocate to Mt. Yi—a move that would place Yicun together with other members of the Hongzhou network—but Yicun declined. Another monk, Xingshi 行實 (d. ca. 889), a fellow student of Furong Lingxun, then convinced Yicun to establish his community instead on Mt. Xuefeng, precisely because it had no history as a Daoist site.[28] Whether intentional or not, Yicun's reluctance to settle in a location associated with both local Daoist traditions and monks of the Hongzhou school effectively distinguished his community from other prominent religious movements in Min. Indeed, by the time his memorial inscription was written in the early tenth century, the prominence of Yicun and his community of more than fifteen hundred monks on Mt. Xuefeng had already eclipsed that of both the Hongzhou movement and Daoist cults in Fujian. There would be little incentive to link him with religious networks whose influence was waning.

Mt. Xuefeng

Yicun moved to Mt. Xuefeng in 870.[29] The valley where he established his temple was located deep in the mountains, some 250 kilometers west of the capital (fig. 4). According to his *Discourse Record*, the temple was constructed on land donated by a layman named Lan Wenqing 藍文卿, who "built a hermitage beside the eastern pond among ancient tamarisk trees and invited the master to live there." This was known as the Kumu 枯木 [Withered Tree] Hermitage. Lan Wenqing later built (and subsequently expanded) a temple on the site and invited Yicun to serve as abbot.[30] A later record, preserved in the *Xuefeng Gazetteer*, adds that along with a residence of over 300 bays came a 12-bay granary, 20 tenant fields, and 360 water buffaloes. Together, the fields produced an annual rice harvest of nearly 1,600,000 pounds.[31] The temple also received twenty-four *guan* 貫 (24,000 cash) in annual tax revenue.[32]

The monastery's extensive holdings are alluded to in the regulations Yicun set down for resident monks in 901: "The [supervision of] the two types of landed estates, the monastery's fields and the [lands that are on] long-term [lease], is to be undertaken by monastic officials who will be rotated annually; all should be subject to service. The permanent property of the stupa and the monastery has been donated to the monks of this monastery and should on no account be taken elsewhere."[33] While not nearly as extensive or affluent as the major monastic institutions of Chang'an during the Tang, Yicun's community at Xuefeng enjoyed a substantial endowment. According to his stupa inscription, the *saṃgha* on Mt. Xuefeng comprised fifteen hundred clerics (other contemporaneous inscriptions place the number at one thousand), all of whom would have been supported by a combination of the produce and income generated from their fields and other business ventures, state funds, and private donations.[34]

The size of the monastic estate on Mt. Xuefeng was significant but not unusual. The earliest gazetteer for northern Fujian (compiled in the late

Figure 4. Xuefeng si. Author's photo, 2006.

twelfth century) cites an "old record" that claimed monastic fields made up one half of all the agricultural land holdings in northern Fujian.[35] Other sources assert that on average one monk held a total of 160 *mu* (10.5 hectares or 26 acres) of land, more than ten times the amount of the average peasant.[36] Monks were accused of monopolizing the best, most fertile fields, leaving only the middling and lesser lands for native citizens and immigrants.[37] Even allowing for hyperbole, such accounts convey the significant economic power wielded by the heads of monastic estates like Xuefeng si.

Economic influence, of course, was closely tied to political power. Although Mt. Xuefeng was geographically distant from Min's capital, the relationship between Xuefeng Yicun and the kingdom's rulers was quite close. During his first five years on the mountain, Yicun gained the support of several local leaders, including the Tang-appointed surveillance commissioner for Fuzhou, Wei Xiu 韋岫 (fl. 878), and his successor, Chen Yan. Toward the end of the Tang, Yicun was also honored by Emperor Xizong 僖宗 (r. 873–888), who, through an emissary, awarded him a purple robe and the title Great Master Zhenjue 真覺 (True Awakening).

The alliance between Yicun and Surveillance Commissioner Chen was mutually beneficial, with Yicun receiving political and economic support and Chen receiving the sanction and service of Yicun and his followers. But such arrangements had their hazards. At the time, Chen was struggling with Wang Chao for control of Fuzhou. Just before Chen's death in 891 and Wang's subsequent siege of Fuzhou, Yicun and his followers left Mt. Xuefeng and relocated north to present Zhejiang province.[38] While it was not un-common for monks to spend months or years on pilgrimage, it is unusual for the abbot of a monastery to leave his post for such an extended period of time. Sources are silent on this point, but Yicun's ties to Wang Chao's primary political rival would have been sufficient cause for caution on his part. There can be little doubt that many of those loyal to Chen Yan fared rather poorly under the new regime. Yicun remained in Zhejiang for several years, but if he was in fact keeping a prudent distance from Min's new ruler, such precautions were unnecessary. The author of Yicun's inscription—the court official Huang Tao—reports that during the time that he was away, Wang Chao frequently "faced east and bowed" out of reverence for the distant master.[39] When Yicun finally did return to Mt. Xuefeng in 894, Wang Chao became his most powerful benefactor, reinstituting the patronage relationship that had been initiated by previous Tang commissioners.[40]

The alliance between Yicun and Min's rulers continued after Wang Chao's death in 897. The next surveillance commissioner for Fuzhou, Wang Chao's younger brother Wang Shenzhi, expanded the monastic complex on Mt. Xuefeng and invited Yicun to reside at his personal estate. The king was forty years younger than Yicun, and he seems to have treated the monk as a venerable elder. According to Yicun's stupa inscription, Wang Shenzhi "would often come to hear [Yicun] lecture on the law, listening for hours on end."[41] Years later, when Yicun began to succumb to old age, it was Wang Shenzhi who summoned a doctor, and before finally passing away in 908, Yicun wrote a farewell letter to the king, who wept at the loss.[42] A vegetarian feast was provided for Yicun's funeral at government expense, and Wang Shenzhi sent his son Wang Yanbing 王延稟 (d. 931), then serving as the governor of nearby Jianzhou 建州, to present offerings to the old monk's remains (fig. 5).

Heirs

After Xuefeng Yicun's death, he was succeeded by several of his disciples. His stupa inscription identified five heirs who it claimed represented the sole orthodox Chan lineage: "The six leaves of [the branch of] Bodhidharma ended at Caoxi, where the lineage was divided between north and south. Deshan [Xuanjian] was the fifth leaf of the southern lineage. The master was his heir, making him the sixth leaf. Xuefeng's [branch] was divided among Xuansha [Shibei], Dongyan [Kexiu], Ehu [Zhifu], Zhaoqing [Huileng], and Gushan [Shenyan]. Their ways were all distinct from the Buddhist sutras, and all are revered as the seventh (leaves), a claim that cannot be made by others."[43] The claim to possess the exclusive and authentic inheritance of Bodhidharma and Huineng was, of course, often made by others, a fact that highlights the importance of lineage credentials during this period. As for Xuefeng Yicun's disciples, Xuansha Shibei, Changqing Huileng 長慶慧稜 (854–932), and Gushan Shenyan 鼓山神晏 (d. ca. 936–944)

Figure 5. Xuefeng Yicun's reliquary. Author's photo, 2006.

all remained within the kingdom of Min and maintained close ties with the royal family. Dongyan Kexiu 洞巖可休 (n.d.) and Ehu Zhifu 鵝湖智孚 (n.d.) settled in Wuyue and the Southern Tang, respectively, two kingdoms that later became important enclaves of Xuefeng Yicun's lineage.[44]

The short list of five heirs given in Xuefeng Yicun's memorial inscription contrasts with the twenty-one students listed in the *Patriarch's Hall Collection* and the sixty-four recorded in the *Transmission of the Flame*—an indication, it would seem, of Yicun's ever-increasing importance in the estimation of later generations of monks. The residences of Yicun's disciples given in these lists indicate that most remained in southeastern China. The largest concentration of disciples, according to the *Transmission of the Flame*, was within the kingdom of Min (twenty-one), more than half of whom settled in the capital, Fuzhou. At least twenty of Yicun's disciples and grand-disciples received some form of support from members the Wang family (see appendix 1). Among those with ties to the court, Xuansha Shibei was second perhaps only to Xuefeng Yicun in terms of his prominence and influence within the kingdom of Min and, later, throughout much of southeastern China.

Xuansha Shibei

The biographies of Xuefeng Yicun and Xuansha Shibei are similar in many respects.[45] Like Yicun, Shibei was a native of Fujian. He was born in Fuzhou and became a monk on Mt. Furong in 860, studying first with a monk named Yitong 義通 and later with Yicun's early teacher, the Hongzhou master Lingxun.[46] Shibei then traveled to Kaiyuan Temple in Zhongling 鍾陵 (present-day Jiangxi), where he received the precepts.[47] Thereafter he lived in hermitages in both Hongzhou and eastern Zhejiang, initiating a pattern of seclusion and mendicancy that would later inspire Yicun to nickname him "Shibei the Ascetic" (*toutuo* 頭陀; Skt. *dhūta*). He eventually returned to Mt. Furong around 865, during which time Yicun also came back to Lingxun's community, following the death of Deshan Xuanjian. After about five years, Yicun relocated to Mt. Xuefeng, but Shibei remained on Furong, secluding himself in a cave for the next eight years. He reunited with Yicun on Mt. Xuefeng in 878.

Śūraṃgama Sūtra

Xuansha Shibei differed from Xuefeng Yicun in his ascetic commitments but also, and perhaps more importantly, in his devotion to Buddhist sutras— the (pseudo) *Śūraṃgama Sūtra* (Ch. *Lengyan jing* 楞嚴經) in particular.[48] According to the *Transmission of the Flame*, it was during his time on Mt. Xuefeng that Shibei awakened while reading the *Śūraṃgama* and was subsequently able to "function in accord with all sutras."[49]

The *Śūraṃgama Sūtra* occupies an important place in the biographies of Shibei and his descendants. The text appears to have been composed in China in the early eighth century and expounds the *tathāgata-garbha* position that all beings contain the seeds of future buddhahood. It was likely this teaching that made the *Śūraṃgama* such an important source for Chan monks both before and after Xuansha Shibei's life. The sutra also asserts that an intellectual understanding of Buddhist doctrine is inferior to a direct realization of the truth of the teachings: "The many kalpas you have spent memorizing the Tathāgata's secret and marvelous [teaching] are not equal to a single day of cultivating the karma that is without outflows and that is far removed from the two worldly afflictions of hatred and love."[50] This, of course, was a common refrain in the teachings of Chan monks. Also embedded within the text are warnings against the mistaken, though presumably prevalent, view that traditional practices such as a reverence for stupas, statues, and sutras could and should be dispensed with. Such cautions, though not central to the sutra, suggest that the author or authors of the *Śūraṃgama* sought to counteract the antinomian trends current in some mid-Tang Buddhist communities, a sentiment very much in keeping with the teachings of Xuansha Shibei and his heirs.

The *Śūraṃgama* had previously been promulgated by monks affiliated with the Northern School of Chan. Shenxiu is said to have copied the text, and Moheyan 摩訶衍 (or Mahāyāna, fl. late eighth century) appears to have advocated the teachings of the *Śūraṃgama* when attempting to introduce Chan to Tibet in the late eighth century.[51] The sutra asserts that "if one awakens suddenly to principle (*li*), then the vehicle and awakening merge together. But phenomena (*shi*) are not suddenly removed, [and must be] eliminated gradually."[52] This instruction buttressed the soteriological position of conservative Tang Chan monks like Guifeng Zongmi and was later echoed by Shibei's grand-disciple, Fayan Wenyi. It thus seems as though in some Chan circles the *Śūraṃgama* had taken the place of the *Diamond Sūtra* (which itself had replaced the *Laṅkāvatāra*) as the scripture of choice—another reminder of the importance of sutras as sources of authority and identity for many Chan monks during the Tang and Five Dynasties. In the kingdoms of Min and the Southern Tang, this sutra's affirmation of gradual practice, together with its dual emphasis on metaphysics and meditation, was championed by Xuansha Shibei and his descendants, whose austere training rose from firm foundations in normative Buddhist texts and practices.[53]

Despite the pivotal role that the *Śūraṃgama* played in the life and teachings of Xuansha Shibei, by the Song dynasty he had been reimagined as a classic Chan savant—of ignoble origins, essentially illiterate, yet inherently gifted. The comment that he was "fond of fishing," repeated in Shibei's *Song Biography* and his entry in the *Transmission of the Flame*, was later interpreted to mean that he made his living as a poor fisherman. Eihei Dōgen 永平道元 (1200–1253), the thirteenth-century patriarch of Japanese Sōtō (Ch. Caodong) Zen, further embellished the myth: "Since he had long been a fisherman, even in his dreams Xuansha had seen none of the great multitude of Buddhist sutras and commentaries, but since he put his deep resolve above all else, an aspiration appeared in him that excelled that of his fellow monks."[54] In these later accounts, Shibei was awakened not through reading the sutras but after painfully stubbing his toe and realizing the illusory nature of the body. Just as later authors portrayed Xuefeng Yicun as a slow but persistent student, Xuansha Shibei was imagined as a country rustic whose deep insight into the Buddhist teachings occurred suddenly, independent of doctrinal study.

Serving the Sovereign

The earliest accounts of Shibei's life record that he spent his younger years in austere, solitary training and that, after his time on Mt. Xuefeng, he resumed his eremitic ways, living in hermitages and other small temples throughout the kingdom of Min. Sometime between 898 and 901, however, Wang Shenzhi invited him to head the newly rebuilt Anguo yuan 安國院 outside Min's capital. This was no thatched hut; it housed an assembly of five hundred monks, some from as far away as Koryŏ and Japan.[55] Wang Shenzhi went on to receive the precepts from Xuansha Shibei, whom he called a "living buddha" (*sheng zhi fo* 生之佛). Shibei in turn was given a purple robe and the name Great Master Zongyi 宗一 (First in the Lineage) by the king. In addition to making donations of food and cash to Shibei's assembly at Anguo, Wang Shenzhi also had the complex expanded to accommodate its growing population, just as he had done for Yicun's community at Xuefeng.[56] When Shibei passed away a few months after Yicun in 908, the king is said to have set aside his official duties in mourning for a period of several days and paid to have a small stupa erected for the master's remains.

What did the king see in Xuefeng Yicun and Xuansha Shibei? If we are to believe the *Record of Discussing the Buddha Mind Seal* (*Lun Fo xinyin lu* 論佛心印錄), a text that is included in the discourse records of both Shibei and Yicun, then the king sought the Mind Seal that has been secretly transmitted by Bodhidharma, to see his Nature, to attain buddhahood, and to resolve the Great Matter of birth and death.[57] Although a colophon for the text claims that it is a transcript of a conversation between Yicun, Shibei, and Wang Shenzhi recorded by three court officials, the earliest extant version dates to the seventeenth century. Xuefeng Yicun's inscription does note that the king often summoned him to the capital and attended his teachings, but there is no way to know what he and Xuansha Shibei taught Wang Shenzhi and members of his court.

A contemporaneous inscription for one of the many stupas Wang Shenzhi constructed in his capital, however, does allude to at least some of the king's motivations for supporting Yicun, Shibei, and other clerics.[58] The Baoen dingguang duobao ta 報恩定光多寶塔 (Repaying Kindness Dīpaṃkara and Prabhūtaratna Stupa, popularly known as Bai ta 白塔 or White Stupa) was built in memory of the king's late mother and father (see map 2).[59] To celebrate its completion, Wang Shenzhi staged vegetarian feasts for Yicun's assembly at Mt. Xuefeng and Shibei's community at Mt. Wolong. In the stupa's inscription, a nobleman is quoted enthusing that Buddhist monks "not only pray for our ancestors in the netherworld but also instruct the people in filial piety," and the king's own support for monks and monasteries is also presented as an expression of core Confucian values: "The Golden Sage [the Buddha] taught merit [*gong* 功] and virtue [*de* 德]. The Sage of Lu [Confucius] taught loyalty [*zhong* 忠] and filiality [*xiao* 孝]. In praying for loyalty and filiality, there is nothing greater than merit and virtue." The inscription goes on to equate the Five Constants of Confucianism—namely benevolence (*ren* 仁), propriety (*li* 禮), wisdom (*zhi* 智), fidelity (*xin* 信), and righteousness (*yi* 義)—with the Buddhist virtues of compassion (*cibei* 慈悲), reverence (*gongjing* 恭敬), sagely awareness (*shengjue* 聖覺), honesty (*zhengzhi* 正直), and the end of afflictions (*fannao* 煩惱).[60] Wang Shenzhi's interest in the Buddhist teachings, according to this inscription, came not at the expense of Confucian values but in service of them. We know that Shenzhi also built at least one Buddhist temple to care for the spirit of his deceased mother and likewise had copies of the entire Buddhist canon placed in stupas "for his late father, officials, the late queen, and for the good fortune of all his relations and officials in the netherworld."[61] The king may have had a sincere interest in awakening and liberation from *saṃsāra*, but these acts also make it clear that Shenzhi's support of monastics was also motivated by a (not unrelated) desire to generate merit both for himself and his ancestors. There is nothing particularly remarkable about this: anxieties about ancestors have always fueled the economic engine of Chinese Buddhism. What is noteworthy is that Chan clerics were now being identified as conduits of Confucian values and appointed arbiters of royal ancestral cults.

A Divided Inheritance

The foremost beneficiaries of the king's offerings, Xuefeng Yicun and Xuansha Shibei, are listed as master and disciple in the *Patriarch's Hall Collection* and subsequent Chan sources, but there are several indications that the relationship between them was rather that of close companions. To begin with, Shibei's memorial inscription and *Song Biography* identify Yicun as Shibei's "fellow student and elder dharma-brother" (*tongxue faxiong* 同學法兄 or *xuexiong* 學兄). Aside from stating that the two met frequently and that Yicun often praised Shibei, these sources contain little to suggest a formal teacher-student relationship except for Yicun's seniority in terms of age. The two men led their large monastic communities simultaneously and died in the same year. In the *Record of Discussing the Buddha Mind Seal*, they are summoned as a pair to Wang Shenzhi's court, where they function as equals, even responding to the king's questions in unison.

Despite their apparent similarity, however, passages in the biographies of Yicun's and Shibei's descendants imply that the two monks had different teaching styles and spawned distinct lineages. For example, Shibei's disciple Luohan Guichen 羅漢桂琛 (867–928) is said to have gone "to the gatherings of Xuefeng [Yicun] and Xuansha [Shibei]" only to eventually find accord with the latter. As discussed in more detail below, an attempt was later made to remove Luohan Guichen from Shibei's lineage and place him within Yicun's line. Luohan Guichen's student Fayan Wenyi, moreover, had originally studied with Yicun's disciple Changqing Huileng, but Wenyi's biography claims that it was because Luohan Guichen belonged to a different lineage than Changching Huileng that Fayan Wenyi was finally able to resolve his doubts.[62] Finally, the *Song Biography* of one of Fayan Wenyi's most prominent students, Tiantai Deshao, specifies that he "propagated the law of Xuansha [Shibei] with great success."[63] In each of these examples, the teachings of Shibei are singled out or contrasted with those of Yicun. In times of conflict among secular clans, members of an extended family typically invoke the apical ancestors from whom their branch of the lineage claims descent. The repeated reference to Shibei in the biographies of his descendants appears to function in this way, distinguishing these monks from collateral branches of Yicun's lineage—a trend that only becomes more pronounced over the course of the tenth century.

It is difficult to know for certain how the styles of these two monks might have differed, but there are some indications. In an addendum to Xuefeng Yicun's biography, Zanning addresses those who claim that Xuansha Shibei "surpassed his teacher [Yicun]," noting that at the time of writing (ca. 988), Shibei's teachings were "greatly esteemed in southern China [Jiangbiao 江表]." According to Zanning, the difference in their approaches was that

Yicun emphasized meditation and precepts, and Xuansha Shibei stressed the importance of the "vehicle" (*sheng* 乘; Skt. *yāna*), probably a reference to Mahāyāna sutras.[64] As we have seen, Yicun's memorial inscription claimed that he and his disciples' way was "distinct from the sutras" (其道皆離貝葉), and the biographies of later generations of Yicun's descendants in the kingdom of Wuyue also express skepticism that the truth of the Buddhist teachings could be conveyed through conventional uses of language. In an exchange with his disciple Daofu, for example, Yicun affirms that ancient worthies only used the mind to transmit the mind and asserted that they "did not set up words, letters, or phrases."[65] When another monk who had spent time at Mt. Xuefeng was asked about the teachings there, he reportedly replied that Yicun taught that "the buddhas of the three worlds do not explain it, and the twelve divisions of the teachings do not record it. It is a separate transmission outside the teachings of the three vehicles. When old monks from the ten directions arrive here [at this truth], their mouths are smashed into hundreds of pieces."[66] The teachings of Yicun, at least as recorded in the *Patriarch's Hall Collection* and the *Transmission of the Flame*, thus appear to be quite similar to those of Hongzhou monks like Huangbo, who, according to Pei Xiu, "carried only the seal of the highest vehicle which is apart from writings, and transmitted only the one-mind, without any other dharma."[67] This similarity may stem from Yincun's time with Lingxun, but it just as well could have come from Deshan Xuanjian, whose teachings were often compared with those of Huangbo's most influential heir, Linji Yixuan.[68]

In contrast to Yicun's cautions against an over dependence on language, the records of Shibei and many of his most famous heirs make frequent reference to Buddhist sutras and commentaries. These two approaches may be distinct, but they were not necessarily incompatible. The scriptures studied by Shibei and other monks had always been understood as expedients. In all traditions of Chinese Buddhism, the immediacy of *bodhi* was the goal; texts, rituals, and regulations were provisional devices intended to help devotees realize that goal. The differences between Shibei and Yicun most likely indicate a difference in perspective—one mapping the path, the other exemplifying the destination. Despite this complementarity, it was Shibei's more conventional and ecumenical approach—combining discipline, meditation, and sutra study (*śīla, samādhi*, and *prajñā*)—that attracted the patronage of kings and courtiers in the Southern Tang and Wuyue.

An argument can thus be made for treating the lineages of Yicun and Shibei as separate, but it is important to note that no such distinction was ever made in Chan genealogies, which always categorize Shibei's disciples as the grand-disciples of Yicun. Nor is there any evidence of competition or antagonism between these two monks. However, after their nearly simultaneous deaths, subsequent accounts in the biographies of their disciples signal that divisions did begin to disrupt the cohesiveness of this monastic movement. Pedagogical and other stylistic differences may have influenced this to a certain degree, but the rivalries among Yicun's and Shibei's disciples were almost certainly exacerbated by the political ruptures forming between their respective patrons.

Clerics as Political Capital

While Wang Shenzhi was on the throne, he appointed ostensibly loyal kin to govern the key port cities of Quanzhou and Zhangzhou, both of which profited from the region's lucrative maritime trade with southeast Asia. As provincial hubs, these cities also developed into Buddhist centers, and governors installed clerical leaders aligned with their interests and dependent on their largesse. Even before the death of Wang Shenzhi, these cities were competing not just for political and economic advantage but also for the counsel, ritual efficacy, and cultural capital conveyed by the disciples of Xuefeng Yicun and Xuansha Shibei.

The life of Yicun's disciple Changqing Huileng hints at some of the political motivations behind provincial governors' practice of recruiting prominent clerics to their cities.[69] Huileng was born near Hangzhou, the future capital of Wuyue.[70] After receiving the precepts, he traveled to Min, where he stayed together with Yicun on Mt. Xuefeng for more than thirty years.[71] In 903, near the end of Huileng's time on Mt. Xuefeng, Wang Shenzhi's older brother Wang Shengui governed the city of Quanzhou. When Wang Chao died in 897, Wang Shengui had been next in line to inherit the throne but allowed the younger Shenzhi, who was already established in Fuzhou, to assume the reins instead. Wang Shengui's son Wang Yanbin 王延彬 (866–930) never ceased striving to recoup the power and position that his father ceded to Shenzhi. With his uncle firmly established in Fuzhou, Wang Yanbin labored to build Quanzhou into a rival political, economic, and cultural center. Part of that process involved the acquisition of Xuefeng Yicun's descendants to head the city's major temples.[72]

According to Yicun's discourse record, in 895, just one year after Yicun returned to Fujian, Wang Yanbin established a new cloister in Quanzhou and invited him to serve as abbot. Despite the "profuse courtesy and respect" paid to Yicun, Wang Yanbin could not compete with Wang Shenzhi, who secured Yicun's return to Mt. Xuefeng in the north, requesting his personal instruction and spending 600,000 cash on the construction of new temple buildings.[73] A decade later, in 906, after Wang Yanbin had succeeded his father as governor of Quanzhou, he requested that Yicun's disciple Huileng relocate from Mt. Xuefeng to the newly built Zhaoqing si 昭慶寺 in Quanzhou.[74] (Later flame records go so far as to list Wang Yanbin as Huileng's dharma-heir, though early accounts make no mention of this.[75]) After several years at Zhaoqing, however, Huileng returned to the Fuzhou area to assume the abbacy of Changqing yuan 長慶院 on Mt. Yi.[76] Huileng spent more than twenty years at this temple, from at least 912 to 932, eventually passing away there; he is therefore also known as Changqing Huileng. Following his death, he was eulogized by Wang Shenzhi's son and successor Wang Yanjun 王延鈞 (r. 926–935), and awarded the posthumous title Chao-jue 超覺 ("Superior Understanding"). As was commonly done for eminent court clerics, the court bore the costs of his funeral and stupa construction.

The stele inscription composed by an administrative assistant named Lin Wensheng 林文盛 (n.d.) and titled "Stele for the Elder Monk Huileng of Zhaoqing Temple" has been lost, but the title and date alone raise a number of questions.[77] The inscription is dated to 914, two years after Huileng had returned to Fuzhou and eighteen years before his death. At that time, Huileng was living at Changqing Temple in Fuzhou under the patronage of Wang Shenzhi. Steles are generally not commissioned during a person's lifetime. Why then was this stele erected so many years before Huileng's death? Why did it link him not with his final place of residence, but with Zhaoqing in Quanzhou, where he had lived no more than six years? Suzuki Tetsuo has argued persuasively that this inscription reflects the political maneuvering of Wang Yanbin in Quanzhou in opposition to his uncle Wang Shenzhi in Fuzhou.[78] By claiming that one of Min's leading Chan monks resided in *his* territory and served *his* interests, Yanbin was representing himself as the preeminent ruler of the region.

Wang Yanbin had involved monks in his political campaigns before. Shortly after Huileng returned to Fuzhou, the appearance of a white deer and purple mushrooms in Quanzhou were interpreted by an otherwise unknown monk named Haoyuan 浩源 (d. 921) as portents of Wang Yanbin's regal destiny. Encouraged by these auguries, Yanbin secretly dispatched Haoyuan to the Liang court to request the title of military commissioner of Quanzhou. Such a position would have made Yanbin the political equal of his uncle, but the plan was foiled when Shenzhi intercepted and executed the monk.[79] Official accounts claim that Wang Yanbin was thereafter dismissed from office and returned to his private residence, but he clearly continued to orchestrate the movements of monastics in Quanzhou.[80] After losing Huileng to Fuzhou, Yanbin next invited Huileng's disciple Daokuang 道匡 (n.d.) to assume the abbacy of Zhaoqing Temple.[81] This effectively established a Quanzhou-based faction of Xuefeng Yicun's heirs (Yicun–Huileng–Daokuang) to rival the primary leadership ensconced in Fuzhou (Yicun–Shenyan–Qinghu).

In Xuefeng Yicun's regulations, he cited an old adage: "A family does not have two masters; a country does not have two kings." "If there were two masters," he cautioned, "there would inevitably be conflicts; if there were two kings, there would be competition."[82] Some decades after his death, however, Min did indeed have multiple rulers, and Yicun's monastic family did split into different branches under the leadership of different masters. As feared, conflicts and competition ensued.

Family Rivalries

In Min as elsewhere, there was a close correlation between the political power of a ruler and the prestige of the clerics under his patronage. The most prominent monks in Min were called to or remained in the capital to serve the king, while clerics of lesser renown accepted appointments in provincial cities. Fuzhou hosted the largest concentration of clerics in the region as well as many of the kingdom's best-endowed monasteries, and most of the clerics who would later spread the lineage of Xuefeng Yicun and Xuansha Shibei to neighboring kingdoms did so after a period of training in or around the capital. The port cities of Quanzhou and Zhangzhou were, respectively, second and third to Fuzhou in terms of political and economic significance.

The biography of the monk Luohan Guichen—the primary conduit through which Min's Chan movement passed to the Southern Tang and Wuyue—highlights the relationship between geographical location, patronage, and lineage during this period. Luohan Guichen was, like Huileng, originally from present-day Zhejiang (Changshan 常山). He became a monk under Master Wuxiang 無相 (n.d.) of Wansui Temple 萬歲寺.[83] According to his *Song Biography*, "After ascending the precept platform, [Guichen] commenced studying the Vinaya. Mounting the dais to expound the precepts books for the congregation, he knew that his aspirations were great. How could they be restricted to the minor teachings? He announced, 'To be bound by the maintenance or transgression [of the precepts] is not liberation. Relying on texts for understanding, how could one become a sage?'[84] Thereupon he vowed to visit [masters of] the Southern School and journeyed nearly ten-thousand *li*."[85] Dissatisfied with the mainstream Vinaya tradition of his native Zhejiang, Luohan Guichen first traveled south to Jiangxi, where he studied with Dongshan Liangjie's disciple Yunju Daoying in Hongzhou. From there he continued on to Fuzhou, training under both Xuefeng Yicun and Xuansha Shibei and eventually succeeding the latter.

Xuansha Shibei reportedly had some seven hundred disciples but "among those who had received the dharma [from Shibei], all praised Guichen as endowed with extraordinary powers. Today [ca. 980] monasteries throughout the Zhejiang region transmit his teachings and his heirs are multiplying."[86] Zanning, the author of this passage, was writing with the benefit of hindsight. By the end of the tenth century, many of the most renowned Chan masters in southeastern China traced their lineage through Luohan Guichen, and it may be that that Guichen was retrospectively invested with significance due to the later success of his descendants. During his life, however, Guichen appears to have been somewhat less prominent than other disciples of Xuansha Shibei or Xuefeng Yicun. While he did secure the patronage of at least two minor members of the Wang family, he remained on the margins—both geographically and politically—of Min's prevailing religio-political networks.

Some years before Xuansha Shibei's death, Guichen was invited by one Wang Cheng 王誠 (n.d.)—presumably a member of the royal clan—to head a small cloister outside of Fuzhou, known as Dizang yuan 地藏院.[87] Eighteen years later, in 920, Guichen relocated to Luohan yuan 羅漢院 in distant Zhangzhou at the request of another little-known member of the Wang family, Wang Zhi 王志 (n.d.).[88] Why did Guichen move from the capital to the city of Zhangzhou in the far south, and why did none of his heirs receive temple appointments in Min? Perhaps Guichen's position on the periphery was intentional; maybe he was wisely avoiding the distractions and obligations that came with serving as abbot of a temple in the capital. After eight years in Zhangzhou, however, Guichen returned to Fuzhou, where he passed away and was cremated "in the hills east of the Western Temple"—a move that seems to imply that Guichen's time in Zhangzhou was something akin to exile.[89] There is also an intriguing passage at the end of Luohan Guichen's entry in the *Song Biographies* that suggests Guichen may have left Fuzhou after having been purposefully excluded from patronage networks in Min's capital. The passage reads: "[Gui]chen obtained the dharma [from Shibei] through a secret dispensation. At that time, Great Master Shenyan was revered by Wang [Shenzhi]. It is said that [Shenyan] tried to coerce [Guichen] to abandon Xuansha [Shibei] and succeed Xuefeng [Yicun], but [Guichen] could not be swayed. In the end [Guichen] suffered from Shen[yan]'s insult. What a pity!"[90] This unsavory episode, of a type rarely seen in hagiographic collections like the *Song Biographies*, not only underscores the importance of lineage identity during this period but also makes it clear that rival factions were forming between groups of Xuefeng Yicun's and Xuansha Shibei's disciples.

The antagonist of this episode, Xuefeng Yicun's disciple Gushan Shenyan, was the most powerful monk in Fuzhou during Guichen's life. His biographies note that he was connected by place of birth to Min's royal clan and by ancestry to the emperors of the Tang dynasty. (Shenyan was originally from Daliang 大梁 in Henan, the natal region of the Wang family. His family name was Li 李, and the *Patriarch's Hall Collection* records that he was descended from the Tang imperial line.[91]) After dreaming that a foreign monk told him that it was time to leave home, Shenyan went to study with Chan Master Daogui 道規 (n.d.) at Mt. Bailu 白鹿山 in Weizhou 衛州 and received the precepts on Mt. Song in 882. Traveling south, he settled on Mt. Xuefeng as one of Yicun's younger disciples. Following Yicun's death, Wang Shenzhi named Shenyan national teacher with the title Xingsheng 興聖 ("Rising Sage"), an honor that effectively made Shenyan Yicun's primary successor in the capital. Shenyan then took up residence in the temple Wang Shenzhi established for him twenty *li* east of the capital on Mt. Gu 鼓山, Yongquan si 湧泉寺, and remained there until his death at the age of seventy-three.[92]

Shenyan's position as *paterfamilias* of Xuefeng Yicun's heirs in Fuzhou is evident from the role he apparently played in recommending monks for the abbacies of Fuzhou's major monasteries. The entry for Xuansha Shibei's disciple Huiqiu Jizhao 慧球寂照 (d. 913) in the *Transmission of the Flame* points to some of the power dynamics involved in temple appointments.[93]

> In the second year of the Kaiping era [909], Shibei was about to pass away. The Min Commander Wang [Shenzhi] sent his son to inquire about the illness and to ask secretly who would succeed him in preaching the dharma. Shibei said,

"It will be [Hui]qiu." Wang remembered this testimony and later asked National Teacher Gushan [Shenyan], "Who should be appointed to the dharma
seat at [Mt.] Wolong [Anguo Temple]?" Gushan summoned all the worthies
living in the city who possessed the eye of the way. There were twelve of them,
each qualified for the appointment.[94] Wang said nothing [about what he had
been told]. On the day when the hall was to be opened, officials and monks
all gathered around the dharma seat. Wang suddenly asked the assembly, "Who
is Head Seat Qiu?" Those in the assembly pointed out the master. Wang then
invited him to ascend the seat.[95]

This passage is revealing in a number of ways. For one, it indicates that
the model of monastic succession at some Min temples may have been similar
to the procedures implemented in the "public" Chan monasteries that later
became ubiquitous in the Song.[96] As Morten Schlütter has discussed, during the Song, when there was a vacancy at a public Chan monastery, prefectural officials would have the monastic controller call a meeting of the
abbots of other public monasteries. Those abbots would then nominate a
monk of high standing for the position of abbot, and their nomination
would then be presented to the authorities for final approval.[97] A very similar system seems to be described in Huiqiu Jizhao's biography. In response
to the king's question about succession, Shenyan summoned the senior
monks in the area, apparently to confer with them about who would assume
the abbacy. The king and his officials were present at the meeting to wit-
ness the event but also probably to ratify the decision reached by the senior clerics. Although the passage in Huiqiu Jizhao's biography implies that
the ultimate decision rested with the dying Xuansha Shibei, it also shows
that both Gushan Shenyan (as ranking monk) and Wang Shenzhi (as king)
exercised a degree of authority over temple appointments in the capital.

But why did the king keep his conversation with Shibei secret, pretending to authorize Shenyan to oversee the process of succession and then
waiting until the last minute to announce the candidate that had already
been selected by Shibei? We cannot rule out the possibility that this is just
a fictional account and these events may have been inserted simply to dra-
matize the narrative. Or it may also be that the disciples and devotees of
Huiqiu Jizhao transmitted this account to portray Jizhao as the chosen heir
of Xuansha Shibei and a personal favorite of Min's king. However, Shenyan's
other attempts to manipulate the lineage affiliation of Guichen allow for
yet another reading: the king's intervention may have been a tactic to ensure that Shibei's temple did not fall under the control of Shenyan and his
circle.

Both Mt. Gu, the headquarters of Shenyan, and Mt. Wolong, the home
base of Shibei, were located in very close proximity to Min's imperial precincts in Fuzhou. These mountains both hosted large populations of clerics supported by the court. Their abbots ostensibly belonged to the same
lineage family, though each represented distinct branches of that lineage.
Shenyan, as national teacher, was presumably the most prominent cleric in

the capital, and his disciples continued to serve as abbots of Yongquan si on Mt. Gu for several generations. Although six of Shibei's disciples assumed the abbacies of temples in and around Fuzhou, after Jizhao's tenure as abbot of Anguo on Mt. Wolong, control of that important temple passed to a direct disciple of Xuefeng Yicun, the monk Hongtao 弘瑫 (n.d.), and thereafter seems to have remained within Hongtao's lineage.[98] Shibei's heirs effectively lost control of their home monastery. These events may explain why Shibei's inscription, which identifies him as the founding abbot of Anguo Chan Cloister, was erected at the site in 930, more than two decades after his death. Were his heirs trying to reassert his fading legacy? It may be that Shenyan was positioning himself, his dharma-brothers, and his disciples as the primary representatives of Xuefeng Yicun's lineage in Min, marking other branches of the lineage—particularly the descendants of Xuansha Shibei—as peripheral and relegating them to the margins.

Drawing so close to the court had obvious benefits, but it also entailed a significant amount of risk. In the case of Gushan Shenyan, the close ties between this cleric, his disciples, and the Wang family in Fuzhou ultimately became a liability as the political and economic stability of the capital began to dissolve under the tenures of Wang Shenzhi's sons and grandsons. Those pushed to the periphery, however, had more success surviving the collapse of the kingdom.

A House in Ruins

Following the death of Wang Shenzhi, his corpse was entrusted to the saṃgha, which effectively became its caretaker and custodian. At Yongquan si, the monastery of National Teacher Gushan Shenyan, funerary services were performed to expedite the king's journey to a propitious rebirth.[99] Wang Shenzhi was thereafter buried next to his wife on Mt. Fengchi 風池, where a temple was established with four monks appointed to tend to the grave.[100] The burial site was later moved to Mt. Lianhua 蓮花, where another temple was constructed, fields were provided for its support, a statue of Shenzhi was enshrined, and monks were again appointed to perform requisite rituals and maintain the site. The temple's name, Lianhua yongxing chansi 蓮花永興禪寺, designates it a "Chan temple"—an indication, most likely, that the temple's abbot belonged to a Chan lineage—but it was also popularly known as the ancestral hall of King Zhongyi (Zhongyi wang citang 忠懿王祠堂).[101] The grave of Shenzhi's son Wang Yanzheng 王延政 (r. 944–946), the fifth ruler of Min, was also later moved to this site.[102]

The selection of Chan clerics as caretakers of the royal ancestral cult in Min established a pattern that would be replicated in the Southern Tang, Wuyue, and, ultimately, the Song dynasty. That Chan monks began to assume responsibilities for the ancestral shrines of royal families during the Five Dynasties reflects their position as leaders of the Buddhist establishment. It also makes it plain that they were valued for their abilities to liberate the dead as well as awaken the living, a fact that has been noted in studies of medieval Japanese Zen but often goes unmentioned in discussions of Chinese Chan.

Wang Shenzhi's death marked the end of the prosperity and stability that had characterized his nearly thirty-year reign. The inter-clan conflicts that Shenzhi had managed to suppress during his life quickly surfaced after his death and began to tear the kingdom apart. According to Ouyang Xiu (quoting one of Min's military commanders), Shenzhi's descendants squandered the noble achievements of their forebear: "Formerly, the Martial Emperor Taizu [Wang Shenzhi] personally withstood the arrows and catapults of war to inaugurate Min rule, but his sons and grandsons are debauched and depraved beyond all description. Heaven now repudiates the Wang house."[103] While Shenzhi's sons and grandsons allowed border skirmishes with neighboring kingdoms to escalate into war, murder and intrigue plagued the Min court at home. None of Shenzhi's descendants were able to maintain control of the territory for any extended period of time. From 925 to 946, five members of the Wang family and two outsiders successively controlled Fuzhou in the north, while a succession of eight governors administered Quanzhou.[104]

The rapid and often violent succession of rulers destabilized the region as a whole and must have crippled Buddhist communities. Two of Wang Shenzhi's sons and successors, Wang Yanjun and Wang Yanxi 王延羲 (r. 939–944), sponsored mass ordinations of Buddhist monks (possibly to generate income from the sale of ordination certificates), but the influence of Buddhist clerics at court declined as subsequent kings took the counsel of Daoist masters.[105] The enthronement and murder of the monk Zhuo Yanming in 944, described at the beginning of this chapter, paradoxically points to both the prestige of Buddhist monks and their utter expendability during this tumultuous period.

With Min weakened by fratricidal infighting, the neighboring kingdoms of the Southern Tang and Wuyue moved in to seize its lands and wealth. In 944, Li Jing 李璟 (r. 943–961), the second of the Southern Tang's three kings, launched an invasion of three of Min's interior counties. These were eventually captured and reconstituted as the new Jian 劍 prefecture, governed by the Southern Tang appointee Chen Hui 陳誨 (n.d.). Wuyue later annexed the northeastern portion of Min to just south of Fuzhou. The Quanzhou and Zhangzhou regions became the quasi-autonomous Qingyuan 清源 commandery, governed by the Southern Tang appointee Liu Congxiao 留從效 (906–978) (see map 3). By 946, the kingdom of Min had ceased to exist.

The overthrow of the Wang clan and the occupation of Min's cities deprived many monastic communities of the political and economic support on which they had grown dependent. Much of Min's economic, political, and cultural resources were transferred to its conquerors. By the mid-tenth century, the capital cities of Jinling (present-day Nanjing) in the Southern Tang and Hangzhou in Wuyue were the most powerful and prosperous cities in southeastern China. Monks from throughout China had once flowed into Min to join the Buddhist renaissance initiated by Xuefeng Yicun and Xuansha Shibei and underwritten through the patronage of Wang Shenzhi. With the onset of the kingdom's collapse, that tide reversed itself as monks fled the embattled region for the shelter and support offered by neighboring states.[106] Some members of Yicun's and Shibei's lineage settled in the kingdoms of Chu, while others rallied around Yicun's disciple Yunmen Wenyan 雲門文偃 (864–949) in the Southern Han. But most members of this clerical network made their way to Wuyue and the Southern Tang—two kingdoms that quickly developed into the new strongholds of this movement.

The late Tang and Five Dynasties was once idealized as an era of liberation and innovation, when Chan monks constituted a radical, grassroots movement oriented more toward the common people than the court. It is quite clear, however, that leading Chan clerics in Min established strong institutional bases and were fully integrated into the kingdom's political power structures. It was by means of their court connections that the descendants of Xuefeng Yicun and Xuansha Sheibei came to occupy affluent, state-sponsored temples throughout the kingdom, to serve as national teachers and royal preceptors, to compile extensive genealogical records, and to preside over the mortuary rites of the royal family. Griffith Foulk once suggested that the work of monks in southeastern China around the mid-tenth century—their formation of an exclusive lineage, their close connections with regional rulers, and their role in the establishment and management of Chan lineage temples—offer some of the earliest evidence of a recognizable Chan school.[107] I have argued that these characteristics were in evidence in Fujian as far back as the early tenth century but would agree that the origins of Chan as an organized, self-consciously sectarian movement can be traced to southeastern China during the Five Dynasties and Ten Kingdoms.

The patron-client relationships that developed between the descendants of Xuefeng Yicun and Xuansha Shibei and patriarchs of the Wang clan elevated members of this Chan lineage network to positions of significant authority and influence—positions members of this network continued to maintain and extend over the course of the tenth century. The initial rise of these monks in Min does not, however, appear to have been predicated on particularly innovative doctrinal interpretations or practice regimens; there was little to differentiate them from the Hongzhou monks that had been supported by the Wang family in the early years of its reign or other Chan clerics active in the region. It is probably no coincidence that the decline of the Hongzhou school corresponded with the fall of the Tang dynasty. The alliance that ensued between the Wang family and Xuefeng Yicun's lineage effectively established new networks of political and monastic leadership, both asserting the authority of new sets of ancestors.

Wang Shenzhi's support for the descendants of Xuefeng Yicun and Xuansha Shibei established a model that was adopted by subsidiary patriarchs of the Wang family serving as governors of Min's major cities. A self-perpetuating system took hold whereby the presence of prominent clerics conferred credibility on regional governors and the support of regional rulers augmented the resources and reputations of favored monks and monasteries. This series of clergy-court alliances created something like an affinal kin group, related not through intermarriage but through patronage. Sub-branches of these two "families," distinguished by locale, continued to ally with one another over the course of several generations—a phenomenon rarely, if ever, seen during the Tang.

One of the results of this process was the formation of sub-lineages that were defined not solely through doctrine or practice but through place-based patronage networks, as monastic communities grew dependent on local resources and were obligated to serve specific branches of the royal clan. Although Min was ostensibly a single kingdom united under one king, in reality it functioned as a series of sub-states that were often in open conflict with one another. Regional governors maintained their own militaries, managed their own economies, and relied on the counsel and ritual protection of their own clerics. Ruptures among members of the Wang clan appear to have led to divisions among Yicun's and Shibei's heirs in Min—divisions that cleaved along the lines of loyalty and affiliation rather than, or perhaps in addition to, ideology.

In the late 930s and early 940s, as leading members of the Wang family were successively murdered or deposed, many of the monastic communities these men had maintained trailed then into obscurity. The once-powerful monks and monasteries in cities like Fuzhou and Quanzhou were relegated to the sidelines. Monks who fled the region entirely or were operating at a safer distance from more violent political power struggles became instrumental in transmitting the Chan lineages, literary traditions, and institutions of Min to the neighboring kingdoms of the Southern Tang and Wuyue.

4

Filial Sons

The Southern Tang

For a brief period, the kingdom of Min was ruled by a monk from Mt. Xuefeng, the monastic headquarters of Xuefeng Yicun and his disciples in Fujian. The kingdom of the Southern Tang, by contrast, was for fourteen years ruled by a monarch in the guise of a monk. The last ruler of the Southern Tang, Li Yu 李煜 (r. 961–975), and his wife reportedly dressed in monastic robes, chanted sutras, made mudras, and bowed until sores formed on their foreheads.[1] Ouyang Xiu charged that Li Yu "tended toward arrogant extravagance and addiction to sensual pleasures. He had an affinity with Buddhism as well, engaging in lofty discourse without due concern for affairs of government."[2] Other Song historians would claim that the ruler "built more than ten Buddhist temples within the palace compound and gave gold to recruit commoners and Daoists to become monks. Within the capital, there were thousands of monks well-versed in extracting resources from the county magistrate."[3] These clerics all but inundated the capital, exceeding ten thousand in number. The ruler, we are told, personally supplied them all with grain, silk, and cash.[4]

Such critiques, written by Song literati with a pronounced distaste for both the Southern Tang's last ruler and Buddhist clerics in general, are far from objective accounts, but the close relationship they describe between the Southern Tang clergy and the court is corroborated in both Buddhist canonical sources and inscriptions written by local literati. The presence of so many monks in the cities along the lower reaches of the Yangzi River during the tenth century may have been condemned as an economic burden by some, but it was nothing new. Long before the establishment of the Southern Tang, the Jiangnan region had served as an important center of Buddhist culture, and later writers often compared the rulers of the Southern Tang with Emperor Wu (r. 502–549) of the Liang dynasty, a famously open-handed patron of the *saṃgha* who ruled southern China from present-day Nanjing. Buddhist monks and monasteries maintained an influential presence in the region throughout the Tang and during the subsequent short-lived kingdom of Wu, so it is little surprise that Buddhist traditions continued to flourish under the tenure of all three of the Southern Tang's rulers. Both Li Yu's grandfather, Li Bian 李昇 (r. 937–943), and his father,

71

Li Jing 李璟 (r. 943–961), the first and second rulers, were also generous patrons of Buddhist monks and frequent sponsors of vegetarian feasts.[5]

Although the Jiangnan region had produced some of the most prominent Chan movements of the late Tang period—the Hongzhou, Caodong, and Oxhead lineages—and fostered an abundance of local clerics and native traditions, most of the monastic beneficiaries of the Southern Tang court's largesse were not native to the area but had migrated north after a period of study in Fujian. Of the twenty-five monks known to have been supported by the Li family, nineteen were members of Xuefeng Yicun's and Xuansha Shibei's lineages; of those nineteen, ten were the heirs of Shibei's disciple Luohan Guichen. While the religious culture of the Southern Tang was undoubtedly more diverse than extant canonical sources suggest, monastic biographies make it possible to document the spread of Yicun's descendants into the Southern Tang, as well as the Southern Han and Wuyue—a process that transformed what had been a local clerical network into a transregional Buddhist movement.[6]

Scholarship on Chan in the Southern Tang has tended to focus on the life and teachings of Luohan Guichen's most influential disciple in that kingdom, Fayan Wenyi 法眼文益 (885–958). While the historical details of Wenyi's life and teachings are reasonably clear, his and his disciples' role in the historical development of Chan traditions remains a topic of some debate. Suzuki Tetsuo has done the most to document the political and social prominence of this clerical network, and in his view the presence of these clerics in the capital and their connections to the court hastened their decline. He compares these "urban" Chan monks with their counterparts in mountain temples, who he presumes avoided the obligations associated with political patronage and were thus free to focus on their training. Clerics in the capital, in contrast, were beholden to officials and affluent merchants, and their energies were necessarily channeled into preaching and proselytizing rather than practice. Although Fayan Wenyi and his disciples in the Southern Tang capital played a critical part in promoting the Chan movement and securing the support of powerful benefactors, Suzuki maintains that their close association with the Southern Tang court sapped the spiritual strength of their movement. For reasons that were both philosophical and political, these monks were swept aside after the Song came to power.[7]

Yanagida Seizan also argued that the movement of Chan monks from the mountains to the capitals of southeastern kingdoms, particularly the Southern Tang, represented a major turning point in the historical development of the Chan movement, but he saw the Fayan lineage not as a dead end but as a bridge linking the Chan traditions of the Tang and with those of the Song. During the late Tang and Five Dynasties, according to Yanagida, two different interpretations of Chan prevailed in China. In Hebei in the north, Linji Yixuan, Zhaozhao Congshen 趙州從諗 (778–897), and their descendants developed an earthy, immediate, muscular style that appealed to the militarists who governed the region. In southern Jiangnan, by contrast, monks associated with Fayan Wenyi and Yunmen Wenyan maintained

a more cultured, classicist approach better suited to the educated, aristocratic cultures of southeastern cities. It was this latter style that Yanagida
believed developed into the mainstream of the Chan tradition of the Song
dynasty.[8] Yanagida thus traced a direct line from the Hongzhou school of
the late Tang, through the Fayan network during the Five Dynasties and
Ten Kingdoms, to the teachings of prominent Song Chan masters such as
Juefan Huihong 覺範惠洪 (1071–1128).[9]

This chapter draws on Suzuki's detailed research on the geographical
distributions and patronage networks of Chan monks in the Southern Tang
in support of Yanagida's claim that the traditions and institutions inherited
and developed by this clerical network left an indelible impression on later
generations of Chan clerics. These issues are explored in two sections. The
first charts the movement of Xuefeng Yicun's and Xuansha Shibei's heirs
from the kingdom of Min to the capital of the Southern Tang, assessing the
effects of political patronage on specific members of this lineage as well as
on the development of regional Buddhist cultures more broadly. The second situates the teachings of influential Chan clerics—particularly Fayan
Wenyi and his disciples—within the context of the Southern Tang's literary
cultures and examines the relationship between the activities and intellectual affinities of this group of clerics and those of their primary patrons.

Centripetal Forces

The Southern Tang and neighboring Wuyue were the principal destina-
tions for monks fleeing Min during the political upheavals of the 930s
and 940s.[10] The second ruler of the Southern Tang, Li Jing, had captured
and incorporated Min's interior territories in 946 and, along with the land,
the Southern Tang also absorbed a substantial number of the kingdom's
courtiers, including Min's last king, Wang Yanzheng. Some of these men
had ties to members of Xuefeng Yicun's monastic network in Min and continued to maintain those relationships after resettling in Southern Tang
territory. Along with Min's former officials, several disciples of prominent
Min Chan masters also relocated to the Southern Tang and were awarded
the patronage of both provincial governors and the kingdom's rulers.

The geographical trajectory of Xuefeng Yicun's and Xuansha Shibei's
descendants in the Southern Tang typically progressed in stages from the
northeastern border of Min to the capital at Jinling (present-day Nanjing)
in the north. This was a migration from the mountains to the cities, from
the peripheries to the political center of the state. After leaving the large
monastic estates in or near Min's major cities, many of these monks made
their way northeast, where they were initially appointed to temples in the
Southern Tang's provincial cities, including Jianzhou 劍州 and Linchuan
臨川 (in Fuzhou 撫州, Jiangxi), or to monasteries located at major Buddhist
mountain enclaves, such as Mt. Lu 廬山 or Mt. Cao 曹山 (see map 3).

Unlike in Min, where new monasteries were often constructed for favored
monks, many of the temples in the Southern Tang had long histories.

When the heirs of Xuefeng Yicun and Xuansha Shibei ascended the high seat in these temples, they were replacing outgoing abbots and assuming control of well-established monastic communities. In many cases, the previous abbots of these temples were descendants of Caoshan Benji 曹山本寂 (840–901) and Dongshan Liangjie (referred to collectively as Caodong), prominent clerics in the Jiangxi region after the Huichang persecutions. But by the 940s, the influence of the Caodong lineage was waning and there is no evidence that Southern Tang rulers sought to align themselves with these monks.

Instead, the royal family recruited clerics from other parts of China, particularly from the Fujian and Zhejiang regions. Twenty of the twenty-five monks known to have been supported by the Southern Tang court came from outside the region, a proportion that exceeded the roughly one-third to one-half of officeholders who were non-native.[11] Unlike émigré officials, however, who were often recruited on the basis of ability rather than ancestry, for Chan monks ancestry and efficacy were closely bound. As in the kingdom of Min, lineage affiliation appears to have become a factor of patronage in the Southern Tang.

The Disciples of Yunmen Wenyan

The rulers of the Southern Tang supported three distinct branches of Xuefeng Yicun's and Xuansha Shibei's lineage: the disciples of Yunmen Wenyan, of Gushan Shenyan, and of Luohan Guichen. The third group was by far the most influential, but disciples of Wenyan and Shenyan also received royal appointments to several major monasteries—many of which, it is worth highlighting, also functioned as royal ancestral shrines. While these monks were not dominant figures in the region's religio-political networks, they were significant enough to warrant a brief introduction before discussing the better-known faction centered on Fayan Wenyi.

Yunmen Wenyan is a central figure in the history of Chan, but he and his disciples play only peripheral roles in the clergy-court relations of the Southern Tang. Wenyan hailed from Suzhou, trained as a young monk in northern Jiangxi, and eventually traveled to the kingdom of Min, where he joined Xuefeng Yicun's assembly.[12] While the precise chronology is unclear, Wenyan apparently left Mt. Xuefeng sometime prior to Yicun's death in 908.[13] In the ensuing forty years, as Yicun's heirs assumed the abbacies of major temples in Min, the Southern Tang, and Wuyue, Wenyan and his disciples rose to prominence in the kingdom of the Southern Han 南漢 (917–971; corresponding to present-day Guangdong and Guangxi provinces) under the patronage of the ruling Liu 劉 family.[14] The second ruler of the Southern Han, Liu Yan 劉龑 (also known as Nanhan Gaozu 南漢高祖; r. 917–941), promoted Wenyan to the position of inspector of monks in the capital, granted him a purple robe, and funded the construction of a new monastic complex on Mt. Yunmen, located near the city of Shaoguan, along the primary transportation route linking the Southern Han with the rest of the continent.[15] At the time of his death, Wenyan had sixty-one heirs according to the *Transmission of the Flame*, twenty-three of whom remained in the Southern Han.[16]

Some of Wenyan's heirs relocated to northern China, where they eventually won the support of powerful Song officials during the second half of the eleventh century. The success of Wenyan's distant descendants retrospectively elevated Wenyan to one of the best known of Xuefeng Yicun's disciples, and he came to be honored as the founding patriarch of the so-called Yunmen house of Chan.[17] During the Five Dynasties and Ten Kingdoms, however, Wenyan's disciples enjoyed only modest success outside their native Southern Han. The two other kingdoms to shelter significant numbers of his disciples were Chu (present-day Hunan province) with eleven, and the Southern Tang with fifteen. (None of Wenyan's immediate disciples settled in the Fujian region.) Of Wenyan's fifteen disciples in the Southern Tang, only three are known to have been awarded imperial appointments.[18] Aside from their brief entries in the *Transmission of the Flame*, very little is known about these monks.[19]

The Disciples of Gushan Shenyan

The lives of Gushan Shenyan's disciples in the Southern Tang are better represented in the literature. At the time of Shenyan's death in 940, Min was on the verge of collapse, yet the majority of his eleven disciples remained in the Fujian region.[20] Five stayed in Fuzhou (which had been annexed by Wuyue) and one settled in Quanzhou (then a semi-autonomous commandery). One of Shenyan's disciples relocated to Hubei, another to Hangzhou. The remaining three, Baoen Qinghu 報恩清護 (916–970), Zhizuo Zhenji 智作真寂 (fl. 945), and Chongxu Huiwu 沖煦慧悟 (916–974), left Min for the Southern Tang and eventually succeeded one another as abbots of a series of temples under the patronage of military and political leaders, first in provincial centers such as Jianzhou 劍州 and Hongzhou and later in the kingdom's capital.[21]

The biography of Gushan Shenyan's disciple Chongxu Huiwu is representative of the temple appointments and patronage relationships of upwardly mobile Chan monks in the Southern Tang. Huiwu's family was from Henan but had immigrated to Fujian along with Wang Chao late in the ninth century. Huiwu was subsequently born in Fuzhou and he later chose another Henan native as his preceptor, receiving ordination from Gushan Shenyan in 931 at the age of sixteen. After completing his training, he settled in Min's capital, but according to his stupa inscription, "At that time the royal family was enfeebled, and seditious ministers did as they pleased. Good people suffered from excessive punishments and baseless gossip, [so] the great Chan master picked up his staff and left."[22] He traveled inland to the city of Linchuan, where he was summoned by Song Qiqiu 宋齊丘 (887–959), then serving as the military commissioner for the Zhennan 鎮南 commandery.[23] Their "words and thoughts were not in accord," however, and Huiwu continued north to Chiyang 池陽 (present-day Guichi City 貴池市, in Anhui province), where he was supported by Wang Jixun 王繼勳 (912–956),

a member of Min's former royal family.[24] Then, sometime between 954 and 959, the second ruler of the Southern Tang, Li Jing, appointed him abbot of Changqing daochang 長慶道場 (Everlasting Prosperity Bodhimaṇḍa), a historic temple in the capital that served as an ancestral shrine for Li Jing's father.[25] Huiwu thus rose through the monastic ranks, winning a series of increasingly prestigious appointments from ever more powerful benefactors, eventually settling in the capital under the care of the ruler.

Thereafter, Huiwu remained in close proximity to the king, who at the time was struggling to maintain control of his kingdom. As a consequence of a failed war against the Zhou in the north, Li Jing was forced to forfeit his imperial title, all his territory north of the Huai River, and any claim of autonomy. Beginning in 958, the Southern Tang, now officially known simply as Jiangnan (the region south of the river), became a vassal state of first the Zhou dynasty and then the Song. That year, as a security precaution, Li Jing began the process of relocating his capital further south to the city of Hongzhou.

During the brief time that the capital was situated in the south, the ruler summoned Huiwu from Jinling to assume the abbacy of Kaixian yuan 開先院 (Opening [the way for] Ancestors Cloister), a temple on nearby Mt. Lu to which the ruler was reportedly "deeply attached." As its name indicates, Kaixian, like Changqing in Jinling, served as an ancestral shrine for the royal family; the portraits of all three Southern Tang rulers were eventually enshrined there.[26] When Jinling was reinstituted as the kingdom's capital after Li Jing's death in 961, Li Yu recalled Huiwu to Jinling to serve as abbot of yet another site of the royal ancestral cult, Baoen (Requiting Kindness) Chan Cloister 報恩禪院, and awarded him the title Chan Master Huiwu 慧悟 (Awakened Wisdom).[27] Huiwu thus appears to have functioned as a ritual specialist in the service of the ruler, charged with maintaining the imperial ancestral cult at several state-sanctioned temples.

The basic pattern of Chongxu Huiwu's biography is similar to that of several other Southern Tang monks who secured the support of the royal family. Like talented officials who ascended the bureaucratic hierarchy to serve in ever more prominent and powerful positions, select monks were promoted through a series of provincial posts until some eventually received appointments to major monasteries within the capital. In the Southern Tang, as elsewhere during the Five Dynasties and Ten Kingdoms, the ruler personally selected the abbots of monasteries that directly served his needs and those of his kingdom. The fact that Huiwu and other heirs of Xuefeng Yicun and Xuansha Shibei were repeatedly posted to temples that functioned as ancestral shrines also makes it clear that, as in Min, their responsibilities included ministering to the ancestors of the royal family. This is not too surprising; these clerics were the stewards of major, state-sanctioned Buddhist institutions and were therefore obliged to serve the state in the conventional ways. More noteworthy is that monks from one particular Chan lineage family were repeatedly posted to these temples, a phenomenon that seems to suggest that lineage affiliations had become indicative of efficacy and that clerics belonging to certain lineages were perceived, in part by virtue of their "ancestry," as more capable of serving the worldly and otherworldly needs of their patrons than monks who lacked equivalent pedigrees. It also indicates that the forebears of this lineage had established reputations for successfully serving the royal family of Min such that their descendants were in high demand in the Southern Tang and elsewhere. Rather than ally themselves with the monastic leadership they had inherited from the Kingdom of Wu, the rulers of the Southern Tang chose instead to adopt the prevailing clerical network of the recently vanquished Kingdom of Min.

Fayan Wenyi

To an even greater extent than heirs of Yunmen Wenyan and Gushan Shenyan, disciples and grand-disciples of Luohan Guichen captured the abbacies of major monasteries throughout Southern Tang territory, including the capital. Among these monks, Fayan Wenyi was by far the most significant and is subsequently the monk most closely associated with Southern Tang Buddhism.[28] Besides personally winning appointments from the second ruler, seven of Fayan Wenyi's heirs secured the support of the Southern Tang court, and more than twice that number received patronage from the court of Wuyue. The ability of these monks to develop and maintain this kind of social capital, securing the support of two ruling families over the course of multiple generations, distinguished Wenyi and his disciples as some of the most influential clerics of the tenth century.

The arc of Fayan Wenyi's career traversed the shifting political and economic centers of southeastern China during the tenth century, tracing a complete circuit of capital cities, beginning in Hangzhou in Wuyue, moving to Fuzhou in Min, then on to Jinling in Southern Tang, and finally, through his disciples, back to Hangzhou. His biography can be summarized briefly. Born in 885 to the Lu 魯 family, in the town of Yuhang 餘杭 (near present-day Hangzhou), Wenyi spent the first decades of his life close to home. He became a monk at the age of seven and received the full precepts thirteen years later in 905 at Kaiyuan Temple 開元寺 in nearby Yuezhou 越州 (present-day Shaoxing).[29] He later went to Ayuwang si on Mt. Mao 鄮山 (present-day Ningbo) to study with the prelate of Wuyue's Nanshan Vinaya tradition, Xijue. After this early mentoring by one the most prominent clerics of his native region, Wenyi left Wuyue to train under the disciples of Xuefeng Yicun and Xuansha Shibei in Min.

In Min, Wenyi joined the assembly of Xuefeng Yicun's disciple Changqing Huileng, presumably during his tenure at Changqing Temple in Fuzhou (912–932). Wenyi's *Song Biography* notes that his "doubts were resolved" under the guidance of Huileng and he soon left Changqing to go on pilgrimage with at least two other monks.[30] The oft-told tale of their travels culminates when the three pilgrims seek shelter from a storm at Dizang Temple and encounter Luohan Guichen. (This chance meeting with Guichen may be another indication of Guichen's marginal status at the time. It may also, of course, just be good storytelling.) According to Zanning's account, "Luohan [Guichen] knew that Wenyi had excelled under Changqing [Huileng] and so gladly accepted and guided him. Because the lineages (*xuemai* 血脈) of Xuansha [Shibei] and Xuefeng [Yicun] were different (*shuyi* 殊異), the mountain of Wenyi's doubts collapsed and he obtained the true road (*zhenglu* 正路)."[31]

This passage makes a clear distinction between the lineages, or more literally the "bloodlines," of Xuefeng Yicun and Xuansha Shibei and insinuates that whatever Wenyi had learned under Changqing Huileng, it fell short of the complete realization he attained with Luohan Guichen. Along these same lines, the *Transmission of the Flame* records that it was due to Wenyi that "Xuansha [Shibei's] teachings prospered in Jiangbiao," that is to say, in the Southern Tang and Wuyue.[32] As mentioned in the previous chapter, the biographies of several of Wenyi's disciples and grand-disciples also emphasize their ties to Xuansha Shibei in an apparent attempt to elevate and distinguish this group from other branches of Xuefeng Yicun's extended lineage—quite possibly the disciples of Yunmen Wenyan and Gushan Shenyan who were also active in the Jiangnan region at the time.

Wenyi left Min at roughly the same time that its first ruler, Wang Shenzhi, passed away. Like many other monks during that period, Wenyi traveled from coastal Fujian into the mountainous interior of northern Jiangxi. He and his companions stopped first in Linchuan, where Wenyi was appointed to the abbacy of Chongshou yuan 崇壽院 (Cloister of Great Longevity) on nearby Mt. Cao by an unspecified regional magistrate. Wenyi purportedly presided over an assembly of one thousand monks at Chongshou before Li Jing summoned him to the capital to assume the abbacy of the aforementioned Baoen Chan Cloister. Significantly, at both Chongshou and Baoen, Wenyi succeeded abbots affiliated with the Caodong lineage.[33]

In 951 Wenyi moved yet again, this time to take over another of the capital's temples, Qingliang si 清涼寺, located in the low-lying hills in the northwestern corner of the walled city (see map 4). There he replaced his late dharma-brother Xiufu Wukong 休復悟空 (d. 951?), remaining until his own death seven years later.[34] Qingliang, like many other large, state-subsidized monasteries, functioned as an elite retreat, cultural center, and ancestral shrine for the ruling family (fig. 6).[35] The Southern Tang's Li family sojourned at Qingliang during the hot summer months and hosted guests of the court within the compound. The temple displayed the ruler's calligraphy and sounded a bell cast by Li Yu as an offering to the spirit of his grandfather, the founder of the Southern Tang, Li Bian.[36]

Given the connections between this temple and the court, it is not surprising that while serving as abbot of Qingliang Wenyi was reportedly on close terms with the ruler. According to the biography of one of Wenyi's students, "When the ruler of Jiangnan became Prince of Zheng [Southern Tang], he obtained the Mind Dharma [*xinfa* 心法] in Jinghui's [Wenyi's] room. He frequently questioned the master up until Jinghui's death."[37] As with representations of Min's king Wang Shenzhi in later Chan texts, here

Figure 6. The current incarnation of Qingliang Temple. Author's photo, 2010.

Li Jing's support of Chan monks is explained by his yearning for awakening. This may very well be true, but imperial support of eminent monks like Wenyi clearly served a number of other purposes as well—ministering to the ancestral cult, instilling morality and discipline, generating merit, and safeguarding the realm. Personal salvation and sociopolitical service were likely indistinguishable as motivating factors in the imperial patronage of Buddhist monks.

As Wenyi's health began to fail, Li Jing personally visited his quarters to inquire after his needs. Following his death, all the monks from Jinling's monasteries are said to have joined in the procession escorting Wenyi's body to Danyang Township 丹陽鄉 outside of Jinling, where it was interred in a stupa called "Markless" (Wuxiang 無相). The last ruler of the Southern Tang, Li Yu, conferred on him the posthumous honorific titles Great Fayan (Dharma Eye) and Great Guiding Master of the Great Wisdom Treasury (Da zhizang da daoshi 大智藏大導師) and personally composed a stele inscription "to sing the praises of the master's virtue."[38]

Fayan Wenyi ranked among the most revered monks in the Southern Tang, but lesser-known members of his lineage enjoyed similar career paths, receiving commissions to increasingly influential posts that drew them closer to the capital and the court. Many of these appointments represented a transfer of temple "ownership," often from members of the Caodong lineage to heirs of Xuefeng Yicun and Xuansha Shibei. After these latter monks were installed, the abbacies of these temples typically remained within their lineage families for multiple generations, indicating a clear shift in patronage from one group of Chan monks to another—a shift that parallels the transfer of political power.

One of the functions of clerics is to serve the interests of the court, so it is not unusual that new rulers often dismissed court clerics appointed by previous regimes and installed new networks of monks in official posts—much as they might replace former military commanders or courtiers. Men elevated by and dependent on the emperor were ostensibly loyal servants of the state. What is less clear is why one particular Chan network was favored above others. Fayan Wenyi may simply have been an unusually capable master, adept at cultivating powerful patrons and attracting talented and insightful monks, but the biographies and teachings of Wenyi and his disciples also reveal congruencies between the broad learning and catholic interests of these monks and the literary culture and social mores of the Southern Tang lay elite.

Chan Monks and the Curation of Culture

The capital of the Southern Tang had a venerable history as a cultured, cosmopolitan city. Song literati, looking back on the Southern Tang, remembered it as a kind of cultural conservatory and conduit, linking the high Tang with the Song. The Song historian Ma Ling, for example, wrote, "In the turbulent times of the Five Dynasties, music and rites were destroyed, documents and archives were all lost; yet Confucian teachings and social etiquette flourished in the Southern Tang. Isn't this because the transmission of culture had not yet been cut off, and Heaven (*Tian*) willed it to reside somewhere? Otherwise, the great classics of sage kings would have been swept away and lost."[39]

Unlike its rivals in the north, the Li family recognized that military strength alone was insufficient to sustain an empire. In emulation of the Tang dynasty they claimed to have restored, the Southern Tang rulers marshaled the "soft power" of culture (*wen* 文) to legitimate the authority they had gained through military force (*wu* 武). As a result, many of the finest landscape painters and lyric poets of the tenth century found refuge in the Southern Tang. (The last ruler, Li Yu, was himself among the most celebrated poets of the Five Dynasties.) The refinement of Southern Tang culture was such that during the Song, the paintings, verse, texts, and ink stones crafted by Southern Tang literati were fetishized and collected as markers of cultural distinction.[40]

Ma Ling attributed the transmission of high culture to Heaven, but practical initiatives certainly deserve some credit. Buddhist monks and monasteries, for their part, were both reservoirs and founts of culture. It was no coincidence that scenic sites within the Southern Tang's borders such as Mt. Lu, Mt. Jiuhua, and Xishan in Hongzhou—places of elite retreat, where officials, artists, and scholars of the capital went to study or unwind—were populated by large Buddhist monasteries as well as Daoist temples and Confucian academies.[41] Monasteries and academies both housed extensive libraries, and during the Five Dynasties and Ten Kingdoms, the Southern Tang preserved one of the largest collections of texts anywhere in China. Wang Yinglin 王應麟 (1223–1296), writing in the Song, recorded that in the Kaibao era (968–976) no fewer than twenty thousand fascicles of texts from Jiangnan were brought to Kaifeng, nearly doubling the size of the imperial library.[42]

Catalogues, Dialogues, and Critiques

At the same time that Buddhist texts were being lost or destroyed in other regions, the *Song Biographies* records that "in Yuzhang [Hongzhou], the scriptures flow like a river and the treatises are as vast as the sea."[43] To consolidate and preserve the collections of Buddhist literature scattered throughout his territory, Li Bian ordered the "Great Chan Worthy" Heng'an 恒安 (n.d.) to compile a comprehensive catalogue of previously unknown translations of Buddhist texts held in monastic libraries.[44] Heng'an first traveled to Mt. Wutai in the far north to obtain the last catalogue produced under the auspices of the Tang court, the *Zhenyuan-Era Catalogue of Newly Selected Buddhist Teachings*.[45] He then visited the "famous mountains" of Jiangnan and catalogued the contents of temple libraries, discovering many texts that had been omitted from the previous catalogue. The result of Heng'an's labors was a collection of 140 works in 413 fascicles, which he presented to the court in 945, six years after the project was initiated.[46]

As indicated by its title, the *Supplement to the Zhenyuan-Era Catalogue of Buddhist Teachings* (*Xu zhenyuan shijiao lu* 續貞元釋教錄) was conceived as a continuation of the project commissioned by Tang emperor Dezong 德宗 (r. 779–805). The preface to the new catalogue makes clear that the project was of symbolic as well as historic import: by curating Buddhist texts, the "emperors" of the Southern Tang (as they are consistently referred to in the text) fulfilled the imperial charge of safeguarding Buddhist scriptures and commentaries and preserving cultural traditions in general.[47] Compilation of the catalogue also demonstrated that a wide range of Buddhist texts still circulated in the Southern Tang, distinguishing the kingdom as one of the last bastions of Buddhist literary culture during those chaotic times. The fact that Li Bian entrusted this task to a Chan monk from the Baoen Chan Cloister—the same temple where Wenyi and his disciples later served as abbots—indicates the important role that members of Chan lineages played in the Southern Tang's cultural renaissance.

Whether or not Heng'an was affiliated with the lineage of Xuefeng Yicun or Xuansha Shibei is not known, but monks from this network definitely did take part in efforts to promote and print classic Buddhist sutras. They were also involved in collecting and compiling explicitly Chan materials like flame records and discourse records. Yunmen Wenyan's disciple Qingbing 清稟 (n.d.), for example, assembled a digest of sayings from prominent Chan monks at the behest of the ruler, while Fayan Wenyi's grand-disciple Daoqi 道齊 (929–997) edited collections of dialogues and

alternate answers to questions posed to Chan masters (*niangu daibie* 拈古代
別).[48] Another of Fayan Wenyi's grand-disciples in the Southern Tang, Qixian Chengti 棲賢澄諟 (n.d.), edited the discourse record of Chan master
Zhaozhou Congshen.[49]

The *Patriarch's Hall Collection* and the *Transmission of the Flame*—Chan
anthologies that were also compiled by clerics affiliated with Yicun's
lineage—contain hundreds of examples of monks quoting and responding
to the words of other Chan masters. The vast majority of these quotations
(531 out of 679) occur within the biographies of members of Yicun's extended lineage.[50] While this may simply reflect the resources available to
or the sectarian agendas of the editors of these texts, it seems more likely
that, as Yanagida Seizan, Ishii Shūdō, and Jia Jinhua have all argued, this
group of clerics was at the forefront of the compilation of the Chan dialogues and discourse records that later evolved into the famous gong'an
(J. kōan) collections of the Song.[51]

Although Fayan Wenyi and his disciples seem to have played a leading
role in the formation of a distinctly Chan style of literature, they did not
limit themselves to the study or production of this kind of material. Whether
this eclecticism was one of the reasons these monks came to be supported
by the court or a result of the positions they attained is difficult to know.
Wenyi's biographies, at least, claim his literary precocity was evident from
early on. The name Wenyi can be translated literally as "Benefiting Culture" and, according to his *Song Biography*, Wenyi's early teacher Xijue reportedly compared him to Confucius's eminent and learned disciples Zi You
子游 and Zi Xia 子夏. Zanning noted that Wenyi "was fond of literary pursuits, especially admiring the style of Zhi 支 and Tang 湯."[52] Wenyi shared
his penchant for composing poetry not only with other members of this
lineage—Luohan Guichen and Xuansha Shibei also have poems recorded
in the *Transmission of the Flame*—but with the last two kings of the Southern
Tang as well, both of whom were famous for their lyrical verse. The *Transmission of the Flame* records that Wenyi's "teachings from three places [Chong-
shou, Baoen, and Qingliang], *gāthās*, hymns, eulogies, inscriptions, notes,
and other works amounted to several tens of thousands of words. Students
copied and circulated them throughout the world."[53]

All that remains of Fayan Wenyi's original work are fourteen poems and
his brief treatise *Ten Admonishments for the Lineage*.[54] These sources, together
with his biographies and discourse records, all indicate Wenyi's familiarity
with Buddhist sutras and commentaries, a fact that is noteworthy only in
the context of Chan's reputation for biblioclasm. In the introduction to his
Ten Admonishments, Wenyi was unequivocal about the importance of canonical teachings. "If people have not read the sutras and commentaries," he
writes, "it will be difficult for them to break free of the intellect and emo-
tions. [If this is the case,] true insight will be driven down dark roads and
false views will be mixed up with the ultimate truth. Later generations will
be needlessly dragged back into the cycle of *saṃsāra*."[55]

As Albert Welter has noted, the biographies and teachings of Wenyi and other Chan monks were most likely edited to conform to the conventions of texts like the *Transmission of the Flame*.[56] Contrary to the rather fastidious master found in the *Ten Admonishments*, in the *Transmission of the Flame*, Wenyi voices the standard warning that the words of the sutras should not be taken at face value but only as pointers to a more fundamental reality, manifest in everyday experience. But here too, his and his audience's familiarity with standard Buddhist sutras and commentaries is taken for granted even as it is challenged:

> All of you have read the *Contemplation on Returning to the Source* (*Huan yuan guan* 還源觀), the *Oceanic Meaning of the Hundred Gates* (*Bai men yi hai* 百門義海), the *Treatise on the Avataṃsaka* (*Huayan lun* 華嚴論), the *Nirvana Sūtra* (*Niepan jing* 涅槃經), and other texts. Is the present moment within these teachings? If it is, let's see it! Is it possible that the present moment is found among the words of these kinds of texts? How do they [the sutras and the present moment] relate? If the subtle words [of the sutras] get stuck in your head, then [your mind] becomes a place for conditioned thought. Reality is right before your eyes, but it gets transformed into the realm of name and form. How does this transformation happen? Once it has happened, how can it be restored? Can you reverse [the process]? If you only read texts this way, what's the use?[57]

In his own writings, Wenyi playfully argued that the study of sutras could be both a problem and, at the same time, its solution: "When people today read the ancient teachings, it is unavoidable that their minds become disturbed. If you want to avoid a disturbed mind, just read the ancient teachings."[58] Wenyi, it seems, freely availed himself of expedient means (*upāya*). Because different circumstances called for different teachings, there was no contradiction in sometimes recommending sutra study and other times cautioning against it. The monk Zhizhao 智昭, writing in the twelfth century, thus characterized the style of the Fayan school as "prescribing medicine based on the illness, tailoring clothes to fit the body."[59]

Wenyi's dual emphasis on *upāya* and immediacy is evident in his own work as well as in secondhand accounts of his teachings. It is also apparent in the records of other members of his circle. Xiufu Wukong, Wenyi's dharma-brother under Luohan Guichen, for instance, also warned that those who only esteem "the ability to interpret [the sutras] are like a slow moving raft while those who [only] take pleasure in stillness [*ningji* 凝寂] repeatedly fall into emptiness."[60]

One of Wenyi's leading disciples in the Southern Tang, Wensui 文遂 (fl. 964), whose name might be rendered as "Succeeding in Culture," was another student of the sutras, particularly the *Śūraṃgama*. According to a passage that has striking similarities to the biography of Xuansha Shibei, Wensui was reportedly able to "distinguish the true from the false, the cause from the effect, the root from the branch, the particular from the universal" after reading the text.[61] Having "deeply accorded with the principle of the sutras," Wensui employed his new insight in the annotation and explication of Buddhist texts and is said to have begun writing a commentary to the *Śūraṃgama*. When Wenyi pressed him on his understanding of the text, however, he was at a loss for words. Wenyi then had him burn all his notes and from then on Wensui "began to forget what he had known."[62] The moral of this story is a familiar one: sutra study is an effective means to an end, but once that end is reached, the means can and should be abandoned.

Wensui's affinity with the *Śūraṃgama* placed him in good company. Not only was this sutra a foundational text for Xuansha Shibei, the patriarch of his lineage, but it was also a favorite of the second ruler of the Southern Tang. Li Jing once ordered his vice director on the left (*Zuo pushe* 左僕射), Feng Yansi 馮延巳 (903–960), to write a preface to the *Śūraṃgama* that was then copied by the monk and calligrapher Yingzhi 應之 (fl. 943–957) and engraved on printing blocks.[63] The ruler also reportedly gave a copy of the sutra to his minister Xu Xuan 徐鉉 (917–992) in a failed attempt to instill in him a greater appreciation for the Buddhist teachings.[64]

While the *Śūraṃgama* was clearly an important text for Chan monks and lay people during this period, it was only one of several sutras promoted by this clerical network in the Southern Tang and Wuyue. Fayan Wenyi himself appears to have been partial to the *Avataṃsaka Sūtra*, which, like the *Śūraṃgama*, was popular among the Southern Tang's rulers. The Li family claimed descent from the same clan as the famous Tang layman and Avataṃsaka exegete, Li Tongxuan 李通玄 (635–730), and in 939 the first ruler of the Southern Tang had Li Tongxuan's commentary on the *Avataṃsaka Sūtra* copied and bound together with illustrations and a portrait of the author.[65] The second ruler commissioned the portrait of a local Avataṃsaka exegete, and the third ruler invited the monk Xuanji 玄寂 (907–967) to the palace to lecture on the "Pure Practices" (*fanxing* 梵行; Skt. *brahmacaryā*) chapter of the text.[66]

Fayan Wenyi's interest in the teachings of the *Avataṃsaka* thus reflected and reinforced the prominent place the sutra already occupied among the Southern Tang elite. The inspiration he drew from Avataṃsaka metaphysics also situated him within the intellectual lineage of Guifeng Zongmi, the great Tang-dynasty Chan scholar-monk, whose writings on Chan and Huayan had an unmistakable influence on the development of Wenyi's thought.[67] In his preface to the *Ten Admonishments*, Wenyi invokes the Huayan lexicon to state his position on the ongoing debate between sudden and gradual awakening, claiming that while an insight into one's original nature occurs suddenly, that initial realization must be refined through a process of gradual cultivation: "Although principle [*li* 理] is illuminated suddenly, phenomena [*shi* 事] must be realized gradually."[68] This model— sudden enlightenment followed by gradual cultivation—is advocated in the *Śūraṃgama* and was made famous by Zongmi in the ninth century in his attempt to reconcile the subitist rhetoric of some Chan monks with more conventional and systematic approaches to Buddhist practice. By advancing this same position, Wenyi distanced himself from those Chan monks, like Wuzhu 無住 (714–774) of the Baotang school, who claimed that sudden enlightenment rendered normative, sequential Buddhist practices—doctrinal study, precept adherence, ritual practice—superfluous. The sudden-gradual synthesis effectively defused an incendiary critique of conventional Buddhism, thereby collapsing the distinctions between Chan and other forms of Buddhism. Wenyi and his disciples were thus able to transform Zongmi's vision of Chan as the repository of the essence of the entire Buddhist tradition into social and institutional realities.

As a representative of state-sanctioned Buddhism in the Southern Tang, Wenyi acknowledged the value of different approaches to practice even as he reserved his highest praise for Tang-dynasty Chan masters. His *Ten Admonishments for the Lineage*, a ten-point critique of the Chan movement of his generation, however, takes aim at antinomian monks—actual or imagined—who espoused more extreme and divisive interpretations of the doctrines of emptiness and sudden awakening. Wenyi was no doubt distancing himself from both iconoclasts and what he saw as the suspect intentions and lax discipline of a monastic population that had swelled in the absence of governmental regulations and in response to an abundance of state resources.[69]

Admonishments of rank-and-file monks by court clerics were not uncommon. They served to police the *saṃgha* but were also performative in the sense that they established their authors as moral authorities and elevated them above common clerics or competitors. Wenyi was in fact participating in a literary tradition of monastic admonitions by Chan monks that reached back to the Huichang persecutions. In Fujian, for example, Guishan Lingyou 溈山靈祐 (771–853) had written a critique of the transgressive behavior of Buddhist monks.[70] An apparently similar tract was composed by the Southern Tang monk Wuyin 無殷 (884–960), a former student—though not a dharma-heir—of Xuefeng Yicun. According to his *Transmission of the Flame* entry, Wuyin "once narrated admonishments in ten sections. [Monks] from all directions sighed and submitted [to them]. Everyone said that Heshan [Wuyin] was a model for the monastic community."[71]

In his own admonishments, Wenyi ridiculed the "small group of deceptive jokers" that parroted masters like Guishan, Deshan, and Linji by striking, shouting, and drawing circles without really understanding their real meaning.[72] Monks like these confused unconventional behavior with awakening, and in so doing they sullied the reputation of the *saṃgha*. As Wenyi described:

> There are those who are on the lookout for [dharma] transmission and [seek to] usurp the position of abbot. They claim to have obtained the highest vehicle and gone beyond the ways of the world. They defend their own shortcomings while slandering the strengths of others. They are "wrapped in their delusions like a silkworm in its cocoon."[73] They lick their lips in front of the

slaughter houses. They advertise their strengths and brag about their eloquence in debate. They expose the faults of others and consider it compassion. They take laziness to be virtuous action. They break the Buddhist precepts and abandon the dignified comportment of monks. They destroy the two vehicles and topple the three teachings. Although unable to untie the great knot, they praise themselves as men of attainment. Now at the end of the age of semblance dharma, demons are strong and the dharma is weak.[74] The robes of the Tathāgata are worn in order to steal the benevolence and might of kings. With their mouths they speak about the causes of emancipation, but with their minds they play the same tricks as ghosts and spirits. Since they have no shame, how can they avoid committing transgressions?[75]

Wenyi goes on to compare the wild talk of vulgar monks with the "brilliant and eloquent, entirely refined and pure" verses of the *Avataṃsaka Sūtra* and ancestral teachers. "How could these [words] be mixed up with what is vulgar or be compared with silly games?"[76]

In the Southern Tang, Fayan Wenyi and his disciples distinguished themselves both through their Chan lineage credentials and their conservative, ecumenical approach to the Buddhist teachings, claiming the authority of mind-to-mind transmission while validating the broad spectrum of Buddhist doctrine and practice. In so doing, this clerical network was able to encompass and incorporate the prevailing Buddhist cultures of the region while maintaining, through the exclusivity of their lineage, their privileged position as the court's favored clerics.

These were not the first Chan monks to have a significant presence in a regional capital or to serve kings and officials, but their activities in Jinling marked the beginning of a new phase in the development of the Chan movement. As stewards of well-established, state-sanctioned Buddhist institutions, these monks took on the responsibilities of court clerics. From these influential positions, they transformed the normative Buddhist traditions of the region, primarily through successfully equating dharma ancestry with efficacy and yoking patronage to their lineage, but they were also transformed in the process. As intermediaries between the *saṃgha* and the state, Fayan Wenyi and his disciples championed a wide range of traditions. In a region that sought to preserve the literary legacies of the Tang, they composed poetry, promoted the study of sutras, produced commentaries, and collected, compiled, and edited the teachings of Chan monks. In a kingdom vying to reunify a fractured empire, these monks also preached a non-divisive, inclusive, and transregional vision of Buddhism that rejected sectarian rhetoric in favor of ecumenical unity.

Many of the characteristics of Min's Chan culture—the close relationship between specific Chan lineages and branches of the royal family, imperial appointments to the abbacies of monasteries with close ties to the state, the role of Chan monks in ministering to the imperial ancestral cult, and the development of distinctive literary forms—are also evident in the Southern Tang, though often in more pronounced, more fully developed forms. While the structure and culture of clergy-court relations in the Southern Tang appear to derive in part from models established in Min, the shift toward a more cultured, catholic, almost Confucian Chan, represented, if not a complete departure, at least a new iteration of the teachings of Xuefeng Yicun and Xuansha Shibei.[77] The commentaries, essays, and poems attributed to Fayan Wenyi and his disciples are thus often credited with fostering a more "literary" (*wenzi* 文字) turn in the teachings and writings of later generations of Chan clerics.[78]

Yanagida Seizan argued that the mainstream of Chan culture in the Northern Song stemmed, in large part, from traditions developed by the Fayan network in the Southern Tang, but the influence of this network on the Chan traditions of the early Song flowed both from the Jiangsu/Jiangxi regions (the Southern Tang) and, perhaps even more significantly, from Zhejiang (Wuyue). Shortly after Fayan Wenyi's death, the political and economic autonomy of the Southern Tang was deeply eroded by northern dynasties—a process that culminated in the invasion and destruction of the Southern Tang capital in 975. Probably as a consequence of this slow but steady decline, beginning in the 950s several of Wenyi's most prominent disciples relocated to the kingdom of Wuyue, where they prospered under the support of the ruling Qian family.

The following chapter takes up the careers of Wenyi's descendants in Wuyue within the context of clergy-court relations in that kingdom. As for the Southern Tang, it continued to serve as an important base for Wenyi's disciples after their master's death. Of Wenyi's sixty-three heirs listed in the *Transmission of the Flame*, forty-one remained somewhere within the kingdom.[79] Major groupings were found in the kingdom's principle Buddhist centers: nine heirs in Jinling; ten on Mt. Lu; and eleven in Hongzhou. At least seven of these men are known to have received support from the royal family, but resources and optimism about the future of the kingdom must have been in short supply. Indulgence in poetry and other pleasures at Li Yu's court is often cited as a cause of the kingdom's downfall, but the poorly conceived military offensives launched by the Li Yu's father, Li Jing, in the 950s bear much of the blame. In quick succession, Li Jing had successfully invaded the kingdom of Chu, seized the interior provinces of Min, and established strategic alliances with the Khitans and Turks further north, but the campaigns exhausted his resources and he was ultimately unable to sustain his offensive. After their defeat by the Zhou, in 958, the Southern Tang was forced to cede all provinces north of the Yangzi River, the center of the lucrative salt trade, and accept vassal status.

Seventeen years later, when Song emperor Taizu finally grew impatient with Li Yu's incessant stalling instead of surrender, he marshaled his troops. Song historians claim that Taizu, in a cunning attempt to exploit Li Yu's Buddhist piety, sent agent-provocateurs disguised as monks to lay the groundwork for invasion.[80] Once the offensive was underway, however, Southern Tang monks reportedly took up arms to fight against the invaders.

Lu You's *Book of the Southern Tang* reports that the ruler did not permit such patriotism, but other accounts claim that some of Southern Tang's monks did indeed enter the fray.[81] One author claims that these monks were conscripted into the Southern Tang army while another implies that monks volunteered their services.[82]

Whether coerced or participating of their own free will, members of Fayan Wenyi's lineage appear to have been part of the resistance. According to the twelfth-century *Duxing zazhi* 獨醒雜志, monks from Yuantong si 圓通寺 on Mt. Lu, a temple built by Li Yu for the Chan monk Yuande 緣德 (898–977), a grand-disciple of Luohan Guichen, stood together with Southern Tang soldiers:[83] "[Yuantong si] was once granted a thousand *qing* of arable land. The hundreds of disciples [of this temple] cared for the land and became extremely rich. When the [Song] emperor's troops crossed the river, the temple's monks one after the other joined the vanguard in resistance. Before long, the city of Jinling fell and they absconded. If Li Yu had cared for his people like he cared for monks, then the people would also know how repay their kingdom!"[84] There is no record of what became of Yuande and his assembly after their failed attempt to stave off the Song invasion, but a later source claims that 60 to 70 percent of the monks and nuns in the region were laicized after the defeat of the Southern Tang. Some suffered facial tattooing, while others were forced to serve in the Song army.[85]

Following the Song invasion of the Southern Tang, the captive Li Yu, along with members of his family and his defunct court, was taken north along the Grand Canal to Kaifeng. For refusing to surrender peacefully, Li Yu might have expected execution, but instead Emperor Taizu granted him a modest residence in the capital where he could live out the remainder of his days under house arrest. Plagued by memories of his former life, Li Yu wrote (or at least was credited with) poems nostalgic for life in Jinling and lamenting the isolation of his final years:

> When will the autumn moon and spring flowers end?
> I have seen so many things.
> The east wind came to my room again last night;
> I cannot bear to remember the bright moon of my old country.
> The marble steps and carved balustrades must still be there,
> Only the flush of youth has changed.
> How much sorrow can one man bear?
> As much as a spring river flowing east.[86]

The marble steps and balustrades of Li Yu's former palace eventually crumbled to ruins. When Ouyang Xiu visited Jinling in the middle of the eleventh century, the site was a wasteland: "Rivers and mountains still survive but the abandoned palace walls have collapsed and are shrouded in mist and weeds. Everyone who passes by lingers and reflects on the heartbreaking scene."[87]

5

Heirs and Ancestors

The Kingdom of Wuyue

IN 947 THE THIRD KING of Wuyue appointed his eighteen-year-old younger brother, Qian Chu 錢俶 (929–988), governor of Taizhou, a coastal county whose assets included the famous Buddhist center of Mt. Tiantai. During Qian Chu's tenure as governor, the Tiantai range was home to Fayan Wenyi's disciple Deshao 德韶 (891–972), and it was not long before the two men met. At that time, Deshao, renowned for his powers of prognostication, reportedly told the governor that he was destined to rule Wuyue and that he would become a great benefactor of the Buddhist teachings. The latter prediction would have been utterly unremarkable, considering that Qian Chu's brother, father, and grandfather had all been loyal patrons of Buddhist monks and monasteries, but the first prophecy would have come as a surprise. Qian Chu was the ninth son of Qian Yuanguan 錢元瓘 (r. 932–941), Wuyue's second king, and advancement to the throne seemed unlikely. The sitting king, Qian Zuo 錢佐 (r. 941–947), was himself only nineteen at the time, and even if he should die prematurely, another brother, Qian Zong 錢倧 (r. 947), was next in succession. Three months later, however, Qian Zuo did pass away, and after just six months of Qian Zong's rule, senior Wuyue officials, suspecting that the new king was plotting against them, installed the younger (and perhaps more pliable) Qian Chu.[1]

Shortly after assuming the throne, Qian Chu sent emissaries to Mt. Tiantai requesting that Deshao serve as national teacher of Wuyue and granting him the title of Great Chan Master.[2] This appointment may have stemmed from personal admiration for the monk but it was also politically astute. As a disciple of Fayan Wenyi, the Guiding Master of the Southern Tang, and also a great-grand-disciple of Xuansha Shibei, the personal teacher to the king of Min, Deshao belonged to a noble lineage that had served generations of rulers.

The monastic descendants of Xuefeng Yicun and Xuansha Shibei had been active in the Wuyue region since the turn of the tenth century, and some of these men had previously secured the support of Qian Chu's grandfather Qian Liu, the founder of the kingdom. Qian Liu had cultivated a diverse field of religious specialists, however, and appeared to harbor no special preference for Chan monks in general, or for Yicun's and Shibei's disciples in particular. That pattern changed among Qian Liu's successors such that by the reign of Wuyue's last king, Qian Chu, the royal family appears to have channeled its support almost exclusively to monks affiliated with the lineage of Xuansha Shibei, particularly disciples and grand-disciples of Fayan Wenyi (see appendix 1).

The development of Wuyue's Buddhist culture is relatively well documented, thanks in part to the kingdom's stability—eighty prosperous years, roughly double the length of Min and the Southern Tang—but also to the existence of a more complete and detailed textual record. Both Zanning, the compiler of the *Song Biographies*, and Daoyuan, the editor of the *Transmission of the Flame*, were Wuyue natives. They were personally familiar with the leading Buddhist monks of that kingdom and had ready access to local inscriptions, manuscripts, and lore. Their collections, along with other, non-monastic sources, contain a wealth of information regarding patronage relationships, temple appointments, and the teachings and practices of hundreds of Wuyue monks, making it possible to reconstruct the institutional ascent of Chan clerics, at least in so far as they are represented in the surviving literature.

These sources make it clear that although Chan transmission lineages became increasingly important as markers of authority and efficacy during this period, lineage identities did not coincide with particular constellations of practice or doctrine. In fact, when the recipients of court patronage under Wuyue's first and last kings are compared, it becomes evident that the types of activities monks engaged in—asceticism, exegesis, Pure Land devotion, thaumaturgy, and ancestral appeasement—and the texts that served as touchstones (including the *Lotus, Avataṃsaka, Śūraṃgama,* and other sutras) remained more or less the same. What had changed was that many of the monks heralded as masters of these disciplines were now affiliated with Chan transmission lineages. The rise of Chan monks in Wuyue thus does not appear to reflect a radical shift in the region's Buddhist culture or signal some kind of a Chan revolution. Rather, the dominance of Fayan Wenyi's heirs in Wuyue might be better characterized as a reformation of prevailing Buddhist traditions under the name of Chan.

The eclectic character of Chan in Wuyue is now well known. Scholars have also long noted the broad range of religious figures and institutions supported by the Wuyue court.[3] In English-language scholarship, the Buddhist culture of Wuyue has been viewed primarily through the life and work of Yongming Yanshou, an erudite Chan monk, prominent court cleric, and prolific author. This chapter places the career of Yongming Yanshou in a broad historical and cultural context in an effort to account for and interpret the growing influence of specific Chan networks in Wuyue over the course of the tenth century.

The rise of Chan lineage families in Wuyue also provides an opportunity to delve deeper into the issues of identity and authority raised in the introduction to this book and touched on briefly in previous chapters. What did it mean to be a Chan monk or to belong to a Chan lineage? While it is common to associate the Chan tradition with particular kinds of practices (notably meditation) and pedagogical methods (such as dialogues), the lives and teachings of Chan monks in Wuyue, which encompass almost the entire spectrum of normative Buddhist activities, do not support such a view. Moreover, although Chan lineages are often characterized by distinctive "house styles"—the Guiyang lineage's use of circle and squares, for instance, or the Hongzhou school's use of slaps and blows—in Wuyue, lineage seems to have functioned less as a vehicle for transmitting particular kinds of knowledge and techniques than as a means of conferring authority and establishing orthodoxy. If that is indeed the case, it has important implications for how we understand the development and spread of Chan and of Buddhist traditions more broadly. Who defines orthodoxy? Is it the community of monks and nuns? The abbots of major monasteries? The national teacher or other officers serving in the state's monastic administration? Or is it the regional rulers, who select the abbots of major temples and appoint monks to leadership positions? I return to these questions at the end of this chapter after surveying clergy-court relations and the rise of Chan clerics in Wuyue.

Chan Monks during the Reign of Qian Liu

Like the founders of Min and the Southern Tang, Wuyue's first king was a stalwart patron of the *saṃgha*. Qian Liu is known to have supported at least twenty-five Buddhist clerics (including one of his sons and one of his daughters). Some of these monastics were renowned for the breadth of their learning, but most specialized in a limited range of texts and practices. As noted in chapter 2, many were monks versed in the Nanshan Vinaya tradition who had relocated to Hangzhou from Chang'an, but others were associated with different disciplines—*Abhidharma-kośa* studies, Yogācāra, Tiantai scholasticism, the cult of the *Lotus Sūtra*, rituals of state protection, ancestral appeasement, asceticism (self-immolation and renunciation), and meditation. Of the nineteen monks Zanning depicted in the *Song Biographies* interacting with the king, he categorized seven as either Vinaya masters or textual exegetes. Five monks, the next largest group, he placed under the heading of *dhyāna* practitioners (*xichan* 習禪). All five of these men, not coincidentally, were affiliated with Chan lineages.

Hongzhou Monks

Qian Liu's relationship with the *saṃgha* reportedly began well before his investiture as king of Wuyue, while he was still serving the Tang dynasty as a military commander. At the time, monks of the Hongzhou network remained the most influential Chan clerics in the Zhejiang region, and Qian Liu's political ascent is said to have been foreseen by one of them. This was the monk Hongyin 洪諲 (d. 901), who met Qian Liu during his campaign to subdue rebels around Hangzhou.[4] By that juncture, Hongyin had already risen to a position of considerable stature in the *saṃgha*. Having become a monk decades earlier under Jianzong 鑒宗 (793–866), a grand-disciple of

Mazu Daoyi, he had spent his early years adhering to the precepts and mastering the Vinaya and had begun lecturing on the scriptures. When Jianzong chastised him for "counting the sand in the sea" instead of directly realizing the truth taught by the buddhas and patriarchs, Hongyin went to study with Guishan Lingyou, another grand-disciple of Mazu Daoyi, and eventually became "a master of his craft." He reunited with Jianzong in 865, while the latter was serving as abbot of Jingshan 徑山 in Hangzhou, and when Jianzong died the following year, the assembly asked Hongyin to assume the abbacy.[5] Imperial honors followed; in 883, Tang emperor Xizong granted the monastery at Jingshan an imperial name placard and awarded Hongyin a purple robe.[6]

Hongyin's first meeting with Qian Liu thus brought together formidable forces in the region, reportedly occasioning a prediction remarkably similar to the one that Deshao would offer Qian Chu fifty years later: telling Qian Liu to take care of himself, Hongyin said, "One day you will attain an extremely high position and will be guided by the Buddha Law." When, after a string of military victories, Qian Liu was named governor of Hangzhou, he requested the Tang court to grant Hongyin the name Grand Master Faji 法濟 ("Savior of the Law"), and himself made lavish donations to support the master. Hongyin's prophecy and Qian Liu's subsequent support adheres to a common prediction motif that simultaneously serves to establish the paranormal powers of the monk and the great virtue of the ruler. In the case of Hongyin, his biographers emphasize his eminence by recording that Wuyue's future king respectfully bowed and kneeled before him while alive and bore the cost of his funeral after he passed away. Hongyin, in short, recognized the nobility of Qian Liu and Qian Liu, in turn, acknowledged the efficacy of Hongyin.

After assuming the governorship of Hangzhou, Qian Liu extended his support to at least two other monks from Hongyin's lineage. These were Chu'nan 楚南 (813–888) and Wenxi 文喜 (821–900), both monks who, like Hongyin, had initially studied the scriptures and regulations but later reportedly came to see these pursuits as inferior to the "sudden teaching" of Chan.[7] The biography of Chu'nan may give some sense of the teachings of Chan monks in Wuyue during this early period. Chu'nan was a native of Min and, as a young monk, the first master he called on was Furong Lingxun, the early teacher of both Xuefeng Yicun and Xuansha Shibei. Furong sent Chu'nan to train with Mazu Daoyi's grand-disciple Huangbo Xiyun. After obtaining Huangbo's "dharma eye," Chu'nan reportedly remained in meditation for months at a time, not leaving his monastery in Suzhou for twenty years. Tang emperor Zhaozong later granted Chu'nan a purple robe along with a five-piece robe apparently (and inexplicably) made of deer placenta (鹿胎衣五事).[8]

During his long sequestration in Suzhou, according to the *Transmission of the Flame*, a monk once asked Chu'nan, "What is easy?" Chu'nan replied, "Wearing clothes, eating, and drinking. There is no need to read scriptures or study the teachings. No need to practice the Way, make obeisance, burn your body, or scorch your head. What isn't easy?" The monk pressed on. "If that is easy, what is difficult?" Chu'nan explained, "Once the slightest thought (*nian* 念) arises, the five *skandhas* are present. The cycle of birth and death among the three realms all follow from the arising of your thought.[9] Therefore, the Buddha taught all bodhisattvas that buddhas guard [their] thoughts (*hunian* 護念)."[10] In a somewhat ironic but hardly unusual move, Chu'nan quoted a line that appears in several sutras, notably the *Lotus* and *Avataṃsaka*, to argue that the study of sutras, along with other forms of conventional Buddhist practice, is ultimately unnecessary. Instead, he asserted that the most effective practice is maintaining a mind free from thought.

Chu'nan's emphasis on the quality of mind, as opposed to the content of canonical teachings, was characteristic of other influential Hongzhou monks in the Zhejiang region. To cite just one additional example, when Zongche 宗徹 (n.d.), another of Huangbo's students supported by a governor in the Zhejiang region, was asked about the ultimate truth (*zong* 宗) of the Northern and Southern schools, he reportedly responded that Mind is the ultimate truth. The monk then asked, "Should the teachings still be read or not?" Zongche replied, "The teachings are Mind."[11]

As a teaching, the equation of one's own ordinary mind with the extraordinary mind of a buddha may have been radical in its expression, even dangerous in its potential for misunderstanding, but it was entirely conventional in terms of doctrine. It represented a provocative but theoretically consistent interpretation of *tathāgata-garbha* theory, which asserts that all beings, regardless of their mental states, are inherently awakened. By suggesting that sutra study was inferior, perhaps even detrimental, to realizing the fundamental nature of Mind, monks like Chu'nan and Zongche were merely following *tathāgata-garbha* doctrine to its logical conclusion. This particular interpretation or expression of Buddha-nature and sudden awakening appears to have been popular with Chan monks in the Zhejiang region at the turn of the tenth century, though it is doubtful that it was limited to Chan monks alone. However, these sorts of teachings are largely absent from the recorded sermons and dialogues of Wuyue Chan clerics in the latter half of the tenth century, suggesting a shift in presentation, if not in perspective.

Despite his initial gestures of support, Qian Liu's patronage of Hongzhou monks did not last long; among the many clerics that he and subsequent Wuyue rulers supported, only one, Quanfu 全付 (882–947), was affiliated with the Hongzhou network.[12] This apparent loss of patronage, so similar to what occurred in the kingdom of Min, bears no clear relationship to any change on the part of Hongzhou monks. Biographical collections portray these clerics living and teaching in the same manner as the other Chan monks to whom Qian Liu and his sons redirected their largesse. Perhaps Qian Liu and his heirs sought to distance their court from certain Tang traditions, forging their own identity and asserting their sovereignty, but the timing of the shift suggests another, probably more important factor:

patronage of Hongzhou monks came to an end during the same period that Xuefeng Yicun's disciples began settling in Wuyue.

Xuefeng Yicun's Disciples

Xuefeng Yicun himself arrived in Zhejiang shortly after Qian Liu was appointed governor of Hangzhou and stayed roughly four years, from 891 to 994. Whatever the immediate effects of his own sojourn, at least fourteen of Yicun's disciples later assumed the abbacies of temples in Wuyue, and nine of them are known to have received some form of support from Wuyue's kings. (Two are linked with Qian Liu, one with Qian Zuo, one with Qian Chu; the remaining five simply with "King Qian.") At least three of the fourteen were Zhejiang natives who had traveled to Min specifically to study Chan. Three others were originally from Fujian but left in the wake of Wang Shenzhi's death and the ensuing regional instability, a period that coincided with the latter part of Qian Liu's reign.

Both the *Song Biographies* and the *Transmission of the Flame* trace the beginning of the ascent of Chan monks in Wuyue to Xuefeng Yicun's disciple Daofu 道怤 (868–937).[13] Born in Yongjia, within the borders of what would become the kingdom of Wuyue, Daofu took the tonsure before leaving to study first in Jiangsu with Caoshan Benji and then in Fujian with Xuefeng Yicun. One of the exchanges between Daofu and Yicun recorded in the *Patriarch's Hall Collection* offers some indication of Daofu's education under Yicun. Daofu reportedly asked, "Among the ancient worthies, were there any who did not use the mind to transmit the mind?" Xuefeng Yicun, echoing lines traditionally attributed to Bodhidharma, said, "They also did not set up words, letters, or phrases."[14] Daofu then asked, "Without setting up words, letters, or phrases, how does a master transmit [anything]?" Yicun, in response, remained silent.[15]

It is of course impossible to know if this dialogue accurately reflects Daofu's dharma legacy from Yicun, but the distinction it draws between the awakened mind, as transmitted by Chan masters, and the Buddha's teachings, as transmitted by sutras and commentaries, tallies with other passages in Yicun's record. It also jibes with the teachings of Hongzhou monks, which may simply reflect a common Chan culture in Min or may derive from Yicun's study with his early teacher, the Hongzhou monk Furong Lingxun. In either case, it appears unlikely that Daofu's subsequent success in Wuyue—or the shift in court support from the Hongzhou network to disciples of Yicun—was predicated on doctrinal or soteriological differences.

After returning to Wuyue from Min, Daofu settled at Jianqing yuan 鑑清院 in Yuezhou, where he earned the admiration of Wuyue's assistant commissioner, the poet and Chan enthusiast Pi Guangye 皮光業 (d. 943). Shortly thereafter, Qian Liu appointed Daofu to Tianlong si 天龍寺 in the capital and awarded him the name Great Master Shunde 順德 ("Pursuing Virtue"). It was at this point, according to the *Transmission of the Flame*, that Chan began to prosper in Wuyue: "King Qian wanted to expand the Chan groups within the capital and ordered [Daofu] to live at Tianlong si. When he first saw the master he said, '[You are] a true person of the Way' and treated him ceremoniously, generously providing for his needs. Because of this, dark learning [*xuanxue* 玄學] flourished in Wuyue."[16] Zanning, for his part, attributes the "flourishing of Chan studies [*chanxue* 禪學] in Wuyue" to Daofu's later tenure at Longce si 龍冊寺, a temple built for him in 934 by Qian Liu's son and successor, Qian Yuanguan.[17]

Why did Qian Liu, Qian Yuanguan, or both want to encourage the growth of "Chan groups" in Wuyue? What qualified Daofu, rather than some other cleric, to head a state-sanctioned monastic center? There is no cause to doubt that Daofu's insight and abilities impressed Wuyue's kings, but the ruling family may have also been seeking to align themselves with a leading figure in the monastic network that had served the Min court for nearly four decades. Daofu and other members of his cohort not only had powerful connections to several secular leaders, they also enjoyed a good reputation, both for their dharma ancestry and also as strict ascetics who, even while serving at regional courts, reportedly managed to remain aloof from the allures of the material world.

The practice of austerities was understood to generate supernormal powers, and it seems likely that the ascetic reputations of this group of clerics endowed them with a kind of charisma and efficacy that enhanced their appeal among potential patrons. Daofu himself was known as "Little Fu of the Patched Robe" (Xiaodao buna 小怤布納) out of respect for his austere habits, and biographies of his fellow monks make plain that they matched or exceeded his rigor. For example, Yicun's Korean disciple Lingzhao 靈照 (870–947), also "only wore a single patched-robe and worked hard to serve the assembly. In Min he was called 'Patch-robed Zhao.' "[18] Lingzhao later relocated to Hangzhou to head Longxing si 龍興寺 before an unidentified member of the Qian family serving as governor of Huzhou 湖州 appointed him abbot of the newly constructed Baoci yuan 報慈院.[19] Giving to his good influences, "Chan disciples lived in harmony and countless monks from throughout the Wu and Kuai [Southern Jiangsu, Northern Zhejiang] regions abandoned the [traditional] three robes for the five-patched robes [characteristic of *dhyana* practitioners]."[20] When the third king of Wuyue, Qian Zuo, had the relics of the famous ascetic and thaumaturge Mahāsattva Fu 傅大士 (497–569) brought from the city of Jinhua to Hangzhou to be reinterred at another new temple, Longhua yuan 龍華院 (see map 5), Lingzhao was designated abbot, and he oversaw that temple for the rest of his life.[21]

The ascetic inclinations of Yicun's disciples in Wuyue are also recounted in the biography of his disciple Zongjing 宗靖 (871–954), which claims that Zongjing's inability later in life to attract renunciant disciples was a kind of retribution for a lapse in protocol he made during his training. Although Zongjing had diligently served more than ten years as a cook and laborer at Yicun's temple, once when nailing up a curtain in the monk's hall, he stripped to the waist (demonstrating a concern with personal comfort that was apparently at odds with the ascetic culture on Mt. Xuefeng). Seeing this,

Yicun is said to have reprimanded him, predicting that when he later became the abbot of a temple, he would have a thousand students but none of them would be a "patch-robed monk"—a term that by the Song would become synonymous with Chan clerics. Zongjing repented and left the assembly. When the king of Wuyue later appointed him to Longxing si, replacing Lingzhao, Zongjing did preside over more than a thousand monks, but they were "only" interested in the three studies (*śīla*, *dhyāna*, and *prajñā*), preaching, and recitation.[22] The lack of patched-robe monks is represented here as a mark of failure, and it may be for this reason that Chan flame records do not credit Zongjing with any heirs.

The biographies of these monks demonstrate that Xuefeng Yicun's students in Wuyue maintained (or at least claimed) a tradition of mendicancy that privileged bodily cultivation over erudition or verbal expression.[23] But other Buddhist monks in Wuyue also pursued ascetic lifestyles, emphasized direct engagement over scholasticism, and left relics or mummies after they died (as was the case with many of the monks previously described), making it clear that while Yicun's disciples may have been well regarded by Wuyue's royal family, they were also participating in a common Buddhist culture that valorized and rewarded a wide range of behavior.[24] Wuyue's first and second kings, moreover, did not ally themselves exclusively with monks of this Chan lineage, and other recipients of the rulers' patronage engaged in scholarship, preaching, and recitation—the very practices Yicun's disciples are said to have disparaged.

By the reign of Qian Liu's grandson Qian Chu, however, members of Yicun's lineage had fallen from favor, and the heirs of Xuansha Shibei came to dominate court patronage in Wuyue. Of the clerics known to have been supported by Qian Chu, 85 percent were members of this network, but this was not a zero-sum game; the rise of Xuansha Shibei's Chan family did not necessitate rejecting other, more conventional forms of Buddhism. As in the Southern Tang, in Wuyue the prevailing Buddhist culture did not assume a character peculiar to Chan; instead Chan monks assumed the character of Wuyue's traditional Buddhist culture. The champions of this broad, inclusive interpretation of Chan were the disciples of Fayan Wenyi.

Chan Monks during the Reign of Qian Chu

Like his grandfather, father, and brother, Qian Chu understood the political expediency of patronizing the *saṃgha*. But more than any of Wuyue's kings, Qian Chu appears to have been personally invested in the teachings. In his preface to Yongming Yanshou's *Zong jing lu* 宗鏡錄, Qian Chu went as far as ranking the three teachings, calling Confucianism (*Ru* 儒) his teacher but then describing Daoism as the teacher of Confucianism and Buddhism as the source of Daoism.[25] Qian Chu had received the bodhisattva precepts from Fayan Wenyi's disciple Daoqian 道潛 (d. 961), and in a postscript to the *Avataṃsaka Sūtra*, he wrote that "In spare moments between myriad affairs of state, my mouth ceaselessly intones Buddhist texts, and my hand con-

stantly unrolls Buddhist sutras."[26] Continuing the examples of his predecessors, Qian Chu built stupas to enshrine Buddha relics, erected *dhāraṇī*
pillars, cast icons, and emulated Aśoka by manufacturing a purported
84,000 reliquaries for distribution throughout East Asia.[27] He also printed
Buddhist texts and images, commissioned copies of the Buddhist canon
(some of them brushed in gold and silver on indigo paper), and is credited
with the construction of sixty-nine temples, more than any other king,
bringing the total number of Buddhist temples and shrines in Hangzhou
during his reign to nearly five hundred.[28] As in Min and the Southern Tang,
some of these temples functioned as ancestral shrines for the patriarchs and
matriarchs of the Qian clan.[29] Most were staffed by monks affiliated with
Chan lineages.

Qian Chu had a broad interest in Buddhist traditions, from questions
of doctrine to the many applications of *dhāraṇī*, yet his patronage policies
appear rather narrow; with some important exceptions, his support seems
to have been channeled primarily to Chan monks. Among the twenty-six
monks known to have been patronized by Qian Chu, no fewer than twenty-
two were members of Chan transmission lineages. Nineteen of these were
descendants of Fayan Wenyi, three others belonged to collateral branches
of Xuefeng Yicun's lineage. In contrast to the exclusivist rhetoric found
in the teachings of some Chan clerics, these monks promoted an eclectic
array of traditions (Esoteric, Huayan, Pure Land, Tiantai) and disciplines
(asceticism, exegesis, meditation), all of which coincided with the interests
of the king and followed the contours of Wuyue's established Buddhist
traditions.

Huiming 慧明 (d. ca. 954–959)

Of Fayan Wenyi's five direct disciples who secured the Qian Chu's patronage, two—Huiming and Deshao—were particularly instrumental in establishing his network in Wuyue. Huiming grew up in and around Hangzhou,
where, as a young monk, he mastered the traditional Buddhist disciplines
of *śīla*, *dhyāna*, and *prajñā*. After meeting Wenyi, he realized that what
"he had previously studied belonged to the category of ephemeral, preju-
dicial views," and thereafter, he returned to Wuyue, settling at Baisha 白沙,
a remote area in the south of the Tiantai range.[30] Like other Wuyue
monks, Huiming engaged in extreme asceticism; he burned off four of his
fingers and built "a straw hut in the style of Xuefeng [Yicun] and Changqing
[Huileng]."[31]

While his *Song Biography* likens his austerities to those of Yicun, the
Transmission of the Flame stresses Huiming's connection to Xuansha Shibei:
"At that time, although the study of Chan was flourishing in Wuyue, the
true lineage of Xuansha [Shibei] was peripheral. The master [Huiming]
wanted to organize and guide [members of this group]."[32] In pursuit of this
goal, Huiming emerged from the mountains sometime between 948
and 950 and was summoned to the capital for an audience with Qian Chu,
who had only recently ascended the throne. At court Huiming asserted the

superiority of his lineage, telling the king that "the highest level of the teachings had been attained by Great Master Xuansha Zongyi [Shibei], Dizang [Guichen], and Fayan [Wenyi]."[33] This would have been a direct challenge to the authority of prominent Wuyue monks descended from different masters. The king accordingly summoned Yicun's students Daofu and Lingcan 令參 (n.d.) along with other Chan monks to the capital to engage Huiming in debate.

According to the account given in the *Transmission of the Flame*, something of a showdown ensued. Daofu—Xuefeng Yicun's most prominent disciple in Wuyue—opened by quoting the *Diamond Sūtra* and challenging Huiming to say something about the source of the teachings: " 'All buddhas and their teachings come from this sutra.' Where does this sutra come from?"[34] Huiming then asked him, "What did you say?" Daofu repeated his question, whereupon Huiming dismissed him, saying, "It's passed." Huiming, it seems, was pointing out that Daofu's question was itself an expression of Buddha-nature, issuing from the same source as the *Diamond Sūtra*. Since this was a standard Mahāyāna position, that Daofu missed it marked him as slow in comparison to Huiming. Another monk, Ziyan 資嚴 (n.d.), then referenced a phrase from the *Avataṃsaka Sūtra* and asked, "What is the *samādhi* that appears before us?" Huiming asked him, "Can you hear?," apparently suggesting that the ordinary functioning of the ears (and, by extension, all sense organs) is itself a manifestation of *samādhi*. But Ziyan, like Daofu, took him literally, saying "I'm not deaf." "Deaf indeed!," Huiming scoffed.

Then it was Huiming's turn, and he chose to quote the opening lines of Xuefeng Yicun's self-composed stupa inscription: "One who comes from the conditioned begins and ends, forms and decays. One who comes from the unconditioned passes through kalpas, [but remains] constant and enduring." By raising these words, Huiming both valorized Yicun's teachings and challenged his leading disciples in Wuyue to live up to them. "Setting aside decay and endurance," he asked them, "where is Xuefeng now?" Nobody, according to Huiming's biographer, was able to reply. Victorious, Huiming received the audience's obeisance. The king thereupon awarded him the name Chan Master Yuantong Puzhou 圓通普照 (All Pervading, Universally Radiant) and invited him to head the newly constructed Great Baoen Temple 大報恩寺 in the capital.[35] Reflecting on Huiming's legacy, Zanning was moved to remark, "If not for Huiming, who could have spread the true eye of Xuansha [Shibei]?"[36]

The story of Huiming's debate with Yicun's heirs asserts the superiority of Shibei's disciples not in terms of the content of their teachings but in the acuteness of their insight. The two groups shared a common, if bifurcated, lineage, upheld similar teachings, and ostensibly sought the same goal. The story seems to claim that disciples of Fayan Wenyi possessed the "true eye," while the eyes of Xuefeng Yicun's disciples were not yet fully opened. Whether Huiming actually bested his competitors in debate and thus rose to prominence or rose to prominence and thus had his history embellished by later generations is impossible to say. It is around the same time that this debate was supposedly staged, however, that the disciples and grand-disciples of Wenyi begin receiving a succession of major temple appointments and the descendants of Yicun start to recede from the historical record.

Deshao 德韶 (891–972)

During the same period that Qian Chu summoned Huiming to the capital, he also dispatched emissaries to Mt. Tiantai to invite Huiming's dharma-brother Deshao to assume the position of national teacher. Like Huiming, Deshao was a Wuyue native who studied with Fayan Wenyi in Linchuan, returned to live at Mt. Tiantai, and prospered under the patronage of Qian Chu. He began his career as a novice monk in his hometown in southern Zhejiang, and received the precepts a year later before going on to study with various Chan masters in the Southern Tang.[37] His biographers highlight his time with Touzi Datong 投子大同 (819–914), a third-generation heir of Shitou, as well as with Shushan Guangren 疎山光仁 (845–935) and Longya Judun 龍牙居遁 (835–923), both disciples of Dongshan Liangjie. According to the *Transmission of the Flame*, Deshao visited a total of fifty-four "good friends," outdoing in his dedication even Sudhana—the legendary youth from the Gaṇḍavyūha chapter of the *Avataṃsaka* who famously visited fifty-three teachers. Finally, reaching Linchuan, Deshao and his companion Shaoyan 紹巖 (899–971) together received "predictions [of future Buddhahood; *shouji* 受記]" from Fayan Wenyi, who reportedly told Deshao, "Later you should become the teacher to the king. In illuminating the way of the ancestors, I am not your equal."[38] When Deshao returned to Wuyue, he settled in the Tiantai mountains at Baisha 白沙, the same place Huiming had lived.[39] It was during this period, when he was "propagating the dharma of Xuansha [Shibei] with great success," that Deshao first encountered Qian Chu, then serving as governor of Taizhou.[40]

Unlike most other monks patronized by the royal family, Deshao never relocated to the capital and remained in the Tiantai range, roughly 175 kilometers southeast of Hangzhou, until his death in 972. From as early as the sixth century, these mountains had served as a major center of religious cultivation, Buddhist as well as Daoist. The mountains are most famously home to the monk Zhiyi 智顗 (538–597), who, together with his disciple Guanding 灌頂 (561–632), formulated an elaborate doctrinal system inspired by the teachings of the *Lotus Sūtra*. The resultant texts and practices, later systematized and elaborated by the monk Zhanran 湛然 (711–782), became the foundation of the Tiantai Buddhist tradition, which spread throughout China, Japan, and Korea during the Tang dynasty. By the late ninth century, however, many of Zhiyi's and Zhanran's writings had been lost and the tradition of Tiantai scholasticism had all but died out. During the Five Dynasties and Ten Kingdoms, several Wuyue monks continued to engage in Tiantai meditation but had to do so without the benefit of the treatises and commentaries of the tradition's great patriarchs.

More than any other monk, Deshao was responsible for restoring the monasteries on Mt. Tiantai and securing the return of Tiantai's lost textual corpus. Deshao had the same surname as Zhiyi, and some claimed he was a reincarnation of the Tiantai patriarch. He is credited with establishing thirteen temples on Mt. Tiantai, referred to as "Zhizhe [Zhiyi] sanctums," and reportedly served as abbot of the headquarters of the Tiantai tradition, Guoqing si 國清寺.[41] When the monk Luoxi Xiji 螺溪義寂 (919–987) sought but failed to find the writings of Zhiyi, he turned to Deshao for help. Deshao, with the backing of Qian Chu, sent a letter along with gold to the abbot of Enryaku-ji on Mt. Hiei in Japan, requesting copies of their Tiantai manuscripts. The texts arrived in China in 953, launching a Tiantai revival that continued well into the Song dynasty.[42]

Given his role in revitalizing the temples and teachings of Tiantai, we might safely assume that Deshao himself was immersed in Tiantai doctrines and cultivation techniques, but we know very little about the kind of practices Deshao advocated or engaged in. His disciple Zhifeng 志逢 (929–985), however, did write a meditation manual that was included in the *Transmission of the Flame*.[43] This short text advocates stopping the thought process and becoming "like a dead man." In terms of technique, Zhifeng recommends breath counting when the mind is agitated or muddled, and contemplation (*guan* 觀) when the mind is focused. He warns against a limited understanding of meditation—sitting facing a wall—arguing instead that meditation should pervade all of one's activities. There should be, he writes, no distinction between sitting and lying down or between living in the wilderness and living in cities.

Zhifeng's references to Bodhidharma's transmission of the dharma eye and the patriarchal transmission of One Mind mark his manual as a Chan text, but there is nothing particularly distinctive about the style of meditation it advocates. Stilling the mind through breath counting and then engaging the mind in contemplation is the basic *śamatha-vipaśyanā* (Ch. *zhiguan* 止觀) model that developed in ancient India and was championed in China by Zhiyi and others. In may not be coincidental then that another of Deshao's disciples, the monk Yuanqi 願齊 (d. ca. 977–984), is said to have practiced the fundamentals of *zhiguan* meditation and studied the Tiantai doctrine of complete merging (*yuanrong* 圓融)—the total interpenetration of all dharmas, such that one dharma encompasses all dharmas and all dharmas are present in a single dharma.[44]

It seems fairly certain that Chan monks in Wuyue advocated doctrinal interpretations and engaged in forms of practice we now typically associate with the Tiantai tradition. Albert Welter has also noted that Deshao's most famous disciple, Yongming Yanshou, frequently relied on Tiantai teachings in his discussions of practice and on Huayan theory in his explications of doctrine.[45] The biographies of Deshao, Yuanqi, and other Chan monks in Wuyue suggest that this approach was not unique to Yanshou but represented a widespread recognition of the relative strengths of various Buddhist disciplines. Rather than competing for favor, these traditions worked in concert with one another. To paraphrase Deshao's teacher Fayan Wenyi, the dharma may consist of many streams, but they all have the same flavor.[46]

Different Roads, Same Destination

If one were to look at Deshao's activities—restoring and presiding over temples on Mt. Tiantai, retrieving the lost corpus of Tiantai texts—one might expect him to be claimed by the Tiantai tradition. But Deshao belonged to a Chan lineage and had his biography recorded in the *Transmission of the Flame*, where he is portrayed, according to the dictates of the genre, giving enigmatic responses to the earnest questions of monks rather than concrete, pragmatic expositions of doctrine or practice.[47] While Deshao was intimately involved with the revitalization of Tiantai, other monks in his circle engaged with other aspects of the broader Buddhist tradition—from the teachings and cults of the *Avataṃsaka* and *Lotus* sutras to the performance of self-immolation and esoteric ritual. That monks affiliated with the same Chan lineage displayed such a wide range of interest and participated in such a broad spectrum of practice is yet another indication that membership in a Chan lineage is a poor predictor of intellectual and behavioral inclinations. The biographies of Fayan Wenyi's descendants in Wuyue discussed in the remainder of this chapter illustrate something of the diverse orientations of clerics affiliated with this network.

Avataṃsaka Sūtra
We have already noted that Fayan Wenyi's teachings, like those of his intellectual forebear Guifeng Zongmi, were infused with Huayan doctrine, so it comes as no surprise that the *Avataṃsaka Sūtra* was equally influential among Wenyi's heirs in Wuyue.[48] The sutra and its commentaries receive the most frequent citations in Yongming Yanshou's famous compendium, the *Zong jing lu* (over 360 citations and compared with 140 for the *Nirvana Sūtra*, the second most cited text in the work).[49] As in the Southern Tang, where the ruler circulated Li Tongxuan's commentary to the *Avataṃsaka*, in Wuyue a different edition of the same commentary was printed by Deshao's disciple Yongan 永安 (911–974).[50]

Sections of the *Avataṃsaka* were also inscribed on the inner walls of the crypt of Hangzhou's Leifeng Stupa. Qian Liu, whose own postface to the sutra was carved alongside it, may have been inspired by Huayan metaphysics, but he also believed the sutra, together with the Buddha's hair and fingernails, transformed the brick tower into a "pillar of great vigor [*vīrya*] that would stand for countless kalpas."[51] In this conception, the Buddha's body and words animated and empowered the stupa, effectively locating Śākyamuni himself on the shores of West Lake.

Some monks went even further, claiming that the mythic geography described in the *Avataṃsaka Sūtra* could be found within the borders of Wuyue. In the thirty-second chapter of the *Avataṃsaka*, the bodhisattva

Mind King 心王 discusses the residences of various bodhisattvas and reveals that in the "southeast" lies a mountain called Zhiti 支提, where all bodhisattvas have dwelled from time immemorial. As Mind King explains, this mountain is currently home to the bodhisattva Tianguan 天冠 (Heavenly Crown), who constantly preaches the dharma there together with a retinue of a thousand other bodhisattvas.[52] According to Zanning, when Qian Chu questioned monks in Hangzhou about the location of this rather obscure site, one cleric explained that Mt. Zhiti was in fact situated on the southern border of Wuyue.[53]

The monk was Fayan Wenyi's student Qingsong 清聳 (n.d.), who had received Wenyi's seal of approval (*yinke* 印可) after "awakening" while reading the *Avataṃsaka*.[54] Qingsong explained to the king that a Korean cleric named Wŏnp'yo 元表 (d. 847) had traveled to India in the mid-eighth century and there met the bodhisattva Mind King. Mind King informed Wŏnp'yo that Mt. Zhiti was not situated somewhere in India, as might have been assumed, but in the mountainous interior of northern Fujian—a region that was, not incidentally, incorporated into Wuyue shortly before Qian Chu assumed the throne. Carrying a copy of the *Avataṃsaka*, Wŏnp'yo duly journeyed to northern Fujian, where he located the Tianguan bodhisattva on Mt. Huotong 霍童.[55] After paying his respects to the bodhisattva, Wŏnp'yo continued on to nearby Mt. Zhiti and settled in one of the mountain's caves. There he remained until, during the Huichang persecutions, he sealed his copy of the *Avataṃsaka Sūtra* in a rosewood box and secreted it away in the cave until the turmoil had subsided. Just after the persecutions, in 847, a Chan master from Baofu 保福 Temple led a group of faithful to the cave. They found Wŏnp'yo gone but the sutra was still there, perfectly preserved.[56]

Acting on this account, Qian Chu reportedly sent an emissary to Mt. Zhiti to retrieve Wŏnp'yo's copy of the sutra. At the cave, the emissary not only obtained the precious text but also a vision of a thousand golden Tianguan bodhisattvas. Upon his return to the capital, he beseeched the king to construct a temple at the site and cast a copper statue of the bodhisattva.[57] Qian Chu accordingly sent gold and silk to pay for the construction of a large temple complex, and when it was completed in 976, dispatched Qingsong's disciple Bianlong 辨隆 (n.d.), then the assistant abbot of Lingyin si in Hangzhou, to serve as the new temple's first abbot.[58]

The report of Tianguan's apparition on Mt. Zhiti, like sightings of Guanyin and Indian arhats elsewhere in the kingdom, verified the sanctity of Wuyue and the sagacity of its king. It also established the presence and authority of the king along a sensitive border region in newly occupied territory. During the reign of the Qian family, more than two hundred new temples were built in the northern Fujian region, many of them staffed by monks loyal to, and often dependent on, the king. While Qian Chu was on the throne, several of Fayan Wenyi's grand-disciples were appointed to the abbacies of temples in this area, effectively returning the heirs of Xuansha Shibei to their ancestral lands.[59] It is important to note, however, that although Bianlong and his master belonged to a Chan lineage, they were remembered primarily for their roles in the promotion of the *Avataṃsaka* and cultic sites associated with the text. Xuefeng Yicun and his leading disciples may have initially distanced themselves, at least rhetorically, from canonical teachings. But by Bianlong's time, this lineage had accommodated other Buddhist traditions to the extent that it could staff the site of a miraculous apparition of a Huayan-related bodhisattva.

Lotus Sūtra and Self-Immolation

Some Chan monks affiliated with Fayan Wenyi's lineage in Wuyue were dedicated to the *Avataṃsaka*, while others promoted the teachings of the Tiantai patriarchs Zhiyi and Zhanran. Still others demonstrated a zealous devotion to the *Lotus Sūtra*. The *Lotus Sūtra* had long been the object of a cult in the Zhejiang region (and elsewhere in China), and devotion to the book and its teachings remained strong during the reign of Wuyue's kings.[60] The contents of the entire sutra were important for exegetes; Yongming Yanshou, who printed and distributed the sutra, cited it and its commentaries more than 130 times in his *Zong jing lu*.[61] Two chapters, however, were particularly influential among Wuyue's monastics and laypeople: "The Universal Gateway of the Bodhisattva Guanshiyin" (chap. 25), which circulated as an independent text and contributed to the burgeoning cult of Guanyin in Wuyue; and "The Former Affairs of the Bodhisattva Medicine King" (chap. 23), which inspired several monks to perform acts of extreme self-sacrifice.

As is well known, the "Medicine King" chapter of the *Lotus* advocates the burning of fingers, toes, or entire bodies as the foremost offering to a buddha.[62] The tradition of emulating Bodhisattva Medicine King's self-immolation in China, studied in detail by James Benn, dates back to at least the end of the fourth century and continued throughout the Six Dynasties and the Tang.[63] During the Five Dynasties and Ten Kingdoms, Wuyue recorded more cases of attempted and actual self-immolations than any other kingdom. The majority of these cases involved monks affiliated with Fayan Wenyi's monastic network.[64]

One of these, Deshao's disciple Wennian 文輦 (895–978), had lived on Mt. Tiantai, where he "studied [the teachings] of Xuansha [Shibei]" under Deshao for more than thirty years. He later read through the Buddhist canon three times to affirm his insight that "different roads lead to the same destination." Wennian later told another monk, "When I die, it would be better for me to burn myself in offering than to take up space on monastic property where food could be grown. I hope that all the virtuous monks will gather by the pyre and chant the Buddha's name to help me to attain a [propitious] rebirth. This is my only request." In 978—the same year, perhaps not coincidentally, that Wuyue surrendered to the Song—Wennian used an ax to carve a sandalwood tree into the shape of a stupa. "He entered through a door in the middle and sat in the lotus posture. Lighting a torch, he vowed, 'With my final breath I burn myself as an offering to the buddhas of the ten directions and all the sages.' When he finished speaking, flames rose into the sky, producing dense, billowing smoke in five colors. The sound of sutra chanting could still be heard but then it suddenly stopped. All who saw this wailed and wept. Innumerable relics were found after the ashes had cooled."[65]

Wennian's dharma-uncle Shaoyan and dharma-brother Shiyun 師蘊 (d. 973) also attempted to make offerings of their bodies but were ultimately unsuccessful. Shaoyan, monastic preceptor to the aforementioned monk Yuanqi, had been Deshao's fellow disciple at Fayan Wenyi's monastery in Linchuan and later settled at Shuixin si 水心寺 in Hangzhou. There he dedicated himself to chanting the *Lotus Sūtra* and in 961 vowed to emulate the Medicine King by setting his body aflame.[66] His *Song Biography* records that "at the time, the ruler of the kingdom of Hannan [Wuyue], Qian [Chu], sincerely pledged his support and requested [Shaoyan] to stop [his plan] and remain [in the world]. [Shaoyan then] stole away and threw his body into the Caoe River 曹娥江 as food for the fish. A fisherman rescued him, and it is said that divine beings supported his feet. [Shaoyan] wanted to drown but it was not permitted. His clothing floated on the water so that even as enormous waves surged around him, it was as if he were sitting on a jeweled dais. Unable to cross over by means of water or fire, he harbored a sadness in his heart."[67]

Deshao's disciple Shiyun had similar aspirations and was similarly thwarted. Although he wanted to end his life in order to expedite his entry into "the ranks of the holy ones," his friends restrained him. When he later fell ill, Shiyun began chanting esoteric spells (*mizhou* 密呪), revealing to those around him that he had "maintained the esoteric practices (*michi* 密持) without rest."[68] The power of Shiyun's recitations was such that after his cremation, his tongue, like his confrere Yongan's, reportedly remained "like a red lotus, soft and delightful"—a phenomenon often associated with pious chanters of the *Lotus Sūtra*.[69]

In contemporary discussions of Buddhism in Wuyue, monks are sometimes categorized according to sect—Vinaya, Tiantai, Huayan, Esoteric, Pure Land, and the conventional five Chan lineages.[70] Shiyun's biography, however, like accounts of other members of Fayan Wenyi's lineage in Wuyue, makes it clear that sectarian categories oversimplify the complex lives of these monastics. Shiyun was a Buddhist monk who belonged to a Chan lineage, had studied esoteric practices, and longed to be reborn in the Pure Land. This was not a case of syncretism—of combining strands hitherto separate—but an example of the many ways that complementary Buddhist aspirations and identities could coalesce in a given individual. Members of Chan lineages like Shiyun clearly did not belong to a "separate" tradition "outside the teachings" but, as Albert Welter has put it, to a "special transmission *within* the scriptures."[71] They represented an elite network that embraced and promoted an array of traditions. Griffith Foulk has argued, "The Ch'an claim to transmit the one mind that is the source of everything . . . was readily interpreted to mean that the Ch'an lineage transmitted all doctrines and practices, or, to state the converse, that it had no particular doctrines or practices that it transmitted to the exclusion of any others."[72] In Wuyue at least, Chan lineage, rather than indicating a specific ideology or soteriology, seems instead to have guaranteed authenticity, verifying that certain monks had been vetted by respected and influential masters within the tradition. The forms of monks' teaching and practice appear to have been less critical that their underlying function.

Chan and the Teachings

No monk exemplified this nonsectarian understanding of Chan more than Yongming Yanshou, arguably the best-known monk of the Five Dynasties period. In his voluminous writings, Yanshou wove together many of the Buddhist texts and traditions previously discussed, articulating not a new vision of Buddhism but a grand synthesis of prevailing trends. Yanshou's life and literary legacy have been studied in detail by Albert Welter, Huang Yi-hsun, and others; here I give only a brief overview by way of recapping the intellectual and cultural climate of Wuyue Buddhism during the latter half of the tenth century.[73]

The trajectory of Yanshou's monastic career ran parallel to those of other elite monks in Wuyue. Raised in Hangzhou, he developed an early and enduring interest in the *Lotus Sūtra*; by the time he passed away, he had reportedly recited the text thirteen thousand times. Despite this youthful affinity with Buddhism, Yanshou initially embarked on the path of a householder, was married, had a child, and worked as garrison commander during the reign of Qian Yuanguan. At the age of twenty-eight, however, he met Xuefeng Yicun's disciple Lingcan at Longce monastery, the temple initially built for Daofu in Hangzhou.[74] Shortly thereafter, King Qian Yuanguan released Yanshou from his position and encouraged him to become a monk. Leaving his family, Yanshou took the tonsure with Lingcan and devoted himself to ascetic practice. At Longce, he "carried out manual labor for the assembly, disregarding his own bodily suffering. He did not wear silken robes and did not eat strongly flavored food. From morning to night he contented himself with wild vegetables and cloth robes."[75] He later left Hangzhou for Tiantai's Tianzhu peak 天柱峯, where he spent three months in a hermitage. Following this period of solitary meditation, he finally descended the peak and went not to Lingcan but to Deshao to ask for verification of his realization (the implications of this move will be explored below). According the *Transmission of the Flame*, Deshao recognized Yanshou as a deep vessel, "secretly taught him the profound meaning," and issued the now-familiar prophecy that Yanshou had an affinity with the ruler and would one day make a great contribution to the Buddhist teachings. After leaving Mt. Tiantai, Yanshou taught at nearby Mt. Xuedou 雪竇 until, in 960, Qian Chu summoned him back to Hangzhou to take over the abbacy of the newly rebuilt Lingyin si 靈隱寺 (see map 5). Just one year later, he was transferred to the nearby Yongming Temple (figs. 7–8)—just outside the imperial compound—to replace the king's preceptor, Fayan Wenyi's recently deceased disciple Daoqian.

Figure 7. Yongming Temple (right) and Leifeng stupa (left), in a detail of a panorama of West Lake attributed to Li Song (active ca. 1190–1230). Collection of the Freer Gallery of Art.

By this date, Wuyue's capital housed a substantial collection of canonical and extra-canonical scriptures and commentaries amassed through the efforts of Qian Chu, Tiantai Deshao, and others. With these resources at hand, some monks had begun preparing massive Buddhist compendia and scholarly reference works. The monk Xingtao 行瑫 (895–956), for example, had already completed his five-hundred-fascicle *Commentary to the Pronunciations of the Great Repository of Scriptures* (*Dazang jing yinshu* 大藏經音疏).[76] Yanshou's own hundred-fascicle *Zong jing lu*, finished in 961, was another attempt to provide a systematic guide to the entire tradition—a single source that would distill the vast sea of Buddhist literature. As Yanshou boasted, the *Zong jing lu* contains passages from "120 Mahāyāna sutras, 120 books of the sayings of the [Chan] patriarchs, and 60 collections of the worthies and noble ones, all together the subtle words of 300 books."[77] Before his death, this bibliophile and prolific writer authored sixty more works, comprising nearly two hundred fascicles of text.[78]

In addition to his own writings, Yanshou was also a major producer and distributor of printed Buddhist materials, availing himself of print technology that had developed in China as early as the seventh century but was still somewhat limited in use.[79] Along with Chengdu in Sichuan and Shazhou in Gansu, during the Five Dynasties, Hangzhou was one of China's major centers of print culture, producing predominantly (though not exclusively) Buddhist materials that ranged from single-sheet images of bodhisattvas or stupas to large texts, like the *Avataṃsaka*, that exceeded one hundred fascicles. The print runs reported for some of the shorter works range from 20,000 to 140,000. These numbers may well be exaggerated, but if accurate they suggest that total production could have run in the millions of units.[80]

Figure 8. Yongming Yanshou's reliquary. Author's photo, 2010. After his death in 975 at the age of seventy-four, Yongming Yanshou's remains were interred in a small stupa on Daci shan (Great Compassion Mountain). His remains were later moved to Jingci si. Today, Yanshou's reliquary is located to the east of the Jingci's main compound in the hall shown here, which is used for Pure Land recitation by local lay devotees.

Of twenty-six individual works known to have been printed in Wuyue during the tenth century, Yanshou was responsible for seventeen (see appendix 4). Yanshou's apparently outsized contribution to Wuyue's print culture is almost certainly the result of the serendipitous survival of documents recording his activities. While other figures undoubtedly produced many other works, the few titles that have come down to us do give some indication of texts and cults popular in Wuyue at the time. The most numerous materials that Yanshou and others printed were *dhāraṇī* texts, a fact that accords with Yanshou's promotion of *dhāraṇī* practices and with King Qian Chu's erection of multiple *dhāraṇī* pillars and broad distribution of the *Baoqieyin jing*.[81] (*Dhāraṇī* texts are also typically quite short, making them easier to print.) Second in number to *dhāraṇī* texts are Pure Land sutras, biographies, and images.[82] Wuyue's Guanyin cult is represented as well, with two editions of the *Guanyin Sūtra* and one image of a twelve-headed Guanyin. An extant copy of the latter lists and illustrates the bodhisattva's twenty-four manifestations and incorporates five *dhāraṇī* (fig. 9).[83] The titles of several other sutras printed in Hangzhou also reflect Wuyue's popular Buddhist culture: the *Lotus*, *Avataṃsaka*, *Śūraṃgama*, *Golden Light*, and the *Sūtra of Perfect Enlightenment*. Yanshou and other Chan monks

Figure 9. *Yingxian Guanyin*, ca. 948–978. This print is a Japanese copy of a print made by Qian Chu in conjunction with Yongming Yanshou. The text at the bottom lists the twenty-four manifestations of Guanyin (depicted in the illustrations surrounding the main image) as well as five *dhāraṇī*. From the collection of the Daitōkyū Kinen Bunko. Reproduced in Nara Kokuritsu Hakubutsukan, *Seichi Ninpō*, 22.

in Wuyue are known to have promoted the teachings contained in all these scriptures.[84] The information we have about the printers of individual texts and, more rarely, the locations of their production is fragmentary at best, but it does seem to demonstrate that Chan monks, if not at the forefront of Wuyue's print culture, were at the very least some of its more active participants.

As Yanshou's printing activity and written work illustrate, and as Albert Welter has emphasized, rather than advance a particular sectarian agenda, Yanshou drew on a wide range of doctrines and practices, attempting to integrate them into a single, comprehensive system.[85] The *Zong jing lu* begins by stating that "Patriarchs reveal the principles of Chan, transmitting the orthodox truth of silent according. Buddhas elaborate the teachings, establishing the great aim of explanation. Therefore, what the former worthies have received, later students have as a refuge."[86]

In other words, Chan and the teachings are complementary components of a unified tradition, the proverbial two wheels of a cart or two wings of a bird.

The writings of Yongming Yanshou make an elaborate and articulate argument for the unity of Chan and the teachings, but this understanding was not unique to Yanshou. Another of Deshao's disciples, the aforementioned Zhifeng, echoed other monks of his lineage when he stated that "the intent of the teachings is the same as the intent of the patriarchs. In the end, expedient means all [lead to] the same truth."[87] Moreover, Zanning, commenting on Chan in his *Song Biographies*, similarly espoused the integration of meditation practice with the maintenance of the precepts and the study of the sutras, asserting that the teachings of Bodhidharma stressed both principle (*li* 理) and practice (*xing* 行). That he appended this comment to Tiantai Deshao's biography was surely intentional. Like Yanshou, Zanning repudiated more radical elements of the Chan community, some of whom, at least for rhetorical purposes, appear to have rejected the sutras and flouted monastic regulations. The point, according to Zanning, was not to do away with the teachings recorded in texts but only to guard against excessive attachment to them. In his view, Chan monks who equated the scriptures with the work of the great demon Māra—fit to be burned—were themselves under Māra's sway:

> They do not realize that Chan contains both principle and practice. One can only speak of liberation when the precepts and the vehicle are both pursued with urgency, when the eye and the feet cooperate. When practice is not abandoned, principle is illuminated. When method is not biased [toward practice or doctrine], one will succeed at both. Only then is one qualified to talk about Chan. It is like the practitioners of dark learning [*xuanxue* 玄學] denouncing lecturers as money-counters who will end up destitute. "They do not see that the sutras are the Buddha's words and Chan is the Buddha's mind. The words and minds of all buddhas are surely in accord."[88]

Only by studying the sutras and putting their teachings into practice could monks "repay the benevolence of the lords and kings who have permitted [their] ordination."[89]

As monks in the service of Wuyue's lords and kings, Yanshou, Zhifeng, Zanning, and others both formed and were formed by this state-sanctioned interpretation of Chan orthopraxy as meditation and renunciation grounded in the precepts and doctrinal study. In the writings and records of these monks, "Chan" is synonymous with an authentic understanding of the Buddhist teachings. While Zanning's and other monks' critiques imply that some Chan monks claimed privileged access to an exclusive, secret, and direct route to awakening, a path bypassing laborious sutra study and ritual practice, few, if any, among Wuyue's elite Chan monks seem to have made such provocative claims. For the leaders of Wuyue's monastic community,

Chan appears to have been conventional Buddhism organized and authenticated by means of lineage.

The Functions of Lineage in Wuyue

The intellectual interests and practice regimens of Fayan Wenyi's heirs in Wuyue were diverse; it was their lineage affiliations that distinguished these state-sanctioned clerics from other, similarly inclined ascetics, exegetes, and scholar-monks. In Chan flame records such as the *Patriarch's Hall Collection* and the *Transmission of the Flame*, Chan monks are regularly described as "heirs" (*si* 嗣) of their masters. However, in contrast to patrilineal societies, in which sons inherit the property or rank of their fathers, or to other Buddhist traditions, where detailed and often closely guarded teachings on texts and rituals pass from master to disciple, most Chan monks assert that their inheritance is formless. In Chan biographical accounts, the moment when a master "transmits" something to his disciple is described in a number of ways with a variety of terms, all of them purposefully vague. Accounts of Deshao's disciples, for example, often use the adverb *mi* 密, which can be translated as "secretly," "mysteriously," or "intimately." *Mi* and other adverbs qualify a range of verbs including "transmitted" (*mi chuan* 密傳), "accorded" (*mi qi* 密契), "imprinted" (*mi yin* 密印), and "conferred" (*mi shou* 密授). The content of this secret or intimate transmission is equally elusive, often designated by adjective-noun compounds like "profound gate" (*xuan guan* 玄關), "profound meaning" (*xuan zhi* 玄旨), "mind source" (*xin yuan* 心源), "mind seal" (*xin yin* 心印), or "mind ground" (*xin di* 心地). We thus have passages stating that Deshao "secretly imprinted the mind ground" 密印心地 or "secretly conferred the profound meaning" 密授玄旨—statements that highlight the extraordinary nature of the exchange but reveal little about what in fact had taken place. The ostensive reason for this was that although dharma-transmission could be indicated in various ways—for example, with the gift of a robe, a bowl, or a fly whisk—the thing itself, the awakened mind of a buddha, was beyond representation. Words like "inheritance" and "transmission," with their implication that some *thing* had been transferred from one person to another, are misleading because awakening, according to tradition, cannot be taught or conveyed but must be individually realized. A monk could only have his insight confirmed or verified (*zheng* 證) by a recognized master. The moment of transmission was thus a moment of verification, when a monk was affirmed as a Chan master by a Chan master and granted entry into that master's lineage family.

While some monks were heirs to their masters in the legal sense of inheriting property, Chan monks also inherited social capital that had accumulated through the good repute of their lineage's ancestors. As in aristocratic clans, where descendants inherit the resources and social standing of their forebears, Chan monks were heir to the collective, routinized charisma of their clan. It may seem counterintuitive that, at the same time that elite Chinese society was moving away from the aristocratic model that prevailed until end of the Tang toward the more meritocratic ethos of the Song, Buddhist systems of authority seemed to be moving in the opposite direction. Unlike in secular clans, however, membership in Chan lineages was not determined by birth, but at the discretion of senior members of the lineage. Chan masters granted or withheld transmission, accepting some monks into their lineage while excluding others, instituting what might be described as a meritocratic aristocracy.

Membership in an illustrious Chan master's lineage gave stature and increased the likelihood that a monk would win support from powerful patrons and be called to support them in turn. As members of an elite Chan lineage, monks were also likely to be sought out by junior clerics. The prestige conveyed through lineage thus played an important role in the perpetuation of patronage as well as the expansion and diversification of lineages themselves. This may be one of the reasons why members from one lineage were supported by generations of rulers in multiple kingdoms, and why the doctrines and practices of these monks spanned such a broad range.[90] It was not that Chan monks began to branch out to study and teach more conventional forms of Buddhism; rather, otherwise conventional Buddhist monks began to associate themselves with Chan lineages.

Yanshou's own biography illustrates this effect. Recall that after extended training in a monastery under the guidance of Lingcan, Yanshou went into the mountains alone, had some kind of insight, and then went to Tiantai Deshao—a master with whom he appears to have had no formal relationship—to have his understanding verified. At that time, Deshao was unquestionably the most powerful monk in the region, and receiving Deshao's sanction lifted Yanshou into his network of clerics. The authority and legitimacy invested in Wuyue's national teacher enabled him to give a talented though still relatively unknown young monk like Yanshou a real advantage in future postings. Deshao's disciples received the vast majority of royal patronage and temple appointments recorded for Wuyue, and Deshao himself appears to have exercised some authority over his disciples' placements.[91] In contrast, Yanshou's mentor Lingcan, whatever his virtues as a teacher, had reportedly lost a public debate with Deshao's confrere Huiming and thereby forfeited his capacity to help his disciples up the institutional ladder. The *Transmission of the Flame* credits Lingcan with only two disciples, neither of whom appears to have been supported by the king. His was a family whose fortunes were in decline.

Monks interested in securing powerful patrons required authorization, not necessarily or not only from the master who had trained them, but also from a monk already well established among the network of powerful benefactors. The monk Xingming 行明 (d. 1001), for example, received ordination from Yanshou on Mt. Xuedou and followed him when he moved to Yongming si in Hangzhou. Later, however, Xingming sought Deshao's sanction in the form of a prediction of future buddhahood. He then returned to Yongming si to "assist and support his original teacher," remaining with Yanshou until the latter's death. Despite his long relationship with and clear devotion to Yanshou, Chan texts consistently identify Xingming as a disciple of Deshao; we can safely assume that his connection with the national teacher played some part in his ensuing temple appointments and imperial honors.[92]

The practice of Wuyue monks seeking the sanction of the national teacher did not always sit well with the masters who had trained them. For example, after the monk Yongan, who had been a disciple of the Vinaya master Huizheng, asked for Deshao's approval, he was upbraided by Huizheng, who scolded that he had "abandoned [his] filial responsibilities and quickly become a disappointment."[93] Some masters, however, appear to have encouraged this kind of affiliation. Pengyan 朋彥 (913–961), a native of Wuzhou (in present-day Zhejiang), had studied under the local Chan master Baozi 寶資 (n.d.), a disciple of the Min master Changqing Huileng, but "later, at Chan master Huiming's urging, he returned to Tiantai [Deshao's] room and awakened the true dharma eye. From this, following conditions, he began to expound the dharma with great success. The commissioner of Gusu, Qian Renfeng treated him with respect, established a temple and invited him to turn the wheel of the dharma."[94]

Examples like these demonstrate that lineage relationships do not necessarily indicate a period of meaningful apprenticeship whereby a master trained a disciple over time, transmitting particular sets of skills. No doubt this did happen, but inclusion in a Chan lineage family could also—and perhaps more often did—mean that a junior monk had been vetted by a cleric in a position of seniority and power. The fact that Chan monks came to nearly monopolize state patronage in Wuyue all but compelled aspiring monks, irrespective of their personal loyalties or doctrinal inclinations, to affiliate themselves with leading Chan lineages. Among the forty-nine monks listed as Deshao's disciples in the *Transmission of the Flame*, there is little to indicate that many spent extended time under his tutelage or collectively championed his particular school of thought or style of practice. What these monks had in common was the imprimatur of Wuyue's most influential cleric.

The link between lineage and patronage does not mean that dharma transmission merely represented clerical cronyism or the self-serving social climbing of ambitious monks. If we grant that monks rose to positions of authority on the strength of their charisma and insight, it makes good sense that junior monks would seek out the approval of respected elders and that senior monks would want to promote talented young clerics. The fact that this arrangement improved the patronage prospects of junior monks need not render these exchanges disingenuous.

Because national teachers and other highly placed monks served as the arbiters of patronage networks, with transmission functioning as a method of authorization, they had a disproportionate influence on the development of regional Buddhist cultures. It is not surprising that these monks' interpretations of Buddhist orthodoxy closely coincided with the interests of the state, given that the monastic elite were essentially selected or approved by the court. The king chose the national teacher, appointed monks to prominent positions within the state's monastic bureaucracy, and often named the abbots of the region's major monastic institutions—the sites where the majority of clerics trained. This was a self-perpetuating system; the king and his courtiers established and supported a monastic leadership sympathetic to their interests while those clerics trained and, together with the court, advanced the next generation of monastic leaders. The transformation of Chan from a small, marginal movement into the bearer of a state-sanctioned and thus state-supporting Buddhist orthodoxy was a natural outcome of this process.

Of course, the symbiotic and reciprocal nature of *saṃgha*-state relations meant that the fortunes of Xuefeng Yicun's and Xuansha Shibei's descendants were bound up, for the better and for the worse, with those of the ruling families of Min, the Southern Han, the Southern Tang, and Wuyue. As these kingdoms self-destructed or submitted to the authority of the nascent Song dynasty, their religio-political networks either disintegrated or were dismantled. Yongming Yanshou, who in the course of his career reportedly ordained 1,700 disciples and conferred the precepts on thousands of others, is credited with a mere two heirs in the *Transmission of the Flame*, neither of whom were even accorded an entry in the collection. This apparently abrupt end to his lineage has often been interpreted as an indictment of Yanshou's "syncretic" approach, but the vagaries of geography and politics were probably more significant factors. By the time the *Transmission of the Flame* was completed in 1004, the kingdom of Wuyue was a fading memory. The political center of China had shifted to north Kaifeng, and a new generation of Chan monks and regional rulers set to work adapting tried and tested models to new circumstances.

6

Reintegration

The North Prevails

WHEN ZHAO KUANGYIN 趙匡胤 (927–976) overthrew the Zhou to establish the Song dynasty in 960, his was only one of seven states competing for control of the empire. With the new the title of Emperor Taizu 太祖 (r. 960–976), Zhao devoted much of his reign to subduing his rivals, and by 976, only Wuyue in the south and the Northern Han in the north remained. That year, Taizu called Qian Chu to Kaifeng with the guarantee of safe passage back to Wuyue. In the Song capital, the king, together with his wife and their son the crown prince, were honored as guests of the emperor, but Taizu's message was clear: Qian Chu would either surrender his kingdom peacefully or would, like the Southern Tang the previous year, be subjugated by force. Taizu underscored his message by holding the crown prince in Kaifeng. After returning to Hangzhou, Qian Chu, hoping to placate Taizu and stall for time, offered to increase his already lavish tributes to the Song court, to disband his army, and to relinquish his royal titles.[1] Despite these gestures of loyalty and submission, when Taizu's son and successor Emperor Taizong 太宗 (r. 976–997) summoned Wuyue's king again to Kaifeng in 978, it was for a one-way journey. With Qian Chu's arrival in Kaifeng, Wuyue, the last of the southern kingdoms, had succumbed.[2] Emperor Taizong bestowed honorary titles on Qian Chu and his sons and provided them a comfortable, if captive, life in the northern capital.[3] After the Song defeat of the Northern Han the following year, the period of the Five Dynasties and Ten Kingdoms had come to an end.

Following reunification, Kaifeng became the focal point of a new empire, a center toward which peripheral concentrations of power were drawn. The processes set in motion at the end of the Tang, with talent and materials flowing toward southern cities, reversed. The capitals of southern kingdoms reverted to their former status as provincial hubs and once again funneled a portion of their resources north to the imperial capital. Along with material treasures—gold, silk, art, rare plants, and foods—some of the kingdoms' human capital also flowed into Kaifeng. Buddhist clerics who had lived in once powerful southern states, finding themselves now on the margins, gravitated toward the capital along with officials, scholars, and craftsmen. The clergy-court relations that played such a defining role in determining Buddhist orthodoxy would henceforth be negotiated in Kaifeng.

While some members of Xuefeng Yicun's and Xuansha Shibei's lineages transitioned successfully to Song patronage, fewer and fewer monks linked themselves to the legacies of masters like Fayan Wenyi, Tiantai Deshao, or Yongming Yanshou, if the decreasing number of heirs listed in Song-era flame records is any indication.[4] Scholars have usually attributed the decline of this clerical network to its teachings, which many have assumed were too scholarly and eclectic for the times. Albert Welter has proposed that the teachings of southeastern monks such as Fayan Wenyi, Tiantai Deshao, and Yongming Yanshou represented "an alternate Chan future, based on the notion of assimilation with doctrinal Buddhism rather than independence from it."[5] This more conservative interpretation of Chan orthodoxy thrived in southeastern China during the tenth century but appears to have been abandoned during the eleventh. Song unification, according to Welter, occasioned a debate between the Fayan faction's "harmony between Chan and the teachings" and the Linji faction's "separate tradition outside the teachings": "The debate associated with this struggle between rival Chan factions in the early Song was instrumental in defining the principles that came to characterize Chan, and served as the foundation for the acceptance of Chan as a leading school of Chinese Buddhism in the Song."[6] During the early Northern Song, members of the Linji lineage advocated an "anticanonical and antiritualistic, iconoclastic, and independent" vision of Chan that was more appealing to Song elites than was the more conservative, ecumenical approach of Chan monks from southeastern China.[7] The Chan orthodoxy that took hold in the Northern Song thus seems to have developed in opposition to the style of Chan that prevailed in southeastern China during the Five Dynasties and Ten Kingdoms.

This chapter offers another interpretation of the rise of Linji clerics and the decline of the Fayan lineage during the early Northern Song. Rather than focusing on the ideological distinctions between these two groups, I explore how the political changes of the Five Dynasties–Song transition might have impacted regional monastic communities and restructured sociocultural networks. The chapter begins with a brief overview of clergy-court relations over the course of the five northern dynasties, both to provide contrast to concurrent events in southeastern kingdoms and to establish the historical context necessary for understanding the changes that were taking place in the early decades of the Song. The second section then explores some of the effects Song unification had on regional and transregional cultures, with particular attention to the importation of southeastern literary, artistic, and religious traditions to the new capital and their role in the formation of Song imperial culture. In the final section, the clerical and patronage associations of prominent Linji clerics are traced to highlight their connections to southeastern social networks and to render connections between the Chan institutions and traditions of the Northern Song and the Buddhist cultures of southeastern China during the Five Dynasties and Ten Kingdoms more visible.

Buddhism in Kaifeng and Luoyang during the Five Dynasties

Very little has been written about the state of Buddhism in northern China during the Five Dynasties.[8] This absence likely stems from a general presumption that northern Buddhist communities were enfeebled throughout this period. The frequent and often violent alternation of northern dynasties meant that most rulers rarely had the luxury—if they ever had the inclination—to nurture cultural traditions. The twin objectives of northern emperors were to amass treasure and maintain strong militaries; literature, rituals, and music were indulgences of little practical value.[9] Buddhist traditions, likewise, were dispensable. With rare exceptions, the rulers of the Five Dynasties were wary of Buddhist monks and covetous of their resources. When Buddhism is mentioned at all in modern historical accounts, the persecution launched by the Zhou emperor Shizong 世宗 (r. 954–959) often receives the focus and is taken as emblematic of the embattled state of the *saṃgha* in the north after the fall of the Tang.

While it is true that Shizong and his predecessors imposed restrictions on Buddhist communities, it is also clear that Buddhist traditions and institutions continued to function in the northern capitals during the tenth century, often with imperial support. Emperors of every northern regime honored Buddhist monks, awarding them purple robes, master titles, and financial resources. Biographies and inscriptions for northern monks demonstrate that, as during the Tang, court patronage of Buddhist monks was predicated on the family backgrounds and accomplishments of individual clerics. Unlike their rivals in the southeast, however, northern emperors never supported extended networks of monks linked through lineage.

Over the course of the Five Dynasties, the succession of rulers in the north was rapid—their reigns averaged just three and a half years (see appendix 3)—and as a consequence, policies toward Buddhist monastics could veer from lavish patronage to harsh persecution.[10] On the whole, though, northern courts were much more assertive than their southern counterparts in regulating Buddhist institutions within their territories. As demonstrated by court documents collected in the *Wudai huiyao*, every northern regime issued edicts in the interest of increasing control and oversight of monks and nuns.[11] The first, circulated in 921, proscribed private ordinations and required those who sought official ordination to submit to exams covering topics such as preaching, recitation, composition, and even meditation. The number of monks allowed to ordain on the occasion of the emperor's birthday was drastically reduced to just fourteen. The position of monastic recorder (*senglu* 僧錄)—the highest rank within the state's monastic bureaucracy, responsible for the behavior and discipline of all monks and nuns—was maintained, but the post of monastic rector (*sengzheng* 僧正), whose responsibilities included maintaining the official registries of monks and nuns, was abolished, its supervisory responsibilities presumably transferred to secular officials.[12] Restrictions were also placed on the awarding of purple robes and honorific titles.[13] The only cleric to receive a purple robe during the reign of Liang emperor Mo (Zhu Youzhen, r. 913–923), for example, was his former schoolmate, the learned monk and abbot of Xiangguo si 相國寺, Guiyu 歸嶼 (862–936).[14]

Two years after Emperor Mo implemented these strictures on the *saṃgha*, Zhuangzong 莊宗 (r. 923–926) overthrew the Liang to establish the Later Tang, and celebrated by authorizing the ordination of three thousand monks.[15] By all accounts, Zhuangzong was an ardent supporter of the clergy, a fact that disapproving historians attributed to the baleful influence of his wife, Empress Liu (Liu Yuniang 劉玉娘, d. 926). According to Ouyang Xiu, Zhuangzong's wife "emerged from obscure origins and leapt above others to become empress, and reasoned this achievement reflected the powers of the Buddha. . . . She personally transcribed Buddhist scripture, while lavishing feasts and presents on monks and nuns. Zhuangzong himself came to be deluded by Buddhism as a consequence."[16] Whether he was deluded, sincerely devoted, or just trying to get along with his wife, other accounts confirm the emperor's interest in Buddhism. He reportedly joined in formal scripture recitations, held feasts for thousands of monastics, granted imperial name plaques to small temples and cloisters, and took monks with him on military expeditions.[17] The clerics patronized by Zhuangzong represented a typically diverse array of traditions, including erudite Vinaya specialists, *Avataṃsaka* devotees, and at least one Chan monk, Xiujing 休靜 (fl. 923).[18]

At the time, such enthusiastic support for the *saṃgha* was an anomaly in the north, and Zhuangzong's successor and adoptive brother, Emperor Mingzong 明宗 (r. 926–933), soon put an end to it. In 927 Mingzong called a halt to all new temple construction, required that ordinations take place only on state-sanctioned ordination platforms, and instituted strict punishments for monks or nuns caught violating the precepts or disregarding state statutes.[19] Mingzong was concerned that the *saṃgha* had grown too large and that quality of monastics was deteriorating, but he also feared the creep of moral corruption, which he saw as a threat to the stability of his state. "Within cities and villages," he warned, "there are many who esteem evil teachings and make spurious claims regarding the teachings of the Sage [i.e., the Buddha]. Some do not differentiate between monks and nuns, [and permit] men and women to live together. Factions gather at night and disperse at dawn. They claim to disseminate [the teachings] in dharma assemblies but secretly indulge in illicit activities. If not eliminated, they will certainly become a pernicious problem." Offenders were to be beaten to death.[20]

The severity of the punishment suggests that Mingzong had concerns well beyond the sex lives of his subjects. Rebellions against Chinese regimes often originated as millenarian movements, and as Chikusa Masaaki and others have pointed out, "gathering at night and dispersing at dawn" later became a catch phrase for Buddhist groups perceived by the state as potential sources of unrest. The expression appears to have originated in Mingzong's edict, however, becoming a stock critique of lay Buddhist groups only in the Northern Song.[21]

In issuing his edict, Mingzong was surely aware of the events that transpired seven years earlier, in the autumn of 920, when a "diabolical renegade" named Wu Yi 母乙 (d. 920) had proclaimed himself Son of Heaven, directly challenging the authority of the last emperor of the Liang dynasty. Government forces swiftly dispatched Wu Yi and his followers, but the northern courts remained wary of the people of Chenzhou 陳州, Wu Yi's center of operations, located just one hundred kilometers south of Kaifeng. According to both the old and new *History of the Five Dynasties*, the people of Chenzhou "delighted in the practice of the left-handed way [i.e., heterodoxy]. Basing themselves on the teachings of the Buddha, they set up their own sect, calling it the Supreme Vehicle (*shang sheng* 上乘). They did not eat meat. They converted the common people to their disorderly and debauched ways, assembling in the evenings and dispersing at dawn."[22] Despite efforts to eradicate it, this movement persisted, resurfacing during the Later Tang and Jin dynasties. Zanning would later identify it as a Manichean group, but whatever their sectarian affiliations, any large movement operating outside the sanction of the state was viewed as a potential threat to social and political stability and was dealt with accordingly.[23] Anxiety over heterodox groups also brought increased restrictions and oversight on mainstream monastic communities.

Throughout the Five Dynasties, tighter control of the *saṃgha* was, not surprisingly, also motivated by the economic and military value of the men and materials within Buddhist monasteries. By the mid-tenth century, northern China had endured decades of internecine war, drastically depleting the stock of soldiers and materiel needed to sustain ongoing military campaigns. Mass-laicization of monks would free up able-bodied men for military service, while confiscation of temple bells and icons could supply copper for the casting of coin.

Fewer monks and nuns also meant fewer wasted resources. In 949 the vice director of the bureau of merit titles, Li Qinming 李欽明 (n.d.), submitted a petition to the Later Han emperor Yindi 隱帝 (r. 948–950) asserting that there were approximately one hundred thousand monks and nuns consuming the state's limited supplies of grain and silk.[24] Every county, he said, had at least twenty Buddhist temples, whose monks sought alms although they had productive fields and paid no taxes. While Buddhist monks lived idly in opulent temples, the common people toiled yet remained impoverished. Li Qinming thus recommended that the Later Han emperor drastically reduce the number of monks and monasteries in his territory.

The Later Han court seems not to have implemented Li's plan, but six years later, a new regime controlled the north, and the second emperor of the Later Zhou dynasty (951–960) proved more responsive to charges of Buddhist excess. In 955, at a time when Wuyue's king was commissioning copies of the Buddhist canon and building dozens of new temples and stupas, Emperor Shizong issued a series of edicts aimed at shrinking the *saṃgha*. He called for the destruction of all temples that lacked official name placards, stipulated that no new temples or hermitages be built outside city walls, and announced that no new requests for temples or ordination platforms within the city would be granted. Private ordinations were forbidden and parental permission was required to leave home. Prospective monks had to be at least fifteen years old and were required to chant a minimum of one hundred pages of scripture to qualify for ordination. Those who met these requirements were obliged to register with the Ministry of Sacrifices and obtain ordination certificates issued by the state. Monastic records were to be updated and submitted to the court each year, rather than every third year as under previous regimes. Clerics absent from the registers would be laicized. Also subject to laicization were monks who engaged in any form of bodily mutilation (sacrificing their bodies, burning arms or fingers, piercing hands or feet, hanging lamps from their skin) or other "perverse" practices (such as the use of talismans, spirit water, and the summoning of spirits).[25]

Authorizing the seizure of monastic assets, Shizong reportedly quipped, "Tradition has it that the Buddha viewed human existence as unreal, yet out of an urge to profit mankind [through his teachings], he chose to retain his true body. Having chosen to forgo personal salvation to profit the world, how could he possibly begrudge us a bunch of bronze statues?"[26] By the end of the year, more than thirty thousand temples had been abolished (their land and other resources, no doubt, requisitioned), leaving just under twenty-seven hundred Buddhist temples in "All under Heaven" (*Tianxia* 天下).[27] Only 42,444 monks and 18,756 nuns remained in the north.[28] If Li Qinming's earlier estimates were accurate, the size of the *saṃgha* had been reduced nearly 40 percent.

Shizong's crackdown undoubtedly brought hardship for the *saṃgha*, but it was a purge rather than a persecution, leaving untouched the elite monks who occupied major temples in northern cities. In planning the proscription, in fact, Shizong consulted with Daopi 道丕 (889–955), one of the most respected clerics of northern China at that time.[29] Daopi conceded that "wild and uncontrollable monks" were everywhere but expressed concern that "when the plowing is done, the orchids might be uprooted along with the weeds. When the water is strained, gold might be lost along with the silt."[30] That some silt had begun to sully the gold appears to have been a foregone conclusion or at least a politic response to a ruler bent on suppressing the *saṃgha*. Whatever the case, Shizong's campaign targeted the lower strata of the monastic population and was limited in both time and space. It did not extend beyond Zhou territory, and like the Huichang persecutions more than a century earlier, it did not last long. Imperial patronage for Buddhist monks and monasteries resumed after the establishment of the Song dynasty, five years later.[31] By 1021, the number of monastics in China appears to have reached an all-time high of nearly 460,000.[32] While

Shizong's suppression is often cited as either the cause or the result of a Buddhist decline during the Five Dynasties, neither seems to be the case.

Chan Monks in Northern Capitals

Tight restrictions on Buddhist monastics in northern China coupled with political instability made the establishment of enduring religio-political alliances extremely difficult. Although a few eminent monks like Daopi received consistent patronage from successive emperors, Buddhist institutions experienced nothing like the sustained imperial support of multigenerational monastic networks that had developed in southeastern China, nor had members of Chan lineages yet emerged as the leaders of mainstream, state-sanctioned Buddhism.

Some Chan monks were active in the northern capitals of the Five Dynasties, however, and at least a few enjoyed the favor of northern emperors. Over the course of the first three dynasties (Liang, Later Tang, and Jin), the only Chan monk known to have had any direct contact with an emperor was Xiujing, whose relationship with the decidedly pro-Buddhist Zhuangzong has already been noted. Xiujing had studied with Dongshan Liangjie at the time when, according to the *Song Biographies*, the latter's style of Chan was in vogue in southeastern China. Unlike most Chan monks of his generation, however, Xiujing later left Jiangnan to settle in Luoyang, the capital of the Later Tang. When Zhuangzong staged a vegetarian feast for the *saṃgha*, Xiujing and his disciples reportedly distinguished themselves by sitting silently while all the other monks chanted sutras. Zhuangzong asked the reason for this and Xiujing is said to have replied, "When the Way is at peace, there is no need to carry out the emperor's commands. At such times, one can stop singing songs [for the sake of] peace." The emperor was delighted with this response and, after Xiujing's death, granted him the posthumous title Great Master Baozhi 寶智 (Precious Wisdom).[33] Despite Xiujing's prominence in Luoyang (his remains were enshrined in no fewer than four stupas), his Caodong lineage, as Morten Schlütter has shown, was virtually defunct throughout most of the Northern Song and only revived in the late eleventh century.[34]

The two most prominent Chan monks in northern China during the Five Dynasties were both disciples of Touzi Datong, a once significant but now largely forgotten fourth-generation heir of Qingyuan Xingsi who was based in the mountains of southern Anhui (near the present city of Anqing).[35] The first of these monks, Yanjun 巖俊 (882–966), had studied with Touzi Datong before settling in Kaifeng, where, years later, he was honored by the emperors and officials of the Zhou dynasty. According to his *Song Biography*, Yanjun had known the Zhou emperors Taizu and Shizong before they had come to power, and when Taizu finally ascended the throne, he showered Yanjun with "lavish donations." Yanjun's prominence in the capital was such that Zanning made the incredible claim that "in the space of fifty years he provided for the needs of hundreds of thousands of monks. The Chan monasteries (*chanlin* 禪林) of the capital took him as their shield"—the latter statement an indication, perhaps, that Yanjun was able to soften the blow of Emperor Shizong's purges. After Yanjun's death, tens of thousands of clerics and laypeople are said to have attended the enshrinement of his relics.[36]

The second of Touzi Datong's disciples to rise to prominence in Kaifeng was Shihui 師會 (879–946), a monk of aristocratic birth who had become a novice under the tutelage of Daopi while both men were living in Chang'an.[37] After the fall of the Tang, Shihui traveled to Kaifeng, where he first met Yanjun. Yanjun, in turn, referred him to Touzi Datong. After spending time in Touzi's assembly, in 914 Shihui returned to Kaifeng and rejoined Yanjun at his temple, the Guanyin Chan Cloister 觀音禪院. With the support of Later Liang ministers, Shihui soon established his own monastery, the Tianshou Chan Cloister 天壽禪院, and at this temple, his biographer claims, Shihui "provided for more than two million monks" over the course of thirty-five years—an impossible number clearly intended to convey his great prominence.[38] That stature is further attested by the fact that in 942 he was granted a purple robe by the Jin emperor Gaozu 高祖 (r. 936–942), and two years later, Gaozu's successor awarded him the name Faxiang 法相 (Dharma Mark).

The influence of Touzi Datong's disciples in the northern capital spanned the length of the Five Dynasties and was known as far south as Wuyue, where Touzi's discourse record was compiled and printed on Mt. Mao in Mingzhou in 961.[39] But the repute of Touzi and his disciples does not appear to have extended into the Song. Despite the vast number of monks Shihui is said to have trained, none of his disciples left any surviving records and he himself has no entry in the *Transmission of the Flame* or any subsequent Chan flame record. As for Yanjun, though he is included in the *Transmission of the Flame* and acknowledged to have provided for "hundreds of thousands of monks," he is not credited with any heirs.

The surprisingly short-lived legacies of Touzi Datong's disciples is part of a larger pattern. Very few of the monks supported by Zhou court were subsequently adopted by the first emperors of the Song, a fact that suggests the architects of the new Song state sought to install a new monastic leadership rather than build on power structures inherited from the Zhou, much as they replaced nearly all the Zhou's military commanders.[40] The rise of Chan monks in the north with the advent of the new regime thus did not flow from the activities of those few Chan clerics that were patronized by the emperors of the Five Dynasties. It was instead another, relatively obscure network of Chan monks, the descendants of Linji Yixuan, together with a small but powerful group of officials that were responsible for elevating Chan monks to positions of influence during the Northern Song.

Cultural Consolidation in the Early Song

The rulers of the Five Dynasties necessarily privileged military strength over cultural refinement, and it was only after Song Taizong completed the task of reunifying the empire that he could turn much attention to reconstructing civil society.[41] Taizong's transition from martial to civil rule, as Peter Lorge has noted, marked the true beginning of social and political stability for the Song: "The Five Dynasties and Ten Kingdoms came to an end when the northern military and political power center absorbed and incorporated southern culture into its imperial culture. When southern culture became Song culture, and when southern men became Song officials at the highest levels, then the period of diverse Chinese polities ended."[42]

The southern orientation of the early Song state is significant. During the tenth century, the Southern Tang, Wuyue, and the Later Shu were the most populous kingdoms in southern China (table 5). The capitals of these kingdoms preserved and developed literary and artistic traditions, and after reunification, Taizong tapped these regional reserves to replenish the depleted cultural capital of the north. He had entire southern libraries transported to Kaifeng and consolidated at the Institute of History (*Shi guan* 史館), increasing the holdings from approximately 12,000 scrolls when the dynasty was established in 960 to more than 46,000 scrolls by the end of his reign. The expansion was made possible primarily through the acquisition of literary collections from the annexed kingdoms of Shu (in 965), which provided 13,000 scrolls, and the Southern Tang (in 975), which sent some 20,000 scrolls.[43] Several southern scholars, including men like former Southern Tang official Xu Xuan who had ties to prominent southern clerics, were set to work distilling local histories and traditions into massive, transregional compendia—notably the *Taiping guangji* 太平廣記 (978), *Taiping yulan* 太平御覽 (983), and *Wenyuan yinghua* 文苑英華 (986).[44] Decrees calling

TABLE 5   Population statistics for various states at the time of their defeat by the Song

Kingdom	Terminal year	Total population	Average population per county
Zhou	960	967,353	<1,500
Nanping	963	142,300	<8,300
Chu	963	97,388	<1,500
Later Shu	965	534,039	<2,600
Southern Han	971	170,263	>800
Southern Tang	975	655,065	<6,000
Zhangquan	978	151,978	<10,000
Wuyue	978	550,680	≈ 6,400
Northern Han	979	35,225	<880

Source: Data derived from Song gazetteers. Chart adapted from Yan G., "Wudai shiguo pian," 9.

for the construction or renovation of dozens of temples throughout the empire (972), the establishment of the Institute for the Translation of Sutras (982), the first printing of the Buddhist canon (983), and the compilation of major, transregional Buddhist collections like the *Song Biographies* (988) and the *Transmission of the Flame* (1004) were all imperial initiatives that served to establish the unity and legitimacy of the Song through authoritative displays of regional integration and cultural stewardship.[45]

Along with books, other elements of the material culture of southeastern states also migrated to Kaifeng. Just as artisans and officials fled Chang'an for the cities of Chengdu and Hangzhou at the beginning of the tenth century, their descendants left southern cities to travel to the new northern court following Song unification. Richard Barnhart has noted that the artistic traditions of Shu—particularly bird-and-flower and figure painting—were brought to Kaifeng, where they became the basis for Song styles.[46] Tracy Miller, in her study of architecture during the Five Dynasties and early Song, has also shown that the architectural designs of Zhejiang were imported to Kaifeng in the early Song and served as models for the construction of official buildings. The prominence of southeastern architectural styles in the capital, she writes, made Kaifeng "a southern 'cultural capital' in its appearance as much as internal content."[47]

Northern buildings in the southeastern style were not limited to governmental structures but also included Buddhist stupas (and presumably temples). Emperor Taizong, for example, ordered the Zhejiang native Yu Hao 喻皓 (fl. 964–989), the same architect who had restored the Baota stupa in Hangzhou for Wuyue's kings, to design a new stupa at Kaifeng's Kaibao Monastery 開寶寺.[48] This new stupa was built to house the famed Aśokan relic that Qian Liu had brought to Hangzhou early in his reign but now resided in the Song capital.

Possession of Śākyamuni's skull relic was a marker of imperial authority, and the *Song Biographies* contains a firsthand account of its presentation to Emperor Taizong. The bone had been carried to Kaifeng by at least three of Wuyue's most eminent monks: Zanning and two of Tiantai Deshao's disciples (all of whom were subsequently awarded purple robes and titles by the emperor).[49] Once the relic was enshrined in the palace sanctum, Zanning wrote, it began to exhibit "marvelous auspicious omens." The Buddha's skull shard, evidently, was pleased to have arrived at the Song court. On the day that the relic was interred in the stupa's crypt, divine lights illuminated the heavens. Monks and laypeople burned their heads and fingers, just as they had when Tang emperors had the Buddha's finger bone displayed in Chang'an. "If not for bodhisattvas of great means and deva-kings of great merit," Zanning marveled, "how could the common people be moved to sacrifice the jewels of their bodies?"[50] The Buddha, bodhisattvas, venerable monks, and pious laypeople were thus drawn to Kaifeng, the residence of the emperor, a "deva-king of great merit," and their presence was described—in a text compiled by imperial decree—as a confirmation of the legitimacy of the nascent dynasty and the centrality of the new capital.[51]

By concentrating Buddhist icons, relics, and clerics in his capital, Taizong successfully incorporated regional Buddhist traditions, most prominently those of southeastern China, into the imperial culture emanating from his capital. Given the relative prosperity of Buddhism in southeastern kingdoms and the difficulties monastic communities had endured in the northern cities, it made good sense for Taizong to construct the official Song Buddhist establishment on models that had successfully served southern courts for more than a century. Indeed, the emperor reportedly once asked a "barefoot person of the way" to tell him about "how Chan and Vinaya had transformed things in the south"—an indication, perhaps, that he was contemplating similar strategies for the Song.[52]

The Buddhist culture of southeastern states was clearly of significant interest to the Song court, but leading clerics from the Southern Tang and Wuyue enjoyed only a relatively brief period of influence during the early Song. Some of these men were called to the northern court while others impressed Song officials posted to administrative positions in former southern capitals like Fuzhou, Hangzhou, and Nanjing, where these monks retained considerable prestige.[53] Since the ecumenical approach of Fayan Wenyi and his descendants nicely complemented the Song project of regional integration, these monks could easily have filled positions in the Song monastic bureaucracy, as they had in so many southern courts. Rather than Wenyi's descendants, however, it was heirs of Linji Yixuan who thrived during the early Song.[54] Why?

The Rise of the Linji Lineage

The Linji lineage grew out of the Hongzhou school, the most politically influential Chan movement of the late Tang dynasty, and many observers have assumed that the dominant position of Linji monks in the early Song represented the culmination of a linear, if briefly obscured or waylaid, progression to power. As we have seen, however, the Hongzhou network was in decline in southeastern China at the beginning of the tenth century, and its representatives in the north, including Linji's descendants, fared little better.[55] Although a grand-disciple of Linji accompanied Tang emperor Xizong 僖宗 (r. 873–888) to Sichuan when Chang'an was occupied by Huang Chao's forces, there are no records of Linji monks receiving patronage from any of the emperors of the five northern dynasties.[56] It is all the more remarkable, then, how sharply Linji fortunes had turned around by the early decades of the eleventh century. By that date, monks affiliated with this network had risen to become some of the most prominent Chan clerics in the empire.

The history of the Linji movement during the Song dynasty has already been treated in detail by a number of scholars.[57] My intention here is not to provide a comprehensive overview of the ascent of these clerics or to survey the history of clergy-court relations during the early Song. Instead, I want to situate early Song developments within the context of the Five

Dynasties–Song transition to underscore some of the political and geo-graphical factors that I suspect contributed to the success of the Linji lineage.

Scholars of Chinese Buddhist history have generally attributed the tri-umph of the Linji faction to an inherent superiority of style, assuming that the unsentimental immediacy and unconventional approach of Linji masters appealed to Song literati more than the conservative, conciliatory, text-based teachings of Fayan Wenyi and his disciples. While the rise of the Linji network may have been facilitated by their irreverent, austere, and of-ten ingenious teachings, the position of Linji monks in northern China at a time when Kaifeng was emerging as the political center of the empire was also significant. The incorporation of southern cultural traditions conveyed the Chan zeitgeist of the southeast to northern cities near the capital where Chan masters were scarce. As noted previously, few other Chan lineage holders held on anywhere in northern China during the late Tang and early Five Dynasties, whereas for decades, the descendants of Linji had been headquartered in Ruzhou 汝州, a city in present-day Henan province situ-ated relatively close to the two northern capitals of Kaifeng and Luoyang (see map 3).[58] Just as the ascent of Xuefeng Yicun, Xuansha Shibei, and their disciples in southeastern China derived, in part, from being in the right place at the right time, the proximity of Linji clerics to prominent Song officials gave them an important strategic advantage over Chan networks located at a further remove from the capital.

Linji Monks and Song Officials

The city of Ruzhou appears to have managed somewhat better than most northern cities during the Five Dynasties, being governed by a succession of pious warlords for much of the tenth century. From 888 through 926, the region was under the authority of Zhang Quanyi 張全義 (852–926), a peasant-turned-ruler who is said to have "revered the teachings of Śākyamuni and Laozi without indulging in the left-handed way."[59] Ruzhou was later admin-istered by Military Commissioner Song Yanyun 宋彥筠 (879–956), who turned to Buddhism, we are told, as a means of atoning for his past crimes. According to the *Old History of the Five Dynasties*, he constructed temples and stupas to offset his karmic debts, mourned before a Buddha image on the anniversary of the Buddha's death, and had his maidservants shave their heads and become nuns.[60] In 951, Song Yanyun also had one of his residences converted to a temple named Guanghui si 廣慧寺 (Temple of Expansive Wisdom). The monk he appointed abbot of this new monastery, Fengxue Yanzhao 風穴延沼 (886–973), was a third-generation heir of Linji Yixuan (see appendix 5).[61]

Like many prominent Chan monks and laymen in northern China dur-ing the early decades of the Northern Song, Fengxue Yanzhao was a trans-plant from the south. He was born and reared in Hangzhou, and his early career paralleled those of other elite monks in Wuyue; versed in the Con-fucian classics in his youth, he practiced *zhiguan* meditation as a young monk.[62] At the age of twenty-five, Yanzhao called on Xuefeng Yicun's disciple Daofu, who, as noted previously, drew credit for popularizing Chan in Wuyue. Yanzhao, however, was "not able to reach the deepest level" with Daofu, and so, moving against the current of the times, he traveled from peaceful Hangzhou to the troubled north, settling in Ruzhou in 925 and joining the assembly of Xinghua Cunjiang's disciple, Nanyuan Huiyong 南院慧顒 (d. 952).[63] Yanzhao spent six years with Huiyong, during which time he "completely penetrated the profound meaning." Thereafter, he taught in several places before answering the summons of Song Yanyun and assuming the abbacy at Guanghui si.[64]

The relationship between Fengxue Yanzhao and Military Commissioner Song Yanyun marked the first phase of a multi-decade alliance between monks of the Linji lineage and Ruzhou's governors. As the north reestablished itself as the administrative heart of the empire, monks based in northern cities, many of whom had endured decades of instability and deprivation, were now well-placed to benefit from the political and economic transformation of the region. Yanzhao's most prominent disciple in Ruzhou, Shoushan Shengnian 首山省念 (926–993), acknowledged in one of his sermons that the existence of the Buddha-dharma depended on the patronage of kings and ministers, and presumably he was expressing a debt to his own benefactors about whom nothing is known.[65] In light of this statement, though, it certainly comes as no surprise that Shengnian's monastic and lay disciples went on to score remarkable success in securing the support of Ruzhou's governors and other influential Song officials. As Suzuki Tetsuo and Albert Welter have both shown, these laypeople proved instrumental in transforming the Linji lineage from a regional to an empire-wide movement.[66]

Flame records credit Shoushan Shengnian with fourteen disciples. At least five of these men are known to have been supported by Song officials and one, the layman Wang Sui 王隨 (ca. 973–1039), was an official himself.[67] Two of Shengnian's disciples, Guanghui Yuanlian 廣慧元璉 (951–1036) and Guyin Yuncong 谷隱蘊聰 (965–1032), also gave dharma-transmission to Song officials—a characteristic, though not an innovation, of Linji masters during the Song. Most of the lay disciples and benefactors of Shengnian's heirs had held administrative posts in Ruzhou and other northern cities where Linji monks were based. It was, of course, common practice for governors to ally with prominent clerics within their territories, but what is noteworthy in this context is that a string of officials lent their support to several monks, all of whom were members of the same Chan lineage—a phenomenon that was common in the south but had little precedent in the north. The relationships that were forming between clerics of the Linji lineage and these governors thus closely resembled the kind of clergy-court alliances that had developed in the kingdoms of Min, the Southern Han, the Southern Tang, and Wuyue. The fact that many of the monks and officials entering into these relationships in Henan were natives of southern China raises the possibility, if not the probability, that the clergy-court alliances established between monks of Xuefeng Yicun's lineage and the ruling families of southeastern kingdoms were serving as templates for the clerics and governors of northern cities.

Not all of Shoushan Shengnian's disciples were from southern China but two of his most influential heirs were: Guanghui Yuanlian was from Fujian and Guyin Yuncong was from Guangdong.[68] These two regions were major centers for Xuefeng Yicun's lineage, and as young monks, both Guanghui Yuanlian and Guyin Yuncong had studied with Yicun's dharma-heirs.[69] It is probably no coincidence that these two monks relocated to northern cities around the same time that southern states were falling before the northern Song. Just as monks during the late ninth and tenth centuries traveled from one region to another in search of stability and support, Yuanlian and Yuncong may have been drawn north by the prospect of patronage. Whether or not they actively sought the backing of well-placed benefactors, that is indeed what they obtained. In the respective cities of Ruzhou and Xiangzhou 襄州, Yuanlian and Yuncong developed close ties with Song officials who not only appointed them to the abbacies of local temples but also began to promote their teachings and their lineage at the Song court.

Guanghui Yuanlian's most prominent lay disciple, the influential Song scholar-official Yang Yi 楊億 (974–1020), like Yuanlian himself, was from Fujian. Before arriving in Ruzhou, Yang Yi had studied with two of Fayan Wenyi's disciples—probably, as Welter has proposed, during his tenure as prefect of Chuzhou in Zhejiang from 998 to 1000.[70] Yang Yi went on to play an important role in shaping the popular image of Chan during the early Song through his editing of Daoyuan's *Transmission of the Flame*, a collection that foregrounds the descendants of Xuefeng Yicun and Xuansha Shibei, particularly the heirs of Fayan Wenyi. In transferring from Zhejiang in the south to assume of the governorship Ruzhou in the north, however, Yang Yi moved from the cradle of Fayan Wenyi's network to the headquarters of the Linji lineage, and his loyalties accordingly shifted from the heirs of Wenyi to the descendants of Linji.

Before arriving in Ruzhou in 1014, Yang Yi had most likely already heard about the Linji master Guanghui Yuanlian. Yang Yi's predecessor as governor of Ruzhou, an official named Wang Shu 王曙 (963–1034), had served as Yang Yi's collaborator in editing the *Transmission of the Flame*. During his own tenure in Ruzhou, Wang Shu had visited Yuanlian at Guanghui si, reportedly engaging him in Chan-style dialogue, and sometime thereafter, when Wang Shu was transferred further south to the city of Yingzhou, he took up with Yuanlian's dharma-brother, the aforementioned Guyin Yuncong, who was living in the nearby city of Xiangzhou.[71] Wang Shu eventually received dharma-transmission from Yuncong, and Yang Yi received transmission from Yuanlian, making the two Song officials dharma-cousins. Given their adoption into this lineage, it comes as no surprise that Wang Shu and Yang Yi championed the teachings of their masters and other monks associated with the Linji network.[72]

Guyin Yuncong's prominence and his presence in the city of Xiangzhou extended the reach of the Linji network beyond the confines of Ruzhou. Xiangzhou was located at the terminus of the Han canal and along one of the major highways connecting southern China to Kaifeng, making it a major crossroads and bringing Yuncong into contact with transiting as well as local officials. Xiangzhou's governor Cha Dao 查道 (955–1018) was one of Yuncong's earliest benefactors. Cha Dao was also a southerner. A native of Anhui, he was the son of a Southern Tang official who had served as assistant commissioner of Jianzhou 劍州 under Li Yu and as governor of Quanzhou during the reign of Song Taizu. It was in Quanzhou that the young Cha Dao developed an interest in Buddhism, and given the Chan-centric Buddhist cultures of Min and the Southern Tang, it makes sense that he sought out the leader of Xiangzhou's Chan community upon his appointment to govern that region.[73] In 1006, he appointed Yuncong abbot of Xiangzhou's Shimen si 石門寺.

As far as we know, Cha Dao never became a direct disciple of Yuncong, but a later governor of Xiangzhou, Xia Song 夏竦 (985–1051), did. Xia Song—like Cha Dao and Yuncong—had also spent his formative years in Southern Tang territory. He was born in the Jiangxi region, grew up in Jiangsu, and like many literati from southeastern China, he was versed in a range of literary traditions, including Buddhist and Daoist texts. After joining the Song bureaucracy, Xia Song cycled through various administrative posts, eventually arriving in Xiangzhou sometime around 1020. There he appointed Yuncong to the abbacy of a temple whose name, Taiping xing-guo chanyuan 太平興國禪院 (Taiping-era Chan Cloister for Rejuvenating the Empire), suggests that it was an imperially sanctioned public Chan monastery.[74]

Chan flame records list both Xia Song and Wang Shu among Yuncong's dharma-descendants, but a third lay disciple likely played an even more high-profile role in promoting Shengnian's disciples. This was the son-in-law of Emperor Taizong, Li Zunxu 李遵勖 (988–1038), who probably met Yuncong through the recommendation of his friend Yang Yi. Li Zunxu went on to become one of the most powerful proponents of the Linji lineage, using his position to catapult these previously little-known monks onto the imperial stage. Some thirty years after Yang Yi and Wang Shu had edited the landmark *Transmission of the Flame*, Li Zunxu produced a second flame record, the *Tiansheng-Era Extensive Flame Record* 天聖廣燈錄, to document the rise of Linji monks that had occurred in northern cities in the interim. Li Zunxu's collection, compiled between 1023 and 1031, was published in 1036 with a preface by Song emperor Renzong 仁宗 (r. 1022–1063), an honor that elevated what was essentially a polemical sectarian text to mainstream representation of Chan teachings and history. Yanagida Seizan argued that Li Zunxu compiled the *Extensive Flame Record* "to promote the lineage of Mazu, Baizhang, Huangbo, and Linji by recording the sermons, statements, and teaching devices of these masters in as much detail as possible," an observation that has also been born out in Welter's detailed research on this text.[75] While it is important to stress that the publication of the *Extensive Flame Record* was not the primary cause of the Linji faction's rise, it remains one of its most visible effects, representing the culmination of alliances that had been forming between Linji masters and Song officials for decades.

The web of connections linking Linji monks, members of Xuefeng Yicun's extended lineage, and Song officials is tightly woven and it is easy to get lost in the details. Stepping back from biographical and geographical particulars, however, some larger patterns do emerge. At the most basic level, it is evident that many prominent Linji monks, their disciples, and their lay supporters during the early Song hailed from southeastern China and had spent time with the dharma-descendants of Xuefeng Yicun and Xuansha Shibei. After these men assumed posts in northern cities, they joined forces with members of Linji Yixuan's lineage—one of the few Chan networks based in northern China at the time. This movement away from Fayan clerics to Linji monks has typically been read in terms of conversion. The assumption, in short, is that there were two Chan factions, one based in the north, the other in the south, each maintaining irreconcilable interpretations of the Chan tradition. Linji monks and laymen had initially studied under Fayan Wenyi's heirs in southeastern China and found them wanting. They then encountered Linji masters in the north and were won over by their superior teachings. Welter has proposed that Song reunification precipitated a power struggle for control of the Chan movement, similar in scope to the famous sudden-and-gradual-awakening debates of the eighth century. During the early Song, he argues, the harmony between Chan and the teachings advocated by the descendants of Fayan Wenyi was pitted against the Linji faction's position that Chan represented a separate transmission outside the teachings. Linji monks and their lay supporters mounted a successful assault on Fayan monks and their teachings, the end result of which was the demise of the Fayan network and the normalization of the Linji vision of Chan orthodoxy.[76]

This chapter has proposed an alternative reading of the rise of Linji clerics and the decline of the Fayan network during the early Song—one that places a greater emphasis on political rather than philosophical or rhetorical factors. It remains unclear whether or not the change in imperial patronage from the Fayan lineage to Linji monks represented a doctrinal confrontation or even a significant shift in notions of orthodoxy. Morten Schlütter has argued that "sectarianism, in the sense of different factions of Chan disputing the authenticity of one another's teachings and practices, was largely absent from Northern Song Chan."[77] If there ever was an explicit ideological conflict between members of the Fayan and Linji factions, we find little trace of it in later Chan sources. On the contrary, the legacies of Wenyi and his descendants remained influential well into the Song dynasty, and the discourse records of Xuefeng Yicun, Xuansha Shibei, and Yunmen Wenyan were among the first printed during the Northern Song.[78] The dialogues of Fayan Wenyi, Tiantai Deshao, and others are well represented in later *gong'an* collections, and there is scant evidence to suggest that the teachings of these masters were ever disparaged when the descendants of Linji or Yunmen assumed the leadership of Song Chan institutions.[79]

Moreover, despite Linji monks' reliance on the slogans that Chan represented a "separate transmission outside the scriptures," which "did not depend on words and letters," most prominent Linji monks and other Chan masters of the Northern Song were literati in their own right, learned in both Buddhist and non-Buddhist literary traditions.[80] The sutras that exerted such a strong influence on the Chan monks of southeastern China—the *Lotus, Avataṃsaka*, and *Śūraṃgama*—remained influential in Northern Song Chan circles as well.[81] There is thus little indication that the exclusivist, antinomian rhetoric found in the discourse records of Linji monks during the Northern Song reflected any kind of institutional reality.

Linji monks clearly superseded their Fayan brethren at court, but the transition from the Five Dynasties to the Song appears to be characterized more by continuity than rupture. In the eleventh century, Linji (and later Yunmen) monks and their lay devotees asserted their distinctive identity through the compilation of flame histories and discourse records, and their role in the production of these kinds of texts is sometimes cited as a factor in their success. There is no reason to doubt that the lively, idiosyncratic style of such texts enhanced the appeal of these Chan monks among literati, but members of the Linji network were not innovating new literary traditions; they were building on textual forms that were developed in southeastern China during the Five Dynasties and Ten Kingdoms.

The structure of clergy-court relations in the Northern Song also bears a striking resemblance to those in Min, the Southern Tang, and Wuyue. Lineage played an increasingly important role in patronage, and the ties between aristocratic families and Chan lineage families were normalized and often spanned multiple generations.[82] Emperors and officials established state-sanctioned, public Chan monasteries; the abbacies of these temples were filled at the discretion of the court; and Chan monks regularly performed mortuary rites for the imperial family and high officials.[83]

While the evidence marshaled here is only circumstantial, it suggests that the transition from Fayan to Linji may have had less to do with doctrinal or pedagogical differences than with the shifting political landscape of the Five Dynasties–Song transition. Just as the literary, artistic, and political cultures of southeastern China were imported to Kaifeng and incorporated into the imperial culture of the Song dynasty, it seems as though the Buddhist traditions of southeastern China also initially served as the foundation of the Song's official Buddhist establishment. The descendants of Xuefeng Yicun, however, may simply have been too closely tied to the Song's former rivals for them to hold positions of power in the new administration. For a Song court intent on both eradicating the deeply entrenched regionalism of the Five Dynasties and dismantling the power-structures of rival regimes, the political associations of these monks could have been viewed as a liability.

Shortly after Song reunification, the first two emperors sought to reg-
ulate and restrict the size of the *saṃgha*, specifically in the former territories of Min, the Southern Tang, and Wuyue.[84] This may simply reflect their
concern over the large number of monastics in southeastern China, but it
can also be read as an attempt to disrupt or at least exert much tighter control over the religio-political networks that had dominated southeastern
states—their former rivals—for more than a century. There were historical precedents for this kind of policy: after the Tang dynasty overthrew the
Sui, for example, it systematically destroyed monasteries loyal to the old regime and laicized the clerics that had served them.[85]

Following Song reunification, several of the leaders of Wuyue's Buddhist institutions were initially summoned to Kaifeng, where, like members
of Wuyue's royal family, they were accorded honors but kept isolated from
their networks of support in the south. Behind the apparent honor of an
imperial summons lay the reality that many of these monks were effectively
removed from positions of power and influence in their home regions.
Rather than link themselves directly with the standard-bearers of southeastern Buddhist culture, Song courtiers instead constructed new networks of
affiliation and obligation, allying themselves with monastic communities
that had an established presence in northern China and had demonstrated
their loyalty to the Song court.

In the city of Ruzhou, Linji monks formed ties with regional rulers before the advent of the Song and continued to forge alliances with Song officials in the early decades of the dynasty. The men who served successful
warlords during the Five Dynasties, as Nicolas Tackett has shown, typically
rose to positions of prominence once their leader seized power or entered
the service of an established ruler.[86] For Buddhist clerics, those allied with
the victors were rewarded with privileged positions in the emerging system
of state-sponsored and state-regulated Buddhist institutions, while those
who cast their lot with the rulers of southern China found themselves in a
vulnerable position after those kingdoms fell to the Song. The demise of
Fayan Chan, then, might best be characterized as the demise of a network
of affiliation, not necessarily the downfall of a particular style of teaching
or practice. The identities of those occupying positions of power had
changed, but the nature of clergy-court relations and the culture of court
Buddhism do not appear to have been radically altered during the Five
Dynasties–Song transition.

Imperial patronage of the Linji network undoubtedly enhanced its appeal. As Linji monks secured the support of powerful politicians and
patrons, monks seeking the authority conferred by the sanction of an eminent Chan master would have gravitated toward leading clerics of the Linji
lineage, just as Wuyue monks had once sought the sanction of Wuyue's national teacher. By the early eleventh century, Tiantai Deshao and Yongming Yanshou were long gone, and the royal families that had supported
them had been removed from power. Monks affiliated with the Fayan network continued to hold support for a time in southeastern China, but their

lineage—as opposed to their teachings or their reputations—irrevocably lost its luster. The value of membership in Wenyi's lineage ebbed as the Linji and later Yunmen networks climbed in the esteem of the Song imperial family. Following their success in the north, monks affiliated with these two lineages began to spread to other parts of China—Yunmen in Zhejiang and Linji in Jiangxi, Hunan, Hubei, and Sichuan.[87] By the second half of the eleventh century, many of the strongholds of Fayan Wenyi's network in the south had been taken over by members of the Linji and Yunmen lineages.

Would the Linji network have become such a powerful force during the Song if it had been based in southern rather than northern China? Would Fayan Wenyi's lineage have come to dominate China if the Southern Tang had succeeded in its bid to unify the empire? We will, of course, never know. But the circumstances of the Five Dynasties–Song transition suggest that place-based patronage networks played a critical role in the success (and failure) of Buddhist movements in general and Chan lineages in particular.

Conclusion

DURING THE SECOND HALF of the Tang dynasty, the monk Wuye 無業 (761–823), a disciple of Mazu Daoyi, expressed his disdain for clerics who curried favor with powerful patrons. Chan monks, he said, were different:

> After ancient worthies of the Way attained realization, they went to live in thatched huts and stone chambers. They would pass twenty or thirty years using old cauldrons with broken legs to cook their food. They were unconcerned with fame and fortune and never thought of money and riches. Completely forgetting human affairs, they concealed their traces among cliffs and forests. When summoned by sovereigns, they would not respond; when invited by lords, they would not go. How could [other clerics] be the same as us? Greedy for fame and cherishing fortune, they sink into worldly ways.[1]

Wuye's rhapsody for renunciation is, paradoxically, recorded in the *Transmission of the Flame*, a text commissioned by Song emperor Zhenzong and compiled by Daoyuan, a member of a Chan lineage that had been serving kings and courtiers for well over a century. Were it not for the connections Chan clerics had forged with regional rulers during the tenth century, Wuye and his teachings might actually have obtained the obscurity he so vividly extolled.

This book has traced the development of one network of Chan monks as they emerged from "thatched huts and stone chambers" to mingle with monarchs and assume the abbacies of affluent, state-sanctioned monasteries. While the geographic distributions and chronologies of these monks are relatively clear, the reasons for their success and their broader historical significance remain matters of speculation. Without pretending to draw definitive conclusions, then, in these final pages I offer a brief synopsis of my arguments, in the hope that additional research will confirm or improve on them.

The forces propelling Chan clerics to prominence, I have proposed, did not flow directly from the destruction of elite Buddhist institutions and traditions of the capitals during the late Tang or from the favorable political and cultural conditions of the Northern Song. The ascent of Chan clerics appears instead to have been set in motion by the political and geographical reorientations taking place during the Tang–Five Dynasties transition. Although elite Buddhist exegetical traditions were disrupted by the upheavals of the late ninth century, they were neither destroyed nor irreparably damaged. In the aftermath of Huang Chao's rebellion, several former Tang officials and court clerics successfully relocated to southern cities, where regional rulers appointed them to positions within their administrations. In major urban centers like Chengdu and Hangzhou, newly named kings recruited former Tang officials as well as some of the same textual exegetes, ritual specialists, and Vinaya masters who had served Tang emperors. The relocation of these clerics from northern capitals to southern cities effectively distributed aspects of Chang'an's Buddhist culture to the capitals of some southern states.

In other, less economically developed and less densely populated regions like Jiangxi and Fujian, meanwhile, a different pattern of patronage seems to have prevailed. Because these areas did not attract many northern elites, regional rulers relied instead on local leaders to establish their political authority and to manage their nascent bureaucracies. Southeastern China had long hosted large populations of Chan monks, and the transformation of these hinterlands into autonomous kingdoms repositioned prominent local clerics at the centers of rapidly developing states. The political and economic decentralization of the Tang–Five Dynasties transition thus had the dual effect of disseminating Chang'an's imperial culture to some regions while elevating local traditions and empowering regional sociocultural networks in others—a process that catapulted Chan monks to positions of significant influence in some southeastern territories.

During the late Tang, multiple warlords were competing for control of southern China, and many of these men naturally sought the sanction and service of leading local clerics. As military conflicts resolved and stable political administrations emerged during the early decades of the tenth century, monks allied with the rulers of new southern kingdoms were awarded imperial honors and appointments to the abbacies of major monasteries. Those aligned with defeated rivals, in contrast, were often relegated to the margins. The ebb and flow of Chan lineages in southeastern China during the late Tang and early Five Dynasties—the fluctuating social and political statures of the disciples of Mazu Daoyi, Dongshan Liangjie, Xuefeng Yicun, and Fayan Wenyi—thus followed the ever-changing contours of political contingencies and patronage networks.

Regional rulers reached out to clerics who were loyal, capable, and close at hand. In Fujian, for example, when the Wang family was based in the southern city of Quanzhou, it initially supported several local clerics affiliated with the Hongzhou school. After the capital of Min was established in Fuzhou, however, the patriarchs of the Wang clan began to patronize Chan monks based in northern Fujian. The most significant of these, as we have seen, was Xuefeng Yicun, a monk who had spent many years in the assembly of a Hongzhou master but claimed the inheritance of Deshan Xuanjian in distant Hunan. Just as effectively as the Wang family deposed Fujian's aristocratic Tang overlords, Xuefeng Yicun and his disciples supplanted members of the imperially honored Hongzhou lineage as the preeminent clerics in the region. The first king of Min and the kingdom's most prominent cleric thus both claimed an authority and an identity independent of Tang precedents.

The close relationship between Min's royal family and members of Xuefeng Yicun's lineage suggests a shift in patterns of imperial patronage. During the Tang, emperors distributed patronage broadly on the basis of clerics' exceptional qualities and capabilities rather than sectarian identities or lineage affiliations. Textual traditions and ritual technologies came in and out of vogue, but imperial patronage rarely passed on to the disciples and grand-disciples of prominent court clerics. Toward the end of the Tang, however, that began to change, as regional rulers in southeastern China channeled resources to monks whose authority and efficacy derived from membership in established lineages.

The premise that the awakened mind of the Buddha had been transmitted directly from master to disciple through an unbroken, undiluted succession of masters meant that members of Chan lineages could be seen as possessed of the same insight and powers as buddhas. With lineage both conferring and confirming authenticity, it followed that the disciples of Chan masters were as capable and qualified to serve the needs of their patrons as their illustrious (and much mythologized) predecessors. Patronage rewarded efficacy and efficacy was linked to ancestry; this routinization of charisma effectively encouraged the institutionalization of patronage.

A kind of monastic aristocracy began to take shape, first in theory and then in practice, whereby a socially and politically privileged class of clerics drew authority and advantage from monastic family connections. The patron-client relationships established among the royal families of southeastern kingdoms and the lineages of Xuefeng Yicun and Xuansha Shibei brought together powerful secular and monastic clans. Like the practice of continuous intermarriage among aristocratic families, this arrangement often endured for generations, as the alliances formed between monarchs and monks were replicated and regularized by their descendants.

Allegiances among royal families and Chan lineages had obvious benefits for monks with the right credentials, but they also bound the fortunes of monastic communities to the fates of their benefactors. The political or economic ruin of major patrons could deprive monks and monasteries of support, and those clerics who had loyally served one regime might be discarded by an incoming administration. Just as some rulers took the precaution of replacing former military commanders and courtiers with trusted allies, some also installed new cadres of monks in the abbacies of major monasteries within their territories. In the kingdom of Min, patronage shifted from Hongzhou monks to Xuefeng Yicun and his disciples, while in the Southern Tang, Xuefeng Yicun's descendants rose into positions formerly dominated by Caodong clerics, and in the early Song, monks from the line of Linji Yixuan came to the fore.

In each instance, rulers installed networks of clerics with no direct ties to the outgoing regime. This changing of the guard was a recurring pattern in the clergy-court relations of southern kingdoms, though a somewhat unpredictable one. While some rulers dismantled or reconstituted inherited power structures, others retained them. The success of Xuefeng Yicun's and Xuansha Shibei's descendants in the Southern Han, the Southern Tang, and Wuyue demonstrates that the most successful monastic factions managed not only to maintain or strengthen their positions during periods of political transition but also to serve rival regimes simultaneously. After several decades in the service of Min's kings and courtiers, members of Xuefeng Yicun's and Xuansha Shibei's lineages had amassed a stock of political and spiritual capital significant enough to elicit the attention of neighboring rulers. No doubt these monks were in demand for the depth of their insights and the dynamism of their teachings, but their presence in the capitals, major cities, and mountain retreats of southeastern states also served to sanction prevailing political orders. Once their networks were established as "imperial" lineages, regional rulers retained members of these lineages as advisors, administrators, and emblems of imperial authority.

For all their ellipses and obfuscations, Buddhist biographical sources do make it possible to chart the formation and dissolution of major regional patronage networks. We can see, for instance, a gradual change in the patronage practices of regional rulers over the course of the Five Dynasties and Ten Kingdoms, transitioning from support for a diverse array of clerics representing a wide range of traditions to the promotion of monks affiliated with one particular lineage, that of Xuansha Shibei. This process was particularly visible in the kingdom of Wuyue, but biographies of prominent monks in that kingdom also reveal continuities in doctrine and practice despite the increasingly privileged positions accorded to a single, interconnected group of Chan clerics. Rather than indicating a transition from ecumenism to sectarianism, then, the data seem to indicate a shift in systems of self-representation, as monks specializing in different disciplines associated with Chan lineages. The strengthening relationship between patronage and lineage gave monks good reason to seek transmission in elite Chan lineage families. The number and diversity of clerics aligning themselves with imperially favored lineages increased exponentially as more and more monks sought the sanction of well-connected clerics whose imprimatur conferred considerable prestige.

In the kingdom of Wuyue, Chan lineage appears to have functioned as a formal network of affiliation, a means of establishing credibility, and a system for safeguarding the integrity of the Buddhist teachings. Senior clerics served as gatekeepers of elite social and institutional networks, promoting monks they deemed most capable of furthering the interests and agendas of the *saṃgha* through training disciples and engaging with the laity. Adoption into a Chan lineage demonstrated that a junior monk had met a senior cleric's expectations and that the two shared the same broad understanding and appreciation of the tradition. It did not necessarily correlate with shared doctrinal interpretations, cultivation techniques, or pedagogical methods. The diversity of teachings and practices among the heirs of Xuefeng Yicun and Xuansha Shibei in the Southern Tang and Wuyue points to a process of expansion and diversification within politically prominent Chan lineages; as lineage identity took on greater significance, talented young monks expanded the epistemological and soteriological range of the movement as a whole.

This ecumenism likely encouraged—and was encouraged by—the support of the court. *Saṃgha*-state relations were never relations between equals, since monks needed rulers much more than rulers needed monks, but they were mutually advantageous. Like other civil servants, monks were supported with the expectation that they were able and willing to serve the interests of the state. The Chan monks patronized by the rulers of southeastern kingdoms were thus both the beneficiaries and the victims of what Peter Brown has described as the "crushing patronage" of lay elites.[2] These men assumed the privileges of court clerics but also invariably accepted the accompanying restrictions and responsibilities.

While the elevation of particular lineages undoubtedly facilitated the spread of those groups' central teachings, as leaders of regional monastic populations, court clerics also necessarily embraced the state's vision of Buddhist orthodoxy and were obliged to respond to the needs of their patrons and their communities. Their teachings and practices naturally came to reflect their regions' prevailing traditions. In cities like Nanjing and Hangzhou that served as centers of literary and artistic culture, for example, Chan monks were involved in preserving, cataloguing, and printing texts; compiling biographical collections and discourse records; writing commentaries and compendia; and composing poetry. They did, in other words, what court clerics were expected to do.

It may finally be impossible to determine whether Chan monks rose to positions of prominence because they best embodied local sensibilities or came to embrace regional traditions as a requisite of their positions, but it is reasonably clear that Chan clerics in southeastern kingdoms moved from the margins to the mainstream ideologically as well as socially, politically, and geographically. The gradual shift in the rhetoric of prominent Chan clerics from the exclusivist position of Xuefeng Yicun and his immediate heirs to the more catholic approach of Fayan Wenyi, Yongming Yanshou, and others seems to reflect a change in presentation, if not perspective, over the course of the tenth century. As these men assumed leadership roles in areas with diverse monastic populations, they muted the polarizing rhetoric characteristic of outsiders and adopted an inclusive approach that stressed both the compatibility of diverse doctrines and practices and the interdependence of the *saṃgha* and the state.

By the early decades of the eleventh century, the descendants of Linji Yixuan had replaced the heirs of Xuefeng Yicun and Xuansha Shibei as the most prominent Chan clerics in the realm. In relatively short order, Linji monks secured powerful benefactors, obtained imperial endorsements for their flame records, and occupied the abbacies of major monasteries throughout the empire. The remarkable success of this group of clerics in the early Song has often been interpreted either as a resumption of the imperial support that Hongzhou monks had enjoyed in the late Tang or as the result of an ideologically charged battle for control of the Chan movement during the early Song. In this latter view, the iconoclastic style of Linji Chan during the Northern Song offered an interpretation of the tradition that was better attuned with the Song vision of cultural revival than was the Tang-inflected, conservative approach of Chan monks from southeastern China.

I have proposed instead that the shift in imperial patronage may have been driven mainly by issues of affiliation and loyalty rather than by preferences in rhetorical styles, modes of practice, or ideologies. This not to say that doctrine and practice were of no concern to lay benefactors but simply to highlight how the politics of patronage influence the development and institutionalization of religious movements and their traditions. Doctrinal debates inevitably occur within socioeconomic, political, and military contexts. As monastic communities representing different traditions of thought and practice were supported by rival political factions and lent them support in return, the outcome of power struggles often determined which monks occupied positions of power and which doctrines were enshrined as orthodoxy.

Philip Jenkins, commenting on the history of Roman Catholicism, observed a similar process in a very different context:

> If religion shaped the political world, then politics forged the character of religion. When we look at what became the church's orthodoxy, so many of those core beliefs gained the status they did as a result of what appears to be historical accident, of the workings of raw chance. . . . This was not a case of one side producing better arguments in its cause, of a deeper familiarity with Scripture or patristic texts: all sides had excellent justifications for their positions. All, equally, produced men and women who practiced heroic asceticism and who demonstrated obvious sanctity. What mattered were the interests and obsessions of rival emperors and queens, the role of competing ecclesiastical princes and their churches, and the empire's military successes or failures against particular barbarian nations.[3]

Jenkins' conclusion that the canonization of Catholic doctrines was often "a political matter, shaped by geographical accident and military success" has some resonance with the history of medieval Chinese Buddhism. From the perspective of patrons, allegiance and loyalty must have been at least as important as ideology. To view the rapid rise of Chan clerics and their traditions as merely an instance of intellectual hegemony gives short shrift to the larger sociopolitical processes at play: the breakdown of centralized rule in the late Tang, the rise of regional powers during the Five Dynasties, and the cultural and political consolidation of the Song dynasty.

In this vein, I have suggested that Linji clerics in the early Song were beneficiaries of Kaifeng's establishment as the northern imperial capital, the dismantling of political and religious networks in southern China, and the appointment of a new secular and clerical leadership to serve the new dynasty. While the lineage affiliations and systems of self-representation championed by Linji clerics were distinct from those of their southern cohorts, their privileged positions within political hierarchies, their roles as arbiters of Buddhist orthodoxy, their strategic deployments of lineage alliances, their literary traditions, and their social and political functions were all quite similar. If lineages convey identity and authority rather than closely guarded traditions of teaching or practice, the rise of the Linji lineage may not indicate an ideological shift in the trajectory of the tradition. By the Northern Song, monks had little incentive to affiliate themselves with the fading Fayan lineage, whose credentials carried little authority. Linji and Yunmen monks, in contrast, served as abbots of major monasteries and commanded the support of powerful and affluent lay benefactors. To choose Linji or Yunmen over Fayan was not necessarily to choose one vision of Chan over another but to choose opportunity over irrelevance, to look to the future rather than the past.

Chan lineages flourished and declined, but the contributions of past generations of Chan monks—the development of genealogies, literary genres, pedagogical styles, and cultivation techniques—were a common heritage. Good ideas are not proprietary, at least not for long. The dissolution of the Tang dynasty initiated a series of changes that ultimately led to the elevation of Chan lineages in southeastern China, while Song unification incorporated and restructured the cultural and material resources of regional powers into the political, social, and economic order of the new empire. Along with traditions of art, architecture, and literature, the Buddhist traditions of southeastern kingdoms were absorbed into Song imperial culture. Chan clerics and Song courtiers thus drew from and expanded on the traditions and institutions they had inherited from their predecessors—and often their fellow countrymen—in Min, the Southern Tang, Wuyue, and elsewhere. The heirs of Xuefeng Yicun and Xuansha Shibei in these kingdoms were at the forefront of developing and popularizing literary forms that came to define the later Chan tradition: flame records, discourse records, collections of questions and responses (*wenda*), and commentaries on past exchanges (*niangu*). These monks were among the first to regularly receive imperial appointments to the abbacies of monasteries that functioned very much like the public Chan monasteries that became ubiquitous in the Song. They were also posted to temples that served

as ancestral shrines for the royal family, just as Chan clerics in the eleventh
century were regularly called to perform funerary rites for the imperial
family and to preside over the ancestral temples of elite lay clans. These
continuities make it reasonably clear that many of the defining features of
the Chan movement in the early Northern Song were, in fact, not innovations but elaborations on traditions and institutions that took shape in the
Buddhist cultures of southeastern China during the Five Dynasties and Ten
Kingdoms.

Finally, lest these conclusions read as declaratives, let me reiterate
that I regard them largely as provisional. As a kind of archeological report
from the archive, this book represents an attempt at reconstruction—a
piecing together of some genuine relics, some reproductions, and no doubt
some forgeries—held together by an act of imagination and will. On
the whole, it offers some answers; more important, it raises a number of
questions.

Monks living in southeastern kingdoms appear to have been the architects or at least the curators of what later became definitive Chan traditions
and institutions, but until we know more about the literary practices, institutional structures, and social and political positions of clerics in other regions we cannot be certain where and when these forms developed, how
they were disseminated, and how they might have evolved over time and
region. We also cannot be certain, at present, of the extent to which the
intellectual affinities, modes of practice, social connections, and geographical distributions of Xuefeng Yicun's and Xuansha Shibei's clerical networks reflect broader trends among monastic populations, both those who
were affiliated with Chan lineages and those who were not. To differentiate between distinctive group identities, regional developments, and larger,
transregional sociocultural patterns would require a comprehensive analysis of all clerics represented in biographical collections, inscriptions, and
secular histories. The development of biographical databases linked with
social-networking software now underway at Dharma Drum Buddhist College may make this Herculean task more manageable in the near future.
In addition, the relative abundance of medieval Chan sources, coupled with
a modern tradition of sectarian scholarship, tends to obscure the real diversity of post-Tang Buddhism. It is easy to forget that Chan monks represented only a very small fraction of the total monastic population. Without
a more complete understanding of the broader religious landscape—not
only other Buddhist clerics but also laypeople, Daoist adepts, philosophers,
diviners, healers, mediums, millenarians, and others—it is difficult to know
how different groups defined and distinguished themselves in relation to
others. Chan clerics may have occupied positions of some prominence during the early Northern Song, but it is significant that the first public Chan
temple in Kaifeng was not established until in 1050, a full ninety years into
the dynasty.[4] Clearly, the Song court relied on other clerics to perform their
requisite ritual functions. A more comprehensive understanding of the Buddhist culture of Kaifeng will help to clarify both the positions Chan monks

occupied in the larger imperial system and the degree to which clergy-court relations in the Song represented a continuation of or departure from the traditions of the late Tang and Five Dynasties.

When that first public Chan monastery was finally inaugurated in the Song capital, the opening ceremonies were reportedly performed "in the style of southern Chan temples."[5] The first abbot, Dajue Huailian 大覺懷璉 (1010–1090), was a native of Fujian and had been called north from Mt. Lu in Jiangxi. Ascending the high seat, he addressed the emperor: "In ancient Buddha halls, there were no different views. In the teachings that circulate, [however,] there are many different expressions. Those who get this always have a marvelous function. Those who miss it are immediately mired in the mud."[6]

In assuming control of a sectarian institution, Huailian stressed the common cause of all Buddhist traditions. While drawing authority and authenticity from southern Chan traditions, he spoke of the universality of the dharma. This book has tried to demonstrate that place, patronage, and lineage played an important part in the success of Chan monks and their teachings, but Huailian surely would have seen things differently. "Creeks, mountains, and the moon in the clouds are all touched by the same wind," he said. "Waters, birds, and forests all manifest the Way." The dharma, in other words, makes no distinctions between north and south, high and low, noble and commoner.

The emperor, we are told, was greatly pleased.

Appendix 1

Members of Xuefeng Yicun's Lineage Supported by the Royal Families of Min, the Southern Tang, and Wuyue

Names are listed alphabetically by generation. Patrons are given after the semicolon: Wang (Min), Li (Southern Tang), and Qian (Wuyue).

1st	2nd	3rd	4th	5th	6th

Xuefeng Yicun 雪峯義存 (822–908); Wang

    Anguo Hongtao 安國弘瑫 (n.d.); Wang

    Baofu Congzhan 保福從展 (d. 928); Wang

        Zhaoqing Wendeng 昭慶文僜 (892–972); Wang

    Changqing Huileng 長慶慧稜 (854–932); Wang

        Guangyun Huijue 光雲慧覺 (n.d.); Wang

        Longhua Qiying 龍華契盈 (n.d.); Qian

        Longhua Yanqiu 龍華彥球 (n.d.); Qian

        Shaozhong Yuanzhi 紹宗圓智 (n.d.); Li

        Zhaoqing Daokuang 招慶道匡 (n.d.); Wang

    Changsheng Jiaoran 長生皎然 (n.d.); Wang

    Cuiyan Lingcan 翠巖令參 (n.d.); Qian

    Daqian Congxi 大錢從襲 (n.d.); Qian

    Erxiang Xingxiu 耳相行脩 (d. 951); Qian

    Fuqing Xuanne 福清玄訥 (n.d.); Wang

    Gushan Shenyan 鼓山神晏 (d. ca. 936–944); Wang

        Baoen Qinghu 報恩清護 (916–970); Wang, Li

        Chongxu Huiwu 沖煦慧悟 (916–974); Li

        Tianzhu Ziyi 天竺子儀 (d. 986); Qian

        Zhizuo Zhenji 智作真寂 (fl. 945); Li

    Helong Miaokong 和龍妙空 (n.d.); Wang

    Huadu Wuzhen 化度悟真 (n.d.); Qian

    Koubing Zaoxian 扣氷藻先 (844–928); Wang

1st 2nd 3rd 4th 5th 6th (*continued*)

Longce Daofu 龍冊道怤 (868–937); Qian

    Wuju Yiyan 烏巨儀晏 (876–990); Qian

Longhua Lingzhao 龍華靈照 (870–947); Qian

Longshou Shaoqing 隆壽紹卿 (n.d.); Wang

Longxing Zongjing 龍興宗靖 (871–954); Qian

Mengbi 夢筆 (n.d.); Wang

Renhui Xingtao 仁慧行瑫 (n.d.); Wang

Siming Wuzuo 四明無作 (d. ca. 907–912); Qian

Xuansha Shibei 玄沙師備 (835–908); Wang

    Huiqiu Jizhao 慧球寂照 (d. 913); Wang

        Luohan Guichen 羅漢桂琛 (867–928); Wang

            Fayan Wenyi 法眼文益 (885–958); Li

                Baoci Wensui 報慈文遂 (fl. 964); Li

                Baoen Huiming 報恩慧明 (d. ca. 954–959); Qian

                Baoen Kuangyi 報恩匡逸 (n.d.); Li

                Baota Shaoyan 寶塔紹巖 (899–971); Qian

                Daguan Zhiyun 達觀智筠 (906–969); Li

                Fa'an Huiji 法安慧濟 (n.d.); Li

                Fadeng Taiqin 法燈泰欽 (d. 974); Li

                Jianfu Shaoming 薦福紹明 (n.d.); Qian

                Lingyin Qingsong 靈隱清聳 (n.d.); Qian

                  Zhiti Bianlong 支提辯隆 (n.d.); Qian

                Tiantai Deshao 天台德韶 (891–972); Qian

                  Baoen Yongan 報恩永安 (911–974); Qian

                  Bore Youchan 般若友蟾 (d. ca. 990–991); Qian

                  Changshou Pengyan 長壽朋彥 (913–961); Qian

                    Changshou Faqi 長壽法齊 (912–1000); Qian

                  Fengxian Qingyu 奉先清昱 (n.d.); Qian

                  Guangping Shouwei 廣平守威 (n.d.); Qian

                  Guangqing Yu'an 光慶遇安 (d. 992); Qian

                  Guanyin Wenqian 觀音文謙 (fl. 964); Qian

                  Kaihua Xingming 開化行明 (932–1001); Qian

                  Longhua Huiju 龍華慧居 (n.d.); Qian

                  Pumen Xibian 普門希辯 (921–997); Qian

                  Wuyun Zhifeng 五雲志逢 (912–986); Qian

                  Yandang Yuanqi 雁蕩願齊 (d. ca. 977–984); Qian

                  Yongming Yanshou 永明延壽 (905–976); Qian

                  Yunmen Zhongyao 雲門重曜 (n.d.); Qian

1st   2nd   3rd   4th   5th   6th (*continued*)

Xuanjue Xingyan 玄覺行言 (n.d.); Li

Yongming Daoqian 永明道潛 (d. 961); Qian

Qianguang Guisheng 千光璟省 (906–972); Qian

Zhangyi Daoqin 章義道欽 (fl. 943–961); Li

Qingliang Xiufu 清涼休復 (d. 951?); Li

Qingxi Hongjin 清谿洪進 (n.d.)

Yuantong Yuande 圓通緣德 (898–977); Li

Yong Xinglu 永興祿 (n.d.); Wang

Zongji Mingzhen 重機明真 (n.d.); Qian

Yongfu Congyan 永福從弇 (n.d.); Wang

Yueshan Shinai 越山師鼐 (n.d.); Wang, Qian

Yunmen Wenyan 雲門文偃 (864–949); Liu

Dongshan Qingbing 洞山清稟 (n.d.); Li

Fengxian Daoshen 奉先道深 (n.d.); Li

Qingliang Zhimeng 清涼智明 (n.d.); Li

Names and Reign Dates for the Rulers of Min, Wu, Southern Tang, and Wuyue

Temple Name	Personal Name	Dates	Reign
Min (909–946), capital at Fuzhou			
Taizu 太祖	Wang Shenzhi 王審知	862–925	909–925
Siwang 嗣土	Wang Yanhan 王延翰	d. 927	925–926
Huizong 惠宗	Wang Yanjun 王延鈞	d. 935	926–935
Kangzong 康宗	Wang Jipeng 王繼鵬	d. 939	935–939
Jingzong 景宗	Wang Yanxi 王延羲	d. 944	939–944
Yindi 殷帝	Wang Yanzheng 王延政	d. 951	944–946
Wu (902–937), capital at Yangzhou			
Taizu 太祖	Yang Xingmi 楊行密	852–905	902–905
Liezu 烈祖	Yang Wo 楊渥	886–908	905–908
Gaozu 高祖	Yang Longyan 楊隆演	897–920	908–920
Ruidi 睿帝	Yang Pu 楊溥	900–938	920–937
Southern Tang (937–975), capital at Nanjing			
Liezu 烈祖	Xu Zhigao 徐知誥 (a.k.a. Li Bian 李昪)	889–943	937–943
Yuanzong 元宗	Li Jing 李璟	916–961	943–961
Last Ruler 後主	Li Yu 李煜	937–978	961–975
Wuyue (907–978), capital at Hangzhou			
Wusu 武肅	Qian Liu 錢鏐	852–932	907–932
Wenmu 文穆	Qian Yuanguan 錢元瓘	887–941	932–941
Zhongxian 忠獻	Qian Zuo 錢佐	928–947	941–947
Zhongxun 忠遜	Qian Zong 錢倧	n.d.	947
Zhongyi 忠懿	Qian Chu 錢俶	929–988	948–978

Appendix 3

Names and Reign Dates for the Rulers of Northern Dynasties

Temple Name	Personal Name	Life Dates	Reign
Tang (618–907), capitals at Chang'an and Luoyang			
Wuzong 武宗	Li Yan 李炎	814–846	840–846
Xuanzong 宣宗	Li Chen 李忱	810–859	846–859
Yizong 懿宗	Li Cui 李漼	833–873	859–873
Xizong 僖宗	Li Xuan 李儇	862–888	873–888
Zhaozong 昭宗	Li Ye 李曄	867–904	888–904
Aidi 哀帝	Li Zhu 李柷	892–908	904–907
Liang (907–923), capital at Kaifeng			
Taizu 太祖	Zhu Wen 朱溫	852–912	907–912
Prince of Ying 郢王	Zhu Yougui 朱友珪		912–913
Modi 末帝	Zhu Youzhen 朱友貞	888–923	913–923
Later Tang (923–937), capital at Luoyang			
Taizu 太祖	Li Keyong 李克用	856–908	
Zhuangzong 莊宗	Li Cunxu 李存勖	885–926	923–926
Mingzong 明宗	Li Siyuan 嗣源	867–933	926–933
Mindi 閔帝	Li Conghou 李從厚	914–937	933–934
Feidi 廢帝	Li Congke 李從珂	887–937	934–936
Jin (937–947), capital at Kaifeng			
Gaozu 高祖	Shi Jingtang 石敬瑭	892–942	936–942
Chudi 出帝	Shi Chonggui 石重貴	b. 914	942–946

(continued)

Temple Name	Personal Name	Life Dates	Reign
Han (947–951), capital at Kaifeng			
Gaozu 高祖	Liu Zhiyuan 劉知遠	895–948	947–948
Yindi 隱帝	Liu Chengyou 劉承祐	932–951	948–950
Duke of Xiangyin 湘陰公	Liu Yun 劉贇	d. 951	951
Later Zhou (951–960), capital at Kaifeng			
Taizu 太祖	Guo Wei 郭威	904–954	951–954
Shizong 世宗	Chai Rong 柴榮	921–959	954–959
Gongdi 恭帝	Chai Zongxun 柴宗訓	953–973	959
Northern Song (960–1127), capital at Kaifeng			
Taizu 太祖	Zhao Kuangyin 趙匡胤	927–976	960–976
Taizong 太宗	Zhao Kuangyi 趙匡義	939–997	976–997
Zhenzong 真宗	Zhao Heng 趙恆	968–1022	997–1022
Renzong 仁宗	Zhao Zhen 趙禎	1010–1063	1022–1063

Appendix 4

Buddhist Texts Printed
in the Kingdom of Wuyue

	Text/Image	Printer	Date	Location	Number
1	Depictions of the Nine Levels of the Western [Pure] Land 西方九品變相	Yanshou 延壽			100,000
2	Stupa images 塔圖	Wang Chengyi 王承益	976		
3	Amitābha stupa images 彌陀塔圖	Yanshou			140,000
4	Amitābha Sūtra 彌陀經	Yanshou	972		
5	Sūtra on the Contemplation of the Buddha of Infinite Life 佛說觀無量壽佛經		ca. 960	Fachang yuan? 法昌院	
6	Abridged Biographies [of those who obtained] Auspicious Responses and Rebirth in the Western Pure Land 往生西方淨土瑞應刪傳*	Daoshen 道詵		Yongxin chanyuan 永心禪院†	
7	Sūtra of Perfect Enlightenment 大方廣圓覺修多羅了義經		ca. 960	Fachang yuan?	
8	Golden Light Sūtra 金光明經		ca. 960	Fachang yuan?	
9	Avataṃsaka Sūtra with [Li Tongxuan's] Commentary 華嚴經合論	Yongan 永安		Baoen guangjiao si 報恩光教寺	
10	Śūraṃgama Sūtra 楞嚴經	Yanshou	ca. 939		
11	Lotus Sūtra 法華經	Yanshou	ca. 939		
12	Guanyin Sūtra 觀音經	Yanshou	ca. 939		
13	Guanyin Sūtra 佛說觀世音經		ca. 960	Fachang yuan	
14	Image of the twenty-four manifestations of Guanyin 二十四應觀音像	Yanshou, Qian Chu 錢俶	974		20,000
15	Bodhisattva Names 菩薩名	Yanshou			100,000

No.	Title	Compiler	Copies	Date	Location
16	Buddha-uṣṇīṣa-dhāraṇī 佛頂咒 (a.k.a. Śuraṃgama-dhāraṇī 楞嚴咒)	Yanshou		ca. 939	
17	Great Compassion dhāraṇī 大悲咒	Yanshou		ca. 939	
18	Mahāmāyūrī-dhāraṇī 孔雀王咒	Yanshou	100,000		
19	Dhāraṇī for Eradicating Disaster 消災咒	Yanshou	100,000		
20	Dhāraṇī for Gathering Blessings 集福咒	Yanshou	100,000		
21	Dhāraṇī of Vairocana, Eliminator of Evil Rebirths 毘盧遮那滅惡趣咒	Yanshou	100,000		
22	Dhāraṇī of Akṣobhya Buddha 阿閦佛咒	Yanshou			
23	The Dhāraṇī Sūtra of the Seal on the Precious Casket of the Secret Whole-Body Relic of the Mind of All Tathāgatas 一切如來心祕密全身舍利寶篋印陀羅尼經	Qian Chu	84,000	956, 965, 975	
24	Notes on the Rhapsody of Mind 心賦注	Yanshou			
25	Chart of the Heart of the Dharma Realm 法界心圖	Yanshou			
26	Discourse Record of the Monk Touzi 投子和尚語錄	Yanshou	70,000	961	Mt. Mao 鄮山, Siming 四明

Notes:

* This appears to be the same text as *Taishō shinshū daizōkyō*, 51n2070, which was taken from Wuyue to Japan by the Japanese monk Nichien 日延 (fl. 945)—the cleric responsible for returning the lost Tiantai texts—in the 950s.

† I suspect that this may be the same temple as Shuixin si 水心寺, previously mentioned in connection with Shaoyan's biography. In addition to similarities in the two temples' names, Shaoyan, like the monks included in this collection, was famed for his attempts to gain rebirth in the Pure Land.

Items 5, 7, 8, and 13 were found in 1960 in the ruins of a stupa in Bihuzhen 碧湖鎮, Zhejiang. (See Zhao, "Wudai shiqi diaoban yinshua shiye de fazhan," 163.) Items 1, 3–4, 10–12, 14–22, and 24–25 are all recorded in an 1160 reprint of Yongming Yanshou's *Notes on the Rhapsody of Mind*. Copies of item 2 were found after the collapse of the Leifeng stupa but have since disappeared. A copy of item 6 is preserved in Japan. (See Zhang, "Wudai Wuyue guo de yinshua," 74–76.) Item 23 exists in multiple copies of different printings. (See Baba, "*Hōkyō inkyō* no denpa to tenkai"; Edgren, "The Printed Dhāraṇī Sūtra of A.D. 956"; and E. Wang, "Tope and Topos.") Details regarding the printing of Touzi's discourse record are given in *Guzunsu yulu*, 237c23–238a8.

Appendix 5

Members of Linji Yixuan's Lineage Supported by Song Officials

Members of Linji Yixuan's lineage beginning with the third generation. Song officials shown in bold; patrons listed after the semicolon; disciples listed below.

3rd 4th 5th 6th 7th

Fengxue Yanzhao 風穴延沼 (886–973); **Li Shijun** 李史君 (n.d.), **Song Yanyun** 宋彥筠 (879–956).

    Shoushan Shengnian 首山省念 (926–993)

        Fenyang Shanzhao 汾陽善昭 (946–1023); **Li Chongze** 李充則 (fl. 1021–1026), **Liu Changyan** 劉昌言 (942–999), **Zhang Maozong** 張茂宗 (fl. 991).

            Cuiyan Shouzhi 翠巖守芝 (n.d.); **Li Mijian** 李密諫 (fl. 1026), **Yang Yi** 楊億 (974–1020).

            Shishuang Chuyuan 石霜楚圓 (986–1039); **Huang Zongdan** 黃宗旦 (*jinshi*, 998–1003), **Li Zunxu** 李遵勖 (988–1038), **Yang Yi.**

                Yang Tian 楊畋 (1007–1062)

        Guanghui Yuanlian 廣慧元璉 (951–1036); **Wang Shu** 王曙 (963–1034), **Xu Shi** 許式 (n.d.).

            Yang Yi

        Guyin Yuncong 谷隱蘊聰 (965–1032); **Cha Dao** 查道 (955–1018).

            Jinshan Tanying 金山曇潁 (989–1060); **Diao Jingchun** 刁景純 (n.d.), **Wang Shu**, **Xia Song** 夏竦 (985–1051), **Yang Yi.**

                Li Duanyuan 李端愿 (d. 1091)

            Li Zunxu

            Wang Shu

            Xia Song

3rd   4th   5th   6th   7th (*continued*)

Lumen Huizhao 鹿門慧昭 (n.d.); **Xu Shi**

Sanjiao Zhisong 三交智嵩 (n.d.); **Zhang Yongde** 張永德
(928–1000), **Zheng Gongbu** 鄭工部 (n.d.).

Wang Sui 王隨 (973–1039)

Notes

Introduction

1. Some of these issues have been addressed elsewhere. For a discussion of Daoism and local cults in Fujian, see Clark, "The Religious Culture in the Minnan Region of Southern Fujian through the Middle Period (750–1450)." The religious world of the Southern Tang official Xu Xuan 徐鉉 (917–992) has been treated in detail in Woolley, "Religion and Politics in the Writings of Xu Xuan." For an analysis of Buddhism, Daoism, and other religious traditions as reflected in the writings of the tenth-century literatus Sun Guangxian 孫光憲 (896–968), see Halperin, "Heroes, Rogues, and Religion in a Tenth-Century Chinese Miscellany." Finally, Suzuki Tetsuo, Yang Zengwen, and Tsuchiya Taisuke have all discussed some of the salient doctrinal developments of Chan during the late Tang and Five Dynasties and Ten Kingdoms.

2. Foulk, "Prolegomenon," in "Histories of Zen," 35–36.

3. Foulk, "The Ch'an Tsung in Medieval China," 28–29.

4. For a discussion of official historiographical representations of the Five Dynasties, see Liu P., "Zhengtong lunxia de Wudai shiguan."

5. *Xin Wudai shi*, 467. Translations from this text are from Davis, *Historical Records of the Five Dynasties*. Unless otherwise noted, all other translations are my own.

6. On the influence of Naka Michiyo's work in China, see Hon, "Educating the Citizens." For an overview of modern Japanese historiography, see Tanaka, *Japan's Orient*.

7. Naka Michiyo's periodization scheme was also adopted in the influential *Newest Chinese History Textbook for Middle School* (*Zuixin zhongxue Zhongguo lishi jiaokeshu* 最新中學中國歷史教科書, 1904) written by the prominent Chinese historian and Buddhist layman Xia Zengyou 夏曾佑 (1863–1924).

8. See Hiyazuki, "An Outline of the Naitō Hypothesis"; and Fogel, *Politics and Sinology*, 168–199.

9. For representative examples, see Eberhard, *A History of China*; and Gernet, *A History of Chinese Civilization*.

10. Hu, *The Chinese Renaissance*, 45, 78–93; and Hu, "Religion and Philosophy in Chinese History," 27. See also McRae, "Religion as Revolution in Chinese Historiography."

11. A similar sentiment was expressed by some secular historians in Japan. In "Tōyō no runessansu to seiyō no runessansu" (Eastern Renaissance and Western Renaissance), the prominent sinologist Miyazaki Ichisada 宮崎市定 (1901–1995) also identified the Song as the beginning of modern China and compared Neo-Confucianism's triumph over Buddhism with the revival of the Greek classics in Italy. See Hiyazuki, "An Outline of the Naitō Hypothesis."

12. Hu, "Religion and Philosophy in Chinese History," 49.

13. Hu, "Ch'an (Zen) Buddhism in China," 17.

14. Hu, "Religion and Philosophy in Chinese History," 54–55. As is well known, several leading scholars of Chinese religion and history in Europe and the United States also presumed that Buddhism after the Tang was intellectually exhausted. Erik Zürcher, to cite just one example, once suggested that the shift to Confucianism in the Song "ultimately reduced Buddhism to a despised creed of the lower classes" (*Buddhism*, 6). John Fairbank's *China: A New History* informs readers that "the splendor of the Tang and of Chinese Buddhism declined together" (86).

15. For a summary of Japanese scholars' views on the ossification of Chan during the Song, see Foulk, "Prolegomenon," in "Histories of Zen," 79–82.

16. Exceptions include Eric Cunningham's *Zen: Past and Present*, published by the Association for Asian Studies as part of its Key Issues in Asian Studies series. In China, the Museum of Chinese Buddhist Culture (Zhongguo Fojiao wenhua bowuguan 中国佛教文化博物馆), built in Yangzhou in 2008, has an exhibit titled "Evolution of Buddhism in China," which identifies the Sui-Tang period as "the prime," the Song-Yuan era as "past the prime," and the Ming and Qing dynasties as having fallen into "decay and desacralization."

17. See Faure, *The Rhetoric of Immediacy* and "Chan and Zen Studies"; Sharf, "The Zen of Japanese Nationalism"; and McRae, "Buddhism."

18. See Abe, *Chūgoku Zenshū shi no kenkyū*; Ishii, *Sōdai Zenshūshi no kenkyū*; Foulk, "The 'Ch'an School,'" "Myth, Ritual, and Monastic Practice," and "Sung Controversies"; Gregory and Getz, *Buddhism in the Sung*; Welter, "A Buddhist Response to the Confucian Revival"; and Schlütter, *How Zen Became Zen*.

19. Records of the transmission of the flame (a.k.a. records of the transmission of the lamp) purport to document the unbroken transmission of the awakened mind of Śākyamuni Buddha to later generations of monastics, just as the flame from a single lamp can be used to light a succession of other lamps.

20. Welter, "A Buddhist Response to the Confucian Revival."

21. Schlütter, *How Zen Became Zen*.

22. Schlütter, *How Zen Became Zen*, 49–50; Welter, "A Buddhist Response to the Confucian Revival," 162; Foulk, "Prolegomenon," in "Histories of Zen," 36.

23. On the Ten Kingdoms in general, see Clark, "The Southern Kingdoms." On the Southern Tang, see Kurz, *China's Southern Tang Dynasty*; and Tackett, "The Transformation of Medieval Chinese Elites." On Shu, see Verellen, "Liturgy and Sovereignty," "A Forgotten T'ang Restoration," and "Shu as Hallowed Land"; and Shields, *Crafting a Collection*. On Min, see Schafer, *The Empire of Min*; and Clark, "Quanzhou (Fujian) during the Tang-Song Interregnum," *Community, Trade, and Networks*, "The Religious Culture in the Minnan Region," and *Portrait of a Community*. On Wuyue, see Chavannes, "Le Royaume de Wou et de Yue"; and Worthy, "Diplo-

macy for Survival." On the political histories of the northern dynasties, see Wang G., *Divided China*; Hon, "Military Governance versus Civil Governance"; Fang, "Power Structures and Cultural Identities"; and, most recently, Standen, "The Five Dynasties."

24. Welter, *Monks, Rulers, and Literati*, 162.

25. For a summary of extant and lost historical sources for the Five Dynasties and Ten Kingdoms, see Kurz, "A Survey of Historical Sources." Kurz's "Sources for the History of the Southern Tang" also provides a detailed discussion of Southern Tang sources. Nicolas Tackett has compiled a list of inscriptions dating from the late Tang through the end of the Five Dynasties, though his survey unfortunately omits Buddhist inscriptions. See Tackett, *Tomb Epitaphs from the Tang-Song Transition*.

26. The date "tenth year of the Baoda era of [Nan]tang" [南]唐保大十年 (952) occurs five times throughout the *Patriarch's Hall Collection*, all within the first two fascicles. The monk Wendeng, who wrote a preface for the text, was awarded the name Chan Master Zhenjue 真覺禪師 during the Song, but this title in not mentioned in the text, which records Wendeng's biography only up until the year 949. For these reasons, Yanagida Seizan and others initially concluded that the present version of the text must have been completed by 952. See, for example, Yanagida, "*Sodōshū* no shiryō kachi," 35–36.

27. For summaries of the early development of Chan lineages, see Adamek, *The Mystique of Transmission*, chap. 5; and Morrison, *The Power of Patriarchs*, chap. 2.

28. Yanagida, "*Sodōshū* no shiryō kachi," "*Sodōshū* no honbun kenkyū (I)," *Sodōshū*, and *Zenrin sōhōden yakuchū*; Kinugawa, "*Sodōshū* no kōri" and "*Senshū senbutsu shinjaku sho soshi ju* to *Sodōshū*"; Ishii, "*Senshū Fukusen Shōkei in no Jōshu Zenji Shōtō* to *Sodōshū*"; and Welter, *Monks, Rulers, and Literati*. See also Anderl, *Studies in the Language of Zu-tang ji*; and Jorgensen, *Inventing Hui-neng, the Sixth Patriarch*, 729–752.

29. *Song gaoseng zhuan*, 818c7–8; and *Jingde chuan deng lu*, 360b13–15.

30. On Daoyuan, see Ishii, *Sōdai Zenshūshi no kenkyū*, 26–44.

31. As Welter has noted, the text underwent several revisions after it was first completed by Daoyuan in 1004. Neither Daoyuan's original text nor Yang Yi's initial revision survives. The earliest edition, now kept at Tōji 東寺 in Kyoto, dates from a 1080 printing from Dongchan si 東禪寺 in Fuzhou. A second edition of the *Transmission of the Flame* was included in the *Sibu congkan* 四部叢刊. This version, which is also the one reproduced in the Taishō canon, dates to 1316 but appears to be based on the now lost Sijian 思鑒 woodblock edition of 1134. Despite the fact that the Dongchan si edition predates that of the *Sibu congkan* text, textual analysis suggests that the latter may actually be closer to the original work than the former. See Welter, *Monks, Rulers, and Literati*, 116–118.

32. See, e.g., Yang Z., *Tang Wudai Chanzong shi*, 600–601.

33. *Jingde chuan deng lu*, 196c23–25; translated in Welter, *Monks, Rulers, and Literati*, 180.

34. For classic examples of this process, see Faure's "Bodhidharma as Textual and Religious Paradigm" on Bodhidharma and Jorgensen's *Inventing Hui-neng, the Sixth Patriarch* on Huineng. As Mark Halperin has noted, the historical accuracy of

Chan genealogies was also doubted by some tenth-century literati. Halperin, "Heroes, Rogues, and Religion in a Tenth-Century Chinese Miscellany," 436.

35. These numbers represent the actual number of biographies found in the work, which are slightly different from those mentioned in Yang Yi's preface.

36. On Zanning, see Dalia, "The 'Political Career' of the Buddhist Historian Tsan-ning"; Welter, "A Buddhist Response to the Confucian Revival"; and Makita, "Kunshu dokusai shakai ni okeru Bukkyōdan no tachiba (jō)" and "Sannei to sono jidai."

37. *Song gaoseng zhuan*, 709c23–26; translated in Kieschnick, *The Eminent Monk*, 60.

38. On Song dynasty representations of Buddhist monks and regional rulers of the Five Dynasties and Ten Kingdoms, see Brose, "Credulous Kings and Immoral Monks."

39. For an overview of the prosopographical method and a collection of case studies, see Keats-Rohan, *Prosopography Approaches and Applications*. Anne Gerritsen has assessed the applicability of prosopography for middle-period China in "Prosopography and Its Potential for Middle Period Research." The most significant prosopographical database for China is maintained by Peter Bol and his team at Harvard's China Biographical Database Project (http://isites.harvard.edu/icb/icb .do?keyword=k16229). This database does not at present include information on monastics.

40. Stone, "Prosopography," 46–47.

41. Wetherell, "Historical Social Network Analysis," 126. For an overview of the networks approach and its application in the field of religious studies, see Vásquez, "Studying Religion in Motion." Jason Neelis has recently demonstrated the potential of this method for Buddhist studies in his *Early Buddhist Transmission and Trade Networks*.

42. For a discussion of secular biographical writing during the tenth century, see Kurz, "Biographical Writing in Tenth-Century China." Kurz argues that, although the form of biographies was standardized, the contents were idiosyncratic.

43. Certeau, *The Writing of History*, 276.

44. On the central motifs of Buddhist hagiography, see Kieschnick, *The Eminent Monk*.

45. For a discussion of the historical value and biases of canonical sources, see Zürcher, "Perspectives in the Study of Chinese Buddhism."

46. Gernet, *A History of Chinese Civilization*, 295.

1: Disintegration

1. *Xin Wudai shi*, 363–365.

2. Zhu Wen affected shock when he heard about the murders. He then had Li Yanwei executed.

3. The most comprehensive English-language accounts of this era are Standen, "The Five Dynasties"; and Clark, "The Southern Kingdoms between the T'ang and the Sung."

4. For the standard account of the fall of the Tang dynasty, see Somers, "The End of the T'ang." The impact of late Tang political and economic changes on the

Tang aristocracy is discussed in Tackett, *The Destruction of the Medieval Chinese Aristocracy*.

5. Tackett, *The Destruction of the Medieval Chinese Aristocracy*, chap. 4.

6. On taxation during the Tang, see Twitchett, *Financial Administration under the T'ang Dynasty*, chap. 2.

7. Somers, "The End of the T'ang," 720.

8. Wei Zhuang 韋莊 (d. 910), "Lament of Lady of Qin"; translated in Yates, *Washing Silk*, 111–112.

9. Hartwell, "Demographic, Political, and Social Transformations of China," 369, table 1; and Clark, *Community, Trade, and Networks*.

10. *Lunyu*, 2:1.

11. For a discussion of conceptions of loyalty during the Five Dynasties and earlier eras, see Standen, *Unbounded Loyalty*, esp. chap. 2.

12. On the founding patriarchs of the Southern Kingdoms, see Clark, "Scoundrels, Rogues, and Refugees."

13. *Xin Wudai shi*, 572.

14. Ibid., 505. In "Images of the South in Ouyang Xiu's Historical Records of the Five Dynasties," Richard L. Davis discusses Ouyang Xiu's portrayals of southern rulers.

15. For an overview of the history of the former and latter Shu, see Shields, *Crafting a Collection*, 78–89.

16. *Zizhi tongjian*, 266:8685; translated in Shields, *Crafting a Collection*, 83.

17. The substantial source material pertaining to the life of Qian Liu has been collected and punctuated by Qian Ji'e 錢濟鄂. For the standard Song-dynasty history of Wuyue, see *Xin Wudai shi*, 561–572. For an overview of the history of Wuyue, see Chavannes, "Le Royaume de Wou et de Yue." Henri Maspero visited Zhejiang in 1914 and published a detailed archaeological report of the region in the same year: "Rapport sommaire sur une mission archéologique au Tchö-Kiang." Wuyue's diplomatic relations are discussed in Worthy, "Diplomacy for Survival."

18. Nicolas Tackett estimates that more than four-fifths of the populations of the prefectures of Runzhou and Changzhou may have died during the five-year period (887–892) when Qian Liu, Yang Xingmi 楊行密 (852–905), and Sun Ru 孫儒 (d. 892) battled for control of the region. See Tackett, *The Destruction of the Medieval Chinese Aristocracy*, 214.

19. The iron pledge is now kept in a shrine to the Qian family on the eastern shore of West Lake in Hangzhou. For an image and description of the pledge, see National Museum of Chinese History, *Sui Dynasty to Northern and Southern Song Dynasties*, 214–215.

20. The names Wu and Yue designated different states as far back as the Spring and Autumn period (ca. 770–476 BCE). Wu had its capital in present-day Suzhou while Yue's capital was in Shaoxing. Since the Han dynasty, this region—corresponding roughly to modern southern Jiangsu and northern Zhejiang provinces—was referred to collectively as Wuyue.

21. The Yangzi traverses China from east to west, beginning in Sichuan and terminating at the coast of Jiangsu. It also provides access to southern China and southeast Asia through two important tributaries: the Gan River 贛江, which links

northern Guangzhou to Jiangxi, and the Xiang River 湘江 further west, which begins in northern Guangxi, passes through Hunan, and terminates in the Yangzi at the southern border of Hubei.

22. For transportation during the Five Dynasties, see Hino, "Godai nanboku Shina rikujō kōtsūro ni tsuite." A brief summary of Hino's findings can be found in Clark, "The Southern Kingdoms between the T'ang and the Sung," 178–183.

23. Wuyue's population totalled approximately 550,700 households distributed among 13 prefectures and 86 sub-prefectures. At its height, its territory corresponded to present-day Zhejiang as well as Jiangsu south of the mouth of the Yangzi and east of Lake Tai and the northeast quadrant of Fujian, including Fuzhou (appended in 947). See Worthy, "Diplomacy for Survival." 19.

24. For the standard historical account of Wu, see *Xin Wudai shi*, 467–485. The background of Wu's and Southern Tang's secular elites is discussed in Tackett, "The Transformation of Medieval Chinese Elites." Other important recent studies of Southern Tang history and culture in English include Woolley, "Religion and Politics in the Writings of Xu Xuan"; Sun, "Rewriting the Southern Tang"; and Kurz, *China's Southern Tang Dynasty.*

25. The *Song gaoseng zhuan* (771c28–772a17) portrays Gao Pian as a pious lay Buddhist and claims that he observed a vegetarian diet for more than twenty years. When his granddaughter was promised in marriage to a military commissioner from Shu, the wedding ceremony entailed the customary butchering of animals for the feast. Gao was pressured by his relatives to exempt the guests from his own strictures, but he did not make up his mind before the animals were killed. For this offense, we are told, Gao fell into hell but was soon spared because of his ability to recite Buddhist texts.

26. *Xin Wudai shi*, 468; translation modified from that of Richard L. Davis.

27. The full title was *Da chengxiang dudu zhongwai zhu junshi* 大丞相都督中外諸軍事.

28. *Xin Wudai shi*, 480.

29. Before reunification under the Sui (581–618), Jinling had served as the capital of various southern kingdoms over the course of several centuries: Wu (222–280), Eastern Jin (317–420), Liu Song (420–479), Southern Qi (479–502), Liang (502–557), and Chen (557–589).

30. *Nantang shu* (Ma), 1:1b; translation modified from Clark, "The Southern Kingdoms between the T'ang and the Sung," 161. For similar sentiments, see *Xin Wudai shi*, 487.

31. Kurz, *China's Southern Tang Dynasty*, 18.

32. Incidentally, Li Bian's brothers (by adoption), Xu Zhizheng 徐知證 and Xu Zhie 徐知諤, were the focus of a spirit-medium cult based in Fujian during the Northern Song. See Schipper and Verellun, *The Taoist Canon*, 1210–1216.

33. The Kingdom of Min comprised five prefectures, listed here with their respective number of households as of 980: Fu 福 (94,475); Quan 泉 (76,851); Zhang 漳 (41,662); Jian 建 (90,492); and Ding 汀 (24,007). Census numbers given in the *Taiping huanyuji* 太平寰宇記; cited in Clark, *Community, Trade, and Networks*, 59.

34. For the standard history of Min, see the *Xin Wudai shi*, 573–584. Edward Schafer's *The Empire of Min* also includes a wealth of information, especially related to the political and material cultures of the kingdom.

35. In terms of seniority, Wang Shenzhi's older brother Wang Shengui 王審邦 (ca. 858–904) should have succeeded Wang Chao, but he remained in Quanzhou, allowing Shenzhi to head the emerging state. This unorthodox succession later led to fratricidal feuds among branches of the Wang family. See chap. 3.

36. Population statistics for Fujian gathered by Robert Hartwell show a general reduction in numbers from the early eighth century to the early ninth, followed by a significant rise in the tenth and eleventh centuries. Fuzhou is listed with a population of 38,200 households (with one household equaling approximately five individuals) in 720; 94,500 in 980; and 211,600 in 1080. More than half the population in 980 was composed of immigrants, according to the *Taiping huanyuji*. As often noted, the population boom in the tenth century coincided with the introduction of new rice strains to Fujian from Cambodia. See Hartwell, "Demographic, Political, and Social Transformations of China," 428, 390n22. On the economic development of Min, see Clark, *Community, Trade, and Networks* and *Portrait of a Community*; and Schottenhammer, "Local Politico-Economic Particulars of the Quanzhou Region."

37. *Xin Wudai shi*, 574–575.

38. Schafer, *The Empire of Min*, 34.

39. The same approach was employed by Wang Shenzhi's elder brother in Quanzhou. According to his biography in the *Xin Tang shu* (190:15a), Wang Shengui "was a fine civil administrator; he loaned oxen and ploughs to returned refugees, and boarding houses were built and kept in perfect shape. When Northern China was in a chaotic state, a large number of government officials were accommodated in [these buildings] and given financial assistance." Translation adapted from Aoyama, "The Newly-Risen Bureaucrats in Fukien at the Five Dynasty-Sung Period," 3.

40. *Wang Shenzhi dezheng beiming*.

41. *Zhongyi wang miao beiwen*.

42. *Wuyue beishi*, 1:18b–19a. The *Wuyue beishi*, the earliest reference to this story that I am aware of, does not name the monk, but in later accounts, such as that contained in *Shuo fu*, 17(下):45a, the prophet is identified as a cleric from Suishi 碎石僧. The *Jingde chuan deng lu* (308c29) lists a monk by this name as a disciple of Shitou Xiqian 石頭希遷 (701–791).

43. Another monk, Zhiguang 智廣 (n.d.), is credited with foretelling the length of the Wang family's reign with an augury of his own: "Riding a horse they come, riding a horse they go." The statement was interpreted to mean that Wang Chao would seize control of Min in the *bingwu* 丙午 year of the Guangqi 光啟 era (886) and lose control on the *bingwu* year of the Baoda 保大 era (946), both of which were "horse" years according to the Chinese zodiac. See *Quan Tang shi*, 878:10b; and *Shiguo chunqiu*, 99:1b.

44. Kieschnick, *The Eminent Monk*, 76.

45. In 923 Wang Shenzhi sent his second-born son to Luoyang to offer tribute to the newly established court of the Later Tang. The son was held hostage in the capital until 926, when the Later Tang emperor Mingzong 明宗 (r. 926–933) came to power. Following his father's death, Shenzhi's son shaved his head, donned monk's robes, and fled to Sichuan. With the new name of Xingzun 行遵 (fl. 923–944),

he took up residence at Guangguo Cloister 光國院 in Langzhou 閬州. According to the *Song gaoseng zhuan*, the monks there were at first skeptical of his intentions but eventually came to admire his powers of prognostication (850b14–c3).

46. *Fujian tongzhi* 福建通志 (1867); cited in Schafer, *The Empire of Min*, 16, 92.

47. *Song gaoseng zhuan*, 782b13.

48. Tackett, *The Destruction of the Medieval Chinese Aristocracy*, 218.

2: Improvisation

1. Ch'en, *Buddhism in China*, 232.

2. Variations on this theme can be found in Hu, "Ch'an (Zen) Buddhism in China," 18; Yanagida, "The Life of Lin-chi I-hsuan," 61–63; Ch'en, *Buddhism in China*, 363; Dumoulin, *India and China*, 212–213; Weinstein, *Buddhism under the T'ang*, 148–150; Wright, *Studies in Chinese Buddhism*, 83–85; de Bary, *East Asian Civilizations*, 45; Yampolsky, *The Platform Sūtra of the Sixth Patriarch*, 56–57; Jia, *The Hongzhou School of Chan Buddhism*, 116; Welter, *Monks, Rulers, and Literati*, 9–10; and Suzuki T., *Seppō*, 31–37.

3. During the Tang, the Jiangnan region was divided into eastern and western circuits. Together they were bordered on the north by the Yangzi River and on the east by the East China Sea. To the south, they extended approximately to the present southern borders of Fujian, Jiangxi, and Hunan provinces, and to the west they reached the present western border of Hunan province.

4. Yan G., "Tang dai pian," 56–57.

5. Textual references to temples before and after the Huichang persecutions (755–845 and 846–907) gathered by Li Yinghui indicate that temple numbers decreased in almost every region of China after Wuzong's purge, though these numbers are probably too low to be statistically relevant. Li, *Tangdai Fojiao dili yanjiu*, 95.

6. Translated in Weinstein, *Buddhism under the T'ang*, 142.

7. For Zhixuan's biography, see the *Song gaoseng zhuan*, 743b5–744c14.

8. The tradition of clerics receiving purple robes from the emperor originated in 690, when Wu Zetian 武則天 (r. 690–705) gave purple robes to the monks responsible for associating her with Maitreya and the *Da yun jing* 大雲經. After Wu Zetian's reign, the tradition was reinstituted by Tang emperor Xuanzong. Subsequently, it became common practice for emperors to award purple robes to high-ranking monastic officials or other highly regarded clerics. On monks' robes in China, see Kieschnick, "The Symbolism of the Monk's Robe in China"; and Adamek, "Robes Purple and Gold."

9. According to his *Song Biography*, Zhixuan composed a total of three hundred thousand words, including the *Combined Commentary and Explanation to the Sūtra of the Repository of the Tathāgata* (*Rulaizang jing hui shi shu* 如來藏經會釋疏) in two fascicles, the *Commentary to the Great Sūtra of Life Everlasting* (*Da wuliangshou jing shu* 大無量壽經疏) in two fascicles, a *Commentary on the Sūtra of the Supreme Victor* (*Shengman jing shu* 勝鬘經疏) in four fascicles, commentaries on the *Heart Sūtra* and the *Diamond Sūtra*, texts on ritual and confession, and "miscellaneous Buddhist writings, treatises on key points in non-Buddhist literature, stele inscriptions, songs,

and poetry." *Song gaoseng zhuan*, 744b28–c5. Sengche, in addition to writing several subcommentaries on Zhixuan's work, also narrated three volumes of *Notes on the Law* (*Fa chao* 法鈔). Enchin's catalogue records texts collected in China between 853 and 858. See *Nihon biku Enchin nittō guhō mokuroku*, 1097b6–1101c26.

10. One of the most prominent monks of the late Tang period, the tantric master Zhihuilun 智慧輪 (Pranjñacakra, d. 875/6), served as both monastic recorder on the left in the capital and national teacher under Emperor Xizong. Zhihuilin provided many of the offerings that were later discovered in the famous crypt of Famen si, demonstrating the continued prominence of esoteric traditions in the capital long after the Huichang persecutions. *Song gaoseng zhuan*, 723a4–12; and Orzech, "After Amoghavajra," 328–330.

11. A passage from the memoir of Wang Renyu 王仁裕 (880–956) claims that several thousand monks were executed by the Tang army out of suspicion that they were aiding the rebels. See Dudbridge, *A Portrait of Five Dynasties China*, 45.

12. Hartwell, "Demographic, Political, and Social Transformations of China," 369–371.

13. According to the population data gathered and analyzed by Robert Hartwell, at the mid-point of the Tang dynasty, in 744, the regions of greatest population density were (in descending order) northern China, the lower Yangzi (including northern Zhejiang and southern Jiangsu), the northwest, and the upper Yangzi (including Sichuan). See ibid., esp. 369–371.

14. *Xin Wudai shi*, 572.

15. Verellen, "Liturgy and Sovereignty." For a discussion of the religious practices of lay elite in Shu as reflected in Du Guanting's *Guang cheng ji* 廣成集, as well as an argument that Du was trying to position Shu as the inheritor of Tang Daoist traditions, see Mitamura, "Tōmatsu Godai ni okeru shūkyō katsudō to setsudoshi."

16. On efforts to sacralize Shu, see Verellen, "Shu as Hallowed Land."

17. On Qian Liu's support of Daoist individuals and institutions, particularly Luo Yin 羅隱 (833–910), Lüqiu Fangyuan 閭丘方遠 (d. 902), and Tianzhu guan 天柱觀, see He, *Qianshi Wuyue guo shi lunqiao*, 352–381.

18. For an overview of the history of this relic and its reliquary, see Brose, "Buddhist Empires," chap. 6.

19. *Fozu tongji*, 90c1–4. This story is also recounted in the *Wuyue beishi* (2:16a), which only records that the king built a stupa in the south of the city to house the reliquary. Lingyin was Qian Liu's nineteenth son. His father sent him to Luohan si before he had taken the tonsure. After becoming a monk, Qian Liu appointed him abbot and granted him thirty years of monastic seniority. The best source for information of Lingyin is his stupa inscription, *Wuyue guo gu seng Huiyin puguang dashi taming* 吳越國故僧慧因普光大師塔銘, reproduced in the *Liangzhe jinshi zhi*, 4:5a–7b.

20. Baota si was also known as Shijia zhenshen sheli ta 釋迦真身舍利塔 and Hangta si 杭塔寺. Its name was changed to Fantian si 梵天寺 between 1064 and 1067. See *Chūgoku Zenshū jimei sanmei jiten*, 388–389, 412.

21. The monk was Zhitong 志通 (fl. 939). *Song gaoseng zhuan*, 858c13–859a15.

22. Along with the small silver stupa containing two Buddha relics, the well also reportedly contained "strange pearls and jades," various ancient coins, gems,

bells, and mirrors. The earliest mention of its discovery is found in the *Wuyue beishi* (2:29a), but the most detailed account is given in the *Shiguo chunqiu* (78:24a). This latter version provides a catalogue of the thirty-four items discovered in the well and reproduces Qian Liu's inscription commemorating their discovery.

23. Durt, "The Meaning of Archeology in Ancient Buddhism." The *Luoyang qielan ji* records similar discoveries when Luoyang was established as the new capital in the fifth century. See, for example, Yi-t'ung Wang's translation, 16, 55–56, 78–79, 131, and 177.

24. *Xianchun Lin'an zhi*, 23:4a. These beautifully carved cliffs and caves are located beside Lingyin Temple in Hangzhou and are known as "The Peak That Has Flown Over" (Feilai feng 飛來峰).

25. For the earliest biography of Guanxiu, see *Song gaoseng zhuan*, 897a11–b18.

26. "Old Frontier Song"; translated in Egan, *Clouds Thick, Whereabouts Unknown*, 92.

27. The *Song gaoseng zhuan* (897a11–b18) records that when Qian Liu ascended the throne, he had one of Guanxiu's poems engraved on the back of a stele erected to record the names of the military officers who had pacified the region. But there is another, often repeated account of Guanxiu's presentation of a poem to Qian Liu. The poem "For the Venerable Qian" 獻錢尚父, contains the lines 滿堂花醉三千客 / 一劍霜寒十四州: "Flowers fill the halls, intoxicating three thousand guests / One sword pacifies fourteen prefectures." According to the *Shishi tongjian* (125b21–c4) and other sources, after reading the poem, Qian Liu refused to meet with Guanxiu until he changed the words "fourteen prefectures" to read "forty prefectures"—an intimation of Qian Liu's imperial ambitions. Guanxiu is said to have replied that, just as prefectures were hard to increase, poems were difficult to change. Soon thereafter, he left Wuyue.

28. *Song gaoseng zhuan*, 897a11–b18.

29. Guanxiu's collected poems, known as the *Chanyue ji* 禪月集 (or *Chanyue shiji* 禪月詩集) in twenty-six fascicles (the *Song shi* lists the same text in thirty fascicles), was first printed in 923 in the kingdom of Shu. As for Guanxiu's paintings, only one of his famous series of sixteen arhats survives. It was discovered in 2008, in a storage facility in Chengdu, and is the subject of a study by Yang Xin: *Wudai Guanxiu luohan tu*. Two other sets of sixteen arhats, believed to be copies of Guanxiu's originals, are now preserved in Japan: one in the Imperial Household Collection, the other at Kodaiji. The latter series, thought to have been brought to Japan during the Song or Yuan dynasty, contains a near replica of the Sichuan find.

30. The celebrated poet Qiji was a disciple of Deshan Xuanjian 德山宣鑒 (782–865). See *Song gaoseng zhuan*, 897c22–24. Yifeng is identified as a "Chan Master" in the *Jingde chuan deng lu* (233a8), but nothing more is known about his background.

31. Guangye was also known as National Teacher Yousheng 祐聖國師. *Song gaoseng zhuan*, 743b5–744c14.

32. Given the flow of talent and resources from Chang'an to Chengdu during the Tang–Five Dynasties transition, it is probably no coincidence that Chengdu developed into a new center for esoteric Buddhism during the same period that Chang'an's Buddhist institutions were deprived of imperial support. On the devel-

opment of esoteric Buddhism in Sichuan, see Sørensen, "Esoteric Buddhism in Sichuan," 394; and Lü, *Zhongguo Mijiao shi*, 437–439.

33. *Song gaoseng zhuan*, 747b10–c8.

34. The eminent literatus Luo Yin, along with fifty other court officials, composed poems in Bianguang's honor. *Song gaoseng zhuan*, 898a29–b19.

35. See, for example, the biography of Wuzuo 無作 (d. 907–910) in the *Song gaoseng zhuan*, 896c7–897a9.

36. The *Four-Part Vinaya* was first translated into Chinese by Buddhayaśas 佛陀耶舍 (n.d.) and Zhu Fonian 竺佛念 (n.d.) in 408. During the first half of the Tang, Daoxuan's work represented one of three major Chinese interpretations of the Vinaya, the other two being those of the Xiangbu school 相部宗 of Fali 法礪 (569–635), and of the Dongta school 東塔宗 of Huaisu 懷素 (634–707). The influence of these last two traditions in southern China declined toward the end of the Tang, leaving Daoxuan's Nanshan tradition (named after the location of Daoxuan's temple in the Zhongnan Mountains 終南山, south of Chang'an), as the orthodox interpretation of the Vinaya. In the north, the Dongta tradition, under the leadership of monks such as Zhenjun 貞峻 (847–924) and Chengchu 澄楚 (889–959), retained considerable influence.

37. *Song gaoseng zhuan*, 818a20–b19.

38. Ibid., 809b2–10.

39. Ibid., 810a. One of Changqing Huileng's disciples, Yanqiu 彥球 (d. ca. 960–962), also studied with Jingxiao. After returning to Wuyue from Min, King Qian Chu appointed Yanqiu first to Gongchen yuan 功臣院 and later to Longhua si 龍華寺. *Song gaoseng zhuan*, 884c; and *Jingde chuan deng lu*, 374c17–375a5.

40. *Song gaoseng zhuan*, 809a12–b2.

41. The platform was probably located at Kaiyuan si 開元寺. *Song gaoseng zhuan*, 809a–b.

42. On Luo Yin and his teachings, see He, *Qianshi Wuyue guo shi lunqiao*, 352–381; and Schipper and Verellen, *The Taoist Canon*, 314–316.

43. Qian Liu's younger brother Qian Hua had Xijue released without questioning when charges were brought against him by another monk. Wuyue's second king, Qian Yuanguan, built the Qianfo (Thousand Buddha) Saṃgha-ārāma 千佛伽藍 for Xijue, conferred a purple robe, and awarded him the name Wenguang 文光 (Literary Brilliance). *Song gaoseng zhuan*, 810b–c.

44. *Song gaoseng zhuan*, 750c–751a. Xuanzhu was at one time recognized as the tenth patriarch of the Tiantai school, but his lineage was eventually eclipsed by the line stemming from Xiji. Haoduan was also supported by the Qian family. Qian Liu invited Haoduan to lecture at Luohan and Baota Temples and Qian Liu's grandson, Qian Zuo 錢佐 (the third king of Wuyue, [r. 941–947]), granted him a purple robe and various titles. *Song gaoseng zhuan*, 750c25–27. On the development of the Tiantai tradition during the tenth and eleventh centuries, see Shinohara, "From Local History to Universal History."

45. The range of Xijue's influence may extend even further, given the probability that he was also known by the name Huizheng 彙征. Makita Tairyō was the first to point out the overlapping identities of these two figures, noting that the preface for Huizheng's collected works ("Foshi Huizheng bieji xu" 佛氏彙征別集序,

in *Xianju bian*, 881a14–b5) records that Huizheng was originally from Yongjia and that, although Xijue was a native of Jiangsu, he later trained in Yongjia. Makita also cites the *Zhengqiao tongzhi bieji lei* 鄭樵通志別集類, which records that the collected works of Huizheng were compiled by Xijue. It is worth noting, however, that although the *Huizheng ji* 彙征集 is listed in several other Song catalogues, the *Song shi* (j. 208), *Tongzhi* 通志 (j. 70), and *Chongwen zongmu* 崇文總目 (j. 11) do not attribute its authorship to Xijue. Both monks also served in the position of monastic controller in Wuyue during the same period. See Makita, "Kunshu dokusai shakai ni okeru Bukkyōdan no tachiba (jō)," 78–79n30. Makita's observations are bolstered by the fact that both men were also friends with Luo Yin, and both appear to have lived for a time at Ayuwang si in Mingzhou. Additionally, Xijue was awarded the title Great Master Wenguang 文光大師, and the biography of Daoqian in the *Song gaoseng zhuan* refers to Huizheng by the very similar title of Great Master Guangwen 光文大師. Huizheng is credited with instructing two prominent Chan monks, Fayan Wenyi's disciple Daoqian and his grand-disciple Yong'an 永安, both of whom were also supported by Wuyue's kings. Huizheng also authored the stupa inscriptions for the monk Quanfu 全付 (882–947) and Xuefeng Yicun's disciple Daofu 道怤 (868–937).

46. *Xing shi chao zhujia ji biaomu*, 304b21–c22; and Wang J., *Zhongguo lüzong tongshi*, 333–342.

47. See the classic studies of the Northern school: McRae, *The Northern School and Formation of Early Ch'an Buddhism*; and Faure, *The Will to Orthodoxy*.

48. McRae, *The Northern School and Formation of Early Ch'an Buddhism*, 70.

49. Shenhui's career and teachings are the topic of McRae's unpublished manuscript, "Evangelical Zen: Shenhui (684–758), the Sudden Teaching, and the Southern School of Chinese Ch'an Buddhism."

50. In 831, Guifeng Zongmi 圭峰宗密 (780–841) listed the four major Chan traditions active in the early ninth century in his *Chan Chart*: the disciples of Shenxiu (the "Northern school"); of Farong 法融 (594–657; the "Oxhead school"); of Shenhui (the "Heze 荷澤 school"); and of Mazu Daoyi (the "Hongzhou school"). The epitaph of Ehu Dayi 鵝湖大義 (746–818) also mentions these same four groups, while that of Hualin Yuntan 華林雲坦 (708–816), written in 825, singled out only the Heze and Hongzhou lines. See Jia, *The Hongzhou School of Chan Buddhism*, 104–105. Suzuki Tetsuo has proposed a general periodization scheme for Chan during the Tang and Five Dynasties, beginning with a "developmental period" from the fifth ancestor Hongren to Shitou and Mazu (lasting up until 790). Next came a "period of expansion" (790–880), from Yaoshan and Baizhang to Dongshan, Yangshan, Deshan, Shishuang, and Jiashan. This was followed by a "period of flourishing," consisting of an early phase (880–940)—from Yunju, Caoshan, and Xuefeng to Deshan Yuanmi and Fayan Wenyi—and a later phase, from Liangshan, Yuanguan, and Tiantai Deshao to the compilation of the *Jingde chuan deng lu* (940–1000). Suzuki T., *Tō Godai Zenshū shi*, 7–9.

51. The Oxhead (Niutou 牛頭) lineage of Chan was initially based in Jiangsu province, just south of present-day Nanjing. Representatives of the Niutou school rose to prominence in Chang'an in the late eighth century; Faqin 法欽 (715–793; a.k.a. Daoqin 道欽) and his disciple Chonghui 崇慧 (n.d.) were both summoned

to the Tang court in 768 by Emperor Daizong 代宗(r. 762–779). These two monks were the eighth- and ninth-generation descendants of Niutou Farong 牛頭法融 (594–657), the purported first patriarch of this lineage. Niutou monks maintained a presence in southeastern China during the late eighth and early ninth centuries, especially in their native region of Jiangsu and in neighboring Zhejiang. By the end of the Tang, however, the Oxhead lineage was virtually defunct. On the history of the Caodong lineage, see Schlütter, *How Zen Became Zen*, chap. 4.

52. On Pei Xiu, see Yoshikawa T., "Haikyū den."

53. On the relationship between Pei Xiu and Zongmi, see Gregory, *Tsung-mi and the Sinification of Buddhism*, 73–77. For a discussion and translation of the *Chan Chart* and Zongmi's critique of contemporary Chan traditions, see Broughton, *Zongmi on Chan*.

54. See Zongmi's critiques of the Hongzhou lineage in his "Chan Letter"; translated in Broughton, *Zongmi on Chan*, 89–96. See also the discussion in Gregory, *Tsung-mi and the Sinification of Buddhism*, 237–244.

55. See, for example, *Jingde chuan deng lu*, 444c1–6.

56. One of these was Huaiyun 懷惲 (755–816), whose own disciple Hongbian 弘辯 (fl. 846–859) was among the few monks known to have been called to Xuanzong's court after the Huichang persecutions. *Jingde chuan deng lu*, 269a27–c12; *Fozu tongji*, 467a5.

57. Pei Xiu compiled two collections of Huangbo's teachings, the *Chuanxin fayao* and the *Wanling lu*.

58. Poceski, *Ordinary Mind as the Way*, 112; Jia, *The Hongzhou School of Chan Buddhism*, 118.

59. For Zhong Chuan's recruitment of scholar-officials, see Tackett, "The Transformation of Medieval Chinese Elites," 193–194, and the sources cited therein.

60. *Zu tang ji*, j. 8, 298; and *Jingde chuan deng lu*, 332a24–b7. These texts record only a few lines of Chan-style dialogue between the two men, but other contemporaneous accounts make it clear that Shanglan was revered not just for his witty repartee but also for his prophetic vision. For instance, when Zhong Chuan was plotting to assassinate Wang Chao, the future king of Min, Shanglan reportedly predicted dire consequences and recommended instead an alliance between the two warlords. Shanglan later purportedly lent his services to Wang Chao's successor in Min, Wang Shenzhi: "At his height, Yang Xingmi sought to swallow up the southeast [of China], and [Wang] Shenzhi was often worried about him. [He knew that] his late [brother] had been good friends with Shanglan, so he sent an emissary to present him with gold and silk and ask about his kingdom's future. The emissary returned with Shanglan's ten-character response. It said, 'Do not fear a lamb entering your room, only fear money [*qian*] entering your stomach.' When Shenzhi saw this, he sighed and said, 'The lamb [*yang*] is Yang [Xingmi]. The stomach [*fu*] is Fu[zhou]. Could it be that the danger for Fuzhou comes not from Yang Xingmi but from someone named Qian? At present there are no commanders named Qian. This is something that my children and grandchildren should be worried about.'" *Wudai shi bu*, 2:6b–7b. The "Qian," of course, referred to the Qian family who would come to power in Wuyue and would eventually invade and annex northern Fujian. The monk also warned Zhong Chuan of an imminent attack by

his rival in the north, Yang Xingmi, though the commissioner was unable to decipher his cryptic message. *Wudai shi bu*, 1:13a. Even assuming that such accounts were written retrospectively, they demonstrate that Shanglan was remembered and valorized primarily for his ability to divine the future—a common characteristic of other prominent Chan clerics during this period. One can only speculate that Zhong Chuan's support for several other Chan monks might have been similarly inspired.

61. Other monks supported by Zhong Chuan include Nanta Guangyong 南塔 光湧 (850–938), a disciple of Yangshan Huiji 仰山慧寂 (807–883). According to his stupa inscription (*Yangshan Guangyong zhanglao taming* 仰山光涌長老塔銘, *Qinding quan Tang wen*, 870:14b–16b), Zhong Chuan made several attempts to lure Nanta Guangyong to his court. The monk initially refused but eventually allowed himself to be set up in a place called the Stone Pavilion (Shiting 石亭). Another inscription transcribed in the *Qinding quan Tang wen* (*Hongzhou yungai shan longshou yuan Guanghua dashi baolu beiming* 洪州雲蓋山龍壽院光化大師寶錄碑銘, 869:11b–14b) records that Zhong Chuan established Longshou yuan 龍壽院 for Master Guanghua 光化 (a.k.a. Yungai Huaiyi 雲蓋懷溢 [847–934]). The inscription stresses the monk's Chan credentials but does not document his lineage or other affiliations. Zhong Chuan also made overtures to at least two disciples of Shishuang Qingzhu 石霜慶諸 (807–888). The first was Huaiyou 懷祐 (n.d.), for whom he restored Qixian si 棲賢寺 on Mt. Lu sometime between 892 and 893 (*Lushan ji*, 1035a14–25; and *Jingde chuan deng lu*, 329a4–12). The second was Nanji Sengyi 南際僧一 (n.d.), whom he invited to take up residence at Mt. Mo 末山. Nanji later accepted an offer from the king of Min to live at the Western Cloister 西院 in Fuzhou (*Zu tang ji*, j. 9, 318; and *Jingde chuan deng lu*, 328c7–14).

62. Jiufeng Puman (a.k.a. Tongxuan 通玄) first studied with the elderly Deshan Xuanjian before becoming a disciple of Dongshan Liangjie (*Chanlin sengbao zhuan*, 506b18). Zhong Chuan had one of his residences on Mt. Mo converted into a temple named Longji 隆濟 for Puman and his disciples. According to the *Ruizhou fu zhi* (3:29b–30a), sometime between 894 and 898 the temple was renamed Hongji 宏濟. A few years later the name was changed again to Jiufeng chongfu si 九峰崇福寺. Puman is generally credited as the founding abbot. See Suzuki T., "Kanton no Zenshū ni kansuru shiryō," 218. The *Chanlin sengbao zhuan* simply states that Zhong Chuan purchased the land on Mt. Mo and had a temple built for Puman (506b7–507a3). The second and third abbots of Puli chanyuan were Daoquan 道全 (d. 894) and Qinglin Shiqian 青林師虔 (d. 904). See *Yunzhou dongshan Puli chanyuan chuan fa ji* 筠州洞山普利禪院傳法記, in the *Wuxi ji*, 9:14a–18a.

63. *Zu tang ji*, j. 8, 263–271; and *Song gaoseng zhuan*, 781b10–c6. See also *Jingde chuan deng lu*, 334c15–336a3.

64. On Daoying, see Ishii, "Ungosan to Ungo Doyo."

65. While there is some evidence to suggest that the rulers of Wu, like Qian Liu in Wuyue, initially patronized monks of the Nanshan Vinaya tradition, the *saṃgha*-state relations in the capital Yangzhou during this period are difficult to trace. The *Fei shang yingxiong xiaolu* 淝上英雄小錄 of Xindou Hao 信都鎬 (n.d.), dating from the first half of the tenth century, purportedly discussed prominent Buddhist and Daoist figures from the kingdom of Wu, but the text has been lost. See

Kurz, "A Survey of Historical Sources," 215. The collected works of Gao Pian's Korean administrator Choe Chiwon (Ch. Cui Zhiyuan 催致遠; *jinshi* 874) preserves a request that a monk named Hongding 弘鼎 (n.d.) be appointed monastic controller and awarded a purple robe. The request was granted, but nothing else is known about this cleric (*Guiyuan bigeng ji jiaozhu*, 93–96). Finally, one subentry in the *Song Biographies* does note that the founding patriarch of Wu, Yang Xingmi, made frequent donations to a monk known as Acārya Shou 壽闍黎, a master of the Nanshan Vinaya tradition (*Song gaoseng zhuan*, 809b26–c3).

    66. The teachings and traditions of Buddhism were initially introduced to the southern coast of China through sea-trade with south and southeast Asia, and Fujian's first temples were constructed toward the end of the third century. Estimates of temple numbers during different historical periods vary. According to the earliest gazetteer for northern Fujian—*San shan zhi*, compiled in 1182—the first two temples in the Fujian region were constructed during the Jin dynasty (265–316). These were supplemented by one in the Qi (479–502), seventeen in the Liang (502–557), thirteen in the Chen (557–589), and another three in the Sui (581–618). The 222 years that spanned the reign of Tang Gaozu 高祖 (618–626) and that of Wenzong (826–840) saw the construction of a further thirty-nine temples. After the Huichang era, temples were built at a much more rapid pace. Forty-one were constructed during the reign of Emperor Xuanzong (846–859), 102 during Yizong's reign (859–873), 56 under Xizong 僖宗 (875–888), and 18 during Zhaozong's reign (888–904), totaling 236 temples in greater Fuzhou by the end of the Tang. During the Five Dynasties, the Wang family added another 267 temples, and when northern Fujian came under the control of the kingdom of Wuyue, 221 more temples were constructed (*San shan zhi*, 512). In *Fujian zongjiao shi*, Chen Zhiping has estimated the total number of temples in all of modern Fujian at the end of the Tang at 547 out of a total of approximately 40,000 throughout greater China (136–137). Another study by Wei Yingqi, "Wudai Min shigao zhiyi," concludes that there were 320 temples in Fujian by the end of the Tang, an additional 337 added during the reign of the Wang family, and another 140 built when the region was controlled by Wuyue (see p. 3005 and all three appendices). For a breakdown of temples in Fujian by region from the Six Dynasties through the Qing, see Suzuki T., "Tō Godai jidai no Fukken ni okeru Zenshū," 3–4.

    67. The biography of Mazu's student Wuliao 無了 (n.d.), originally from Quanzhou, notes that when his tomb was flooded and his body remained afloat, Wang Shenzhi had the corpse transported to Fuzhou, where it was worshipped before being reinterred in a newly constructed stupa on Mt. Guiyang 龜洋 in Quanzhou (*Jingde chuan deng lu*, 260b29–c19). A stele inscription for Wuliao's stupa was later composed by the Min literatus Huang Tao 黃滔 (ca. 840–911; *jinshi* 895) who also wrote memorials for Wang Chao, Wang Shenzhi, and Xuefeng Yicun. According to the *Zu tang ji*, one of Mazu's grand-disciples, Zhengyuan 正原 (792–870), was also buried nearby and had his stupa rebuilt by Wang Shenzhi, in 905 (j. 17, 573–574; and *Jingde chuan deng lu*, 279c15–26). Together these two monks were known as the Two True Bodies of Guiyang (*Guiyang er zhenshen* 龜洋二真身) (*Jingde chuan deng lu*, 260b29–c19). In addition to the posthumous honors accorded these monks, Shenzhi also built the Guohuan chanyuan 國歡禪院 for Huiri 慧日 (d. 894–898), another

grand-disciple of Mazu. Like the Guiyang stupas, this temple was established in Quanzhou.

3: Founding Fathers

1. *Zizhi tongjian*, 284:25b–26a; *Xin Wudai shi*, 583; *San shan zhi*, 5; and *Wuyue beishi*, 3:28b–29a. The *Wu guo gushi* (2:11a) claims that a red snake would slither in and out of Yanming's nose while he slept. Aside from these miraculous accounts and a later tradition that claimed Zhuo Yanming was originally from Shenguang si 神光寺, little else is known about this monk.

2. Tokiwa, "Bukkyō shijō ni okeru futari no Chūiō"; and Chikusa, "Tōmatsu Godai ni okeru Fukken Bukkyō no tenkai."

3. Yanagida, "*Sodōshū* no shiryō kachi," 35.

4. Yanagida, "Seppō to sono yūjintachi," 53.

5. Ibid., 62.

6. Yanagida, *Junzen no jidai*. When addressing an audience at San Francisco Zen Center in September 1989, Yanagida quoted this passage and said, "Reading these words of mine again, I have nothing to add." See Yanagida, "Passion for Zen," 25.

7. For an overview of Yanagida's work on the *Patriarch's Hall Collection*, see Kinugawa, "Yanagida Seizan no *Sodōshū* kenkyū."

8. Suzuki T., "Tō Godai jidai no Fukken ni okeru Zenshū," "Sekkō no Zenshū ni kansuru shiryō," *Tō Godai Zenshū shi*, and "Minkoku Chūiō Ō Shinchi ni okeru Bukkyō."

9. Kinugawa, "*Sodōshū* no kōri." The preface to the 1245 Korean printing makes reference to an earlier version of the text in a single fascicle, which later grew to ten and then twenty fascicles: "[Wendeng's] preface and the *Patriarch's Hall Collection* in a single fascicle previously circulated in this land. Subsequently, it reached ten fascicles. Cautiously basing ourselves on this version, we wanted to make new printing blocks so that it could be widely circulated. It was therefore divided into twenty fascicles." *Zu tang ji*, 2. Two other Song texts—the *Chongwen zongmu* 崇文總目 (1041), and the *Tongzhi* 通志 (1161)—also state that the *Patriarch's Hall Collection* originally circulated in a one fascicle edition. "A Sung Colloquial Story from the Tsu-t'ang chi," a short article written by Arthur Waley and published posthumously in 1968, demonstrates that at least a portion of the *Patriarch's Hall Collection* must have been composed sometime after 990. Waley noted the use of the place name Guangnan 廣南 to refer to the region known as Lingnan 嶺南 prior to the Chunhua era (990–994) of the Song. Moreover, he speculated that the character *kuang* 匡 used in the text was a substitute for the tabooed character *guang* 廣 in the personal name of the Song emperor Taizu (r. 960–976). Kinugawa has expanded on Waley's discoveries and shown that other portions of the text were also undoubtedly composed after 952. To cite just one important example, the entry for Yunmen Wenyan quotes from his stele inscription composed in 958. Based on textual and linguistic evidence, Kinugawa has suggested that that the *Patriarch's Hall Collection* was probably composed in three successive stages (see "*Sodōshū* no kōri"). The first two fascicles of the present version, covering the period from the seven ancient buddhas up through Huineng, were composed by Jing and Yun and originally cir-

culated with Wendeng's preface as a single fascicle. This version was then expanded, probably in Korea, sometime in the late tenth or early eleventh century, most likely before the completion of the *Transmission of the Flame* in 1004. It may have been at this time that the biographies of Korean monks were added to the collection. This ten-fascicle version was then subdivided into the twenty smaller fascicles that were printed and circulated in 1245. The Korean expansion of the text is further supported by John Jorgensen's discovery of three entries that quote from a memorial stele that would only have been available in Korea. See Jorgensen, *Inventing Huineng, the Sixth Patriarch*, 731–733.

10. Ishii, "Senshū Fukusen Shōkei in no Jōshu Zenji Shōtō to *Sodōshū.*" In *Zenrin sōhōden yakuchū* (73–87), Yanagida Seizan revisited his older work on the *Patriarch's Hall Collection* in light of new sources introduced in Ishii's "Senshū Fukusen Shōkei in no Jōshu Zenji Shōtō to *Sodōshū*" and Shiina Kōyū's "*Sodōshū* no hensei."

11. Welter, *Monks, Rulers, and Literati*, chap. 4.

12. The most comprehensive modern account of Yicun's life and teachings is found in Suzuki, *Seppō*. The best discussion of Yicun in English is Welter, *Monks, Rulers, and Literati*, 90–101.

13. Huang Tao's inscription, *Fuzhou Xuefeng shan gu Zhenjue dashi beiming* 福州雪峯山故真覺大師碑銘, is reproduced in the *Huang yu shi ji*, 5:31a–36b. Subsequent biographies for Yicun are found in *Zu tang ji*, j. 7, 249–262; *Song gaoseng zhuan*, 781c28–782c8; and *Jingde chuan deng lu*, 327a–328b. A version of the discourse record existed as early as 1032, when Wang Sui 王隨 (ca. 973–1039) wrote a preface for the work. Yicun's record was first printed in 1080, the same year as Xuansha Shibei's discourse record, though neither of these printings is extant. See Shiina, "Tōdai Zenseki no Sōdai kankō ni tsuite," 524–525. The received edition of the *Xuefeng zhenjue chanshi yulu* 雪峰真覺禪師語錄 (*Wan xu zang jing*, 69n1333), was edited and printed by Lin Hongyan 林弘衍 (fl. 1638).

14. Xuefeng Yicun's inscription identifies this monk as "Hongzhao dashi Furong Lingxun" 宏照大師芙蓉靈訓. However, Yicun's biography in the *Song gaoseng zhuan* names this monk Hengzhao 恒照, while his entry in the *Zu tang ji* gives Yuanzhao 圓照 and in the *Jingde chuan deng lu* he is called Changzhao 常照. Lingxun's own biographies in the *Jingde chuan deng lu* (280c23–281a21) and *Zu tang ji* (j. 15, 575) give his posthumous title as Hongzhao 弘照. The *Jingde chuan deng lu* lists him as a grand-disciple of Mazu Daoyi through Guizong Zhichang 歸宗智常 (n.d.).

15. *Zu tang ji*, j. 7, 249–50.

16. *Song gaoseng zhuan*, 782a10–12.

17. *Fuzhou Xuefeng shan gu Zhenjue dashi beiming* (*Huang yu shi ji* 5:32b).

18. *Zu tang ji*, j. 7, 250.

19. See the *Jingde chuan deng lu* biography of Touzi Datong 投子大同 (819–914; 319a2–320b5).

20. See, for example, *Wu deng hui yuan*, 145a22– b3; and case five of the *Biyan lu*, 145a13–16.

21. *Xuefeng zhenjue chanshi yulu*, 87b5–20. Huang Tao's inscription notes that Yicun left Deshan's monastery in 865 but does not indicate when he arrived.

22. Welter, *Monks, Rulers, and Literati*, 67.

23. *Jingde chuan deng lu*, 359b20–23. Unfortunately, nothing is recorded about Ruti's history, making it impossible to know if he had some connection with Lingxun or the Furong community independent of his relationship with Yicun.

24. The *Shi gui zhi* 師規制 (85c7–86a8) and the *Shi yi jie* 師遺誡 (86a9–b2) are both contained within the *Xuefeng zhenjue chanshi yulu*. The *Shi gui zhi* has been translated by Mario Poceski in "Xuefeng's Code and the Chan School's Participation in the Development of Monastic Regulations."

25. Jia Jinhua has speculated that "it is highly possible that, in order to build an independent, distinct house, Dongshan [Liangjie] deliberately elevated Shitou's teaching, broke away from the Hongzhou line, and attributed himself to the Shitou line exclusively." Jia, *The Hongzhou School of Chan Buddhism*, 113.

26. The precise identity of Yuanji is unclear. The *Song gaoseng zhuan* (777c13–21) contains an account of Xuance 玄策 (d. 854), whose posthumous title was Yuanji, but the biographical details do not match. Suzuki Tetsuo has suggested that Yuanji was Baizhang Huaihai's grand-disciple Yishan Da'an 怡山大安 (793–883). See Suzuki T., *Tō Godai Zenshū shi*, 90–91. The information and the dates given in Da'an's *Song Biography* do coincide with Yuanji's chronology, and Da'an's master, Weishan Lingyou 潙山靈祐 (771–853), was based on Mt. Wei. Moreover, the first character of Da'an's posthumous title, Yuanzhi 圓智, is the same "Yuan" as in Yuanji. Further evidence linking Yuanji with Da'an derives from the *San shan zhi* (546), which notes that in 867, Surveillance Commissioner Li Jingwen 李景溫 (fl. 860–873) invited Da'an to relocate from Mt. Wei to Mt. Yi. This record correlates with Xuefeng Yicun's *Discourse Record* (*Xuefeng zhenjue chanshi yulu*, 87c12–15), which also states that it was Li Jing (the second character of his surname is omitted) who requested that Yicun move to Mt. Yi.

27. Wang zhen jun is often identified as Wang Ziqiao, the legendary immortal, but in this case the title probably refers to Wang Ba 王霸 (ca. 1st century), who reportedly lived on Mt. Yi as a Daoist adept before ascending to heaven. According to legend, he prophesized that his descendants would become the rulers of the region. *Wudai shibu*, 2:6a.

28. In the stupa inscription Yicun wrote for Xingshi, he refers to him as "uncle" (*bo* 伯). See *Xuefeng zhenjue chanshi yulu*, 88c7–15.

29. Mt. Xuefeng was originally known as Mt. Xianggu 象骨 (Elephant Bone). Yicun's *Song gaoseng zhuan* biography credits Xingshi with locating and naming the mountain, but the *Yudi jisheng* 輿地紀勝 (cited in Schafer, *The Empire of Min*, 12) claims that Wang Shenzhi was responsible for the name. See also the *San shan zhi*, 546–547.

30. *Xuefeng zhenjue chanshi yulu*, 89b4–9; see also *Xushi bijing*, 7:25b–26a. Incidentally, a small temple is now built around the dead tree at the location of Yicun's original temple. The inside of the hollowed trunk contains a brief inscription dating the founding of the hermitage to 905.

31. The measurement is given as 10,100 *shi* 石, with one *shi* equaling 120 *jin* 斤 (approximately 158 pounds).

32. *Xuefeng zhi*, 186–187. The estate is also described in the *San shan zhi*, 546–547.

33. *Xuefeng zhenjue chanshi yulu*, 85c17–18; translation from Poceski, "Xuefeng's Code and the Chan School's Participation in the Development of Monastic Regulations," 55.

34. Huang Tao, *Datang Fuzhou baoen dingguang duobao ta beiji* 大唐福州報恩定光多寶塔碑記 (*Huang yu shi ji*, 5:4a–11b). On this and other Min inscriptions, see Suzuki T., "Minkoku Chūiō Ō Shinchi ni okeru Bukkyō."

35. According to the *San shan zhi* (127), the populace had 82,000 *qing* of land for 579,000 citizens (not including the old and young), while monks controlled over 2,000 *qing* for a population of just 14,000.

36. Chikusa, *Chūgoku Bukkyō shakaishi kenkyū*, 151. For a comparison of land purportedly owned by monks and non-monks, see Huang M., *Songdai Fojiao shehui jingji shi lunji*, 122–123.

37. *Song shi*, 173:12a–b. Some blamed the existence of these vast monastic estates on Min's rulers. According to the Song dynasty official and Fujian local Cai Xiang 蔡襄 (1012–1067), the "illegal autocratic kings [of Min] took the land of the people and gave it to the Buddhists." See Schottenhammer, "Local Politico-Economic Particulars of the Quanzhou Region," 18, 30.

38. The *Song gaoseng zhuan* notes that Yicun and his companions traveled to Siming 四明 and Danqiu 丹丘 (782b12). Yicun's *Discourse Record* elaborates that he stopped at Lingyin, Guoqing, and Yuwang temples, in Hangzhou, Tiantai, and Mingzhou, respectively (*Xuefeng zhenjue chanshi yulu*, 88c20–21).

39. *Fuzhou Xuefeng shan gu Zhenjue dashi beiming* (*Huang yu shi ji*, 5:33b–34a). This passage in the inscription has some illegible characters and the wording is somewhat ambiguous. Welter has suggested that Yicun was in the service of Yang Xingmi in the kingdom of Wu at this point, but the subject of the passage is more likely Wang Chao. See Welter, *Monks, Rulers, and Literati*, 94.

40. The date of Yicun's return to Min is based on his discourse record and thus is of late provenance. Both his stupa inscription and *Song Biography* refer only to the "prince of Min" 閩王, which, given the dates, I have assumed refers to Wang Chao, but it is possible that it refers to Wang Shenzhi. The biography for Youzhang 幼璋 (841–927) in the *Jingde chuan deng lu* (367b2–3) mentions that sometime during the Qianning 乾寧 era (894–898), Yicun met Youzhang in eastern Zhejiang and gave him a palm whisk. If accurate, this would place Yicun in Zhejiang until at least 894.

41. *Fuzhou Xuefeng shan gu Zhenjue dashi beiming* (*Huang yu shi ji*, 5:34a).

42. Before his death, Yicun left final instructions to his disciples concerning the disposal of his corpse and the future functioning of the monastery. In the document, preserved in his discourse record and dated to the year of his death, he wrote: "Recently the Buddha-dharma has become faint. People only attend to worldly truths and only believe in the distribution of alms. Whether for master or monk, death comes at the end of a hundred years. If kindness is not repaid, people's rituals will obtain no response, and there will be little self-examination. I seem to be dispersing into the four elements. Some days ago a wooden casket and a stone niche were arranged in accord with the ancient annals. Do not provide me with a separate stupa and do not set up a spirit feast. Do not uphold the conventional period

of mourning or wear [garments of] thick cloth. Anyone who sheds a tear is no *śramaṇa* and is no heir of mine." (*Xuefeng zhenjue chanshi yulu*, 86). According to a later tradition, Yicun's body was not cremated but stored in its coffin for a hundred years. Every month it was brought out and people marveled to see that the corpse had not decomposed and the hair and nails had continued to grow. It was only during later wars that the body was burned and Yicun's remains were interred in the small stupa that still stands on the monastery's grounds. See *Yuzhi tang tan hui*, 14:33a.

43. *Fuzhou Xuefeng shan gu Zhenjue dashi beiming* (*Huang yu shi ji*, 5:35b–36a).

44. Dongyan Kexiu has an entry in the *Jingde chuan deng lu* (354b8–11). Ehu Zhifu is represented in both the *Jingde chuan deng lu* (350b2–23) and the *Zu tang ji* (j. 10, 340–341).

45. The earliest biographical account of Xuansha Shibei is a stele inscription composed by Lin Cheng 林澄 (n.d.) titled *Tang Fuzhou Anguo chanyuan xian kaishan Zongyi dashi beiwen* 唐福州安國禪院先開山宗一大師碑文, found in Shibei's *Extensive Record* (*Fuzhou Xuansha Zongyi chanshi yulu*, 25b7–26c20). The text of the inscription contains a colophon stating that the stele was erected with the support of Wang Yanjun 王延鈞 (r. 926–935). The inscription itself is undated but the *San shan zhi* (617) and other sources date it to 930. Shibei's biography in the *Song gaoseng zhuan* (785c19–786a8) appears to have been based on this inscription. For other biographical accounts, see the *Zu tang ji*, j. 10, 333–338; *Jingde chuan deng lu*, 343c–347b; and *Chanlin sengbao zhuan*, 499a7–500a17.

46. The *Jingde chuan deng lu* gives the date of Shibei's arrival at Furong as 864. Shibei's inscription also records that he took the tonsure under Lingxun early in the Xiantong 咸通 era (860–873).

47. The *Song gaoseng zhuan* gives Yuzhang, also in Jiangxi, as the location of the temple.

48. *Da foding rulai miyin xiuzheng liaoyi zhu pusa wanxing shoulengyan jing* 大佛頂如來密因修證了義諸菩薩萬行首楞嚴經 (*Taishō shinshū daizōkyō*, 19n945).

49. *Jingde chuan deng lu*, 344a811. For a review of the debate over the authenticity of the *Śūraṃgama*, see Benn, "Another Look at the Pseudo-*Śūraṃgama sūtra*," and the scholarship cited therein.

50. *Lengyan jing*, 122a4–5. It is worth noting that the core practice advocated in the *Śūraṃgama* is markedly different from what is described in Chan meditation manuals written during the Five Dynasties and the Song. The *Śūraṃgama* promotes detaching one of the sense faculties—hearing is singled out as the most efficacious—from its object (e.g., sound) and redirecting that faculty inward to ascertain its true nature. Once one faculty is thus disengaged, other faculties can be made to follow suit. This contrasts with the more conventional calming and contemplation (*zhiguan*) model advocated by at least one of Xuansha Shibei's descendants, Zhifeng (discussed in chap. 6).

51. See *Song gaoseng zhuan*, 738c4–6; Demiéville, *Le Concile de Lhasa*, 43–52; and Faure, *The Will to Orthodoxy*, 65, 195.

52. *Lengyan jing*, 155a8–9.

53. Suzuki Tetsuo's "Hōgenshū no keisei (I)" discusses the influence of the *Śūraṃgama* on Chan monks from the Tang through the Song, and particularly on Xuansha Shibei and his descendants.

54. *Ikka Myōju* 一顆明珠; translation modified from Waddell and Abe, *The Heart of Dōgen's Shōbōgenzō*, 32.

55. An earlier temple existed at this site but it was destroyed during the Huichang persecutions. Wang Shenzhi rebuilt the temple, also known as Wolong shan 臥龍山, in 896. The *San shan zhi* (617) records that "during the Kaiyun era of the Jin [944–946] troops from Huai invaded and laid [the temple] to waste. During the fourth year of the Yangfu era of the Song [1011] the old site was made anew."

56. *Fuzhou Xuansha Zongyi chanshi yulu*, 26a2–3.

57. This text is found in the discourse records of both Xuefeng Yicun (*Wan xu zang jing*, 69n1333, 78b3–79c8) and Xuansha Shibei (ibid., 73n1445, 23c7–25a13). A partial translation is provided in Welter, *Monks, Rulers, and Literati*, 96–98.

58. Many of the stupas built by Min's kings functioned as memorials for the dead. The Dazhong 大中 and Shenguang 神光 stupas, for example, were built for the pacification of the military and civilian dead. *Zhangliu jinshen bei* 丈六金身碑 (*Huang yu shi ji*, 5:17a–23a).

59. According to its inscription, this stupa, like others found throughout China, was inspired by the story of Prabhūtaratna's stupa emerging from the earth in the eleventh chapter of the *Lotus Sūtra* (*Huang yu shi ji*, 5:6a).

60. *Datang Fuzhou Baoen dingguang duobao ta beiji* (*Huang yu shi ji*, 5:9a). Cf. the *Tiwei boli jing* 提謂波利經, composed in northern China by Tanjing 曇靖 (n.d.) around 460, which pairs the Confucian constants with the five Buddhist precepts: *ren* is not taking life, *yi* is not taking what is not given, *li* is not engaging in illicit sexual activity, *zhi* is not drinking intoxicating beverages, and *xin* is not lying. The same system of correspondences was promoted by Zongmi. See Gregory, *Tsung-mi and the Sinification of Buddhism*, 282–284.

61. *Datang Fuzhou Baoen dingguang duobao ta beiji* (*Huang yu shi ji*, 5:4a–b). In 923, Wang Shenzhi also had the monk Yiying 義英 (n.d.) calligraph four copies of the canon that were scrolled on sandalwood spools. The scrolls, along with bronze statues of Śākyamuni and Maitreya, were enshrined at Jinshen baoguo si 金身報國寺, where a seven-storied stupa was erected (*San shan zhi*, 519; and Zhuge and Yin, *Minguo shishi biannian*, 108). These, like other collections of the Buddhist canon commissioned by Shenzhi, were probably housed in revolving, two-storied, octagonal libraries, painted with bright red lacquer and trimmed with gold and bronze, as described in the *Datang Fuzhou Baoen dingguang duobao ta beiji* (*Huang yu shi ji*, 5:6–7a).

62. *Song gaoseng zhuan*, 788b1–2.

63. Ibid., 789a25–26. A separate biography for the monk Wennian 文輦 (895–978) also records that when he "met the Chan elder Deshao of Mt. Tiantai, [Deshao] was preaching the way of Great Master Zongyi [Shibei]." Ibid., 860c5–6.

64. Ibid., 782c9–17.

65. *Zu tang ji*, j. 10, 342; and *Jingde chuan deng lu*, 348c9–11.

66. *Zu tang ji*, j. 6, 233. Cf. Welter, *Monks, Rulers, and Literati*, 202.

67. *Huangbo shan Duanji chanshi chuanxin fayao*, 379b28–29. Translated in Jia, *The Hongzhou School of Chan Buddhism*, 88.

68. Yanagida, "The Life of Lin-chi I-hsuan," 73.

69. The characters 長慶 are sometimes romanized as *zhangqing* but should probably be read as *changqing*, as in the Tang reign era (821–824). Thus, the name Changqing Huileng is sometimes given as Zhangqing Huileng.

70. Biographies for Huileng are found in *Zu tang ji*, j. 10, 360–368; *Song gaoseng zhuan*, 787a5–17; and *Jingde chuan deng lu*, 347b–348b.

71. Accordingly, Huileng must have arrived sometime before 876, not long after the community was first established.

72. Kaiyuan si was one of the most prominent temples in Quanzhou during this period. According to the *Quanzhou Kaiyuan si zhi* 泉州開元寺志, a temple gazetteer published in 1643, Wang Yanbin, along with his son and successor Wang Jichong, constructed a number of sub-temples at Kaiyuan si and appointed their abbots. The names of eleven monks are listed: three are identified as Chan masters (*chanshi*), two as Vinaya masters (*lüshi*), two as Dharma masters (*fashi*), one as Lecturer (*jiangshi*), and three without titles. See Ishii, "Senshū Fukusen Shōkei in no Jōshu Zenji Shōtō to *Sodōshū*," 176–177; and Nichols, "History, Material Culture and Auspicious Events at the Purple Cloud," 46–60. Yanagida Seizan has argued that Qianfo si 千佛寺, a branch temple of Kaiyuan si, was another name for Fuxian Zhaoqing yuan 福先招慶院, the location where Wendeng wrote the verses that were eventually incorporated into the *Patriarch's Hall Collection*. Kinugawa Kenji has refuted this point, arguing that Qianfo si and Fuxian Zhaoqing yuan were in fact two different temples. See Yanagida, *Zenrin sōhōden yakuchū*, 79; and Kinugawa, "Yanagida Seizan no *Sodōshū* kenkyū," 47.

73. *Xuefeng zhenjue chanshi yulu*, 89a14–18.

74. For the history Zhaoqing si, see Yanagida, *Zenrin sōhōden yakuchū*, 73–87.

75. Some dialogue between the two is recorded in Wang Yanbin's entry in the *Wu deng hui yuan* (172b3–14).

76. Changqing was a later name for Xichan si 西禪寺 on Mt. Yi, the same mountain where Mazu Daoyi's grand-disciple Da'an had lived and where Xuefeng Yicun was invited to reside before he moved to Mt. Xuefeng. The name of Xichan si was changed to Changqing by Wang Yanjun in the Changxing era (930–933).

77. *Zhaoqing si zhanglao seng Huileng bei* 招慶寺長老僧慧稜碑. See Makita, *Godai shūkyōshi kenkyū*, 19.

78. See Suzuki T., *Tō Godai Zenshū shi*, 110–111.

79. *Zizhi tongjian*, 271:12b–13a.

80. Ibid., 271:13a.

81. *Zu tang ji*, j. 13, 438–444; *Jingde chuan deng lu*, 374b2–c16; and *Wu deng hui yuan*, 169b11–170a2. Daokuang followed Huileng from Zhaoqing in Quanzhou to Changqing in Fuzhou and assumed the abbacy of Zhaoqing shortly after Huileng's death. Ishii Shūdō has suggested that the order of the second abbots of Zhaoqing si should be reversed, with Daokuang succeeding Wendeng. Ishii, "Senshū Fukusen Shōkei in no Jōshu Zenji Shōtō to *Sodōshū*," 173.

82. *Wan xu zang jing*, 69n1333, 85c11–12.

83. *Song gaoseng zhuan*, 786c5–787a3. Later sources for biographical information on Luohan Guichen include *Jingde chuan deng lu*, 371a–372a, 453b–c; *Chanlin sengbao zhuan*, 229b–230a; and *Wu deng hui yuan*, 446–450.

84. Luohan Guichen's critique of the ability of language to either describe or encompass awakening is also evident in his "Song of Illuminating the Way" (*Mingdao song* 明道頌), which opens with the lines: "The Way is deep and vast. Do not use words to describe it. Words are not the point. Who ever said they were?" *Jingde chuan deng lu*, 453b26–c6.

85. *Song gaoseng zhuan*, 786c9–13; see also *Jingde chuan deng lu*, 371a4–7.

86. *Song gaoseng zhuan*, 786a4–6.

87. Dizang Temple was located on Mt. Shi 石山, near Mt. Yi to the west of Fuzhou and not in Zhangzhou as is sometimes assumed. Guichen's initial patron is identified as Wang Cheng of Taiyuan 太原, governor of Zhang[zhou], in both the *Song gaoseng zhuan* and the *Jingde chuan deng lu*. This may refer to Wang Yanzheng's son Wang Jicheng 王継成 (n.d.).

88. Wang Zhi also bore the titles deputy commander of Longxi 龍溪, grand guardian of Qinzhou 勤州太保, and Duke of Langye 瑯琊公. Given the dates, it seems likely that this was the same figure who also patronized Baofu Congzhan, but his precise identity is unclear. Incidentally, two of Guichen's grand-disciples, students of Fayan Wenyi, later settled at Luohan Temple, suggesting that the temple remained within Guichen's lineage after his death. See the biographies of Zhiyi 智依 (n.d.) and Shouren 守仁 (n.d.) in the *Jingde chuan deng lu* (410c25–411a18 and 412a14–b14).

89. "Chapi yu cheng xi yuan zhi donggang" 茶毘於城西院之東崗 (*Song gaoseng zhuan*, 786c28). Although the language of the passage is somewhat ambiguous, if this temple is the same as the Western Chan Cloister (Xichan yuan 西禪院), also known as Changqing Temple, on Mt. Yi, Guichen's cremation may have been presided over by Huileng (with whom Guichen shared his most famous student, Fayan Wenyi). The *Transmission of the Flame* lists seven disciples for Guichen, but the *Song Biographies* singles out only two: Fayan Wenyi and Xiufu Wukong 休復悟空 (d. 951?), both of whom rose to prominence in the Southern Tang under the patronage of that kingdom's ruling family. Significantly, none of Guichen's disciples appear to have remained within the kingdom of Min.

90. *Song gaoseng zhuan*, 787a1–3.

91. *Jingde chuan deng lu*, 351a2–c14; and *Zu tang ji*, j. 10, 353–355. Shenyan's dates are unclear. The *Shishi tongjian* (131c12–16) gives 945 as the date of his death while the *Guzunsu yulu* 古尊宿語錄 (246a1–3) dates his death to the middle of the Tianfu 天福 era (936–943). The *Guzunsu yulu* also contains a collection of Shenyan's teachings, *Gushan xian xingsheng guoshi heshang fatang xuanyao guangji* 鼓山先興聖國師和尚法堂玄要廣集, with a preface dated to 965.

92. The site was originally known as Huayan Terrace. The monastery was given the name Yongquan 湧泉 by Wang Shenzhi in 915 (*San shan zhi*, 526). After Shenyan's death, control of the temple was successively passed to three of his disciples: Liaojue Zhiyan 了覺智嚴 (939–959), Liaozong Zhiyue 了宗智岳 (959–967), and Liaowu Qing'e 了悟清諤 (968–985). The fact that the first character is the same in all three of these tonsure names suggests that they were ordained by the same master, presumably Shenyan, and that the succession at Yongquan si on Mt. Gu was hereditary, with direct disciples inheriting the temple according to seniority. The *Zengjia*

Gushan liezu lianfang ji, printed in 1936 at Yongquan si, lists the temple's abbots beginning with Shenyan and continuing up through the early twentieth century.

93. Huiqiu Jizhao was also known as Zhongta Huiqui 中塔慧救. He has a brief entry in the *Zu tang ji*, j. 12, 433–435.

94. The *Jingde chuan deng lu* lists exactly twelve of Xuefeng Yicun's disciples in Fuzhou.

95. *Jingde chuan deng lu*, 372a24–b2.

96. The earliest references to "ten directions" (i.e., "public") Chan monasteries that I am aware of are Tiantong si 天童寺 (in Ningbo, present-day Zhejiang province), 847 (*Tiantong si zhi*, 2:2a); Xuedou shan zisheng chansi 雪竇山資聖禪寺 (also in Ningbo), 892 (*Xuedou si zhi lüe*, 5a); and Kaihua chanyuan 開化禪院 (in present-day Anhui province), 904 (*Huizhou fu zhi*, 4.4:3a). Morten Schlütter dismisses the first two (he does not mention the third) as late attributions and concludes that, while monasteries of a similar type must have existed earlier, "it was only in the Song that public monasteries became a legal and well defined category." Schlütter, *How Zen Became Zen*, 39, 193–194n54.

97. Schlütter, "Vinaya Monasteries, Public Abbacies, and State Control of Buddhism."

98. *Zu tang ji*, j. 10, 356–359.

99. Zhuge and Yin, *Minguo shishi biannian*, 132.

100. Ibid., 122.

101. *San shan zhi*, 616; and Zhuge and Yin, *Minguo shishi biannian*, 123, 133. "Zhongyi" 忠懿 (loyal and virtuous) was one of Wang Shenzhi's titles. The same title was also held by the last king of Wuyue, Qian Chu.

102. See Schafer, *The Empire of Min*, 28.

103. *Xin Wudai shi*, 582.

104. Wang Shenzhi was succeeded by his eldest son, Wang Yanhan 王延翰 (r. 925–926). Yanhan was soon murdered by his adoptive brother Wang Yanbing, who in turn enthroned yet another brother, Wang Yanjun. Yanjun reigned for nine years, during which time he had his brother Yanbing killed. Yanjun was succeeded by his son Wang Jipeng 王繼鵬 (r. 935–939), who reigned for three years before he was forced to flee the capital, pursued by his cousin. After Jipeng was found hiding in the wilderness, he was executed along with his wife and sons. Thereafter, the kingdom of Min was briefly ruled by two successive members of the Wang family, Wang Yanxi 王延羲 (r. 939–944) and Wang Yanzheng.

105. Wang Yanjun reportedly permitted the ordination of twenty thousand citizens (*min* 民) as monks in 928. During the Northern Song, it was claimed that no fewer than two thousand new monks were ordained every year during Yanjun's reign. Yanjun's brother Yanxi followed suit in 940, ordaining another eleven thousand. See *Zizhi tongjian*, 276:22a, 282:22a–b. A later account relates that, after assuming the throne, Yanjun also fed three million monks and made three hundred copies of the Buddhist canon (*Shuo fu*, 17[下]:45b). Such numbers are obviously exaggerated and intended to convey the tremendous strain the Wang family's support of the *saṃgha* placed on the region's economy. As for Daoist masters at the Min court, Wang Yanjun was allied with Chen Shouyan 陳守元 (n.d.). This same figure, along with Tan Zixiao 譚紫霄 (fl. 935–963), was also close to Wang Yanjun's

son Wang Jipeng. Tan Zixiao was known in Min as Dongxuan Tianshi, Zhenyi Xiansheng 洞玄天師貞一先生 (Master of True Unity, Celestial Master of Cavernous Mystery), and it was under his influence that Wang Jipeng purportedly used "several thousand catties of gold" to cast images of the Precious Emperor 寶皇 and Laozi. The king, according to some accounts, also searched for the divine elixir that would grant him immortality. See *Xin Wudai shi*, 576, 580. Like many Buddhist monks, after the fall of Min, Tan Zixiao traveled to the Southern Tang and established an abbey on Mt. Lu. The *Lushan ji* (1033c29–1034a2) notes that he was given the honorific name Jinmen Yuke 金門羽客 (Feathered Guest of the Golden Portal), presumably by the ruler of the Southern Tang, Li Jing 李璟 (r. 943–961). For more on Chen Shouyan and Tan Zixiao, see Qing Xitai, *Zhongguo Daojiao shi*, 2:395–396; and Schipper and Verellen, *The Taoist Canon*, 1064–1065. For discussions of Daoism and popular cults in the Fujian region, see Clark, *Portrait of a Community*, 187–211; and "The Religious Culture in the Minnan Region of Southern Fujian."

106. The Wang family was apparently able to maintain its position and privilege even after the fall of Min. During the Song, the Fujian region became a major source of bureaucratic and scholastic talent, and the descendants of the Wang family occupied a disproportionately large share of the province's *jinshi* degree holders. See Clark, "The Southern Kingdoms between the T'ang and the Sung," 190.

107. Foulk, "The Ch'an Tsung in Medieval China," 27.

4: Filial Sons

1. *Nantang shu* (Ma), 26:1b–2a; and *Nantang shu* (Lu), 18:2a.

2. *Xin Wudai shi*, 503.

3. *Nantang shu* (Lu), 18:2a.

4. *Jiangnan yeshi*, 3:7a.

5. *Qing xiang za ji*, 7:1b. The best overview of the history of the Southern Tang in English is Kurz, *China's Southern Tang Dynasty*. On the relationship between the Southern Tang court and Buddhist monks, see Tsukamoto Shunkō, "Godai Nantō no ōshitsu to Bukkyō"; and Chen B., "Nantang sanzhu yu Fojiao xinyang." While some Song-dynasty accounts claim Li Bian was inclined toward Daoist traditions, other authors asserted that that had an early affinity with Buddhism. His biological father, Li Rong 李榮 (n.d.), reportedly "enjoyed traveling with monks and retired to a temple," and Li Bian himself is said to have spent part of his childhood in a Buddhist monastery. While still in the service of the kingdom of Wu, Bian had a great residence built in Jianye 建業 (Nanjing). The compound was reportedly so large and ornate that its construction is said to have exhausted the region's resources. Once it was finished, Bian had it converted to a Buddhist temple. Moreover, rather than indulge in his harem, Li Bian purportedly sequestered his concubines and eventually had them all become Buddhist nuns. See *Nantang shu* (Ma), 6:3a; and *Nantang shu* (Lu), 16:2a.

6. The writings of the Southern Tang official Xu Xuan 徐鉉 (917–992), for example, reflect a popular religious culture of which Chan clerics represented only one facet. See Woolley, "Religion and Politics in the Writings of Xu Xuan."

7. Suzuki T., *Tō Godai Zenshū shi*, 291, 315–316.

8. Yanagida, "Tōmatsu Godai no Kahoku chihō," 185, and *Zenrin sōhōden yakuchū*, 58.

9. Yanagida, *Zenrin sōhōden yakuchū*, 92–97, and "Tōmatsu Godai no Kahoku chihō," 185.

10. Suzuki T., *Tō Godai Zenshū shi*, 80, 82.

11. On the provenance of Southern Tang bureaucrats, see Tackett, "The Transformation of Medieval Chinese Elites," 162–173.

12. The earliest sources for Yunmen Wenyan's life are two stelae erected in 958 and 964. The 958 inscription was authored by Lei Yue 雷岳 (n.d.) and titled *Dahan shaozhou yunmen shan Guangtai chanyuan gu Kuangzhen dashi shixing bei bing xu* 大漢韶州雲門山光泰禪院故匡真大師實性碑并序. For a translation of this inscription and a study of Wenyan's life and teachings, see App, "Facets of the Life and Teaching of Chan Master Yunmen Wenyan." The 964 inscription, *Dahan shaozhou yunmen shan Dajue chansi Da ciyun kuangsheng hongming dashi beiming* 大漢韶州雲門山大覺禪寺大慈雲匡聖弘明大師碑銘, was written by Chen Shouzhong 陳守中 (n.d.). Both inscriptions are transcribed in *Nanhan jinshi zhi*, in fascicles one and two, respectively. Wenyan was not among the five successors listed in Xuefeng Yicun's memorial inscription, nor was he accorded an entry in the *Song gaoseng zhuan*. This may be because at the time Yicun's inscription was composed, Wenyan had yet to be recognized as one of his most influential disciples. There is some evidence, however, that he may have been intentionally excluded from the historical record. The Song monk Juefan Huihong claimed, "When I first traveled to the Wu region and read Zanning's *Song Biographies*, I thought it strange that he did not include a biography of Yunmen [Wenyan]. I asked an elderly man about this, and he said that he had once heard his teacher, who was from the Wu region, say that he had met Zanning, who explained that he had deleted Yunmen's biography because he was 'no scholar.'" Translation slightly modified from Kieschnick, *The Eminent Monk*, 135. The first biographical collection to list Wenyan as one of Yicun's heirs was the *Zu tang ji*, but Kinugawa Kenji in his "*Sodōshū no kōri*" has shown that Wenyan's biography is a later addition to the 952 text.

13. App, "Facets of the Life and Teaching of Chan Master Yunmen Wenyan," 12.

14. On Buddhism in the Southern Han during the Five Dynasties, see Lin, "Godai Nankan no Bukkyō."

15. It is worth noting that in Shaozhou, Yunmen Wenyan first lived at Lingshu Cloister 靈樹院, whose abbot Rumin 如敏 (n.d.) was purportedly a disciple of Yishan Da'an (Yuanji), a Hongzhou school monk and associate of Xuefeng Yicun.

16. According to legend, Yunmen Wenyan's corpse, like that of Xuefeng Yicun, did not decay after death. According to the *Fozu tongji* (467a14–15), during the early Song, when Emperor Taizu ordered Wenyan's reliquary opened, the body appeared "life-like." The corpse was then shipped to the imperial palace to receive offerings. Later generations prayed to the body in times of drought, as they did with the mummified body of the sixth ancestor, Huineng, enshrined at Nanhua si 南華寺, located a short distance from Yunmen si.

17. The Yunmen, Guiyang, Caodong, Linji, and Fayan lineages were grouped together as the Five Houses (*wujia* 五家) of Chan in the mid-eleventh century. On the formation of this scheme, see Schlütter, *How Zen Became Zen*, 20–24.

18. These were Qingbing 清稟 (n.d.), Daoshen 道深 (n.d.), and Zhiming 智明 (n.d.). *Jingde chuan deng lu*, 390a22–b4, 390b26–28, and 390b29–c5.

19. Only Zhiming had a disciple of any discernable historical significance. In 1010, Yunhuo 雲豁 (n.d.), a monk renowned for his ability to remain in *samādhi* for extended periods, was called to the Song court, where Emperor Zhenzong 真宗 (r. 997–1022) had him reside in the northern imperial garden. Following Yunhuo, the next member of the Yunmen lineage to be supported by the Song court was Dajue Huailian 大覺懷璉 (1010–1090), who was summoned by Emperor Renzong 仁宗 (r. 1022–1063) in 1050. Thereafter, several monks of the Yunmen lineage began to receive imperial appointments. On the Yunmen faction during the Northern Song, see Huang C., "Yunmen zong yu Bei Song conglin zhi fazhan"; and Protass, "Mapping the Rise and Decline of the Yunmen Chan Lineage."

20. *Jingde chuan deng lu*, 370c22–28.

21. The Min prefecture of Jianzhou 建州 bordered the Southern Tang and lay on the primary land route connecting Fuzhou with interior and northern China. Not surprisingly, this was the first city to be occupied by the Southern Tang's armies. Just as Jianzhou would later supply the Southern Tang with former Min officials, the region was also an important staging ground for Min monks on their way to Jinling. On the prevalence of native Jianzhou officials at the Southern Tang court, see Aoyama, "The Newly-Risen Bureaucrats in Fukien at the Five Dynasty-Sung Period."

22. Xu Xuan's *Gu Tang Huiwu dashi muzhiming* 故唐慧悟大禪師墓志銘 is collected in the *Qisheng ji*, 30:1a–3a, and reproduced in Suzuki T., *Tō Godai Zenshū shi*, 282. The *Jingde chuan deng lu* (379a29–b6) also contains a brief biography of Huiwu.

23. Song Qiqiu was the son of Song Cheng 宋誠 (n.d.), who, together with Zhong Chuan 鍾傳 (d. 906), commanded troops in Jiangxi. Gao Pian 高駢 (ca. 822–887) subsequently recommended Zhong Chuan as military commissioner of Hongzhou and Song Cheng as assistant commissioner. After Zhong Chuan's death, amid power struggles for control of Jiangxi, Song Qiqiu fled to Huainan, where he was taken in by Li Bian (a.k.a. Xu Zhigao). Later, when Li Bian deposed Yang Pu and established the Southern Tang, he appointed Song Qiqiu to the position of prime minster and later to military commissioner of Zhennan. Following the death of Li Bian, his son and successor, Li Jing, named Song Qiqiu the head of the secretariat. In addition to Huiwu, Song Qiqiu was involved with several other Buddhist monks, including Fayan Wenyi's disciple Huilang 慧朗 (n.d.) from Huacheng Temple 化城寺 on Mt. Lu (*Jingde chuan deng lu*, 420a3–11); Luohan Guichen's grand-disciple Yuande 緣德 (898–977); and Mazu Daoyi's great-grand-disciple Guangxiao Huijue 光孝慧覺 (n.d.). Later in life, Song Qiqiu ran afoul of Li Jing's ministers, the so-called five devils, and was repeatedly demoted. He was eventually confined to Mt. Jiuhua, where he reportedly hanged himself at the age of seventy-three.

24. *Gu Tang Huiwu daishi muzhiming* (*Qisheng ji*, 30:1b–2a). According to his biography in the *Song shi* (274:5b–6a), Wang Jixun was the son of Wang Yanmei 王延美 (fl. 934) and the grandson of Wang Shengui. Formerly the prefect of Quanzhou (944–945), he was relocated to the Southern Tang capital by Liu Congxiao and appointed prefectural magistrate (*junshou* 郡守) of Chiyang sometime thereafter. Wang Jixun was eventually buried in the Southern Tang capital, Jinling; his

tomb epitaph was recently excavated in Nanjing. (A version of the inscription is found in the *Qinding quan Tang wen*, 875:11a–13b; see Tackett, "The Transformation of Medieval Chinese Elites," 163, 204.) In addition to corresponding with Huiwu, Wang Jixun also maintained contact with at least one of Xuefeng Yicun's disciples, Helong Miaokong 和龍妙空 (n.d.), who had also left Min for the Southern Tang (*Jingde chuan deng lu*, 359a26–b4). One of the poems Wang Jixun sent to Helong Miaokong, when the monk was in residence at Lingqing yuan 靈慶院 (in present-day Anhui province), reads: "South of Mt. Baimian at Lingqing Cloister, / a man of the Way practices Xuefeng Chan in a thatched hut. / He dwells among the clouds and trees on two or three acres / and hasn't descended into the haze for four or five years. / He can distinguish the calls of apes and birds; / his unwavering determination subdues dragons and spirits. / Who knows that today on the banks of Autumn River / the Medicine King walks alone, laying out a Dharma feast?" (*Quan Tang shi*, 763:4b–5a.) Another poem to Miaokong, composed by Xia Hong 夏鴻 (n.d.), is also reproduced in the *Quan Tang shi*: "In the ruins of a scholar's [hut] before a still pool, / a solitary and lofty monk practices Chan. / Emerging, he preaches and converts believers for days. / Sitting, he brings years of peace and tranquility to our kingdom. / His body is as radiant and penetrating as a *maṇi* jewel. / His words are like swords of wisdom, daggers of determination. / The fruit of his way has already ripened, his name is already established. / Look! People come from all around [to offer] incense and food" (763:5b–6a).

25. Changqing si had originally been established for the Indian translator Guṇabhadra 求那跋陀羅 (394–468) as Zhihuan si 祇洹寺 (Jetavana Temple). The name was changed to Changqing in the Kaiyuan era of the Tang (713–741). During the Baoda era of the Southern Tang (943–958), Li Jing changed the name again to Fengxian 奉先 (Revering Ancestors) in honor of his late father. In the Taiping xingguo era of the Song (976–983), the name was changed yet again to Baoning 保寧 (Protecting the Peace). *Jingding Jiankang zhi*, 46:1a–3a; and *Nanchao Fosi zhi*, 52–59.

26. The *Lushan ji* (1033c29–1034a13) also records that the monks at four monasteries on the mountain (Kaixian 開先, Qixian 棲賢, Guizong 歸宗, and Yuantong 圓通), all of which were headed by monks from Xuefeng Yicun's lineage, conducted mortuary rites for each of the three Southern Tang rulers.

27. Because of the ubiquity of temples bearing the name Baoen (Repaying Kindness) and the frequency of name changes during this period, the identity of this temple is difficult to trace. Most likely, the temple mentioned here was first established in 425 by Song Emperor Wendi (r. 424–453), who gave it the name Baoen and designated it an ancestral shrine for his late father Gaozu (r. 420–422). The original structure was destroyed during the Huichang persecutions but rebuilt around 934, during the reign of the Yang family of Wu, with the new name Baoxian 報先 (Repaying the Ancestors). The name was changed again to Xingci 興慈 (Flourishing Compassion) during the Shengyuan era of the Southern Tang (937–942). The temple was destroyed during the Kaibao era of the Song (968–975), probably when the city was invaded by Song troops, and subsequently rebuilt in 978. Early in the twelfth century, the name was changed yet again to Nengren si 能仁寺 (Śākyamuni Temple). See *Jingding Jiankang zhi*, 46:4a–b; *Chūgoku Zenshū jimei sanmei jiten*, 341–342, 400; and Suzuki T., *Tō Godai Zenshū shi*, 281.

28. On Fayan Wenyi's life and teachings, see also Deng, *Fayan Wenyi chanshi zhi yanjiu*; and Welter, *Monks, Rulers, and Literati*, 139–144.

29. This was at Zhitong Cloister 智通院 in Xinding 新定 under the tutelage of Chan Master Quanwei 全偉 (n.d.).

30. The two monks were Shaoxiu 紹修 (n.d.) and Fajin 法進 (n.d.). Shaoxiu was a disciple of Luohan Guichen. He later settled on Mt. Longji 龍濟山 in Fuzhou 撫州 (*Jingde chuan deng lu*, 400c9–401a25). Although Shaoxiu gained some notice for his teachings (the *Song shi* [205:12b] lists a collection of his talks in one fascicle titled *Seng Shaoxiu yuyao* 僧紹修語要), there is no evidence that he was ever patronized by the Southern Tang court. Fajin was a grand-disciple of Xuefeng Yicun through Ehu Zhifu 鵝湖智孚 (n.d.).

31. *Song gaoseng zhuan*, 788a29–b2.

32. *Jingde chuan deng lu*, 399c26–27.

33. Before Fayan Wenyi, a grand-disciple of Dongshan Liangjie, Chongshou Daoqin 崇壽道欽 (n.d.) served as abbot of Chongshou yuan. At Baoen, the previous abbot was Caoshan Benyi's disciple Congzhi 從志 (n.d.) (*Jingde chuan deng lu*, 364b3–11). Gushan Shenyan's disciples Qinghu and Huiwu were appointed to Baoen after Wenyi's death.

34. Xiufu was originally from Beihai 北海 (present-day Shandong). He traveled to Min during the same period that Fayan Wenyi was also in Fuzhou and the two appear to have been close. A passage in Wenyi's biography shows him instructing Xiufu: "Master [Wenyi] and Chan Master [Xiufu] Wukong were warming themselves by the fire. [Wenyi] picked up an incense spoon and asked Wukong, 'You cannot call this an incense spoon. What do you call it, brother?' Wukong replied, 'An incense spoon.' Fayan [Wenyi] did not approve. After more than twenty days, Wukong came to understand [Wenyi's] words" (*Jingde chuan deng lu*, 399b28–c2). Xiufu succeeded Wenyi as abbot of Chongshou yuan on Mt. Cao and in 944 was called to serve as abbot of Qingliang si in the capital. Before his death, Xiufu requested that Wenyi succeed him as abbot. He also sent a farewell letter to the king, who in turn dispatched attendants to look after his final needs. Xiufu's death was mourned by the king, and his stupa inscription, like that of Fayan Wenyi, was written by the assistant minister and court literatus Han Xizai 韓熙載 (902–970) (*Baoke congbian*, 419). For Xiufu's biographies see *Jingde chuan deng lu*, 400a29–c8; and *Wu deng hui yuan*, 180b18–181a4. There is some confusion over the date of Xiufu's death. The *Jingde chuan deng lu* contradicts its own statement that he passed away in 943, saying that he was summoned to Qingliang Temple in 944. The titles of four inscriptions for this monk still exist, all of them stating that they were composed in the ninth year of the Baoda era (951), which was likely the year of his death.

35. Qingliang si was originally built by Xu Wen, the father of the first ruler of the Southern Tang, with the name Xingjiao si 興教寺. After Li Bian deposed the last king of Wu, he changed the temple's name to City of Stones, Clear and Cool Great Bodhimaṇḍa (Shicheng qingliang da daochang 石城清涼大道場). *Jingding Jiankang zhi*, 46:8a–10a.

36. According to popular legend, one of Li Yu's subjects had died and was resuscitated. While in the netherworld, he saw the first ruler of the Southern Tang,

Li Bian, engaged in forced labor. The subject asked him how he ended up there, and Li Bian replied that he had wronged Song Qiqiu and murdered thousands of people in Hezhou. He then instructed the man that when he returned to the land of the living he should tell the present ruler—his grandson—that the sound of the great bells in Buddhist and Daoist temples temporarily relieves his suffering. On learning this, Li Yu had a bell cast and placed at Qingliang si. Its inscription read, "We pray that the late Liezu 烈祖, Great Filial Emperor, may be freed from the underworld and escape from suffering." *Lei shuo*, 18:22b–23a; *Jingding Jiankang zhi*, 46:8b–9a; and *Fozu tongji*, 392a7–18. Qingliang also contained a miraculous Amitābha image, a dragon painting by the Southern Tang artist Dong Yu 董羽 (n.d.), and the calligraphy of Li Xiaoyuan 李霄遠 (n.d.). *Jingding Jiankang zhi*, 46:9a. On Dong Yu, see *Shiguo chunqiu*, 31:12a–b. On Li Xiaoyuan, see *Liu yi zhi yi lu*, 332:20a–b.

37. *Jingde chuan deng lu*, 415a18–20.

38. The *Song gaoseng zhuan* records the title of Great Fayan, while the *Jingde chuan deng lu* gives Great Guiding Master, Great Wisdom Treasury 大智藏大導師. The title *Daoshi* (Guiding Master) was an honorific reserved for the Southern Tang's most eminent monks, and was the equivalent of the better-known title *Guoshi* 國師, or national teacher (see the *Da Song seng shi lüe*, 244c1–15). In the Southern Tang, only two other monks are known to have received it, both disciples of Fayan Wenyi: Xingyan 行言(n.d.) and Wensui 文遂 (n.d.). Following the death of Fayan Wenyi, the abbacy of Qingliang passed to at least two of his disciples. The first of these was Fadeng Taiqin 法燈泰欽 (d. 974). According to the *Jingde chuan deng lu*, before he passed away, Taiqin publicly addressed his assembly, saying, "This old monk has been the abbot [at Qingliang] for over twelve years and has always received the assistance of the ruler." *Jingde chuan deng lu*, 415b12–14. At Taiqin's request, his remains were interred next to Wenyi's on South Mountain. After his death, Taiqin was succeeded at Qingliang by Wensui.

39. *Nantang shu* (Ma), 13:1; translation modified from Sun, "Rewriting the Southern Tang," 42.

40. Sun, "Rewriting the Southern Tang," 144.

41. Tackett, "The Transformation of Medieval Chinese Elites," 159–160. In 940, Li Bian established the Imperial Academy at Mt. Lu 廬山國學, which functioned as a center of classical learning in the Southern Tang. This academy later evolved into the White Deer Academy 白鹿洞書院 during the Song. Sun, "Rewriting the Southern Tang," 43.

42. *Yu hai*, 52:42a. See also Kurz, "The Compilation and Publication of the *Taiping yulan* and the *Cefu yuangui*," 41.

43. *Song gaoseng zhuan*, 747c12–13.

44. Unfortunately, nothing else is known about this monk.

45. The *Zhenyuan xinding shijiao mulu* 貞元新定釋教目錄 (*Taishō shinshū daizōkyō*, 55n2157) was compiled by the scholar-monk Yuanzhao 圓照 (n.d.) in 800.

46. The first copy of the newly assembled collection was bestowed on the Xizang Cloister 西藏院 of the Shengyuan Temple 昇元寺 within the capital. On this temple, see the *Jingding Jiankang zhi*, 46:13b–14a.

47. At least one foreign monk is said to have traveled to Jinling to present a palm-leaf sutra. Another monk, from Longxing si 龍興寺 in Hangzhou, was then summoned to translate the text (the title is not recorded). It was only during the Northern Song, however, that Jinling developed into a center for the translation of Buddhist texts. One of the monks in charge of these activities was Weijing 惟淨 (d. 1051), a nephew of the Southern Tang's last king. Weijing had studied Sanskrit and headed a team in translating the large collection of sutras that were introduced from the "western regions" during the Jingde and Xiangfu eras (1004–1016). For his efforts he was awarded a purple robe and the name Great Master Guangfan 光梵. See *Nantang shu* (Lu), 18:3b; and *Fozu tongji*, 398:c22–28. Several of Weijing's translations are preserved in the Taishō canon. On translation projects during the Northern Song, see Sen, *Buddhism, Diplomacy, and Trade*, chap. 3.

48. According to Qingbing's entry in the *Jingde chuan deng lu* (390a28–b1), after the ruler appointed Qingbing to Guangmu Cloister, he ordered him to come to the Hall for Clarifying the Mind 澄心堂, a library within the royal palace, to work on compiling a collection of essential sayings (*zhufang yuyao* 諸方語要). Unfortunately, no such work appears to have survived. Daoqi's work is mentioned in the *Jingde chuan deng lu* (428c18–19).

49. Zhaozhou's record, the *Zhaozhou Zhenji chanshi yulu* 趙州真際禪師語錄, is contained in fascicles 13 and 14 of the *Guzunsu yulu*. On the history of this text, see Yanagida, "The Development of the 'Recorded Sayings' Texts of Chinese Ch'an Buddhism," 199–200.

50. Jia, *Gudian Chan yanjiu*, 316.

51. Yanagida, "Goroku no rekishi," 253–254; Yanagida, "The Development of the 'Recorded Sayings' Texts of Chinese Ch'an Buddhism," 199–201; Ishii, *Sōdai Zenshūshi no kenkyū*, 93–104; and Jia, *Gudian Chan yanjiu*, 315–318.

52. *Song gaoseng zhuan*, 788b13–14. "Zhi" probably refers to Zhidun 支遁 (314–366) and "Tang" may refer to Tang Huixiu 湯惠休 (n.d.), a monk and poet who lived during the Liu Song era (420–479).

53. *Jingde chuan deng lu*, 400a6–11. The collections mentioned here most likely refer to the two, single-fascicle compilations of his work listed in the *Song shi* (205:11a): *Wenyi fayan chanshi ji* 文益法眼禪師集 and *Fayan chanshi ji zhenzan* 法眼禪師集眞贊. Wenyi also composed a now lost commentary to the *Cantong qi* 參同契 (J. Sandōkai)—a poem by the eighth-century Chan monk Shitou Xiqian that later became closely associated with Caodong lineage. See *Linjian lu* 林間錄, 253a4–5.

54. The received version of the *Zongmen shi gui lun* contains a postface by the monk Yun Shuzhong 惲恕中 (1310–1386) that was discovered in a Korean library and subsequently appended to the original text. It reads: "During the *bingxu* year of the Yuan (1346), Yue Zangzhu 悅藏主 of [Mt.] Nanping 南屏 [in southern Hangzhou] produced this text and asked me to copy it. The woodblocks [had been kept] in the Jizhao tayuan 寂照塔院 on Mt. Jing 徑山. When Mt. Jing was captured during the war, the blocks were burned. The eminent Min 旻 from [Mt.] Weiyu 委羽 in Tai[zhou] 台[州] contributed his own funds and a new edition was printed using old rubbings" (39a17–24). The earliest surviving textual reference to Fayan Wenyi's *Admonishments* that I am aware of is in the *Congrong lu* 從容錄 (267a22–23), first circulated in 1244.

55. *Zongmen shi gui lun*, 36c3–4.

56. Welter, *Monks, Rulers, and Literati*, 141–142.

57. *Jingde chuan deng lu*, 398c4–11.

58. Ibid., 454b28.

59. *Ren tian yanmu*, 325a5.

60. *Jingde chuan deng lu*, 400b1–3.

61. Wensui was originally from Hangzhou but his parents moved to the city of Xuan 宣 (in present-day Anhui province) when he was still an infant. He became a monk at the age of sixteen in Chizhou 池州 (also in Anhui) and commenced studying meditation and Chan teachings (*guanfang chanjiao* 觀方禪教). He later traveled to Jinling, where he became Fayan Wenyi's disciple. He eventually settled at Zhiguan Temple 止觀 in Jizhou 吉州 (present-day Jiangxi). In Wenyi's *Song Biography*, Wensui is identified by this toponym, so he probably arrived there shortly after Wenyi's death in 958. From Jizhou, the last ruler of the Southern Tang, Li Yu, invited Wensui back to the capital to head Changqing Temple in 964. It was after this that he was appointed abbot of Qingliang Temple and later of Baoci daochang 報慈道場, where he subsequently passed away. See the *Jingde chuan deng lu*, 411c6–412a13.

62. *Jingde chuan deng lu*, 411c8–15.

63. *Nantang shu* (Ma), 26:4a–5a. On the position of *pushe* (or *puye*), see Hucker, *A Dictionary of Official Titles in Imperial China*, 394–395. Yingzhi was from southern Min and bore the family name of Wang, suggesting a possible kinship with the ruling Wang family. He was one of the few monks to elicit praise from Ma Ling in his history of the Southern Tang, and this can probably be credited to his literary abilities. Yingzhi had passed the *jinshi* examination and was well trained in the classic literary arts. He was especially famous for his mastery of the Liu 柳 style of calligraphy. After being dismissed from his official duties, Yingzhi is said to have become disillusioned with secular life and thereafter was ordained as a Buddhist monk. Li Jing ordered him to teach and awarded him a purple robe and the title "Great Worthy" (Dade 大德). Yingzhi declined the position of monastic recorder of the right, preferring instead to retire to the western hermitage of Fengxian Temple 奉先寺 in the capital. *Nantang shu* (Ma), 26:4b. According to the *Lushan ji* (1029a16–19), Yingzhi also had a hermitage on Mt. Lu known as the Five Fir Pavilion (Wushan ge 五杉閣). It was here that he reportedly met with Li Jing and composed the now lost *Wushan ji* 五杉集. This text was said to have been widely circulated and used a preparatory book by monks during the Song. Some of Yingzhi's other works are listed in the *Song shi* 宋史: *Linshu guanyao* 臨書關要 (202:36a), *Sizhu jingang jing* 四注金剛經 (205:12b), and *Yingzhi ji* 應之集 (208:36b). The eleventh-century *Chongwen zongmu* (12:5b) also lists a collection of his poems: *Yingzhi shi* 應之詩.

64. This account is drawn from the writings of Yang Yi; cited in Woolley, "Religion and Politics in the Writings of Xu Xuan," 74.

65. *Xu zhenyuan shijiao lu*, 1049b7–11; and *Nantang shu* (Lu), 18:1b. Li Bian exerted his imperial privilege to have Li Tongxuan's commentary (*Xin Huayan jing lun* 新華嚴經論 [*Taishō shinshū* daizōkyō, 36n1739]—the same text mentioned by Fayan Wenyi—entered into the Buddhist canon.

66. Primary sources on Xuanji include Xu Xuan's inscription for his image hall (*Qisheng ji*, 28:8b–10a), and *Nantang shu* (Lu), where he is listed by the name

Yuanji 元寂 (26:3b–4a). During the reign of the second ruler, Li Jing, the monk Xingyin 行因 (d. ca. 943–957) wrote a commentary on the *Avataṃsaka* in ten fascicles. After Xingyin's death, Li Jing had an artist paint the monk's portrait. *Lushan ji*, 1031a9–12.

67. On Zongmi, see Gregory, *Tsung-mi and the Sinification of Buddhism*; and Broughton, *Zongmi on Chan*.

68. *Zongmen shi gui lun*, 36c1–2. Compare with Zongmi: "While awakening from delusion is sudden, the transformation of an unenlightened person into an enlightened person is gradual." *Chan Chart* (*Wan xu zang jing*, 63n1225), 35b11; translated (and emended) in Gregory, *Tsung-mi and the Sinification of Buddhism*, 194.

69. For accounts of monastic transgression in the Southern Tang, see Brose, "Credulous Kings and Immoral Monks."

70. The earliest surviving edition of *Guishan's Admonitions* (*Guishan jingce* 溈山警策) has been dated to 936. The entire text is translated in Kirchner, "The Admonitions of Zen Master Guishan Dayuan." For a partial translation and study, see Poceski, "*Guishan jingce* (*Guishan's Admonitions*) and the Ethical Foundations of Chan Practice."

71. *Jingde chuan deng lu*, 342c16–343a20. Wuyin was from Fujian and became a monk under Xuefeng Yicun at the age of seven. He went on to train under Jiufeng Daoqian 九峯道虔 (n.d.), presumably in Yunzhou (present-day Jiangxi province), where the latter was teaching. Wuyin later settled in the Southern Tang, where he was patronized by the first and second kings. His epitaph was written by Xu Xuan: *Hongzhou Xishan Cuiyan guanghua yuan gu Chengyuan chanshi beiming* 洪州西山翠巖廣化院故澄源禪師碑銘, in the *Qisheng ji*, 27:1a–3a. See also *Zu tang ji*, j. 12, 413–422. Wuyin's admonishments have not survived.

72. This appears to have been a common critique. The stupa inscription of Yangshan Huiji 仰山慧寂 (807–883) written by Lu Xisheng in 895 noted that Yangshan's students often missed the point of his enigmatic instructions: "Raising eyebrows, twinkling eyes, knocking with a wooden stick, and pointing to objects, they imitated each other, little short of making fun. This was not the Master's fault." Translated in Jia, *The Hongzhou School of Chan Buddhism*, 50.

73. A quote from the *Nirvana Sūtra* (*Taishō shinshū daizōkyō*, 12n375), 613a.

74. Cf. the *Yongjia zhengdao ge* 永嘉證道歌: "Alas it is the wicked age of the end of the dharma. Living beings are unhappy and control is difficult. The sage is long gone and false views run deep. The demons are strong and the dharma is weak. Fear and injury abound." *Taishō shinshū daizōkyō*, 48n2014:396b.

75. *Zongmen shi gui lun*, 38c16–23.

76. Ibid., 38b24–c5.

77. Zhu Xi 朱熹 (1130–1200), the prominent Song-dynasty Confucian scholar and native of Jiangxi, singled out the teachings of Fayan Wenyi and his disciples as the most compatible with his own philosophical principles (*Lixue* 理學). *Zhuzi yulei*, 126:3018.

78. Fayan Wenyi and members of his lineage feature prominently as masters of "literary Chan" in the writings of Juefan Huihong. For a recent study of the literary Chan movement in the Northern Song and its ties to monks of the Fayan lineage, see Xu, "Yi biyan zuo Foshi."

79. *Jingde chuan deng lu*, 400a6–11. Among these sixty-three heirs, four are highlighted: Deshao 德韶 (national teacher of Wuyue), Wensui 文邃 (guiding teacher of the Southern Tang), Huiju 慧炬 (national teacher of Koryŏ), and Fadeng Taiqin 法燈泰欽. The *Song gaoseng zhuan* lists six "disciples who carried on his lineage": Deshao 德韶, Huiming 慧明, Zhiyi 智依, Daoqin 道欽, Guangyi 光逸 (a.k.a. Kuangyi 匡逸), and Wensui 文邃.

80. *Nantang shu* (Ma), 26:2a–3a; and *Nantang shu* (Lu), 18:2b–3b. These events are discussed in more detail in Brose, "Credulous Kings and Immoral Monks."

81. *Nantang shu* (Lu), 18:3b.

82. According to the *Xu zizhi tongjian changbian* (16:28a), the conscripted monks were later freed by the Song government.

83. Yuande was originally from Zhejiang, born to a family of Confucian scholars and painters. He first studied under Xuefeng Yicun's disciple Daofu and later (according to the *Jingde chuan deng lu*) with Luohan Guichen's heir, Hongjin 洪進 (n.d.). Li Yu summoned Yuande to the capital to assume the abbacy of the newly built Luohan Cloister 羅漢院, but Yuande asked to be allowed to remain in the mountains. The king then built Yuantong si on Mt. Lu and appointed Yuande abbot. In addition to the king's support, the *Song gaoseng zhuan* also claims that Song Qiqiu was one of Yuande's disciples. Intriguingly, this same biography hints that Yuande may have also practiced alchemy 黃白術. For Yuande's biographies, see *Jingde chuan deng lu*, 420c20–421a6; and *Song gaoseng zhuan*, 789a6–19.

84. *Duxing zazhi*, 1:8b.

85. *Shuo fu*, 20(下):28b; and Chen B., "Nantang sanzhu yu Fojiao xinyang," 262–263. According to Yuande's *Song gaoseng zhuan* biography, he died in his temple during the Kaibao era (968–975). The *Chanlin sengbao zhuan* gives the more precise date of 977, suggesting that he died some years after the Song invasion.

86. *Quan Tang shi*, 889:10b.

87. *You mei tang ji* 有美堂記 (1057), in *Wen zhong ji*, 40:9a.

5: Heirs and Ancestors

1. *Xin Wudai shi*, 570.

2. Variant versions of this story are found in the *Wuyue beishi*, 4:1a–b; *Song gaoseng zhuan*, 789a26–28; and *Jingde chuan deng lu*, 407c2–5.

3. Abe Chōichi's study of the patronage of Buddhist and Daoist figures by Wuyue's kings in the second section of his *Chūgoku Zenshū shi no kenkyū* remains one of the best treatments of the topic. Lai Jiancheng's *Wuyue Fojiao zhi fazhan* contains a brief discussion of Buddhist patronage in Wuyue as well as more comprehensive coverage of Wuyue's monks and monasteries. The best overview of clergy-court relations in Wuyue in English is Huang Y., *Integrating Chinese Buddhism*, chap. 3.

4. *Song gaoseng zhuan*, 781b3–8. There is a similar story in the *Wuyue beishi* (1:2b) concerning a monk whose name is given as Hongyan 洪渰, which seems to be a scribal error for Hongyin 洪諲.

5. Jingshan was first built for the revered Oxhead Chan master Faqin in the mid-eighth century. After falling into disrepair, the monastery was restored in the mid-ninth century and Jianzong was appointed the second abbot. On the history

of Chan at Mt. Jing from the Tang through the Song, see Furuta, "Zenshū shijō ni okeru Kinzan no kenkyū."

6. Qian Liu later granted Jianzong the posthumous name Wushang 無上 ("Unexcelled"). *Song gaoseng zhuan*, 779c25–27.

7. *Song gaoseng zhuan*, 817c7–818a3. Wenxi studied the *Lotus Sūtra* along with Tiantai teachings and eventually turned to Chan under the guidance of Yangshan Huiyi. Rumors circulated that Wenxi had been given Mazu Daoyi's robe—the paradigmatic symbol of transmission—as a "treasure of trust," and Wenxi's body, like that of Chu'nan, reportedly did not decompose after his death. When rebels opened his tomb, his body was discovered intact, as if sitting in meditation. *Song gaoseng zhuan*, 783c15–784a20; and *Jingde chuan deng lu*, 294a5–25.

8. *Song gaoseng zhuan*, 817c23–24.

9. These words are reminiscent of a passage in the *Varjrasamādhi Sūtra*: "The five *skandhas* all arise in the action of a single moment of thought. In the arising of the five *skandhas* all fifty evils are contained." *Taishō shinshū daizōkyō*, 9n273, 369a13–14; translation from Buswell, *The Formation of Ch'an Ideology in China and Korea*, 208.

10. *Jingde chuan deng lu*, 292c8–10.

11. Ibid., 293a21–22.

12. *Song gaoseng zhuan*, 787b7–c12; and *Jingde chuan deng lu*, 297b1–c1.

13. Also known as Jingqing Daofu 鏡清道怤. *Zu tang ji*, j. 10, 341–350.

14. See, for example, *Chanyuan zhuquan ji duxu*, 400b17–20.

15. *Zu tang ji*, j. 10, 342; and *Jingde chuan deng lu*, 348c9–11.

16. *Jingde chuan deng lu*, 349b7–9.

17. *Song gaoseng zhuan*, 787a29–b1.

18. *Jingde chuan deng lu*, 352a26–27. For Lingzhao's biographies, see also *Zu tang ji*, j. 11, 384–390; and *Song gaoseng zhuan*, 788a6–17.

19. Lingzhao, like Daofu, initially settled at Yuezhou's Jianqing Cloister 鑑清院, where he attracted the attention of Pi Guangye. But whereas Daofu was greatly esteemed by the assistant commissioner, Lingzhao appears to have rubbed him the wrong way and consequently left for Longxing Temple in Hangzhou.

20. *Song gaoseng zhuan*, 788a13–14. In his *Da Song seng shi lüe* (240a24–25), Zanning lists the wearing of soiled five-piece robes as a distinguishing feature of meditation (*chan*) monks.

21. On the extreme asceticism of Mahāsattva Fu (a.k.a. Fuxi 傅翕 or Shanhui 善慧) and his followers, see Benn, *Burning for the Buddha*, 91. Two of Huileng's students, Yanqiu 彦球 (n.d.) (supported by Qian Chu) and Qiying 契盈 (n.d.), followed Lingzhao as abbots of Longhua yuan. The temple's abbacy was later filled by at least two of Deshao's students, Huiju 慧居 (n.d.) (also patronized by Qian Chu) and Shaoluan 紹鑾 (n.d.).

22. *Jingde chuan deng lu*, 355c17–356a3.

23. One disciple of Xuefeng Yicun, Xingxiu 行脩/修 (d. 951), for instance, "did not offer instruction but only sat in silent meditation. When asked a question, he would simply smile." *Song gaoseng zhuan*, 898c29–899a2.

24. Another monk supported by Qian Liu, Congli 從禮 (847–925), reportedly "never slept, ate only once a day, spent most of his time in seated [meditation], and

kept no possessions." He was known for his strict observance of the precepts but was apparently a slow learner. Frustrated with his inability to stay awake when reading scriptures, "he would drive nails into his forehead and the palms of his hands until they ran with blood." His biographer suggests that the depth of his resolve, his purity of conduct, and the power of his *samādhi* gave rise to supernormal powers. At Congli's request, Wang Ziqiao 王子喬 (trad. 6th century BCE), the legendary Daoist immortal and guardian spirit of the Tiantai mountains, conjured rain during a drought and felled trees for monastic water troughs. Qian Liu summoned Congli to the capital, constructed a Golden Light sanctum (presumably for the performance of Golden Light ceremonies), and conferred lavish donations. Despite these resources, Congli is said to have kept only a patched robe and left only relics when he died. *Song gaoseng zhuan*, 809c5–810a3.

25. *Zong jing lu*, 415b10–15. The entire preface, along with the first fascicle of the *Zong jing lu*, has been translated in Welter, *Yongming Yanshou's Conception of Chan in the "Zongjing lu."*

26. Qian Chu's postface, carved on the subterranean crypt of Hangzhou's Leifeng stupa, is reproduced in the *Xianchun Lin'an zhi*, 82:17a–b. A fragment of the original engraving was retrieved after the stupa's collapse. Daoqian was an avid reader of sūtras and a skilled poet. Like several of Fayan Wenyi's students, he left the Southern Tang to settle in Wuyue, where he first paid obeisance to the Buddha's relics at Ayuwang si in Mingzhou. At that time, Daoqian was mentored by the monastic controller Huizheng 彙征 (see chap. 2, n. 45), who invited him to attend a vegetarian feast and Samantabhadra repentance ritual on Mt. Mao. Before long, Daoqian was summoned to confer the bodhisattva precepts on the king. Qian Chu subsequently built a large monastery along the banks of West Lake called Huiri Yongming yuan 慧日永明院 and invited Daoqian to serve as the first abbot. Daoqian was further awarded with a monthly stipend and the name Chan Master Cihua Dinghui 慈化定慧. Daoqian passed away in 961, and some years later Deshao erected a stone stupa for his remains. *Song gaoseng zhuan*, 788c8–789a4; and *Jingde chuan deng lu*, 412b15–c25.

27. The reliquaries, modeled on the Aśokan reliquary Qian Liu retrieved from Ayuwang si in Mingzhou to Baota si in Hangzhou, contained printed scrolls of the *Yiqie rulai xin mimi quanshen sheli baoqieyin tuoluoni jing* 一切如來心秘密全身舍利寶篋印陀羅尼經 (Sanskrit: *Sarvatathāgata-adhiṣṭhāna-hṛdaya-guhyadhātu karaṇḍa-mudrā-dhāraṇī*). For a study and summary of the text, see Edgren, "The Printed Dhāraṇī Sūtra of A.D. 956." On the Baoqieyin stupas, see Yoshikawa I., *Sekizō hōkyōintō no seiritsu*; and Wang L., "Baoqieyin jingta yu Wuyue guo dui Ri wenhua jiaoliu." On Buddhist art in Wuyue, see Falco, "Royal Patronage of Buddhist Art in Tenth-Century Wu Yüeh."

28. Qian Chu's production of Buddhist canons is recorded in the *Xianchun Lin'an zhi*, 76:11b. Qian Chu also sponsored a copy of the Daoist canon written in silver on blue paper, produced by a joint group of Daoist adepts and Buddhist monks. The resulting two hundred cases of texts were housed on Mt. Tiantai at Tongbai Abbey 桐柏觀. See "Chongjian daozang jing ji" 重建道藏經記, in *Tiantai shan zhi* 天台山志, *Zhengtong Daozang*, no. 603, 18:14335–14344. As for Buddhist temples, the *Shiguo chunqiu* (81:8a) records 480 during the reign of Qian Chu, though many

of these must have been small shrines. Suzuki Tetsuo has compiled a list of major temples established by Wuyue kings. In addition to those built by Qian Chu, Qian Liu is credited with sixteen, Qian Yuanguan with twenty-four, and Qian Zuo with thirty-five. See Suzuki T., *Tō Godai Zenshū shi*, 159–160. A much longer list, culled from Song gazetteers and listed by region, can be found in Lai, *Wuyue Fojiao zhi fazhan*, 161–217.

29. Qian Chu had statues of his grandfather Qian Liu; his father, Yuanguan; and his brother Qian Zuo enshrined at Baota si (Zhuge and Yin, *Wuyue shishi biannian*, 343). In 968, in the west of Hangzhou, Qian Chu established another Buddhist temple, named Fengxian 奉先 (Revering Ancestors), in which he also enshrined statues of the Qian patriarchs (ibid., 350, 352–353). Tiantai Deshao's disciple Qingyu 清昱 (d. ca. 968–975) was invited to serve as the first abbot of Fengxian, and Fayan Wenyi's disciple Fagui 法瓌 (n.d.) later occupied the same position. While Baota and Fengxian were clearly key nodes in the Qian family's network of ancestral shrines, Qian Chu did not limit his piety to the patriline. Shortly after his mother's death, he established Baoen yuanjiao si 報恩元教寺 in the north of Hangzhou as a shrine for her spirit. Qian Chu also had statues of his mother cast and enshrined at two nunneries, Fengguo 奉國 and Jinchi 金池. The former temple was originally built for Qian Liu's daughter, who had become a nun in 919. Further afield, King Qian Chu's cousin Qian Renfeng 錢仁奉 (fl. 942–969) built Jianfu yuan 薦福院 at the site of his father's tomb and summoned Fayan Wenyi's disciple Shaoming 紹明 (n.d.) to fill the abbacy. After Renfeng passed away, he too was buried nearby.

30. *Song gaoseng zhuan*, 859b29. In addition to his biography in the *Song gaoseng zhuan*, Huiming also has an entry in the *Jingde chuan deng lu*, 410b13–c24.

31. *Song gaoseng zhuan*, 859b29–c1. The *Jingde chuan deng lu* places his hermitage on Mt. Damei 大梅山.

32. *Jingde chuan deng lu*, 410b16–18.

33. Ibid., 410c2–4.

34. Huiming's interlocutor in this passage is identified as Tianlong 天龍, the name of the temple where Daofu was serving as abbot.

35. *Jingde chuan deng lu*, 410c3–14. Baoen was first established for Huiming sometime around 950. After Huiming's death, this temple was passed on to a series of his dharma-brothers under Deshao: Deqian 德謙 (n.d.), Faduan 法端 (n.d.), Shaoan 紹安 (n.d.), and Yongan 永安 (911–974).

36. *Song gaoseng zhuan*, 859c6.

37. Deshao was first ordained at Longgui si 龍歸寺 and received the full precepts at Kaiyuan si 開元寺 in Xinzhou 信州. For Deshao's biographies, see *Song gaoseng zhuan*, 789a20–b10; and *Jingde chuan deng lu*, 407b7–410b12.

38. *Jingde chuan deng lu*, 407b27.

39. *Song gaoseng zhuan*, 789a25–2. Xieshan Lingmo 浰山靈默 (747–818), a disciple of Mazu Daoyi, had also previously lived at Baisha. *Jingde chuan deng lu*, 254b6–c1.

40. *Song gaoseng zhuan*, 789a25–26.

41. Penkower, "T'ien-t'ai during the T'ang dynasty," 320; and *Guoqing si zhi*, 254. It should be noted that early biographical sources link Deshao only with Baisha, Yunju 雲居, and Bore 般若 Temples. The last of these appears to be the primary

temple managed by Deshao and his disciples. Deshao is also credited with rebuilding one of the three brick stupas that had been established on the peak of Mt. Chicheng (at the base of Mt. Tiantai) during the Liang dynasty (502–557). These stupas, believed to contain forty-nine Buddha relics, had been destroyed during the Huichang persecutions. After the relics were recovered, some were reinterred in a new brick stupa, but twenty-eight others were sent to be enshrined in other stupas throughout the region, including sites at Guoqing si, Yingtian si, and Dongyang's Zhongxing si 中興寺. See the *Song Tiantai bore xin si zhuan ta ji* 宋天台般若新寺甎塔記, in *Liangzhe jinshi zhi*, 5:1a–b.

42. On the loss and return of Tiantai texts, see Brose, "Crossing Ten-Thousand *Li* of Waves."

43. Zhifeng was originally from the Hangzhou area and became a monk at Langzhan Cloister 朗瞻院. According to his entry in the *Jingde chuan deng lu*, he met Deshao at Yunju Temple 雲居道場 during the Tianfu era (936–947) and was later ordered by Qian Chu to head Gongchen Cloister 功臣院 in present-day Lin'an, west of Hangzhou. Sometime between 968 and 972, Qian Chu constructed Pumen Temple 普門精舍 for Zhifeng and installed him as the first abbot. Shortly thereafter Zhifeng was granted permission to retire from his post whereupon a general named Ling Chao 凌超 (n.d.) rebuilt the Huayan Bodhimaṇḍa on Mt. Wuyun for him. It was on Mt. Wuyun that Zhifeng apparently composed his meditation manual, the *Hangzhou Wuyun heshang zuochan zhen* 杭州五雲和尚坐禪箴. *Jingde chuan deng lu*, 422b12–423a3, 459c23–460a13.

44. Ibid., 424a7–16. The doctrine of complete merging is central to Tiantai theories of the three truths of complete merging (*yuanrong sandi* 圓融三諦) and the three contemplations of complete merging (*yuanrong sanguan* 圓融三觀), as well as the *Avataṃsaka* teachings of the unimpeded nature of all phenomena (*shishi wuai* 事事無礙) and the complete merging of the six characteristics (*liuxiang yuanrong* 六相圓融). As for Yuanqi, after visiting Deshao and gaining insight into the "mysterious and profound," he was appointed abbot of Guangqing si 光慶寺, a temple in Hangzhou built by Qian Chu's eldest son. According to the *Jingde chuan deng lu*, Yuanqi was joined at the new temple by three hundred of Hangzhou's most renowned Chan monks.

45. Welter, *Yongming Yanshou's Conception of Chan in the "Zongjing lu,"* 292n28.

46. *Zongmen shi gui lun*, 37b4.

47. See also Albert Welter's discussion of Deshao's life and teachings in *Monks, Rulers, and Literati* (144–149).

48. On the relationship between Chan and Huayan, see Takamine, *Kegon to Zen no tsūro*. See also Jana Benická, "(Huayan-like) Notions of Inseparability (or Unity) of Essence and Its Function (or Principle and Phenomena) in Some Commentaries on 'Five Positions' of Chan Master Dongshan Liangjie."

49. Welter, *Yongming Yanshou's Conception of Chan in the "Zongjing lu,"* 23, 118.

50. This text was likely based on the *Combined Treatise* edited by the Min monk Huiyan 惠[慧]研 (n.d.) in 967. The *Song gaoseng zhuan* biography of Li Tongxuan notes that in the Dazhong era (847–858), the monk Zhining 志寧 (n.d.) combined Li's commentary with the sutra to produce a work of 120 fascicles. Huiyan edited

and circulated the text under the name *Combined Treatises [and Text of] the Flower Adornment Scripture* (*Huayan jing he lun* 華嚴經合論). *Song gaoseng zhuan*, 854a14–20. As for Yongan, he received the tonsure from Huizheng, the monastic controller in Wuyue (possibly the same monk as Xijue, discussed in chapter 2). Because he wished to engage in the traditional twelve ascetic practices (*ershi toutuo* 十二頭陀; Skt. *dvādaśa-dhūta*), he set out for the kingdom of Min sometime between 926 and 930, after the death of Wang Shenzhi and the onset of Min's political turmoil. Yongan's *Song Biography* records that at that time "the situation in the border region was extremely tense," so he was forced to return to Wuyue and settled on Mt. Tiantai, where he joined the assembly of National Teacher Deshao. Qian Chu ordered Yongan to serve as abbot of both Qingtai 清泰院 and Shang 上寺 temples. At the time he was producing his edition of the *Avataṃsaka*, Yongan was serving as abbot, at Qian Chu's behest, of Baoen guangjiao si 報恩光教寺 ("Repaying Kindness, Illuminating the Teachings"). After his death and cremation, it was discovered that Yongan's tongue was impervious to fire. For Yongan's biographies, see *Song gaoseng zhuan*, 887a10–28; and *Jingde chuan deng lu*, 423b6–26. On the phenomenon of the unburnable tongue, see Suwa, *Chūgoku Nanchō Bukkyōshi no kenkyū*, 303–348; and Benn, *Burning for the Buddha*, 70–72.

51. *Xianchun Lin'an zhi*, 82:17a. On the Leifeng stupa, see E. Wang, "Tope and Topos."

52. *Da fangguang fo huayan jing*, 241b26–29. Zhiti transliterates the Sanskrit *caitya*, a synonym for "stupas" or "shrines."

53. Since the early Tang, this chapter of the *Avataṃsaka* had been read by some Chinese Buddhists as revealing that the "northeastern" dwelling place of Mañjuśrī bodhisattva was on Mt. Wutai, in present Shanxi province. The location of Tianguan bodhisattva on a mountain in northern Fujian might have been an attempt to create a new cultic site within Wuyue territory. It is noteworthy that the Putuo islands, off the coast of Zhejiang, were identified as the home of Guanyin and began to develop into a major pilgrimage site during this same period. See Yü, *Kuan-yin*, chap. 9.

54. After his time in the Southern Tang, Qingsong relocated to Mingzhou in Wuyue. He was first supported by Qian Chu's younger brother, Qian Yi 錢億 (929–967), who at that time was serving as military commissioner for the area. From Mingzhou, Qian Chu summoned Qingsong to Hangzhou to assume the abbacy of Lingyin si 靈隱寺, one of the capital's most prominent temples. *Jingde chuan deng lu*, 413a10–b10. Linda Penkower, in "T'ien-t'ai during the T'ang dynasty," suggests that this monk may be the same as Qingsong 清竦, the teacher of Luoxi Xiji, but the evidence is inconclusive (328–333).

55. It is not clear to me why Wŏnp'yo finds the bodhisattva on Mt. Huotong rather than Zhiti, but Huotong is also identified as the home of Tianguan in the *Song gaoseng zhuan* biography of Benjing 本淨 (n.d.), a monk from Baofu si in Fuzhou (847c26–848a8).

56. *Song gaoseng zhuan*, 895b7–c2. Although the text does not specify, this Baofu temple was most likely located in Fuzhou rather than in Quanzhou, where there is a better known temple of the same name.

57. *Shiguo chunqiu*, 89:12a–b.

58. *San shan zhi*, 608–609. The main hall of the temple that currently occupies the site, Huayan si 华严寺, enshrines one thousand small statues of Tianguan bodhisattvas.

59. On temple numbers, see *San shan zhi*, 512. Monks appointed to temples in Fujian include Huiming's disciple Baoming Daocheng 保明道誠 (n.d.) and Deshao's disciples Guangping Shouwei 廣平守威 (n.d.), Yuquan Yilong 玉泉義隆 (n.d.), and Yanfeng Shishu 嚴峰師尗 (n.d.).

60. Seven scrolls of the *Lotus Sūtra*, illustrated with golden pigment on indigo paper, were recently discovered in the ruins of Suzhou's Ruiguang stupa 瑞光塔. They have been tentatively dated to the late Tang dynasty or Five Dynasties period. See S. Huang, "Early Buddhist Illustrated Prints in Hangzhou," 148, 151. One of the early beneficiaries of Qian Liu's patronage, Hongchu 鴻楚 (858–932), reportedly lectured on the *Lotus* more than fifty times and once copied out all seven fascicles in his own blood. *Song gaoseng zhuan*, 870b13–14. Other prominent Wuyue monks known to have studied or lectured on the *Lotus* include Xushou, Kezhou 可周 (d. 926), Wuzuo, and Wenxi.

61. Welter, *Yongming Yanshou's Conception of Chan in the "Zongjing lu,"* 118.

62. Significantly, the same practice was also extolled in the *Śūraṃgama*, one of the most influential sutras for Xuansha Shibei and his descendants.

63. Benn, *Burning for the Buddha*.

64. In addition to the monks discussed later in this section, Shouxian 守賢 (d. ca. 963–968), a disciple of Yunmen Wenyan, also made an offering of his body. Like the future Buddha in the *Vyaghri Jataka*, Shouxian, age seventy-four at the time, threw himself before a hungry tiger. *Song gaoseng zhuan*, 860a2–12.

65. *Song gaoseng zhuan*, 860c12–18; cf. Benn's translation in *Burning for the Buddha*, 156.

66. Originally from the Shaanxi area, Shaoyan first became a monk under a Chan master by the name of Gaoan 高安. This was possibly Dongshan's disciple Gaoan Baishui Benren 高安白水本仁, whose brief *Song Biography* is contained within the entry for Deshao's early teacher Shushan (*Song gaoseng zhuan*, 785b25–c2). See also Benn, *Burning for the Buddha*, 306n90.

67. *Song gaoseng zhuan*, 860b16–21. Shaoyan eventually died a natural death within Wuyue's imperial compound at Baota si 寶塔寺. His funeral was paid for by the court and his epitaph was composed by Sun Chengyou 孫承祐 (936–985), the military commissioner of Wuyue's Army of Great Tranquility 大寧軍.

68. There are some other indications that esoteric Buddhism—beyond the mere use of *dhāraṇī*—was practiced in Wuyue during this period. According to the *Song gaoseng zhuan*, the monk Zhitong 志通 (d. 942) had studied the practice of Yoga with a master named Tripitika Poriluo (Vajra) 嚩日囉三藏 (fl. 935–939) in Luoyang. When Zhitong left Luoyang to travel to Zhejiang in 939, his master gave him Sanskrit tantric texts to translate. In Wuyue, he was posted to Baota si in Hangzhou by Qian Yuanguan—thus replicating the association between Buddha relics and esoteric practices seen at Famen si in the late Tang. Later, seeking rebirth in the Pure Land, he twice threw himself off a cliff on Mt. Tiantai and was injured but not killed (*Song gaoseng zhuan*, 858c13–859a15). A Song gazetteer records that the kings of Wuyue also maintained a Yoga sanctum 瑜伽道場 at Jing'an Temple 靜安寺 (in pre-

sent-day Shanghai). The central Vairocana icon contained five viscera inscribed with the names of the king's concubines. (*Shaoxi*) *Yunjian zhi* (紹熙) 雲間志, in *Xuxiu siku quan shu*, 687:22b. (Thanks to Zhaohua Yang for this reference.) Esoteric traditions appear to have been even more popular in the northern capitals. For example, the monk Daoxian 道賢 (d. ca. 934–936), according to Zanning, "received instruction in the techniques of yoga consecration" and "miraculously understood the Indian Sanskrit *siddham* language." He instructed the monastics and laypeople of Longdi (present-day Gansu province) in the "esoteric canon" and was known as "ācārya." When Li Congke 李從珂 (r. 934–936), the fifth emperor of the Later Tang, was fighting against Li Conghou 李從厚 (r. 933–934), the fourth emperor, for control of the north, Daoxian served as one Li Congke's advisors. After Li Congke was installed as emperor, Daoxian joined him in the capital. As a result of his efforts there, Zanning noted, "those who spread the Great Teaching in the two capitals are all Daoxian's grandsons and great-grandsons in the Law." *Song gaoseng zhuan*, 870c10—871a3. Further evidence of esoteric Buddhism in northern China during this time can be found in other biographies in the *Song gaoseng zhuan*, particularly those for monks patronized by the Han 韓 family of Lingzhou 靈州 (present-day Ningxia autonomous region).

69. *Song gaoseng zhuan*, 860a13–b6.

70. See for example, Lai, *Wuyue Fojiao zhi fazhan*, 47–70.

71. Welter, *Yongming Yanshou's Conception of Chan in the "Zongjing lu."*

72. Foulk, "Sung Controversies Concerning the 'Separate Transmission' of Ch'an," 243.

73. Yanshou's earliest biographies are contained in *Song gaoseng zhuan*, 887b1–16; and *Jingde chuan deng lu*, 421c8–422a20. On the life and work of Yanshou in English, see Welter, *The Meaning of Myriad Good Deeds* and *Yongming Yanshou's Conception of Chan in the "Zongjing lu"*; Huang Y., *Integrating Chinese Buddhism*; and Shih, "The Ch'an-Pure Land Syncretism in China."

74. On Lingcan, see *Zu tang ji*, j. 10, 350–351; and *Jingde chuan deng lu*, 352c15–353a3.

75. *Jingde chuan deng lu*, 421c14–15. For a discussion of how Yanshou is represented differently in different sources, see Welter, *Yongming Yanshou's Conception of Chan in the "Zongjing lu,"* 13–38.

76. Xingtao (not to be confused with Xianzong Xingtao 僊宗行瑫 (n.d.), a disciple of Xuefeng Yicun) was born in Wuyue and received the precepts at Longxing si in Hangzhou. He subsequently studied Nanshan Vinaya and engaged in ascetic practices. Because of his great love of the sutras and his dissatisfaction with the commentaries available to him, he devoted himself to writing the monumental *Dazang jing yinshu*. A single fascicle of his work is preserved in the Kyoto National Library. For Xingtao's biography, see *Song gaoseng zhuan*, 871a22–b16. For a discussion of Xingtao and a reproduction of the surviving fascicle, see Makita, *Godai shūkyōshi kenkyū*, 247–274.

77. *Zong jing lu*, 924a17–19. Translation from Welter, *Yongming Yanshou's Conception of Chan in the "Zongjing lu,"* 65.

78. On works authored by Yanshou, see Welter, *The Meaning of Myriad Good Deeds*, 113–118.

79. On printing during the Five Dynasties, see Zhang, *Zhongguo yinshuashu de faming ji qi yingxiang*, 47–56; and Zhao, "Wudai shiqi diaoban yinshua shiye de fazhan."

80. The print runs here are self-reported and thus may by piously inflated. At the same time, many of these prints were single sheets intended for broad distribution, so the numbers are not entirely unfeasible. On the difficulty of determining print runs, see McDermott, "The Ascendance of the Imprint in China," 59.

81. There is some evidence to suggest that Qian Chu had the Baoqieyin sutras printed at Yongming Yanshou's behest. See Baba, "*Hōkyō inkyō* no denpa to tenkai," 18n37.

82. The ubiquity of Pure Land devotion is apparent in the biographies of several Wuyue monks and in the dedicatory inscriptions of Buddhist monuments commissioned by the royal family and other prominent laypeople. Tiantai Deshao, for example, was responsible for rebuilding the stupa of the famous Tang Pure Land Master Shaokang 少康 (d. 805). Shaokang had been inspired by the works of Shandao 善導 (613–681) and was known as the "Later Shandao." He died and was buried in Zhejiang at Taiziyan (in the modern city of Jiande 建德). His apotropaic powers were such that the earth around his tomb was believed to cure illness when eaten. The stupa had been eroded (or eaten?) to its foundation by 950, when Deshao had it rebuilt (*Song gaoseng zhuan*, 867b12–c20). During this same period, Qian Chu's maternal uncle, Wu Yanshuang 吳延爽 (n.d.), had Shandao's relics brought from Dongyang 東陽 to be enshrined in a new nine-storied stupa in the hills north of West Lake called Yingtian 應天塔. (The stupa, rebuilt several times and now named Baochu 保俶, still stands.) *Xihu youlan zhi*, 8:11a–b; and *Liangzhe jinshi zhi*, 4:46b–47a. For an extended discussion of the Pure Land affinities of Wuyue monks, see Satō, *Sōdai Bukkyōshi no kenkyū*, 123–188.

83. Yongming Yanshou advocated veneration of this rare form of Guanyin as well as some of the *dhāraṇī* printed on the image. See *Quan Tang wen bubian*, 2:1432.

84. For a listing of the sources cited by Yanshou in his *Zong jing lu*, see Welter, *Yongming Yanshou's Conception of Chan in the "Zongjing lu,"* 117–118.

85. On Pure Land, Tiantai, Huayan, and Tantric elements in Yanshou's thought, see Huang Y., "Yongming Yanshou zhi jingtu famen"; and *Integrating Chinese Buddhism*, 80–163.

86. *Zong jing lu*, 417b5–6. Cf. Welter, *Yongming Yanshou's Conception of Chan in the "Zongjing lu,"* 240.

87. *Jingde chuan deng lu*, 422c2–3.

88. *Song gaoseng zhuan*, 790a2–7. The last two lines quote Zongmi (*Chanyuan zhuquan ji duxu*, 400b10–11). See Gregory, *Tsung-mi and the Sinification of Buddhism*, 226. The same statement also occurs in works by Yongming Yanshou and Chinul 知訥 (1158–1210).

89. *Song gaoseng zhuan*, 790a20.

90. This same phenomenon has been noted by T. Griffith Foulk in the context of Song Chan: "Precisely because the lineage was defined in terms of the transmission of something as utterly signless and ineffable as the Buddha-mind, not the transmission of any particular set of doctrines or religious practices, the Ch'an school was able to draw into its ranks monks and laypersons who in fact took a vari-

ety of approaches to Buddhist thought and practice." Foulk, "Myth, Ritual, and Monastic Practice in Sung Ch'an Buddhism," 194.

91. According to an inscription for the Guanyin Chan Cloister 觀音禪院 in Suzhou written shortly after 964 by King Qian Chu's cousin Qian Yan 錢儼 (937–1003), the monk Wenqian 文謙 (fl. 964) assumed the abbacy because Deshao had forbidden him from settling in his native Zhejiang. *Wudu wencui*, 8:21a.

92. Qian Chu appointed Xingming to the abbacies of two temples, Nengren 能仁 and Dahe 大和. Xingming was later awarded a purple robe and the title of master by Song Taizong 太宗 (r. 976–997). *Jingde chuan deng lu*, 425b19–28.

93. *Song gaoseng zhuan*, 887a20.

94. *Jingde chuan deng lu*, 422a28–b11.

6: Reintegration

1. The *Wuyue beishi* (addendum [*buyi*]: 26b–27b) catalogues Qian Chu's gifts to the Song court in 978, the year that he surrendered and relocated to Kaifeng. Among the items listed are 95,000 taels of gold, over a million taels of silver, hundreds of thousands of bolts of silk, various types of teas, ginger, gold and silver wine vessels and cups, silver trays, gold-plated tortoiseshell vessels, engraved tables, beds, several boats, various types of exotic trees, unusual food delicacies, gem-encrusted string instruments, drums, incense, elephant tusks, and rhinoceros horns. See also Worthy, "Diplomacy for Survival," 34.

2. The Qingyuan commandery in Fujian also surrendered in 978.

3. Members of the Qian clan remained prominent in and around Hangzhou throughout the Song. The history of the Qian clan has been studied by Ikezawa Shigeko in his *Wuyue Qianshi wenren qunti yanjiu*.

4. The disappearance of members of Fayan Wenyi's lineage was gradual and by no means total. Tiantai Deshao's disciples Yu'an 遇安 (d. 992), Xibian 希辯 (921–997), and Xingming 行明 (932–1001), as well as and Daoqian's disciple Guisheng 璝省 (906–972), all received purple robes or temple appointments from Emperor Taizong. The Fayan lineage is conventionally documented to seven generations, terminating with Xiangfu Liangqing 祥符良慶 (n.d.) (a.k.a. Xiangfu Liangdu 良度) sometime after the Xiangfu era (1008–1016), but there is some evidence that this network remained vital into the twelfth century. In the *Chuanfa zhenzong ji* 傳法真宗記, Qisong 契嵩 (1007–1072) noted, "Today, the followers of three families of the Yunmen, the Linji, and the Fayan are in great abundance. But the Guiyang [family] has already become extinct, and the Caodong barely exists, feeble like a lonely spring during a great drought." (Translated in Schlütter, *How Zen Became Zen*, 23.) Sometime between 1223 and 1228, while he was staying on Mt. Tiantong, Eihei Dōgen claimed to have seen an inheritance certificate (*sishu* 嗣書) of the Fayan lineage but goes on to say that "the heads of the large monasteries in Jiangsu and Zhejiang now are mostly the heirs of Linji, Yunmen, and Dongshan lineages." ("Shisho," translated in Tanahashi, *Moon in a Dewdrop*, 189–190.) The Republican-era Chan master Xu Yun 虛雲 (d. 1959) is credited with reviving the Fayan lineage in 1933. See Xuyun and Cen Xuelü, *Xuyun heshang fahui*, 264–265.

5. Welter, *The "Linji lu" and the Creation of Chan Orthodoxy*, 32.

6. Welter, *Monks, Rulers, and Literati*, 27.

7. Ibid., 179, 219.

8. An important exception is Makita Tairyō's excellent study, *Godai shūkyōshi kenkyū*. The political and military history of the Five Dynasties has been treated in detail in Wang Gungwu's *Divided China* and, more recently, in Naomi Standen's "The Five Dynasties."

9. Fang, "Power Structures and Cultural Identities in Imperial China," 114.

10. The first Liang emperor, Taizu 太祖 (r. 907–912) sought the legitimacy conferred by Buddhist monks, richly rewarding a Chinese monk who had retrieved Sanskrit texts and relics from India. Zanning notes that the monk Zhixuan 智宣 (n.d.) was ordered to translate the texts but was unable to do so because of the "turmoil of subsequent years." *Song gaoseng zhuan*, 897c2–10. Later rulers had little use for such offerings. When another monk arrived from India and offered one of the Buddha's teeth to Emperor Mingzong 明宗 (r. 926–933), an official smashed it with a hatchet. *Xin Wudai shi*, 235.

11. Imperial edicts regulating the activities of the clergy during all five northern dynasties are collected in the *Wudai huiyao*, 12:1a–10b, 16:5b–6b.

12. The position of Daoist recorder (*daolu* 道錄) was also abolished at this time.

13. *Jiu Wudai shi*, 10:7a.

14. *Song gaoseng zhuan*, 746c5–747a4. Guiyu was a quintessential monastic scholar, versed in classical, non-Buddhist literature as well as the Vinaya, Buddhist logic, Yogācāra, *Abhidharma*, and the *Vimalakīrti* and *Birth Above* sutras. He eventually composed a (now lost) work in twenty fascicles entitled *Notes on Essentials* (*Huiyao caozi* 會要草字), which the emperor approved for entry into the Buddhist canon. The *Fozu tongji* (23a16–18) gives the title of this text as *Essentials of the Sūtras and Śastras* 經論會要. Xiangguo si was first constructed during the Tang and was one of the most prestigious temples in northern China during the Five Dynasties. It served as the center of Vinaya studies in the north, and more than one of the temple's abbots assumed the title of "school authority" (*zong zhu* 宗主) for the so-called New Commentary tradition. The abbots of Xiangguo si during the Five Dynasties were appointed by the emperor and shared many of the same qualities as their forebears who had served at imperial temples in Chang'an: most were learned in both secular and Buddhist literatures and were masters of the Vinaya. See the *Song gaoseng zhuan* biographies for Zhenjun 貞峻 (847–924), Zhenhui 貞誨 (863–935), Guiyu 歸嶼 (862–936), Zhenhui 遵誨 (875–945), and Chengchu 澄楚 (889–959) (810a19–b14, 747c28–748a24, 746c5–747a4, 884b11–c20, and 810c24–811a16). During the Song, the Xiangguo si continued to be frequented by emperors and officials and was the site for the celebration of imperial birthdays and other state ceremonies. Not coincidentally, Zanning, the most influential Vinaya master from the south, was stationed at Xiangguo si some years after his relocation to the north. By the reign of the Song emperor Renzong 仁宗 (r. 1022–1063), however, Chan monks began receiving imperial appointments to cloisters within the Xiangguo complex. The Linji monks Dezhang 德章 (fl. 1048–1050) and Daolong 道隆 (fl. 1054–1056) were appointed respectively to the Xi jingzang yuan 西經藏院 and the Shaozhu yuan 燒朱院, two cloisters within the larger Xiangguo complex. The Yunmen monk Chuxiang 楚祥 (n.d.) was also appointed to a sub-temple (*Yunlu manchao*, 2:12a). In 1082,

when Emperor Shenzong 神宗 (r. 1067–1085) had the sixty-four cloisters of Xiangguo consolidated into eight compounds, six of these were designated as Vinaya (i.e., hereditary) cloisters, while the other two were set aside as Chan cloisters. The first monks invited to assume the abbacies of these two cloisters were affiliated with the Yunmen lineage: Zhengjue Benyi 正覺本逸 (n.d.) at the Zhihai chanyuan 智海禪院, and Yuanzhao Zongben 圓照宗本 (1019–1099) at the Huilin chanyuan 慧林禪院. On the history of Xiangguo si, see Soper, "Hsiang-Kuo-Ssŭ"; Duan, *Xiangguo si*; Xiong, *Xiangguo si kao*; and Chen J., "Images, Legends, Politics, and the Origin of the Great Xiangguo Monastery in Kaifeng."

15. The ordinations were presided over by Zhenjun. See note 18 of this chapter.

16. *Xin Wudai shi*, 133–134; translation slightly modified from Davis, "Historical Records of the Five Dynasties."

17. *Da Song seng shi lüe*, 248b12–13; *Beimeng suoyan*, 18:4b; and Makita, *Godai shūkyōshi* kenkyū, 169.

18. Among the Vinaya specialists, Zhenjun's encyclopedic knowledge of Buddhist texts earned him the nickname "walking scripture case." In addition to overseeing the mass ordination on the occasion of Zhuangzong's inauguration, Zhenjun restored and served as the abbot of Kaifeng's largest monastery, Xiangguo si, and was anointed the "school authority" (*zong zhu* 宗主) for the New Commentary Vinaya tradition, named after the New Commentary of the Tang monk Huaisu 懷素 (625–698): *Si fen lü kai zong ji* 四分律開宗記 (*Wan xu zang jing*, 42n735). Zhuangzong also awarded a purple robe to the *Avataṃsaka* specialist Chenghui 誠慧 (876–925), the leader of the monastic communities of Mt. Wutai (*Song gaoseng zhuan*, 883b12–c7).

19. *Wudai huiyao*, 12:4a–6a. Mingzong's successor, Emperor Min 閔帝 (r. 933–934), imposed further restrictions: ordinations and honors were only granted on the occasion of the emperor's birthday and any monk or nun recommended for the purple robe or the title of master was required to sit for exams on preaching, repentance, composition, recitation, meditation, and eulogizing. *Jiu wudai shi*, 47:3a; and *Wudai huiyao*, 12:6a–b.

20. *Wudai huiyao*, 12:6a.

21. Chikusa, *Chūgoku Bukkyō shakaishi kenkyū*, 207–214. See also ter Haar, *The White Lotus Teachings in Chinese Religious History*, 44–48 and the sources cited therein.

22. *Xin Wudai shi*, 27, 123; and *Jiu Wudai shi*, 10:4b–5a. On official attempts to eradicate heterodox religious movements, see Seiwert, *Popular Religious Movements and Heterodox Sects in Chinese History.*

23. For Zanning's account, see *Da Song seng shi lüe*, 253c8–20. In "The Syncretism of Maitreyan Belief and Manichaeism in Chinese History," Ma Xisha suggests that these types of gatherings may have represented a fusion of Maitreyan and Manichaeistic traditions.

24. "Each day they [each consume] one liter [*sheng* 升] of rice. One hundred thousand people use one thousand hectoliters [*shi* 石] worth of grain each day." This accounting, Li Qinming points out, does not include the many untonsured novices, slaves, and servants living within temples. Moreover, while most people do not dress in fine silks, "in one year, a monk requires sixteen-and-a-half meters [five

pi 匹] of rough silk and fifty ounces [*liang* 兩] of fine silk. One hundred thousand monks use up 1,650,000 meters [500,000 *pi*] of rough silk and 5,000,000 ounces of fine silk." *Cefu yuangui*, 547:29b–30a.

25. *Wudai huiyao*, 12:10a. See also Makita, Godai *shūkyōshi kenkyū*, 176–180.

26. *Xin Wudai shi*, 115.

27. *Wudai huiyao*, 16:6a–b. The *Xin Wudai shi* gives the number of destroyed or decommissioned temples at a more modest 3,336. These numbers likely refer only to temples within Zhou territory, since Shizong's orders do not appear to have been implemented elsewhere. Responding to Shizong's order to eradicate unofficial temples, the king of Wuyue, Qian Chu, reported that the city of Hangzhou alone contained no fewer than 480 Buddhist temples—all officially sanctioned. *Shiguo chunqiu*, 81:8a.

28. *Wudai huiyao*, 16:6b.

29. Daopi was born in the Chang'an region. His father, Li Congyan 李從晏 (n.d.), was a member of the Tang imperial line and his mother was a devotee of Guanyin. Daopi took the tonsure while still a child and was reportedly lecturing on the *Diamond Sūtra* by the age of thirteen. Just a few years later, he was awarded a purple robe by the last Tang emperor (Ai Di 哀帝, r. 904–907). Under both the Liang and Later Tang dynasties, he was called to establish "incense altars" within the imperial palaces and was "often placed in the seat of honor" during audiences with emperors. The Later Tang emperor Zhuangzong awarded him the title Guangzhi 廣智 (Extensive Wisdom). After the fall of the Later Tang, Daopi was again summoned to the capital, this time to serve as the assistant monastic recorder on the left under the Later Jin. Before long, he was promoted to the position of monastic recorder on the left (in 944). As was common among elite monks of the north during that time, Daopi was well-versed in the *Buddha's Names*, *Lotus*, *Diamond*, *Benevolent Kings*, and *Birth Above* sutras. Several officials are said to have taken refuge with him. Daopi fled Kaifeng for Luoyang after the fall of the Later Han but was summoned back to the capital by the first emperor of the Zhou to serve again as monastic recorder on the left. *Song gaoseng zhuan*, 818c15–819b19.

30. *Song gaoseng zhuan*, 819b1–4. It is worth noting that a very similar exchange between an emperor and an eminent monk is found in the late eighth-century Chan text, the *Lidai fabao ji* 歷代法寶記. The relevant passage reads: "At the time of Emperor Huan (Huan Xuan 桓玄, 369–404) of the Jin, [the emperor] wanted to cut back the Buddha-Dharma, and so he summoned Dharma Master Yuan (Huiyuan 慧遠, 334–416) of Mt. Lu. The emperor said, 'We have observed recently that the monks and nuns are not sincere in their practice of the precepts, and there have been many transgressions. We wish to weed out [the Saṅgha]. Shall we at once carry out this culling process?' Gentleman Yuan responded, 'the jade that is extracted from Mt. Kun is covered with dirt and grit. The Li River is rich with gold, yet it is also full of gravel. Your majesty must respect the Dharma and value its representatives; you must not scorn its representatives or treat the Dharma with contempt.' The Jin emperor then issued a general amnesty." Translated in Adamek, *The Mystique of Transmission*, 306.

31. On the policies of the first Song emperors in relation to the Buddhist *saṃgha*, see Wang S., *Songdai zhengjiao guanxi yanjiu*, chap. 1.

32. In 1021, according to the *Song huiyao*, the total monastic population in the Song empire was 378,456 monks and 61,239 nuns. The largest populations (both monks and nuns) were in Zhejiang and Jiangsu (82,220; the original reads 2,220 but this is almost certainly a mistake for 82,220; see Cheng, "Lun Songdai Fojiao de diyu chayi," 38n1), Fujian (71,080), Sichuan and Shaanxi (combined total of 56,221), and Jiangnan (54,316). *Song huiyao jigao*, 618–619. See also Huang M., *Song-dai Fojiao shehui jingji shi lunji*, 349–352. On the state of Buddhism in southeastern China in the Song, see Liu X., "Buddhist Institutions in the Lower Yangtze Region during the Sung Dynasty."

33. *Zu tang ji*, j. 8, 285–287; *Jingde chuan deng lu*, 338a14–16; and *Song gaoseng zhuan*, 785a18–24.

34. Schlütter, *How Zen Became Zen*, chap. 4.

35. For Touzi Datong's biographies, see *Song gaoseng zhuan*, 785b5–16; *Zu tang ji*, j. 6, 203–208; and *Jingde chuan deng lu*, 319a2–320b5. Both Xuefeng Yicun and Tiantai Deshao also reportedly sought this monk's instruction. Touzi's own teacher, Cuiwei Wuxue 翠微無學 (n.d.), was reputedly honored by Tang Emperor Xizong 僖宗 (r. 873–888). *Jingde chuan deng lu*, 313c7–21; see also *Zu tang ji*, j. 5, 175–176.

36. *Song gaoseng zhuan*, 886a12–b15; and *Jingde chuan deng lu*, 325a17–b2.

37. For Shihui's biography, see the *Song gaoseng zhuan*, 885a15–b12.

38. *Song gaoseng zhuan*, 885b3.

39. The *Discourse Record of Monk Touzi* (*Touzi heshang yulu* 投子和尚語錄) is contained within the *Guzunsu yulu*, 233b19–238a11.

40. Lau and Huang, "Founding and Consolidation of the Sung Dynasty," 216.

41. For a historical overview of the early Song, see Lau and Huang, "Founding and Consolidation of the Sung Dynasty"; and Lorge, "The End of the Five Dynasties and Ten Kingdoms." For a discussion of the Buddhist activities of the first four Song emperors, see Huang C., "Imperial Rulership and Buddhism in the Early Northern Song"; and Wang S., *Songdai zhengjiao guanxi yanjiu*.

42. Lorge, "The End of the Five Dynasties and Ten Kingdoms," 241.

43. *Xu zizhi tongjian changbian*, 19:3a. By way of contrast, the 791 catalogue of the Tang imperial library listed 51,852 scrolls in addition to the collection of Buddhist and Daoist texts in 95,000 scrolls. See also Dudbridge, *Lost Books of Medieval China*, 2–3.

44. The editorial work was directed by the northern literatus Li Fang 李昉 (925–996). On the compilation of these texts, see Kurz, "The Politics of Collecting Knowledge." Xu Xuan wrote inscriptions for Xuefeng Yicun's disciple Wuyin (*Hongzhou Xishan Cuiyan Guanghua yuan gu Chengyuan chanshi* 洪州西山翠巖廣化院故澄源禪師), Zhaoqing Daokuang's disciple Xuanji (*Jinling Jile tayuan gu Xuanji chanshi yingtang ji* 金陵寂樂塔院故玄寂禪師影堂記), and Gushan Shenyan's disciple Huiwu (*Fuzhou Yongan chanyuan ji* 撫州永安院記 and *Gu Tang Huiwu da chanshi muzhiming* 故唐慧悟大禪師墓誌銘)—all reproduced in the *Qisheng ji* (27:1–3a, 28:8b–10a, 28:10b–11b, and 30:1a–3a). Zhaoqing Wendeng 招慶文僜 (892–972) was also awarded the title Zhenjue (True Awakening) by Song Emperor Taizu on Xu Xuan's recommendation. See Kinugawa, "*Senshū senbutsu shinjaku sho soshi ju* to *Sodōshū*," 5.

45. In 972, officials were ordered to compose fifty-two inscriptions for temples to be repaired or built by imperial decree throughout the empire. Woolley,

"Religion and Politics in the Writings of Xu Xuan," 128. The Buddhist canon, comprising 5,048 fascicles carved on 130,000 blocks, was printed in Chengdu between 971 and 983. A copy of the Daoist canon kept in the Tiantai mountains was also brought north in 985 as part of a larger effort to collect and collate Daoist texts. See Chen G., *Daozang yuanliu kao*, 127–128. On the revival of state-sponsored translations in the Song, see Sen, *Buddhism, Diplomacy, and Trade*, chap. 3.

46. Barnhart, *Three Thousand Years of Chinese Painting*, 91–92. Incidentally, the work of Gao Wenjin 高文進 (fl. 965–985), who traveled to Kaifeng with the last king of Shu in 965, was found within the famous Seiryōji Buddha in Japan.

47. Miller, "Something Old, Something New, Something Borrowed," 212.

48. *Song bailei chao*, 31:1a.

49. The first of these clerics, Yu'an 遇安 (d. 992), had been appointed to several temples within Hangzhou by Qian Chu. After his audience in the Zifu Hall 滋福殿 of the Song imperial palace, Yu'an was awarded a purple robe and given the name Great Master Langzhi 朗智. The other monk, Xibian, had also been patronized by Qian Chu and was awarded a purple robe and new name (Great Master Huiming 慧明) by Emperor Taizong. *Jingde chuan deng lu*, 424b7–c10, 434a17–b6.

50. *Song gaoseng zhuan*, 861c25–862a5.

51. As a part of the process by which Taizong reoriented the Buddhist world with his court at its center, Xiangguo si, the temple most closely associated with the court in Kaifeng, welcomed five hundred arhat statues from Mt. Lu (in Southern Tang territory) and received a tooth relic of the Buddha from Chang'an. The tooth relic, reportedly obtained in a dream by the celebrated Tang monk Daoxuan, was kept at the Fahua yuan 法華院, a sub-temple of the larger Xiangguo si compound. An account of its enshrinement, taken from a now lost stele, is preserved in the *Shishi jigu lüe* (861b18–26). On the history of this tooth relic in English, see Strong, *Relics of the Buddha*, 187–190. The best description of the relic during the Song is provided by the Japanese pilgrim Jōjin 成尋 (1011–1081) in 1072. See Soper, "Hsiang-Kuo-Ssŭ," 24–26.

52. *Fozu tongji*, 451b16–17.

53. In 1026 the imperial court had the home of the former escort commandant Wu Yuanyi 吳元扆 (962–1011) converted into a temple named Cixiao 慈孝寺, which came to serve as an ancestral shrine for the imperial family. The name placard bore the calligraphy of Emperor Renzong and the temple itself enshrined a portrait of his father, Emperor Zhenzong. The *Tiansheng guang deng lu* (567a12–16) notes that this was the first Chan temple (*chanlin* 禪林) in the capital. The monk initially summoned to serve as its first abbot, Wensheng 文勝 (d. 1026), was a native of Zhejiang and a great-grand-disciple of Fayan Wenyi. Wensheng had lived at Lingyin si in Hangzhou and had served as abbot of Chengtian si 承天寺 (formerly known as Zhaoqing si) in Quanzhou. He died on route before assuming his new post. The abbacy was next offered to Xianci Zhaocong 先慈照聰 (965–1032), a disciple of Shoushan Shengnian 首山省念 (926–993), who turned it down. *Tiansheng guang deng lu*, 501b21–c1.

54. By the end of the eleventh century, heirs of Yunmen Wenyan had risen to positions of significant influence, but during the first century of Song rule their success at securing powerful patrons was limited. Most of Wenyan's direct disciples

remained in Guangdong, but at least six relocated to Hubei. Despite the presence of Wenyan's disciples in northern China, the first of his descendants to receive an invitation to court was Yunhuo, a disciple of the Southern Tang monk Zhifeng. Emperor Taizong summed Yunhuo to the capital from Jizhou in southern Jiangxi, and in 1010, Emperor Zhenzong had him reside in the northern imperial garden. Following Yunhuo, however, it was another forty years until a member of the Yunmen lineage was summoned to court. Only during the second half of the eleventh century did monks of the Yunmen lineage consistently receive imperial appointments. Huang Chi-Chiang has calculated that at least fourteen of Yunmen's descendants (from the third to the eighth generation) were called to audiences with Song emperors. Huang C., "Yunmen zong yu Bei Song conglin zhi fazhan," 15.

55. On the early history of the Linji lineage in Hebei, see Yanagida, "Tōmatsu Godai no Kahoku chihō."

56. This was Yungai Huaiyi 雲蓋懷溢 (847–934); the relevant portion of his funerary inscription reads: "[Yungai] went to the capital early in the Guangming era [880] at the same time that Huang [Chao] invaded. When Emperor Xizong fled to Sanfeng 三峰 to temporarily avoid the crazed bandits, he commanded that ten great worthies skilled in Chan, regulations, sutras, treatises, poetry, and essays be selected to go ahead to make provisions. The monk [Yungai] was one of the [representatives of the] Chan lineage [*Chan zong* 禪宗] and was awarded the [name] Chan Master Futian 福田禪師." *Qinding quan Tang wen*, 869:11b–14b.

57. See Abe, *Chūgoku Zenshū shi no kenkyū*, 248–277; Zheng, *Sō shoki Rinzaishū no kenkyū*; Yan M., *Songdai Linji Chan fazhan yanbian*; and Welter, *Monks, Rulers, and Literati*, 172–204, and *The "Linji lu" and the Creation of Chan Orthodoxy*.

58. Ruzhou is located just over 70 kilometers southeast of Luoyang and about 185 kilometers southwest of Kaifeng. Linji Yixuan's temple, Linji si, is located in present-day Hebei province and one of Linji's most prominent disciples, Xinghua Cunjiang 興化存獎 (830–888), was based in present-day Shandong. After Xinghua Cunjiang, however, the next several generations were based in Ruzhou. For Cunjiang's biography, see the *Jingde chuan deng lu*, 295b1–22. Some biographies of Xinghua Cunjiang claim that he once met with Emperor Zhuangzong of the Later Tang, but Cunjiang died long before Zhuangzong assumed the throne.

59. *Jiu Wudai shi*, 63:6b. His religious inclinations are not mentioned in his biography in the *Xin Wudai shi*, 373–377.

60. *Jiu Wudai shi*, 123:15a–b.

61. *Wu deng hui yuan*, 230b13–15. The temple was awarded an imperial placard by the Zhou emperor Taizu 太祖 (r. 951–954) in 951.

62. The earliest biography for Fengxue Yanzhao is found in the *Jingde chuan deng lu*, 302b2–303c25. This account of his life and teachings was later expanded in the *Tiansheng guang deng lu* (488b22–493b14) and the *Wu deng hui yuan* (229c11–232a2).

63. The chronology here follows a later biographical account in the *Fozu lidai tong zai*, 657a14–658a10. The earliest biography of Nanyuan Huiyong (also known as Baoying Heshang 寶應和尚) is contained in the *Jingde chuan deng lu*, 298b21–c20.

64. Fengxue Yanzhao first lived on Mt. Fengxue 風穴山, outside the city of Ruzhou. When military activity made living in the area too dangerous, an otherwise

unknown official by the name of Li Shijun 李史君 invited Yanzhao to live in the governmental compound in the city of Yingzhou 郢州 (corresponding to the present-day city of Zhongxiang 鍾祥 in Hubei province), located over four hundred kilometers due south of Ruzhou. A well-known *gong'an, Biyan lu* case 38, takes place in the Yingzhou compound, with its governor playing a cameo role.

65. Shoushan Shengnian was originally from Laizhou 萊州 (present-day Shandong) and eventually traveled to Ruzhou to join Yanzhao's assembly on Mt. Fengxue. Sometime later—the details of his biography are sketchy—Shengnian was appointed abbot of two newly built temples in Ruzhou, Shoushan 首山 and Guangjiao yuan 廣教院. He later became the third abbot of Nanyuan Huiyong's old temple, Baoying yuan 寶應院 (the identity of Baoying's second abbot is unclear). For Shengnian's biography, see the *Jingde chuan deng lu*, 304a11–305a6.

66. Suzuki T., "Hokusōki no chishikijin to Zensō to no kōryū"; and Welter, *Monks, Rulers, and Literati*, chap. 6.

67. On Wang Sui, see *Song shi*, 311:10–12; and Suzuki T., "Hokusōki no chishikijin to Zensō to no kōryū," 30–32. Wang Sui's inclusion in Shoushan Shengnian's lineage is found only in later texts: *Taishō shinshū daizōkyō*, 51n2077, 488b8–9; and *Wan xu zang jing*, 81n1570, 350a14. Given their respective dates, Wang Sui could have been only nineteen or twenty when he studied with Shengnian. This would have been before he took the *jinshi* exam and assumed his official duties. (He eventually rose to the position of vice censor in chief during the reign of Song Renzong.) Wang Sui also had some interest in Xuefeng Yicun and his heirs. While serving as supervising secretary of Hangzhou, he befriended one of Deshao's students, Chan Master Xiao Shou 小壽 (n.d.) (*Linjian lu*, 245b14–c1; and *Fofa jin tang bian*, 420b23–c5). He went on to write a preface for Xuefeng Yicun's discourse record in 1032 and, two years later, produced an abridged version of the *Transmission of the Flame*, the *Chuan deng yuying ji* 傳燈玉英集. On this text, see Huang Y., "*Zhao cheng jin zang* yu *chuang deng yuying ji*."

68. Guanghui Yuanlian's biography is found in the *Louhu yelu*, 387b19–c17. Guyin Yuncong's stupa inscription, *Xian Cizhao Cong chanshi taming (bing xu)* 先慈照聰禪師塔銘(并序), is contained in the *Tiansheng guang deng lu*, 501a9–c13. Shengnian's disciple Fenyang Shanzhao 汾陽善昭 (946–1023) is an exception to the trend of southerners relocating to the north. Fenyang was from the Shanxi region and, after a period of wandering, returned there to settle. From that base he attracted several important disciples and lay patrons. His disciple Shishuang Chuyuan 石霜楚圓 (986–1039) seems to have been the first to spread the Linji movement to Hunan in the south.

69. Guanghui Yuanlian initially studied with Baofu Congzhan's disciple Zhaoqing Wendeng in Quanzhou. He reportedly then called on some fifty other teachers in the Fujian area. Apparently dissatisfied with what was on offer in southeastern China, he headed north and completed his training under Shoushan Shengnian. Guyin Yuncong studied with Fayan Wenyi's disciple Baizhang Daochang 百丈道常 (d. 991) in Hongzhou. Yanagida has also noted that Baizhang Daochang's disciple Chengshi 澄諟 (n.d.) was an early teacher of the prominent Linji master Huanglong Huinan 黃龍慧南 (1002–1069). See Yanagida, "The Development of the 'Recorded Sayings' Texts of Chinese Ch'an Buddhism," 200.

70. See Welter, *Monks, Rulers, and Literati*, 181–182.

71. An exchange between Wang Shu and Yuanlian is recorded in *Luohu yelu*, 387c2–6. Wang Shu was also associated with Jinshan Tanying 金山曇穎 (989–1060) and Dayang Jingxuan 大陽警玄 (1043–1027). See Suzuki T., "Hokusōki no chishikijin to Zensō to no kōryū," 6–7.

72. Yang Yi was connected with at least three other monks from this lineage: Fenyang Shanzhao, Lumen Huizhao 鹿門慧昭 (n.d.), and Shishuang Chuyuan. On Yang Yi, see Nishiwaki, "Yō Oku kenkyū *Shōji jutsu* o yomu"; and Welter, *Monks, Rulers, and Literati*, 173–185.

73. Cha Dao reportedly copied sutras in blood in an attempt to cure his mother's sickness and, after her death, traveled to the Wutai mountains to become a monk. Changing his mind, he took and passed the *jinshi* exam in 988. Thereafter, he embarked on an official career that took him through a series of administrative posts, one of which was the governorship of Xiangzhou. On Cha Dao, see *Song shi*, 296:23a–26b; and Suzuki T., "Hokusōki no chishikijin to Zensō to no kōryū," 17.

74. On Xia Song, see *Song shi*, 283:16b–26b; and Suzuki T., "Hokusōki no chishikijin to Zensō to no kōryū," 18–19.

75. Yanagida, "The Life of Lin-chi I-hsuan," 83; and Welter, *Monks, Rulers, and Literati*, 186–207. It is worth pointing out that Li Zunxu was not only interested in Linji monks but also associated with several monks of the Yunmen lineage, including Yuelin Xian 嶽林賢 (n.d.), Xuedou Zhongxian 雪竇重顯 (980–1052), and Dongshan Zibao 洞山自寶 (978–1054).

76. Welter, *The "Linji lu" and the Creation of Chan Orthodoxy*, 24–43.

77. Schlütter, *How Zen Became Zen*, 25.

78. On the printing of Chan texts during the Song, see Shiina, "Tōdai Zenseki no Sōdai kankō ni tsuite."

79. It is worth noting in this context that, at the opening sermon for the new Zhihai Chan cloister in the Song capital, Zhengjue Benyi—a Yunmen monk from Jiangxi—approvingly quoted the teachings of Yongming Yanshou. *Wan xu zang jing*, 78n1556, 676c23–677a11. See also Protass, "Mapping the Rise and Decline of the Yunmen Chan Lineage," 28.

80. Both Paul Demiéville and T. Griffith Foulk have observed that Chan monks during the Song engaged in a broad range of practices and that there was little correlation between lineages and disciplines. See Demiéville, "Le Bouddhisme Chinois," 1314; and Foulk, "Myth, Ritual, and Monastic Practice in Sung Ch'an Buddhism," 161. For an extensive discussion of the literary practices of Chan monks during the Song, see Keyworth, "Transmitting the Lamp of Learning in Classical Chan Buddhism."

81. See Yoshizu, "Kegon kyōgaku no ataeta Sōdai Zenshū e no eikyō."

82. For example, Li Zunxu's son, Li Duanyuan 李端愿 (d. 1091), received transmission from Guyin Yuncong's disciple, Jinshan Tanying. *Wu deng hui yuan*, 254c11–255a1.

83. The Northern Song's imperial cemetery contained several Chan cloisters. See Henan Sheng Wenwu Kaogu Yanjiusuo, 410–439.

84. See *Yanyi yimou lu*, 3:3a–4b; *San shan zhi*, 515.

85. Weinstein, *Buddhism under the T'ang*, 12.

86. Tackett, "The Transformation of Medieval Chinese Elites," 206–207.

87. On the geographical distribution of Chan clerics during the Song, see Protass, "Mapping the Rise and Decline of the Yunmen Chan Lineage," 9.

Conclusion

1. *Jingde chuan deng lu*, 444c1–6. Cf. Poceski, *Sun-Face Buddha*, 128–129. This speech is not found in Wuye's *Song gaoseng zhuan* biography (772b13–773a29).

2. Brown, *Authority and the Sacred*, 63.

3. Jenkins, *Jesus Wars*, 13–14.

4. This was the Ten Directions Pure Cause Chan Cloister 十方淨因禪院. According to Zhipan's *Fozu tongji* (412b10–21), prior to the founding of this monastery, temples in the capital were all devoted to Nanshan Vinaya, Huayan (賢首), Yogācāra (慈恩), and other doctrinal studies (義學). The history of the Pure Cause Chan Cloister is discussed in Protass, "Mapping the Rise and Decline of the Yunmen Chan Lineage."

5. *Linjian lu*, 260a12.

6. *Linjian lu*, 260a16–19.

Bibliography

Abbreviations

SKQS   *Wenyuange siku quanshu*
T   *Taishō shinshū daizōkyō*
X   *Wan xu zang jing*

Primary Sources and Reference Works (by title)

Baoke congbian 寶刻叢編. Chen Si 陳思 (fl. 1225–1264). *Congshu jicheng chubian* 叢書集成初編. Shanghai: Shangwuyin shuguan, 1937.

Beimeng suoyan 北夢瑣言. Sun Guangxian 孫光憲 (900–968). SKQS.

Biyan lu 碧巖錄 (1125). Xuedou Chongxian 雪竇重顯 and Yuanwu Keqin 圓悟克勤. T 48n2003.

Cefu yuangui 冊府元龜 (1013). Wang Qinruo 王欽若, Li Sijing 李嗣京, Hu Weilin 胡維霖, Wen Xiangfeng 文翔鳳, Huang Jiuxi 黄九錫, and Huang Guoqi 黄國琦. SKQS.

Chanlin sengbao zhuan 禪林僧寶傳. Juefan Huihong 覺範慧洪 (1071–1128). X 79n1560.

Chanyuan zhuquan ji duxu 禪源諸詮集都序 (ca. 833). Zongmi 宗密. T 48n2015.

Chongwen zongmu 崇文總目 (1041). Wang Yaochen 王堯臣. SKQS

Chuanxin fayao 傳心法要 (857). Huangbo 黃檗 and Pei Xiu 裴休. T 48n2012a.

Chūgoku Zenshū jimei sanmei jiten 中国禅宗寺名山名辞典. Suzuki Tetsuo 鈴木哲雄, ed. Tokyo: Sankibō busshorin, 2006.

Congrong lu 從容錄. Hongzhi Zhengjue 宏智正覺 (1091–1157) and Wansong Xingxiu 萬松行秀 (1166–1246). T 48n2004.

Da fangguang fo huayan jing 大方廣佛華嚴經. T 10n279.

Da foding rulai miyin xiuzheng liaoyi zhu pusa wanxing shoulengyan jing 大佛頂如來密因修證了義諸菩薩萬行首楞嚴經. T 19n945.

Da Song seng shi lüe 大宋僧史略 (999). Zanning 贊寧. T 54n2126.

Duxing zazhi 獨醒雜志. Zeng Minxing 曾敏行 (1118–1175). SKQS.

Fofa jin tang bian 佛法金湯編 (Ming dynasty). Xintai 心泰. X 87n1628.

Fozu lidai tong zai 佛祖歷代通載 (Yuan dyansty). Nianchang 念常. T 49n2036.

Fozu tongji 佛祖統紀 (1269). Zhipan 志磐. T 49n2035.

Fuzhou Xuansha Zongyi chanshi yulu 福州玄沙宗一禪師語錄 (1626). Lin Hongyan 林弘衍. X 73n1445.

Guitian lu 歸田錄. Ouyang Xiu 歐陽修 (1007–1072). SKQS.

Guiyuan bigeng ji jiaozhu 桂苑筆耕集校注. Ch'i-wŏn 崔致遠 (b. 857). Beijing: Zhonghua shuju, 2007.

Guoqing si zhi 國清寺志. Ding Tiankui 丁天魁. Shanghai: Huadong shifan daxue chubanshe, 1994.

Guzunsu yulu 古尊宿語錄 (1267). Zezang 頤藏. X 68n1315.

Huang yu shi ji 黃御史集. Huang Tao 黃滔 (*jinshi* 895). SKQS.

Huizhou fu zhi 徽州府志, vol. 2 (1827). Ma Buchan 馬步蟾. Taipei: Chengwen chubanshe, 1975.

Jiangnan yeshi 江南野史 (Song dynasty). Long Gun 龍袞. SKQS.

Jianzhong jingguo xudeng lu 建中靖國續燈錄 (1101). Foguo Weibai 佛國惟白. X 78n1556.

Jiatai pudeng lu 嘉泰普燈錄 (1204). Leian Zhengshou 雷庵正受. X 79n1559.

Jingde chuan deng lu 景德傳燈錄 (1004). Daoyuan 道原. T 51n2076.

Jingding Jiankang zhi 景定建康志 (1261). Zhou Yinghe 周應合, ed. Collected in *Song-Yuan difang zhi congshu* 宋元地方志叢書. Taipei: Zhongguo dizhi yanjiu hui, 1978.

Jinling gujin tukao 金陵古今圖考 (1516). Chen Yi 陳沂. Nanjing: Nanjing chu ban she, 2006.

Jinshi cuibian 金石萃編. Wang Chang 王昶 (1724–1806). *Xuxiu siku quanshu* 續修四庫全書, vols. 886–891. Shanghai: Shanghai guji chubanshe, 1995.

Jiu Wudai shi 舊五代史 (974). Xue Juzheng 薛居正. In *Sibu congkan*.

Lei shuo 類說 (Song dynasty). Ceng Zao 曾慥. SKQS.

Lengyan jing. See *Da foding rulai miyin xiuzheng liaoyi zhu pusa wanxing shoulengyan jing.*

Liangzhe jinshi zhi 兩浙金石志. Ruan Yuan 阮元 (1764–1859). Hangzhou: Zhejiang shuju, 1890.

Linjian lu 林間錄 (1107). Juefan Huihong 覺範慧洪. X 87n1624.

Liu yi zhi yi lu 六藝之一錄 (Qing dynasty). Ni Tao 倪濤. SKQS.

Louhu yelu 羅湖野錄 (Song dynasty). Xiaoying 曉瑩. X 83n1577.

Lunyu 論語. Kong Qiu 孔丘. Collected in *The Analects of Confucius: A Philosophical Translation*, translated by Roger T. Ames and Henry Rosemont. New York: Ballantine, 1998.

Luoyang qielan ji 洛陽伽藍記. Yang Xuanzhi 楊衒之 (d. 555). Translated by Yi-t'ung Wang as *A Record of Buddhist Monasteries in Lo-Yang*. Princeton, N.J.: Princeton University Press, 1984.

Lushan ji 廬山記 (Song dynasty). Chen Shunyu 陳舜俞. T 51n2095.

Min du ji 閩都記 (1831). Wang Yingshan 王應山. In *Fujian jiu fangzhi congshu* 福建旧方志丛书. Beijing: Fangzhi chubanshe, 2002.

Nanchao Fosi zhi 南朝佛寺志 (Qing dynasty). In *Zhongguo Fosi zhi congkan* 中國佛寺志叢刊, vol. 28, edited by Sun Wenchuan 孫文川. Yangzhou: Jiangsu guangling guji keyinshe, 1996.

Nanhan jinshi zhi 南漢金石志 (19th century). Wu Lanxiu 吳蘭修. Taipei: Yiwenyin shuguan, 1968.

Nantang shu 南唐書 (1105). Ma Ling 馬令. SKQS.

Nantang shu 南唐書 (1184). Lu You 陸游. SKQS.

Nihon biku Enchin nittō guhō mokuroku 日本比丘圓珍入唐求法目錄. Enchin 圓珍 (814–891). T 55n2172.

Qinding quan Tang wen 欽定全唐文 (1814). Dong Gao 董誥. Taipei: Huiwen shuju, 1961.

Qing xiang za ji 青箱雜記 (Song dynasty). Wu Chuhou 吳處厚. SKQS.

Qisheng ji 騎省集. Xu Xuan 徐鉉 (917–992). SKQS.

Quan Tang shi 全唐詩 (1707). Peng Dingqiu 彭定求. Beijing: Zhonghua shuju, 1999.

Quan Tang wen bubian 全唐文補編. 3 vols. Chen Shangjun 陳尚君. Beijing: Zhonghua shuju, 2005.

Quanzhou qianfo xinzhu zhu zushi song 泉州千佛新著諸祖師頌. Zhaoqing Wendeng 招慶文僜 (892–972). T 85n2861.

Ren tian yanmu 人天眼目 (1188). Zhizhao 智昭. T 48n2006.

Ruizhou fu zhi 瑞州府志 (1873). Xiao Junlan 蕭浚蘭. Taipei: Chengwen chubanshe, 1970.

San shan zhi 三山志 (1182). Liang Kejia 梁克家, ed. Fuzhou: Haifeng chubanshe, 2000.

Shiguo chunqiu 十國春秋. Wu Renchen 吳任臣 (17th century). SKQS.

Shishi jigu lüe 釋氏稽古略 (Yuan dynasty). Jue'an 覺岸. T 49n2037.

Shishi tongjian 釋氏通鑑 (1270). Benjue 本覺. X 76n1516.

Shuo fu 說郛 (preface 1370). Tao Zongyi 陶宗儀, ed. SKQS.

Sibu congkan 四部叢刊. Shanghai: Shangwu yinshu guan, 1919–1936.

Song bailei chao 宋稗類鈔. Pan Yongyin 潘永因 (Qing dynasty). SKQS.

Song gaoseng zhuan 宋高僧傳 (988). Zanning 贊寧. T 50n2061.

Song huiyao jigao: fan yi dao shi 宋會要輯高: 蕃夷道釋. Guo Shengbo 郭聲波, ed. Chengdu: Sichuan daxue chubanshe, 2010.

Song shi 宋史. Tuo Tuo 脫脫 (1313–1355). SKQS.

Taishō shinshū daizōkyō 大正新脩大藏經. Takakusu Junjirō and Watanabe Kaigyoku, eds. Tokyo: Taishō issaikyō kankōkai, 1924–1932.

Tang huiyao 唐會要. Wang Pu 王溥 (922–982). Shanghai: Shanghai guji chubanshe, 1991.

Tiansheng guang deng lu 天聖廣燈錄 (1029). Li Zunxu 李遵勗. X 78n1553.

Tiantong si zhi 天童寺志. Woodblock edition, 1851.

Tōhō nenpyō 東方年表. Fujishima Tatsurō 藤島達朗 and Nogami Shunjō 野上俊靜. Kyoto: Heirakuji Shoten, 1996.

Wang Shenzhi dezheng beiming 王審知德政碑銘. Yu Jing 於競. In *Jinshi cuibian*, 118:10b–13b.

Wanling lu 宛陵錄. Huangbo 黃檗 and Pei Xiu 裴休. T 48n2012b.

Wan xu zang jing 卍續藏經. Taipei: Xinwen feng chuban gongsi, 1977. Originally published as *Dainippon zoku zōkyō* 大日本續藏經. Kyoto: Zōkyō Shoin, 1905–1912.

Wenyuange siku quanshu (dianzi ban) 文淵閣四庫全書 (電子版). 3rd edition. Hong Kong: Zhongwen daxue and Digital Heritage Publishing, 2007.

Wen zhong ji 文忠集 (Song dynasty). Ouyang Xiu 歐陽修. SKQS.

Wudai huiyao 五代會要. Wang Pu 王溥 (922–982). SKQS.

Wudai shi bu 五代史補. Yue Tao 陶岳 (*jinshi* 985). SKQS.

Wu deng hui yuan 五燈會元 (1252). Puji 普濟. X 80n1565.

Wudu wencui 吳都文粹 (Song dynasty). Zheng Huchen 鄭虎臣. SKQS.

Wu guo gushi 五國故事 (Song dynasty). Anonymous. SKQS.

Wuxi ji 武溪集. Yu Jing 余靖 (1000–1064). Shanghai: Shanghai shudian, 1994.

Wuyue beishi 吳越備史. Qian Yan 錢儼 (937–1003). SKQS.

Xianchun Lin'an zhi 咸淳臨安志 (1268). Qian Shuoyou 潛說友. Taipei: Taiwan shangwu yinshuguan, 1983.

Xianju bian 閑居編 (1016). Zhiyuan 智圓. X 56n949.

Xihu youlan zhi 西湖遊覽志 (Ming dynasty). Tian Rucheng 田汝成. SKQS.

Xihu youlan zhi yu 西湖遊覽志餘 (Ming dynasty). Tian Rucheng 田汝成. SKQS.

Xing shi chao zhujia ji biaomu 行事鈔諸家記標目 (Song dynasty). Huixian 慧顯. X 44n741.

Xin Tang shu 新唐書 (1043–1060). Ouyang Xiu 歐陽修. SKQS.

Xin Wudai shi 新五代史 (1072). Ouyang Xiu 歐陽修. Partially translated in *Historical Records of the Five Dynasties*, by Richard L. Davis. New York: Columbia University Press, 2004.

Xuedou si zhi liang zhong 雪竇寺志兩種. 5 vols. Lüping 履平. Shanghai: Shanghai guji chubanshe, 1987.

Xuedou si zhi lüe 雪竇寺志略. Lüping 履平. Vol. 1 of *Xuedou si zhi liang zhong*.

Xuefeng zhenjue chanshi yulu 雪峰真覺禪師語錄 (1639). Lin Hongyan 林弘衍. X 69n1333.

Xuefeng zhi 雪峰志 (Ming dynasty). Xu Bo 徐𤊁. Vol. 103 of *Zhongguo Fosi zhi congkan* 中國佛寺誌叢刊. Zhang Zhi 张智, ed. Yangzhou: Jiangsu guangling guji keyinshe, 1996.

Xushi bijing 徐氏筆精. Xu Bo 徐𤊁 (Ming dynasty). SKQS.

Xuxiu siku quan shu 續修四庫全書. Shanghai: Shanghai guji chubanshe, 1995.

Xu zhenyuan shijiao lu 續貞元釋教錄 (945). Heng'an 恒安. T 55n2158.

Xu zizhi tongjian changbian 續資治通鑑長編 (1183). Li Tao 李燾. SKQS.

Yanyi yimou lu 燕翼詒謀錄 (Song dynasty). Wang Yong 王栐. SKQS.

Yu hai 玉海 (Song dynasty). Wang Yinglin 王應麟. SKQS.

Yunlu manchao 雲麓漫抄 (Song dynasty). Zhao Yanwei 趙彥衛. SKQS.

Yuzhi tang tan hui 玉芝堂談薈 (Ming dynasty). Xu Yingqiu 徐應秋. SKQS.

Zengjia Gushan liezu lianfang ji 增校鼓山列祖聯芳集 (1936). Lingmo 靈默, ed. Woodblock edition. Fujian: Gushan Yongquan chansi.

Zhengtong Daozang 正統道藏. Taipei: Yiwenyin shuguan, 1962.

Zhongyi wang miao beiwen 忠懿王庙碑文. Qian Yu 錢昱 (943–999). In *Qinding quan Tang wen*, 893:11b–19a.

Zhuzi yulei 朱子語類. Zhu Xi 朱熹 (1130–1200). Beijing: Zhonghua shuju, 1986.

Zizhi tongjian 資治通鑑. Sima Guang 司馬光 (1019–1086). Taiwan: Academia Sinica, Hanji dianzi wenxian (Scripta Sinica database).

Zong jing lu 宗鏡錄. Yanshou 延壽 (904–975). T 48n2016.

Zongmen shi gui lun 宗門十規論. Fayan Wenyi 法眼文益 (885–958). X 63n1226.

Zu tang ji 祖堂集. Jing 靜 and Yun 筠, ed. Zhengzhou: Zhongzhou guji chubanshe, 2006.

Secondary Sources (by author)

Abe Chōichi 阿部肇一. *Chūgoku Zenshū shi no kenkyū* 中国禅宗史の研究. Tokyo: Komazawa daigaku rekishigaku kenkyūshitsu, 1960.

Adamek, Wendi Leigh. *The Mystique of Transmission: On an Early Chan History and Its Contexts*. New York: Columbia University Press, 2007.

————. "Robes Purple and Gold: Transmission of the Robe in the *Lidai fabaoji* (Record of the Dharma-Jewel through the Ages)." *History of Religions* 40, no. 1 (2000): 58–81.

Anderl, Christoph. *Studies in the Language of Zu-tang ji.* 2 vols. Oslo: Unipub AS, 2004.

Aoyama Sadao. "The Newly-Risen Bureaucrats in Fukien at the Five Dynasty-Sung Period, with Special Reference to their Genealogies." *Memoirs of the Research Department of the Tōyō Bunkō* 21 (1962): 1–48.

App, Urs E. "Facets of the Life and Teaching of Chan Master Yunmen Wenyan (864–949)." Ph.D. diss., Temple University, 1989.

Baba Norihisa 馬場紀寿. "*Hōkyō inkyō* no denpa to tenkai" 『寶篋印経』 の伝播と展開. *Bukkyōgaku* 仏教学 54 (2013): 1–21.

Banister, Judith. *China's Changing Population.* Stanford, Calif.: Stanford University Press, 1987.

Barnhart, Richard M., ed. *Three Thousand Years of Chinese Painting.* New Haven, Conn.: Yale University Press, 1997.

Barrett, T. H. "The Madness of Emperor Wuzong." *Cahiers d'Extrême-Asie* 14 (2004): 173–186.

Benická, Jana. "(Huayan-like) Notions of Inseparability (or Unity) of Essence and Its Function (or Principle and Phenomena) in Some Commentaries on 'Five Positions' of Chan Master Dongshan Liangjie." In *Reflecting Mirrors: Perspectives on Huayan Buddhism,* edited by Imre Hamar, 231–239. Wiesbaden, Germany: Harrassowitz Verlag, 2007.

Benn, James A. "Another Look at the Pseudo-*Śūraṃgama sūtra*." *Harvard Journal of Asiatic Studies* 68, no. 1 (2008): 57–89.

————. *Burning for the Buddha: Self-Immolation in Chinese Buddhism.* Honolulu: University of Hawai'i Press, 2007.

Brose, Benjamin. "Buddhist Empires: Saṃgha-State Relations in Tenth-Century China." Ph.D. diss., Stanford University, 2009.

————. "Credulous Kings and Immoral Monks: Critiques of Buddhism during the Five Dynasties and Ten Kingdoms." *Asia Major,* 3rd series, 27, no. 1 (2014): 73–98.

————. "Crossing Ten-Thousand *Li* of Waves: The Return of China's Lost Tiantai Texts." *Journal of the International Association of Buddhist Studies* 29, no. 1 (2006–2008): 21–62.

Broughton, Jeffrey L. *Zongmi on Chan.* New York: Columbia University Press, 2009.

Brown, Peter. *Authority and the Sacred: Aspects of the Christianisation of the Roman World.* Cambridge: Cambridge University Press, 1995.

Buswell, Robert E. *The Formation of Ch'an Ideology in China and Korea: The Vajrasamādhi-Sūtra, a Buddhist Apocryphon.* Princeton, N.J.: Princeton University Press, 1989.

Certeau, Michel de. *The Writing of History.* New York: Columbia University Press, 1988.

Chavannes, Édouard. "Le Royaume de Wou et de Yue." *T'oung Pao* 17, no. 2 (1916): 129–264.

Ch'en, Kenneth. *Buddhism in China: A Historical Survey.* Princeton, N.J.: Princeton University Press, 1964.

Chen Baozhen 陳葆真. "Nantang sanzhu yu Fojiao xinyang" 南唐三主與佛教信仰. In *Foxue yu wenxue: Fojiao wenxue yu yishuxue yantaohui lunwen ji (wenxue bufen)* 佛學與文學–佛教文學與藝術學研討會論文集 (文學部份), edited by Li Zhifu 李志夫, 247–264. Taipei: Fagu wenhua shiye gongsi, 1998.

Chen Guofu 陳國符. *Daozang yuanliu kao* 道藏源流考. Beijing: Zhonghua shuju, 1963.

Chen Jinhua. "Images, Legends, Politics, and the Origin of the Great Xiangguo Monastery in Kaifeng: A Case-Study of the Formation and Transformation of Buddhist Sacred Sites in Medieval China." *Journal of the American Oriental Society* 125, no. 3 (2005): 353–378.

Chen Zhiping 陈支平. *Fujian zongjiao shi* 福建宗教史. Fuzhou: Fujian jiaoyu chubanshe, 1996.

Cheng Minsheng 程民生. "Lun Songdai Fojiao de diyu chayi" 论宋代佛教的地域差异. *Shijie zongjiao yanjiu* 世界宗教研究 1 (1997): 38–47.

Chikusa Masaaki 竺沙雅章. *Chūgoku Bukkyō shakaishi kenkyū* 中国仏教社会史研究. Kyoto: Dōhōsha, 1982.

———. "Tōmatsu Godai ni okeru Fukken Bukkyō no tenkai" 唐末五代における福建仏教の展開. *Bukkyō shigaku* 佛教史學 7, no. 1 (1958): 24–45.

Clark, Hugh R. *Community, Trade, and Networks: Southern Fujian from the Third to the Thirteenth Centuries.* Cambridge: Cambridge University Press, 1991.

———. *Portrait of a Community: Society, Culture, and the Structures of Kinship in the Mulan River Valley (Fujian) from the Late Tang through the Song.* Hong Kong: Chinese University Press, 2007.

———. "Quanzhou (Fujian) during the Tang-Song Interregnum, 879–928." *T'oung Pao* 68, no. 1–3 (1982): 132–149.

———. "The Religious Culture in the Minnan Region of Southern Fujian through the Middle Period (750–1450): Preliminary Reflections on a Maritime Frontier." *Asia Major*, 3rd series, 19, no. 12 (2006): 211–240.

———. "Scoundrels, Rogues, and Refugees: The Founders of the Ten Kingdoms in the Late Ninth Century." In Lorge, *Five Dynasties and Ten Kingdoms*, 47–77.

———. "The Southern Kingdoms between the T'ang and the Sung, 907–979." In *The Sung Dynasty and Its Precursors, 907–1279*, edited by Denis Twitchett and Paul Jakov Smith, 133–205. Vol. 5, bk. 1 of *The Cambridge History of China.* Cambridge: Cambridge University Press, 2009.

Cunningham, Erik. *Zen: Past and Present.* Ann Arbor, Mich.: Association for Asian Studies, 2011.

Dalia, Albert A. "The 'Political Career' of the Buddhist Historian Tsan-ning." In *Buddhist and Taoist Practices in Medieval Chinese Society*, edited by David W. Chappell, 146–180. Buddhist and Taoist Studies 2. Honolulu: University of Hawai'i Press, 1987.

Davis, Richard L. "Images of the South in Ouyang Xiu's Historical Records of the Five Dynasties." In *Shixue yu wenxian* 史學與文獻, edited by Shixue yu wenxian xueshu yantaohui 史學與文獻學術研討會, 97–157. Taipei: Xuesheng shuju, 1998.

de Bary, W. T. *East Asian Civilizations: A Dialogue in Five Stages.* Cambridge, Mass.: Harvard University Press, 1988.

Demiéville, Paul. "Le Bouddhisme Chinois." In *Encyclopédie de la Pléiade, Histoire des religions*, 1:1249–1319. Paris: Gallimard, 1970.

———. *Le Concile de Lhasa: Une controverse sur le quiétisme entre bouddhistes de l'Inde et de la Chine au VIIIe siècle de l'ère chrétienne.* Bibliothèque de l'Institut des hautes études chinoises 7. Paris: Institut des Hautes Études Chinoises, Collège de France, 1952.

Deng Keming 鄧克銘. *Fayan Wenyi chanshi zhi yanjiu* 法眼文益禪師之研究. Taipei: Zhonghua foxue yanjiusuo, 1987.

Duan Yuming 段玉明. *Xiangguo si: zai Tang-Song diguo de shensheng yu fansu zhijian* 相国寺：在唐宋帝国的神圣与凡俗之间. Chengdu: Bashu shushe, 2004.

Dudbridge, Glen. *Lost Books of Medieval China.* London: British Library, 2000.

———. *A Portrait of Five Dynasties China: From the Memoirs of Wang Renyu (880–956).* Oxford: Oxford University Press, 2013.

Dumoulin, Heinrich. *India and China.* Vol. 1 of *Zen Buddhism: A History.* New York: Macmillan, 1988.

Durt, Hurbert. "The Meaning of Archeology in Ancient Buddhism: Notes on the Stūpas of Aśoka and the Worship of the 'Buddhas of the Past' According to Three Stories in the *Samguk Yusa*." In *Pulgyo wa chegwahak: Kaegyo p'alsip chunyŏn kinyŏm nonch'ong* 佛教와 諸科學: 開校八十周年紀念論叢, 1223–1241. Seoul: Dongguk University Press, 1987.

Eberhard, Wolfram. *A History of China.* Berkeley: University of California Press, 1977.

Edgren, Sören. "The Printed Dhāraṇī Sūtra of A.D. 956." *Bulletin of the Museum of Far Eastern Antiquities* (Östasiatiska Museet) 44 (1972): 141–146.

Egan, Charles. *Clouds Thick, Whereabouts Unknown: Poems by Zen Monks of China.* New York: Columbia University Press, 2010.

Fairbank, John K., and Merle Goldman. *China: A New History.* Cambridge, Mass.: Harvard University Press, 2006.

Falco, Angela Howard. "Royal Patronage of Buddhist Art in Tenth-Century Wu Yüeh." *Bulletin of the Museum of Far Eastern Antiquities, Stockholm* 57 (1985): 1–60.

Fang, Cheng-hua. "Power Structures and Cultural Identities in Imperial China: Civil and Military Power from Late Tang to Early Song Dynasties (A.D. 875–1063)." Ph.D. diss., Brown University, 2001.

Faure, Bernard. "Bodhidharma as Textual and Religious Paradigm." *History of Religions* 25, no. 3 (1986): 187–198.

———. "Chan and Zen Studies: The State of the Field(s)." *Chan Buddhism in Ritual Context,* 1–35. London: Routledge, 2003.

———. *The Rhetoric of Immediacy: A Cultural Critique of Chan/Zen Buddhism.* Princeton, N.J.: Princeton University Press, 1991.

———. *The Will to Orthodoxy: A Critical Genealogy of Northern Chan Buddhism.* Stanford, Calif.: Stanford University Press, 1997.

Fogel, Joshua A. *Politics and Sinology: The Case of Naitō Konan (1866–1934).* Cambridge, Mass.: Council on East Asian Studies, Harvard University, 1984.

Foulk, T. Griffith. "The 'Ch'an School' and Its Place in the Buddhist Monastic Tradition." Ph.D. diss., University of Michigan, 1987.

———. "The Ch'an Tsung in Medieval China: School, Lineage, or What?" *Pacific World,* new series, 8 (1992): 18–31.

———. "Histories of Zen." Unpublished manuscript, 2012.

————. "Myth, Ritual, and Monastic Practice in Sung Ch'an Buddhism." In *Religion and Society in T'ang and Sung China*, edited by Patricia Buckley Ebrey and Peter N. Gregory, 147–208. Honolulu: University of Hawai'i Press, 1993.

————. "Sung Controversies Concerning the 'Separate Transmission' of Ch'an." In *Buddhism in the Sung*, edited by Peter Gregory and Daniel Getz, 220–294. Honolulu: University of Hawai'i Press, 1999.

Furuta Shōkin 古田紹欽. "Zenshū shijō ni okeru Kinzan no kenkyū" 禅宗史上に於ける徑山の研究. *Shūkyo kenkyū* 宗教研究 2, no. 3 (1940): 118–134.

Gernet, Jacques. *A History of Chinese Civilization*. Cambridge: Cambridge University Press, 1982.

Gerritsen, Anne. "Prosopography and Its Potential for Middle Period Research." *Journal of Sung-Yuan Studies* 38 (2008): 161–201.

Gregory, Peter N. *Tsung-mi and the Sinification of Buddhism*. Honolulu: University of Hawai'i Press, 2002.

Gregory, Peter N., and Daniel A. Getz Jr., eds. *Buddhism in the Sung*. Honolulu: University of Hawai'i Press, 1999.

Halperin, Mark. "Heroes, Rogues, and Religion in a Tenth-Century Chinese Miscellany." *Journal of the American Oriental Society* 129, no. 3 (2009): 413–430.

————. *Out of the Cloister: Literati Perspectives on Buddhism in Sung China, 960–1279*. Cambridge, Mass.: Harvard University Asia Center, 2006.

Hartwell, Robert M. "Demographic, Political, and Social Transformations of China, 750–1550." In *Harvard Journal of Asiatic Studies* 42, no. 2 (1982): 365–442.

He Yongqiang 何勇强. *Qianshi Wuyue guo shi lunqiao* 钱氏吴越国史论稿. Hangzhou: Zhejiang daxue chubanshe, 2002.

Henan Sheng Wenwu Kaogu Yanjiusuo 河南省文物考古研究所. *Bei Song huang ling* 北宋皇陵. Zhengzhou: Zhongzhou guji chubanshe, 1997.

Hino Kaisaburō 日野開三郎. "Godai nanboku Shina rikujō kōtsūro ni tsuite" 五代南北支那陸上交通路について. *Rekishigaku kenkyū* 歴史学研究 11, no. 6 (1941): 2–32.

Hiyazuki Miyakawa. "An Outline of the Naitō Hypothesis and Its Effects on Japanese Studies of China." *Far Eastern Quarterly* 14, no. 4 (1955): 533–552.

Hon, Tze-ki. "Educating the Citizens: Visions of China in Late Qing Historical Textbooks." In *The Politics of Historical Production in Late Qing and Republican China*, edited by Tze-ki Hon and Robert J. Culp, 79–105. Leiden: Brill, 2007.

————. "Military Governance versus Civil Governance: A Comparison of the Old History and the New History of the Five Dynasties." In *Imagining Boundaries: Changing Confucian Doctrines, Texts, and Hermeneutics*, edited by Kai-wing Chow, On-cho Ng, and John B. Henderson, 85–105. Albany: State University of New York Press, 1999.

Hu Shih. "Ch'an (Zen) Buddhism in China: Its History and Method." *Philosophy East and West* 3, no. 1 (1953): 3–24.

————. *The Chinese Renaissance: The Haskell Lectures, 1933*. Chicago: University of Chicago Press, 1934.

————. "Religion and Philosophy in Chinese History." In *Symposium on Chinese Culture*, edited by Sophia H. Chen Zen, 31–58. Shanghai: China Institute of Pacific Relations, 1931.

Huang Chi-Chiang 黃啓江. "Elite and Clergy in Northern Sung Hang-chou: A Convergence of Interest." In Gregory and Getz, *Buddhism in the Sung*, 295–339.

———. "Imperial Rulership and Buddhism in the Early Northern Song." In *Imperial Rulership and Cultural Change in Traditional China*, edited by Fredrick Paul Brandauer, 144–187. Seattle: University of Washington Press, 1994.

———. "Yunmen zong yu Bei Song conglin zhi fazhan" 雲門宗與北宋叢林之發展. *Dalu zazhi* 大陸雜誌 89, no. 6 (1994): 246–267.

Huang Minzhi 黃敏枝. *Songdai Fojiao shehui jingji shi lunji* 宋代佛教社會經濟史論集. Taipei: Taiwan xue sheng shu ju, 1989.

Huang, Shih-shan Susan. "Early Buddhist Illustrated Prints in Hangzhou." In *Knowledge and Text Production in an Age of Print: China, 900–1400*, edited by Lucille Chia and Hilde De Weerdt, 135–165. Leiden and Boston: Brill, 2011.

Huang Yi-hsun 黃繹勳. *Integrating Chinese Buddhism: A Study of Yongming Yanshou's Guanxin Xuanshu*. Taipei: Dharma Drum, 2005.

———. "Yongming Yanshou zhi jingtu famen: Yi *Zhijue chanshi zixing lu* wei zhongxin" 永明延壽之淨土法門—以《智覺禪師自行錄》為中心. In *Ran Yunhua xiansheng bazhi huayan shouqing lunwen ji* 冉雲華先生八秩華誕慶論文集, edited by Wang Sanqing 王三慶, 2003, 329–353. Taipei: Faguang chubanshe.

———. "*Zhao cheng jin zang* yu *chuang deng yuying ji*" 《趙城金藏》與《傳燈玉英集》. *Diyi jie guoji Fojiao da zang jing xueshu yantaohui lunwen ji* 第一屆國際佛教大藏經學術研討會論文集, 255–280. Gaoxiong: Foguang chubanshe, 2010.

Hucker, Charles O. *A Dictionary of Official Titles in Imperial China*. Stanford, Calif.: Stanford University Press, 1985.

Ikezawa Shigeko 池澤滋子. *Wuyue Qianshi wenren qunti yanjiu* 吳越錢氏文人群體研究. Shanghai: Shanghai renmin chubanshe, 2006.

Ishii Shūdō 石井修道. "Senshū Fukusen Shōkei in no Jōshu Zenji Shōtō to *Sodōshū*" 泉州福先招慶院の淨修禪師省澄と『祖堂集』. *Komazawa daigaku bukkyō gakubu kenkyū kiyō* 駒沢大学仏教学部研究紀要 44 (1986): 155–197.

———. *Sōdai Zenshūshi no kenkyū* 宋代禅宗史の研究. Tokyo: Daitō shuppansha, 1987.

———. "Ungosan to Ungo Doyo: Chūgoku shoki Sōtōshū no shūdan no dōkō o kōryo shite" 雲居山と雲居道膺—中国初期曹洞宗の集団の動向を考慮して. *Shūkyōgaku ronshū* 宗教学論集 10 (1980): 153–179.

Jenkins, Philip John. *Jesus Wars: How Four Patriarchs, Three Queens, and Two Emperors Decided What Christians Would Believe for the Next 1,500 Years*. New York: HarperOne, 2010.

Jia Jinhua 賈晉華. *Gudian Chan yanjiu: zhong Tang zhi Wudai Chanzong fazhan xintan* 古典禪研究: 中唐至五代禪宗發展新探. Hong Kong: Oxford University Press, 2010.

———. *The Hongzhou School of Chan Buddhism in Eighth- through Tenth-Century China*. Albany: State University of New York Press, 2006.

Jorgensen, John. "The 'Imperial' Lineage of Ch'an Buddhism: The Role of Confucian Ritual and Ancestor Worship in Ch'an's Search for Legitimation in the Mid-T'ang Dynasty." *Papers on Far Eastern History* 35 (1987): 89–133.

———. *Inventing Hui-neng, the Sixth Patriarch: Hagiography and Biography in Early Ch'an*. Leiden: Brill, 2005.

Keats-Rohan, K. S. B. *Prosopography Approaches and Applications: A Handbook*. Oxford: Unit for Prosopographical Research, Linacre College, University of Oxford, 2007.

Keay, John. *China: A History*. New York: Basic, 2009.

Keyworth, George Albert III. *"Transmitting the Lamp of Learning* in Classical Chan Buddhism: Juefan Huihong (1071–1128) and Literary Chan." Ph.D. diss., University of California, Los Angeles, 2001.

Kieschnick, John. *The Eminent Monk: Buddhist Ideals in Medieval Chinese Hagiography*. Honolulu: University of Hawai'i Press, 1997.

———. "The Symbolism of the Monk's Robe in China." *Asia Major*, 3rd series, 12, no. 1 (1999): 9–32.

Kinugawa Kenji 衣川賢次. *"Senshū senbutsu shinjaku sho soshi ju* to *Sodōshū*—Fu Shōtō (Buntō) Zenji o meguru Senshū no chiri" 『泉州千佛新著諸祖師頌』と『祖堂集』附省燈（文燈）禪師をめぐる泉州の地理. *Zengaku kenkyū* 禪學研究 88 (2010): 1–31.

———. *"Sodōshū* no kōri" 祖堂集の校理. *Tōyō bunka* 東洋文化 83 (2003): 127–151.

———. "Yanagida Seizan no *Sodōshū* kenkyū" 柳田先生の『祖堂集』研究. *Zen bunka kenkyūjo kiyō* 禅文化研究所紀要 30 (2009): 25–69.

Kirchner, Thomas. "The Admonitions of Zen Master Guishan Dayuan." *Hanazono daigaku kokusai Zengaku kenkyūjo ronsō* 花園大学国際禅学研究所論叢 1 (2006): 1–18.

Kurz, Johannes L. "Biographical Writing in Tenth-Century China." In *Biographie als Weltliteratur: Eine Bestandsaufnahme der biographischen Literatur im 10. Jahrhundert*, edited by Susanne Enderwitz, 135–152. Heidelberg: Mattes, 2009.

———. *China's Southern Tang Dynasty, 937–976*. London: Routledge, 2011.

———. "The Compilation and Publication of the *Taiping yulan* and the *Cefu yuangui*." *Extrême-Orient Extrême-Occident* (hors série) 1 (2007): 39–90.

———. "The Politics of Collecting Knowledge: Song Taizong's Compilations Project." *T'oung Pao* 87, no. 4–5 (2001): 289–316.

———. "Sources for the History of the Southern Tang (937–975)." *Journal of Sung-Yuan Studies* 24 (1994): 217–235.

———. "A Survey of Historical Sources for the Five Dynasties and Ten States in Song Times." *Journal of Sung-Yuan Studies* 33 (2003): 187–224.

Lai Jiancheng 賴建成. *Wuyue Fojiao zhi fazhan* 吳越佛教之發展. Taipei: Huamulan wenhua chubanshe, 2010.

Lau Nap-yin and Huang K'uan-chung. "Founding and Consolidation of the Sung Dynasty under T'ai-tsu (960–976), T'ai-tsung (976–997), and Chen-tsung (997–1022)." In *The Sung Dynasty and Its Precursors, 907–1279*, edited by Denis Twitchett and Paul Jakov Smith, 206–278. Vol. 5, bk. 1 of *The Cambridge History of China*. Cambridge: Cambridge University Press, 2009.

Lee, Hui-shu. *Exquisite Moments: West Lake and Southern Song Art*. New York: China Institute Gallery, China Institute, 2001.

Li Yinghui 李映辉. *Tangdai Fojiao dili yanjiu* 唐代佛教地理研究. Changsha: Hunan daxue chubanshe, 2004.

Lin Chuanfang 林傳芳. "Godai Nankan no Bukkyō" 五代南漢の仏教. *Kyōto joshi gakuen Bukkyō bunka kenkyūjo* 京都女子学園仏教文化研究所 13 (1983): 71–93.

Liu Pujiang 刘浦江. "Zhengtong lunxia de Wudai shiguan" 正统论下的五代史观. *Tang yanjiu* 唐研究 11 (2005): 73–94.

Liu Xinru. "Buddhist Institutions in the Lower Yangtze Region during the Sung Dynasty." *Bulletin of Sung-Yüan Studies* 21 (1989): 31–51.

Lorge, Peter. "The End of the Five Dynasties and Ten Kingdoms." In Lorge, *Five Dynasties and Ten Kingdoms*, 223–242.

———, ed. *Five Dynasties and Ten Kingdoms*. Hong Kong: Chinese University Press, 2011.

Lü Jianfu 呂建福. *Zhongguo Mijiao shi* 中国密教史. Beijing: Zhongguo shehui kexue chubanshe, 1995.

Ma Xisha. "The Syncretism of Maitreyan Belief and Manichaeism in Chinese History." In *Popular Religion and Shamanism*, edited by Ma Xisha and Meng Huiying, 19–53. Leiden: Brill, 2011.

Makita Tairyō 牧田諦亮. *Godai shūkyōshi kenkyū* 五代宗教史研究. Kyoto: Heirakuji shoten, 1971.

———. "Kunshu dokusai shakai ni okeru Bukkyōdan no tachiba (jō)—Sōsō Sannei chūshin to shite" 君主獨裁社會に於ける佛教團の立場 (上)—宋僧贊寧中心として. *Bukkyō bunka kenkyū* 佛教文化研究 3 (1953): 63–80.

———. "Sannei to sono jidai" 贊寧とその時代. *Chūgoku kinsei Bukkyōshi kenkyū* 中国近世仏教史研究, 96–133. Kyoto: Heirakuji shoten, 1957.

Maspero, Henri. "Rapport sommaire sur une mission archéologique au Tchö-Kiang." *Bulletin de l'Ecole française d'Extrême-Orient* 14, no. 8 (1914): 1–117.

McDermott. "The Ascendance of the Imprint in China." In *Printing and Book Culture in Late Imperial China*, edited by Cynthia J. Brokaw and Kai-wing Chow, 43–82. Berkeley: University of California Press, 2005.

McRae, John R. "Buddhism." *Journal of Asian Studies* 54, no. 2 (1995): 354–371.

———. *The Northern School and Formation of Early Ch'an Buddhism*. Honolulu: University of Hawai'i Press, 1986.

———. "Religion as Revolution in Chinese Historiography: Hu Shih (1891–1962) on Shen-hui (684–758)." *Cahiers d'Extrême-Asie* 12 (2001): 59–102.

Miller, Tracy. "Something Old, Something New, Something Borrowed: Local Style in the Architecture of Tenth-Century China." In Lorge, *Five Dynasties and Ten Kingdoms*, 167–222.

Mitamura Keiko 三田村圭子. "Tōmatsu Godai ni okeru shūkyō katsudō to setsudoshi" 唐末五代における宗教活動と節度使. *Tōhō shūkyō* 120 (2012): 1–21.

Miyazaki Ichisada 宮崎市定. "Tōyō no runessansu to seiyō no runessansu" 東洋のルネッサンスと西洋のルネッサンス. *Ajiashi kenkyū* アジア史研究 2 (1940): 336–387.

Morrison, Elizabeth. *The Power of Patriarchs: Qisong and Lineage in Chinese Buddhism*. Leiden: Brill, 2010.

Naka Michiyo 那珂通世 and Wada Sei 和田清. *Shina tsūshi* 支那通史. Tokyo: Iwanami shoten, 1938.

Nara Kokuritsu Hakubutsukan. *Hijiri to inja: Sansui ni kokoro o sumasu hitobito; Tokubetsuten* 聖と隠者: 山水に心を澄ます人々: 特別展. Nara: Nara kokuritsu hakubutsukan, 1999.

———. *Seichi Ninpō: Nihon Bukkyō 1300 nen no genryū: Subete wa koko kara yatte kita* 聖地寧波 (ニンボー): 日本仏教1300年の源流: すべてはここからやって来た. Nara: Nara kokuritsu hakubutsukan, 2009.

National Museum of Chinese History. *Sui Dynasty to Northern and Southern Song Dynasties*. Vol. 3 of *A Journey into China's Antiquity*. Beijing: Morning Glory, 1997.

Neelis, Jason. *Early Buddhist Transmission and Trade Networks: Mobility and Exchange within and beyond the Northwestern Borderlands of South Asia*. Leiden: Brill, 2011.

Nichols, Brian J. "History, Material Culture and Auspicious Events at the Purple Cloud: Buddhist Monasticism at Quanzhou Kaiyuan." Ph.D. diss., Rice University, 2011.

Nishiwaki Tsuneki 西脇常記. "Yō Oku kenkyū *Shōji jutsu* o yomu" 楊億研究「殤子述」を読む. In Suzuki, *Sōdai Zenshū no shakaiteki eikyō*, 359–397.

Orzech, Charles. "After Amoghavajra: Esoteric Buddhism in the Late Tang." In *Esoteric Buddhism and the Tantras in East Asia*, edited by Charles Orzech, 315–335. Leiden: Brill, 2010.

Penkower, Linda. "T'ien-t'ai during the T'ang dynasty: Chan-jan and the Sinification of Buddhism." Ph.D. diss., Columbia University, 1993.

Poceski, Mario. "*Guishan jingce* (*Guishan's Admonitions*) and the Ethical Foundations of Chan Practice." In *Zen Classics: Formative Texts in the History of Zen Buddhism*, edited by Steven Heine and Dale S. Wright, 15–42. Oxford: Oxford University Press, 2006.

———. *Ordinary Mind as the Way: The Hongzhou School and the Growth of Chan Buddhism*. Oxford: Oxford University Press, 2007.

——— [Cheng Chien Bhikshu]. *Sun-Face Buddha: The Teachings of Ma-tsu and the Hung-chou School of Ch'an*. Berkeley, Calif.: Asian Humanities Press, 1992.

———. "Xuefeng's Code and the Chan School's Participation in the Development of Monastic Regulations." *Asia Major*, 3rd series, 16, no. 2 (2003): 33–56.

Protass, Jason. "Mapping the Rise and Decline of the Yunmen Chan Lineage." Unpublished paper presented at the American Academy of Religion annual meeting, Baltimore, November 2013.

Qian Ji'e 錢濟鄂. *Wuyue guo Suwang jishi* 吳越國肅王紀事. Taipei: Zongjingxiao Shulin chuban youxian gongsi, 1999.

Qing Xitai 卿希泰. *Zhongguo Daojiao shi* 中國道教史. 4 vols. Chengdu: Sichuan renmin chubanshe, 1992.

Reischauer, Edwin O. *Ennin's Travels in T'ang China*. New York: Ronald Press, 1955.

Satō Seijun 佐藤成順. *Sōdai Bukkyōshi no kenkyū* 宋代仏教史の研究. Tokyo: Sankibō busshorin, 2012.

Schafer, Edward H. *The Empire of Min: A South China Kingdom of the Tenth Century*. Rutland, Vt.: Charles E. Tuttle, 1954.

Schipper, Kristofer, and Franciscus Verellen. *The Taoist Canon: A Historical Companion to the Daozang*. Chicago: University of Chicago Press, 2004.

Schlütter, Morten. *How Zen Became Zen: The Dispute over Enlightenment and the Formation of Chan Buddhism in Song-Dynasty China*. Honolulu: University of Hawai'i Press, 2008.

———. "Vinaya Monasteries, Public Abbacies, and State Control of Buddhism under the Song (960–1279)." In *Going Forth: Visions of Buddhist Vinaya*, edited by William M. Bodiford, 136–160. Honolulu: University of Hawai'i Press, 2005.

Schottenhammer, Angela. "Local Politico-Economic Particulars of the Quanzhou Region during the Tenth Century." *Journal of Sung-Yuan Studies* 29 (1999): 1–41.

Seiwert, Hubert Michael. *Popular Religious Movements and Heterodox Sects in Chinese History*. Leiden: Brill, 2003.

Sen, Tansen. *Buddhism, Diplomacy, and Trade: The Realignment of Sino-Indian Relations, 600–1400.* Honolulu: University of Hawai'i Press, 2003.

Sharf, Robert H. "The Zen of Japanese Nationalism." *History of Religions* 33, no. 1 (1993): 1–43.

Shields, Anna M. *Crafting a Collection: The Cultural Contexts and Poetic Practice of the Huajian ji* 花間集 *(Collection from among the Flowers).* Cambridge, Mass.: Harvard University Asia Center, 2006.

Shih Heng-Ching. "The Ch'an-Pure Land Syncretism in China: With Special Reference to Yung-Ming Yen-Shou." Ph.D. diss., University of Wisconsin, Madison, 1984.

Shiina Kōyū 椎名宏雄. "*Sodōshū* no hensei" 『祖堂集』の編成. *Shūgaku kenkyū* 21 (1979): 66–72.

———. "Tōdai Zenseki no Sōdai kankō ni tsuite" 唐代禅籍の宋代刊行について. In Suzuki, *Sōdai Zenshū no shakaiteki eikyō,* 513–541.

Shinohara, Koichi. "From Local History to Universal History: The Construction of the Sung T'ien-t'ai Lineage." In Gregory and Getz, *Buddhism in the Sung,* 524–576.

Smith, Paul Jakov. "Introduction: The Sung Dynasty and Its Precursors, 907–1279." In *The Sung Dynasty and Its Precursors, 907–1279,* edited by Denis Twitchett and Paul Jakov Smith, 1–37. Vol. 5, bk. 1 of *The Cambridge History of China.* Cambridge: Cambridge University Press, 2009.

Somers, Robert M. "The End of the T'ang." In *Sui and T'ang China, 589–906 AD,* edited by Denis Twitchett, 682–789. Vol. 3 of *The Cambridge History of China.* Cambridge: Cambridge University Press, 1979.

Soper, Alexander C. "Hsiang-Kuo-Ssŭ: An Imperial Temple of Northern Sung." *Journal of the American Oriental Society* 68, no. 1 (1948): 19–45.

Sørensen, Henrik H. "Esoteric Buddhism in Sichuan during the Tang and Five Dynasties Period." In *Esoteric Buddhism and the Tantras in East Asia,* edited by Charles Orzech, 315–335. Leiden: Brill, 2010.

Standen, Naomi. "The Five Dynasties." In *The Sung Dynasty and Its Precursors, 907–1279,* edited by Denis Twitchett and Paul Jakov Smith, 38–132. Vol. 5, bk. 1 of *The Cambridge History of China.* Cambridge: Cambridge University Press, 2009.

———. *Unbounded Loyalty: Frontier Crossing in Liao China.* Honolulu: University of Hawai'i Press, 2007.

Stone, Lawrence. "Prosopography." *Daedalus* 100 (1971): 46–79.

Strong, John S. *Relics of the Buddha.* Princeton, N.J.: Princeton University Press, 2004.

Sun, Chengjuan. "Rewriting the Southern Tang (937–975): Nostalgia and Aesthetic Imagination." Ph.D. diss., Harvard University, 2008.

Suwa Gijun 諏訪義純. *Chūgoku Nanchō Bukkyōshi no kenkyū* 中国南朝仏教史の研究. Kyoto: Hōzōkan, 1997.

Suzuki, Daisetz Teitaro. "Zen: A Reply to Hu Shih." *Philosophy East and West* 3, no. 1 (1953): 25–46.

———. "Zen in T'ang and Sung." Edited by Sueki Fumiko. Translated by Stefan Grace. *Annual Report of Researches of the Matsugaoka Bunko* 25 (2011): 104–143.

Suzuki Tetsuo 鈴木哲雄. "Hōgenshū no keisei (I)" 法眼宗の形成 (一). *Aichi gakuin daigaku bungakubu kiyō* 愛知学院大学文学部紀要 6 (1976): 1–21.

————. "Hokusōki no chishikijin to Zensō to no kōryū" 北宋期の知識人と禅僧との交流. In Suzuki, *Sōdai Zenshū no shakaiteki eikyō*, 3–81.

————. "Kanton no Zenshū ni kansuru shiryō: Tō・Godai" 広東の禅宗に関する資料: 唐・五代. *Aichi gakuin daigaku bungakubu kiyō* 14 (1984): 101–117.

————. "*Kenchū seikoku zokutōroku* no jūchi betsu jinmei sakuin" 建中靖国続燈録の住地別人名索引. *Aichi gakuin daigaku ningen bunka kenkyūjo kiyō* 愛知学院大学人間文化研究所紀要13 (1998): 116–184.

————. "Kohoku no Zenshū ni kansuru shiryō: Tō・Godai" 湖北の禅宗に関する資料: 唐・五代. *Aichi gakuin daigaku bungakubu kiyō* 16 (1986): 92–135.

————. "Konan no Zenshū ni kansuru shiryō: Tō・Godai" 湖南の禅宗に関する資料: 唐・五代. *Aichi gakuin daigaku bungakubu kiyō* 10 (1980): 12–53.

————. "Kōnan no Zenshū ni kansuru shiryō (I): Tō・Godai" 江南の禅宗に関する資料(上): 唐・五代. *Aichi gakuin daigaku bungakubu kiyō* 12 (1982): 35–53.

————. "Kōnan no Zenshū ni kansuru shiryō (II): Tō・Godai" 江南の禅宗に関する資料 (下): 唐・五代. *Aichi gakuin daigaku bungakubu kiyō* 13 (1983): 22–49.

————. "Kōsei no Zenshū ni kansuru shiryō: Tō・Godai" 江西の禅宗に関する資料: 唐・五代. *Aichi gakuin daigaku bungakubu kiyō* 8 (1978): 135–185.

————. "Minkoku Chūiō Ō Shinchi ni okeru Bukkyō" 閩国忠懿王王審知における仏教. In *Tendai shisō to higashiajia bunka no kenkyū: Shioiri Ryōdō sensei tsuitō ronbunshū* 天台思想と東アジア文化の研究: 塩入良道先生追悼論文集, edited by Shioiri Ryōdō Sensei Tsuitō Ronbunshū Kankōkai 塩入良道先生追悼論文集刊行会, 587–597. Tokyo: Sankibō busshorin, 1991.

————. "Sekkō no Zenshū ni kansuru shiryō: Tō・Godai" 浙江の禅宗に関する資料: 唐・五代. *Aichi gakuin daigaku bungakubu kiyō* 5 (1975): 63–101.

————. "Senshū ni okeru Zenshū: Godai jidai o chūshin toshite" 泉州における禅宗: 五代時代を中心として. *Indogaku Bukkyōgaku kenkyū* 印度学仏教学研究 47 (1975): 109–113.

————. *Seppō: Soshi Zen o jissenshita kyōikusha* 雪峰: 祖師禅を実践した教育者. Kyoto: Rinsenshoten, 2009.

————, ed. *Sōdai Zenshū no shakaiteki eikyō* 宋代禅宗の社会的影響. Tokyo: Sankibō busshorin, 2002.

————. "*Tenshō kōtōroku・Katai futōroku* no jūchi betsu jinmei sakuin" 天聖広燈録・嘉泰普燈録の住地別人名索引. *Zen kenkyūjo kiyō* 禅研究所紀要 27 (1999): 139–192.

————. "Tō Godai jidai no Fukken ni okeru Zenshū" 唐五代時代の福建における禅宗. *Aichi gakuin daigaku bungakubu kiyō* 3 (1973): 1–41.

————. *Tō Godai no Zenshū: Konan Kōsei hen* 唐五代の禅宗: 湖南江西篇. Tōkyō: Daitō Shuppansha, 1984.

————. *Tō Godai Zenshū shi* 唐五代禅宗史. Tokyo: Sankibō busshorin, 1985.

————. "Zenshū no tenkei" 禅宗の転型. *Zen kenkyūjo kiyō* 禅研究所紀要 34 (2006): 19–41.

Tackett, Nicolas. *The Destruction of the Medieval Chinese Aristocracy*. Cambridge, Mass.: Harvard University Asia Center, 2014.

————. *Tomb Epitaphs from the Tang-Song Transition*. Shanghai: privately printed, 2005.

————. "The Transformation of Medieval Chinese Elites (850–1000 C.E.)." Ph.D. diss., Columbia University, 2006.

Takamine Ryōshū 高峰了州. *Kegon to Zen no tsūro* 華厳と禅の通路. Nara: Nanto bukkyō kenkūkai, 1956.

Tanahashi, Kazuaki, ed. *Moon in a Dewdrop: Writings of Zen Master Dōgen.* San Francisco: North Point, 1985.

Tanaka, Stefan. *Japan's Orient: Rendering Pasts into History.* Berkeley: University of California Press, 1993.

ter Haar, B. J. *The White Lotus Teachings in Chinese Religious History.* Leiden: Brill, 1992.

Tokiwa Daijō 常盤大定. "Bukkyō shijō ni okeru futari no Chūiō" 仏教史上に於ける二人の忠懿王. *Zoku Shina Bukkyō no kenkyū* 續支那仏教の研究, 453–470. Tokyo: Shunjusha shohakukan, 1941.

Tsuchiya Taisuke 土屋太祐. *Bei Song Chanzong sixiang ji qi yuanyuan* 北宋禅宗思想及其淵源. Chengdu: Bashu shushe, 2008.

Tsukamoto Shunkō 塚本俊孝. "Godai Nantō no ōshitsu to Bukkyō" 五代南唐の王室と仏教. *Bukkyō bunka kenyū* 仏教文化研究 3 (1953): 81–88.

Twitchett, Denis Crispin. *Financial Administration under the T'ang Dynasty.* Cambridge: Cambridge University Press, 1970.

Vásquez, Manuel A. "Studying Religion in Motion: A Networks Approach." *Method and Theory in the Study of Religion* 20 (2008): 151–184.

Verellen, Franciscus. "A Forgotten T'ang Restoration: The Taoist Dispensation after Huang Ch'ao." *Asia Major,* 3rd series, 7, no. 1 (1994): 107–153.

———. "Liturgy and Sovereignty: The Role of Taoist Ritual in the Foundation of the Shu Kingdom (907–925)." *Asia Major,* 3rd series, 2, no. 1 (1989): 59–78.

———. "Shu as Hallowed Land: Du Guangting's Record of Marvels." *Cahiers d'Extrême-Asie* 10 (1998): 213–254.

Waddell, Norman, and Masao Abe. *The Heart of Dōgen's Shōbōgenzō.* Albany: State University of New York Press, 2002.

Waley, Arthur. "A Sung Colloquial Story from the Tsu-t'ang chi." *Asia Major,* new series, 14, no. 2 (1968): 242–246.

Wang, Eugene Y. "The Rhetoric of Book Illustration." In *Treasures of the Yenching: Seventy-Fifth Anniversary of the Harvard-Yenching Library,* edited by Patrick Hanan, 181–217. Cambridge. Mass.: Harvard University Press, 2003.

———. "Tope and *Topos*: The Leifeng Pagoda and the Discourse of the Demonic." In *Writing and Materiality in China: Essays in Honor of Patrick Hanan,* edited by Judith Zeitlin and Lydia Liu, 488–552. Cambridge, Mass.: Harvard University Asia Center, 2003.

Wang Gungwu. *Divided China: Preparing for Reunification, 883–947.* Singapore: World Scientific Publishing, 2007.

Wang Jianguang 王建光. *Zhongguo lüzong tongshi* 中国律宗通史. Nanjing: Fenghuang chubanshe, 2008.

Wang Li 王力. "Baoqieyin jingta yu Wuyue guo dui Ri wenhua jiaoliu" 寶篋印經塔與吳越國對日文化交流. *Zhejiang daxue xuebao (renwen shehui kexue ban)* 浙江大學學報 (人文社會科學版) 32, no. 5 (2002): 27–32.

Wang Shengduo 汪圣铎. *Songdai zhengjiao guanxi yanjiu* 宋代政教关系研究. Beijing: Renmin chubanshe, 2010.

Wei Yingqi 魏應麒. "Wudai Min shigao zhiyi" 五代閩史稿之一. Pts. 1–4. *Guoli zhongshan daxue yuyan lishixue yanjiusuo zhoukan* 國立中山大學語言歷史學研究所週刊 7,

no. 75 (1929): 3001–3015; 7, no. 76 (1929): 3051–3070; 7, no. 77 (1929): 3105–3125; 7, no. 78 (1929): 3165–3173.

Weinstein, Stanley. *Buddhism under the T'ang*. Cambridge: Cambridge University Press, 1987.

———. "Imperial Patronage in T'ang Buddhism." In *Perspectives on the T'ang*, edited by Arthur F. Wright and Dennis Twitchett, 265–306. New Haven, Conn.: Yale University Press, 1973.

Welter, Albert. "A Buddhist Response to the Confucian Revival: Tsan-ning and the Debate over *Wen* in the Early Sung." In Gregory and Getz, *Buddhism in the Sung*, 21–61.

———. *The "Linji lu" and the Creation of Chan Orthodoxy*. Oxford: Oxford University Press, 2008.

———. *The Meaning of Myriad Good Deeds: A Study of Yong-ming Yen shou and the "Wan-shan t'ung-kuei chi."* New York: Peter Lang, 1993.

———. *Monks, Rulers, and Literati: The Political Ascendancy of Chan Buddhism*. Oxford: Oxford University Press, 2006.

———. *Yongming Yanshou's Conception of Chan in the "Zongjing lu": A Special Transmission within the Scriptures*. Oxford: Oxford University Press, 2011.

Wetherell, Charles. "Historical Social Network Analysis." Supplement. *International Review of Social History* 43 (1998): 125–144.

Wong, Kwok-Yiu. "The White Horse Massacre and Changing Literati Culture in the Late-Tang and Five Dynasties China." *Asia Major*, 3rd series, 23, no. 2 (2010): 33–75.

Woolley, Nathan. "Religion and Politics in the Writings of Xu Xuan (917–92)." Ph.D. diss., Australian National University, 2010.

Worthy, Edmund H., Jr. "Diplomacy for Survival: Domestic and Foreign Relations of Wu Yueh." In *China among Equals: The Middle Kingdom and Its Neighbors, Tenth to Fourteenth Centuries*, edited by Morris Rossabi, 17–34. Berkeley: University of California Press, 1983.

Wright, Arthur F. *Studies in Chinese Buddhism*. Edited by Robert M. Somers. New Haven, Conn.: Yale University Press, 1990.

Xiong Bolü 熊伯履. *Xiangguo si kao* 相国寺考. Zhengzhou: Zhongzhou guji chubanshe, 1985.

Xu Mingqian 徐銘謙. "Yi biyan zuo Foshi: Bei Song wenzi Chan yundong liuyan kao" 以筆硯作佛事：北宋文字禪運動流衍考. Ph.D. diss., National Central University, Taiwan, 2012.

Xuyun 虛雲 and Cen Xuelü 岑學呂. *Xuyun heshang fahui* 虛雲和尚法彙. Hong Kong: Xuyun heshang fahui bianyin banshichu, 1953.

Yampolsky, Philip B. *The Platform Sūtra of the Sixth Patriarch*. New York: Columbia University Press, 1967.

Yan Gengwang 嚴耕望. "Tang dai pian" 唐代篇. In *Zhongguo lishi dili* 中國歷史地理 (二), by Shi Zhangru 石璋如 et al., 2:1–62. Taipei: Zhonghua wenhua chuban shiye weiyuan hui, 1954.

———. "Wudai shiguo pian" 五代十國篇. In *Zhongguo lishi dili* 中國歷史地理 (二), by Shi Zhangru 石璋如 et al., 2:1–22. Taipei: Zhonghua wenhua chuban shiye weiyuan hui, 1954.

Yan Mengxiang 闫孟祥. *Songdai Linji Chan fazhan yanbian* 宋代临济禅发展演变. Beijing: Zongjiao wenhua chubanshe, 2006.

Yanagida Seizan 柳田聖山. "The Development of the 'Recorded Sayings' Texts of Chinese Ch'an Buddhism." Translated by John R. McRae. In *Early Ch'an in China and Tibet*, edited by Whalen Lai and Lewis R. Lancaster, 185–205. Berkeley, Calif.: Asian Humanities Press, 1983.

————. "Goroku no rekishi: Zenbunken no seiritsu shiteki kenkyū" 語録の歴史: 禪文献の成立史的研究. *Tōhō gakuhō* 東方學報 57 (1985): 211–663.

————. *Junzen no jidai: Sodōshū monogatari* 純禅の時代: 祖堂集ものがたり. Kyoto: Zenbunka kenkyūjo, 1983.

————. "The Life of Lin-chi I-hsuan." Translated by Ruth Sasaki. Originally published in the *Eastern Buddhist*, new series 5, no. 2 (1972): 70–94. Revised and expanded in *The Record of Linji*, by Sasaki and Thomas Yūhō Kirchner, 59–115. Honolulu: University of Hawai'i Press, 2009.

————. "The *Li-Tai Fa-Pao Chi* and the Ch'an Doctrine of Sudden Awakening." In *Early Ch'an in China and Tibet*, edited by Whalen Lai and Lewis R. Lancaster, 13–49. Berkeley, Calif.: Asian Humanities Press, 1983.

————. "Passion for Zen." Translated by Urs App. *Cahiers d'Extrême-Asie* 7 (1993): 1–29.

———— [Yokoi Seizan]. "Seppō to sono yūjintachi" 雪峯とその友人たち. *Zen bunka* 禅文化 4 (1956): 53–66.

————. *Shoki no zenshi* I 初期の禅史 I. Vol. 2 of *Zen no goroku* 禅の語録. Tokyo: Chikuma shobō, 1971.

————, ed. *Sodōshū* 祖堂集. Kyoto: Chūbun shuppansha, 1974.

————. "*Sodōshū* no honbun kenkyū (I)" 祖堂集の本文研究 (一). *Zengaku kenkyū* 禅学研究 54 (1964): 11–87.

———— [Yokoi Seizan]. "*Sodōshū* no shiryō kachi" 祖堂集の資料価値. *Zengaku kenkyū* 禅学研究 44 (1953): 31–80.

————. "Tōmatsu Godai no Kahoku chihō ni okeru Zenshū kōki no rekishiteki shakaiteki jijō ni tsuite" 唐末五代の河北地方に於ける禅宗興起の歴史的社会的事情について. *Nihon Bukkyō gakkai nenpō* 日本仏教学会年報 25 (1960): 171–186.

————. *Zenrin sōhōden yakuchū* 禪林僧寶傳譯注. Kyōto: Kyōto daigaku jinbun kagaku kenkyūjo, 1988.

Yang Xin 杨新. *Wudai Guanxiu luohan tu* 五代贯休罗汉图. Beijing: Wenwu chubanshe, 2008.

Yang Zengwen 杨曾文. *Tang Wudai Chanzong shi* 唐五代禅宗史. Beijing: Zhongguo shehui kexue chubanshe, 1999.

Yates, Robin. *Washing Silk: The Life and Selected Poetry of Wei Chuang (834?–910)*. Cambridge, Mass.: Harvard University Press, 1988.

Yoshikawa Isao 吉河功. *Sekizō hōkyōintō no seiritsu* 石造宝篋印塔の成立. Tokyo: Daiichi shobō, 2000.

Yoshikawa Tadao 吉川忠夫. "Haikyū den" 裴休傳. *Tōhō gakuhō* 東方學報 64 (1992): 115–277.

Yoshizu Yoshihide 吉津宜英. "Kegon kyōgaku no ataeta Sōdai Zenshū e no eikyō: *Shuryōgongyō* shinkō keisei e no yōin" 華厳教学の与えた宋代禅宗への影響–首楞厳経信仰形成への要因. In Suzuki, *Sōdai Zenshū no shakaiteki eikyō*, 289–328.

Yü, Chün-fang. *Kuan-yin: The Chinese Transformation of Avalokiteśvara*. New York: Columbia University Press, 2001.

Zhang Xiumin 張秀民. "Wudai Wuyue guo de yinshua" 五代吳越國的印刷. *Wenwu* 文物 12 (1978): 74–76.

——. *Zhongguo yinshuashu de faming ji qi yingxiang* 中國印刷術的發明及其影響. Taipei: Wenshizhe chubanshe, 1988.

Zhao Yongdong 趙永東. "Wudai shiqi diaoban yinshua shiye de fazhan" 五代時期雕版印刷事業的發展. *Wen shi* 文史 44 (1998): 151–170.

Zheng Suwen (Tei Shukubun) 鄭夙雯. *Sō shoki Rinzaishū no kenkyū* 宋初期臨済宗の研究. Tokyo: Sankibō busshorin, 2006.

Zhuge Ji 諸葛計 and Yin Yuzhen 銀玉珍. *Minguo shishi biannian* 閩国史事编年. Fuzhou: Fujian renmin chubanshe, 1997.

——. *Wuyue shishi biannian* 吴越史事编年. Hangzhou: Zhejiang guji chubanshe, 1989.

Zürcher, E. *Buddhism: Its Origin and Spread in Words, Maps, and Pictures*. New York: St. Martin's, 1962.

——. "Perspectives in the Study of Chinese Buddhism." *Journal of the Royal Asiatic Society* 2 (1982): 161–176.

Index

Page numbers in boldface type indicate illustrations.

**Kuroda Institute
Studies in East Asian Buddhism**

Studies in Ch'an and Hua-yen
Robert M. Gimello and Peter N. Gregory, editors

Dōgen Studies
William R. LaFleur, editor

The Northern School and the Formation of Early Ch'an Buddhism
John R. McRae

Traditions of Meditation in Chinese Buddhism
Peter N. Gregory, editor

Sudden and Gradual: Approaches to Enlightenment in Chinese Thought
Peter N. Gregory, editor

Buddhist Hermeneutics
Donald S. Lopez, Jr., editor

Paths to Liberation: The Mārga and Its Transformations in Buddhist Thought
Robert E. Buswell, Jr., and Robert M. Gimello, editors

Sōtō Zen in Medieval Japan
William M. Bodiford

The Scripture on the Ten Kings *and the Making of Purgatory in
Medieval Chinese Buddhism*
Stephen F. Teiser

The Eminent Monk: Buddhist Ideals in Medieval Chinese Hagiography
John Kieschnick

Re-Visioning "Kamakura" Buddhism
Richard K. Payne, editor

Original Enlightenment and the Transformation of Medieval Japanese Buddhism
Jacqueline I. Stone

Buddhism in the Sung
Peter N. Gregory and Daniel A. Getz, Jr., editors